The Workers Are Few: Towards the Repair of Pastoral Training

J. Alexander Rutherford

Unless otherwise indicated, all Scripture quotations from the book of Habakkuk or those marked Teleioteti are my own translations. Translations from Habakkuk are taken from the translation published in my commentary on Habakkuk (Vancouver, Teleioteti 2020).

Paperback ISBN-13: 978-1-989560-79-2
Hardcover ISBN-13: 978-1-989560-80-8
eBook ISBN-13: 978-1-989560-81-5

DOI: 10.60080/idwf5931

Teleioteti publishing, Campbell River, BC

Cover image by Photo by Evgeniya Kuzmina on Pexels.

To contact Teleioteti publishing for information or to provide feedback, please visit us at **https://teleioteti.ca** or email us at **info@teleioteti.ca**

DEDICATION

This book is dedicated to my brothers and sisters across the world who have been told you are not competent to serve God as a pastor or to minister his word because you have not formally studied the Bible and who have come to believe that serving the Lord in a ministerial capacity is not for you because of the intellectual and literate study it apparently requires. I pray this book will lead to real change in our denominations and training institutions so that your faithfulness and love for our Lord will be recognised and you will be equipped and empowered for Christian ministry.

CONTENTS

ACKNOWLEDGMENTS

I find myself in a strange yet ideal position to write this book. I have studied the Bible and theology academically for far too long, and I have been well served by the institutions I studied at. By God's grace, I have grown greatly through my time at Pacific Life Bible College, Regent College, and Moore Theological College: God has used these institutions and the students and teachers there to make me into a more godly man and to shape my thinking about his word and his world in innumerable ways. It may seem odd, therefore, that someone who owes such a great debt to Christian institutions of higher education would write so strongly against them.

However, my training has equipped me to speak to those who have studied and work in these institutions as someone who has succeeded there like they have. Yet my time at these colleges has shown me that though they 'worked' for me, the vast majority of my peers had a different experience than I did. This was not because I was smarter or better but because God has his unique (and ironic) way of working.

I don't want to abolish serious Christian thought—I enjoy thinking seriously about my faith! However, my time in Christian higher education has convinced me that for all its merits, this is a terrible context for training pastors. I pray that this book would lead to better pathways for training ministers and new contexts for serious Christian thinking. So I acknowledge that without the input of my teachers—especially Brad Copp, V. Philips Long, and Mark Thompson—I would not be able to write a book like this, which employs the intellectual tools used in higher education to critique Christian higher education. Thank you to all the teachers, markers, and peers who have challenged, rebuked, and encouraged me as I have engaged with God's word and his world over the last 15 years. I am immensely grateful for your grace, patience, and wisdom, and I hope that by attacking a form of pastoral training I do not communicate disdain for your work and ministry to me and many others.

ANALYTICAL OUTLINE

PREFACE

This book emerges from my meditations upon congregational ecclesiology, the present crises of the church, and church history. As a result, it unashamedly approaches the issues of theology and pastoral training through the lens of Congregationalism and, in particular, its rejection of an embodied universal church (a visible, uniform entity, such as the Roman Catholic Church or Anglicanism) and its view of the role of a pastor, as the co-shepherd of an individual congregation.[1] This book simultaneously evolves out of Congregational Ecclesiology and, I believe, forms an argument in favour of it as I seek to commend a holistic picture of the pastoral role and the training of pastors within the local church. However, though this theological tradition is on display in this book, I believe this book still has much to say to other theological traditions, including churches in the magisterial traditions.

In the Reformed tradition, the form of theology I criticise in this book is prominent. Though I personally disagree with this model and do so for what I believe are biblical reasons, this discussion involves philosophical reflections and meditations that take us several steps

---

[1] J. Alexander Rutherford, *The Being of Churches: A Neo-Congregational Polity*, Teleioteti Technical Studies (Campbell River, BC: Teleioteti, 2023), https://doi.org/10.60080/eikd5738.

away from Scripture. This is, therefore, an area where we can disagree and remain in good fellowship.[2] For this scholastic tradition, I believe the argument of the books raises questions about the prominence of a form of philosophical theology. I will argue that this form of theology is a late development and that the biblical requirements for a pastor do not require this view of theology; since the Bible itself does not theologise in this way or commend theology of this sort, the sufficiency of Scripture should lead us to conclude that scholastic theology is not necessary for godly and faithful Christian ministry, nor for piety. Thus, if this theology does generally give us deeper insight into God and his world, and if it gives a comprehensive system for the relation of Christianity to all fields of knowledge and for the defence of the faith, it could certainly be advantageous to offer training in it, but this training is not necessary for the average Christian to live lives pleasing to God or for the average pastor to shepherd the sheep God has given them. If this argument is accepted, then the conclusion suggests some modifications to the curriculum and approach of seminaries within the Reformed tradition.

The argument that our current model of seminary discriminates against those God may be calling to ministry should be taken seriously. However, in the magisterial traditions, eliminating seminaries entirely is probably not a realistic option. For one, the form of theology adopted by these traditions requires an academic context to thrive and is best taught in such a context. Moreover, especially under episcopalian models, training ministers in a centralised context is organic to the structure and reasoning that undergirds this model. So, for the Reformed Presbyterian tradition and churches employing an

---

[2] See J Alexander Rutherford, "Of Metaphysics and Theology," *Journal of The Evangelical Theological Society* 66, no. 4 (2023): 727–49. See the discussion of early Reformed diversity in Richard A. Muller, *Prolegomena to Theology*, 2. ed, Post-Reformation Reformed Dogmatics: The Rise and Development of Reformed Orthodoxy, ca. 1520 to ca. 1725, Vol. 1 (Grand Rapids: Baker Academic, 2003).

episcopalian ecclesiology, I believe this book can function as a challenge to rethink the limitations and hidden curriculum of the seminary model. Recognising that God may call people to ministry who will not thrive in seminaries as they currently exist, efforts could be made to eliminate the barriers to successful training for such people. Perhaps the solution is to direct such people to denominations that are more accommodating in these regards or to invest in alternate training models that stand alongside but not in place of the traditional models, as some in Sydney are exploring.[3] However, the creation of a two-class clergy system within the traditional model of ordination is a significant issue that emerges at this point.

That is, there is a tendency for those trained under the traditional model to look down on those trained in the alternate model as deficient in some way. In light of the argument of this book, such an attitude is entirely inappropriate; both may be adequately trained for God's calling, though they will be uniquely gifted for different contexts and issues. These two models could perhaps be seen as complementary, each filling in what the other is lacking. Clergy from both streams are able to offer something the other does not have. I am ill-equipped to speak into the complex situations of these denominations and traditions, so I offer these preliminary reflections as merely an invitation to read this book and wrestle with its implications for your particular context, even if that context is radically different from my own.

---

3 See "The Well Training," accessed October 31, 2024, https://thewelltraining.org.au/. "Vocational Bible College," accessed October 31, 2024, https://www.vbc.edu.au.

INTRODUCTION

> And I tell you, you are Peter, and on this rock I will build my church, and the gates of hell shall not prevail against it. – Matthew 16:18 (ESV)

> I praise you, Father, Lord of heaven and earth, that you have hidden these things from the wise and intelligent but revealed them to infants. – Matthew 11:25 (my translation)

Matthew 16:18 has been subject to much debate across church history, especially in the last 400 years, yet many would agree that here, Jesus invests great authority in the apostles and, with them at its head, his Church. The apostles were critical to the establishment of the Church in its many local forms; with the completion of the New Testament and the death of John, elders inherited the leadership role (though not all the authority) of the apostles. With the authoritative Scriptures given by God, through his Spirit moving the apostles, the elders were to teach and lead God's people in local churches. This Church, built upon the apostles and led by Christ's under-shepherds, would not succumb to the assaults of the devil. No, Jesus assures us that "the gates of hell shall not prevail against it."

Jesus never breaks a promise, but it does not always feel this way, does it? We read in the New Testament itself of conflict and sin among the churches and even among the apostles. Yet, despite the attacks of the Devil, the first generations of Christians endured, and the Gospel spread to the ends of the earth. Every generation has certainly been deeply aware of its weakness, yet Jesus Christ has been faithful. Despite the unfaithfulness of his churches, Jesus has remained faithful. The Church has not failed; the Kingdom has not failed. No, the forces of Hell have been pushed back progressively over the last 2000 years; the Gospel has spread. However, the grace of God to use broken instruments does not justify that brokenness. God used the first-century churches, but Jesus nevertheless rebuked them for their faithlessness, for losing their first love and for chasing spiritual harlotry (Revelation 2-3).

So, if we look at the church today and say something is broken, we are not denying God's faithfulness or the beauty of his Church. The gates of Hell will not prevail by God's grace, but God does not want us to be lulled into complacency. If we do not address the issues prevailing in our age, God may very well choose other servants to do so; he may choose different churches—maybe he would even remove our lampstand from his midst (Rev 2:5).

Pastors, theologians, and journalists have been speaking of the decline of the Western church for decades, with varying degrees of glee expressed in that observation and numerous failed attempts at prophecy. When I first went to Bible College in 2010, I encountered much of this. However, what struck me was a far deeper issue, an issue that, though occasionally addressed, did not receive nearly as much attention as the bigger narrative of the failure of the "Western Church." I was struck by a failure of pastoral ministry worldwide, by the prevalence of false teaching, the failings of institutions designed to prevent this, and my own serious failures to understand the nature of pastoral ministry. A related problem is much more documented, the decline of Christian seminaries and Bible colleges. However, the obsession with numbers involved in identifying the second problem often disguises the true extent of the first problem.

I am writing this book to convince you that there is a problem plaguing pastoral ministry, a problem that has only gotten worse in the last 14 years since I started studying for Christian ministry. The body of this book will analyse this problem and offer something of a solution, but to feel the force of that argument, you really need to be persuaded that a problem exists. I want to begin with my own experience; limited as it is, I have every reason to believe it is revelatory of bigger issues. I have experienced the same realities across multiple denominations, on two different continents, in three colleges, and have had it confirmed in numerous conversations with pastors, students, and scholars. However, though I am not moved by statistics, I know many readers are, so I will attempt to show that my intuition and experience is supported by the numbers and observations of others.

A. An Intuition

Like many in North America, I first went to Bible College when I was quite young. In 2009, I had serious brain surgery and spent a month at home in recovery. During this time, God hit me with the conviction that I was not living for him. I read 1 Corinthians 10:31, "whether you eat or drink, or whatever you do, do all to the glory of God"; I was struck by just how much my life at that time fell short of this standard. After much prayer and discussion with my parents, we decided I would go to Bible College for a one-year program to get grounded in the Bible before pursuing a career. That first year was life-changing. God began a work in me to challenge my sin and many aspects of my life. However, the most significant result was the firm conviction I developed that God had called me to give everything I had to his kingdom; I knew God had called me to grow in my knowledge of his word and to serve his people. My theology and spirituality were terribly malformed at that time, but God was beginning a good work in me. I signed up for a bachelor's degree and threw myself into my studies for the next three years, then I spent the next four years doing two master's degrees at Regent College. After a 1-year break, I then spent four years doing a PhD at Moore Theological College. I am grateful for the opportunities I was given to study God's word at these institutions, and God certainly used them to grow my character and understanding. However, during these 12 years of study, God continually drew my attention to the cracks in the system and gave me deep discontent with these cracks.

The first crack was biblical interpretation. It became apparent to me after a year or two of studies that the model of interpretation I was being taught could not be accurate. According to the Psalms, God's word gives understanding to children and adults alike and has done so for thousands of years (e.g. Pss 19:7; 119:9-16, 105; cf. Deut 6:4-9). Yet, according to what I was learning in class, properly understanding that word took years of study and massive libraries. As one author has put it,

> The process of learning, at its most basic, involves a deep study of the text of Scripture itself, and for the scholar, a deep study of Scripture calls for the hard work of biblical studies research.... To begin with, we must be able to engage the biblical languages with competence, as well as modern languages that facilitate our dialogue with others in the field. The study of the history of the ancient Near East and the Roman Empire, as well as a wide variety of cultural backgrounds, is mandatory. Since we are dealing with texts in a world of other texts, the ability to access and analyze ancient Near Eastern literature for Old Testament scholars or Second Temple Jewish literature and Greco-Roman literature for those studying the New Testament is mandatory, and increasingly, various aspects of modern linguistic theory play a part in our work as well. To understand and enter into dialogue with others in the field, we also must have some familiarity with the dizzying array of "criticisms," both

> higher and lower, in the history of investigating the biblical literature. Further, since texts are always interpreted, we need an awareness of what is going on in the areas of philosophical hermeneutics and biblical theology. On top of all this, we must keep up with developments in our own areas of focus—and bibliography has become daunting in almost all specializations.[1]

If this is what it takes to read the Bible, it is far from a clear light to our feet, a firm foundation in the shifting sands of our culture.[2] Moreover, what hope do our brothers and sisters across the globe have to understand God's Word?

The second crack was ethical. Upon the completion of a four-year degree in biblical and theological study, people look at you differently; I could have been hired by many churches as a pastor—many of my peers were. However, whatever theological and biblical knowledge my four-year bachelor's degree reflected, I certainly was not competent for Christian ministry. I did not understand—I did not truly love—God's churches; I did not see ministry as, above all, *pastoral* ministry, as soul care and shepherding. My academic gifts perhaps made it easy to think this way, but I certainly saw this reflected among my peers. Not only was my heart not right, but sin still dominated my life. I was still regularly indulging in lust, and pride and self-righteousness were strong in me. God had been changing me in the years since my wake-up call, but four years of theological training did little to equip me for the

---

[1] George H. Guthrie, "The Study of Holy Scripture and the Work of Christian Higher Education," in *Christian Higher Education: Faith, Teaching, and Learning in the Evangelical Tradition*, ed. David S. Dockery and Christopher W. Morgan (Wheaton: Crossway, 2018), 83. Cf. J. Alexander Rutherford, *God's Gifts for the Christian Life — Part 1: The Gift of Knowledge* (Airdrie, AB: Teleioteti, 2021).

[2] Cf. James Rutherford, "Review of When Doctrine Divides (by Rhyne Putman)," *Reformed Theological Review* 79, no. 2 (2020).

reality of pastoral ministry.[3] I was, perhaps, "able to teach," as Paul demands from an elder, but I did not have the character necessary to lead God's people. God, in his kindness, ensured that I would not be inflicted upon his church. He placed mentors in my life who challenged me and continually closed the doors to ministry, to the benefit of my faith and godliness, and then to my marriage.

Though I am no less convinced that God was and is working for the good of my peers, their stories looked very different from mine. Some of them went into pastoral ministry; some of them, by God's grace, have thrived; others have dropped out of ministry. Many of my peers fell away from the faith entirely; for others, I do not know what faith they now claim, but they are not living lives consistent with the Bible. Still others have become Catholic or Orthodox; still others have suffered marriage and family breakdowns. These were men and women who trained for pastoral ministry, or at least for lay ministry, yet instead of coming out with a stronger faith and firm godliness, many have walked away from that faith, or at least Protestant Christianity.[4]

Perhaps this was an issue with us, or with the college's system for vetting prospective students, you may suggest. Certainly, there is some truth to this, but my assumption, and the assumption of those who referred me to bible college (certainly others held this assumption too), was that bible college was a place where someone who was new or weak in faith could grow. That was not, however, the experience of many of us. Indeed, after I finished my bachelor's degree and reflected

---

[3] Cf. Linzay Rinquest, "Caught and Not Taught: A Journey in Integrating the Hidden Curriculum in a South African Seminary," in *Making Connections: Integrative Education in Africa*, ed. Marilyn Naidoo (African Sun Media, 2021), https://www.academia.edu/111133180/Caught_and_not_taught_A_journey_in_integrating_the_hidden_curriculum_in_a_South_African_seminary.

[4] I view my Catholic and Orthodox brothers and sisters as just that, brothers and sisters in Christ. However, I agree with the standard Protestant judgment that the Catholic and Orthodox churches are theologically deficient, and this may and often does create impediments to healthy church structures, discipleship, and evangelism.

on my wife's experience and mine at bible college, it was the class content itself that caused problems for us and our peers. I read broadly enough to overcome the problems I identified in biblical interpretation as I was taught it and to hold fast to the Bible's claims that it was clear, true, and applicable today. However, many of my peers gave up on the clarity of Scripture, sometimes abandoning the faith for this reason, turning to the Catholic church, or justifying ethical and theological positions Scripture explicitly prohibited. In Nicole's experience, her theology classes (with different teachers than mine) would have led her away from the Bible if she hadn't fought that tendency (hers is a lot more complicated story, but now is not the place to share it).

The apparent incongruity between my expectations of bible college—that it would grow my faith and that of others—was not unique to Pacific Life Bible College, where I first studied. This became all the more apparent as I continued to study at Regent College and, most recently, Moore Theological College. At Regent College, I saw peers walk away from the faith or, at least, abandon confidence in God's Word. The latter sort of students often converted to Catholicism or, on occasion, the Orthodox Church. I saw others become disillusioned with their faith and their churches, drifting towards Postmodern forms of Christianity, forms that abandoned the Bible and its ethics, often along with the teaching of the Christian tradition. I did not see this so much at Moore College for various reasons. This was a sign of some genuine advantages the system at Moore had over the others I had experienced; however, the recent track record of this institution is not much brighter than the others.

I talked with students from previous generations who had watched their peers walk away from the faith, go through painful divorces, or embrace heterodox expressions of Christianity. Sydney churches have been effective in employing a system of church mentorship and training that has meant many of their students are already more formed theologically and, to some extent, spiritually than those beginning at Regent College or Pacific Life Bible College. Nevertheless, this seems to confirm my observations from Pacific Life Bible College (PLBC) that our colleges do not do a great job training in godliness and spiritual maturity: the evident differences between Moore College, Regent, and PLBC were because of the church or university-based training apprenticeships most students attended before Moore.[5]

The third crack in our pastoral training institutions was evident to me at all three colleges I attended (and the numerous others I considered). My experience at college did not reinforce my confidence in Scripture but shook it. My experience at PLBC and Regent College didn't grow me in godliness but often gave fuel to my pride. My experience at all three colleges made evident to me the barriers facing prospective ministers of the Gospel. I mentioned above the system of pastoral apprenticeships used here in Sydney. In one influential book, the authors commend this system, but they then indicate that after someone has begun training in their church, they will need to go to bible college for theological training.[6] The message was clear: the church is great at doing certain things, but you really need a theological degree to be competent for ministry.[7] You need *academic* theological training for ministry. Similarly, the Presbyterian churches here in Sydney require their students to have academic theological training, and the Baptists require you to take some components at their college for full accreditation. The message is similar at Regent College; this is a school that, until recently, had specialised in training laypeople for ministry. The message? You need academic theology—or academic theology would certainly be useful—to live a fully Christian life (that is, to be intentionally Christian in all you do).

---

[5] See https://mts.com.au/; Colin Marshall and Tony Payne, *The Trellis and the Vine: The Ministry Mind-Shift That Changes Everything* (Sydney, NSW: Matthias Media, 2021).

[6] Marshall and Payne, 148–49.

[7] Even lay ministry in Sydney Anglican churches requires theological education.

Similarly, PLBC's one-year program was intended to give a theological and biblical foundation for living Christianly. So, the message of all these colleges (and every other college in my experience) is that you need *academic, college-based* knowledge or skills to be competent for ministry or to live an intentionally Christian life.[8] They do not say this explicitly, of course, but it is the *hidden curriculum,* the message communicated by the medium chosen to achieve their task: by choosing an academic institution to achieve these ends, they communicate that the ends are at the very least compatible with if not inextricably linked to higher education.[9]

Think for a moment about that. This raises immediate social, economic, intellectual, and geographical barriers for those considering Christian ministry. Socially, higher education is often associated with more well-off families and communities; those from disadvantaged backgrounds may, and often do, struggle with the particular demands of higher education institutions, not to mention meeting the entrance criteria. If you get accepted, there is an economic barrier: students are required to take on more and more debt as the costs of higher education increase. I have incurred immense debt during my studies, despite receiving many scholarships and working most of the time. Others have had to work to avoid debt and, as a result, have not been able to learn what the courses were intended to teach them. Others

---

8 See John M. Frame, "The Academic Captivity of Theology," in *John Frame's Selected Shorter Writings*, vol. 2 (Phillipsburg: P&R Pub, 2014); John M. Frame, "Seminaries and Academic Accreditation," in *John Frame's Selected Shorter Writings*, vol. 2 (Phillipsburg, NJ: P&R Pub, 2014). Cf. https://www.teleioteti.ca/2021/05/12/ over-intellectualisation/.

9 Cf. Perry W. H. Shaw, "The Hidden Curriculum of Seminary Education," *Journal of Asian Mission* 8, no. 1–2 (2006): 23–51; Terry Anderson, "The Hidden Curriculum in Distance Education: An Updated View," *Change: The Magazine of Higher Learning* 33, no. 6 (November 1, 2001): 28–35, https://doi.org/10.1080/00091380109601824.

choose not to pursue ministry entirely because of the economic costs.[10]

If you can afford it and get accepted, another barrier is intellectual. Higher education is difficult. Academic study not only requires discipline and time management skills but also a base of knowledge and literacy along with natural gifting in research, reading, and argument. Many students have dropped out, or struggled in other ways, because they came to college to pursue Christ and service to his church but were not intellectually wired for higher education. There are geographical barriers as well: in wealthy Western nations, Bible Colleges and Seminaries are usually located in large cities, so prospective students must move to the big cities for four or so years for their studies. If they are willing to do so, this means removal from their home church and the support structures they had developed there, which can exacerbate the social and economic barriers to study. If a student does this, it is hard to escape the pull of the city; fewer students return to the regional and rural areas than left them. There are significant ministry needs in the cities, but so also in the country, yet the model of ministry employed in our seminaries encourages future

---

[10] Cf. Bridget Terry Long, "Addressing the Academic Barriers to Higher Education," Brookings, accessed February 7, 2024, https://www.brookings.edu/articles/addressing-the-academic-barriers-to-higher-education/; Alasdair Forsyth and Andy Furlong, "Socio-Economic Disadvantage and Experience in Higher Education | Joseph Rowntree Foundation," Joseph Rowntree Foundation, May 16, 2003, https://www.jrf.org.uk/socio-economic-disadvantage-and-experience-in-higher-education; William B. Evans, "Whither the Seminary Model?," Reformation21, April 29, 2012, https://www.reformation21.org/blogs/whither-the-seminary-model.php; Alison Sheridan et al., "Four Barriers to Higher Education Regional Students Face – and How to Overcome Them," The Conversation, October 27, 2015, http://theconversation.com/four-barriers-to-higher-education-regional-students-face-and-how-to-overcome-them-49138; Hazel Ferguson, "Regional and Remote Higher Education: A Quick Guide," Government, Parliament of Australia, April 27, 2022, Australia, https://www.aph.gov.au/About_Parliament/Parliamentary_Departments/Parliamentary_Library/pubs/rp/rp2122/Quick_Guides/RegionalRemoteHigherEducation.

pastors to meet the needs of the cities, not the country.[11] That is my concise list of the barriers created by the academic system; surely you can think of more.

It is only within this system that someone could dare write the following lines:

> No one can be an expert in everything, but *statements about God constitute theology*, and theology is a single activity. Anyone who wishes to do theology of *any sort*—from Old Testament exegesis to systematic theology—needs basic competence in all of the following areas: the history of philosophy and theology, biblical languages, biblical hermeneutics, biblical introduction, the history of biblical interpretation, biblical theology, and dogmatic theology. To ask that it be made easier is to ask the impossible; it cannot be less complicated than it is. Asking that theologians without competencies in all these areas be allowed to do theology is like demanding that a person with only high school biology be allowed to perform surgery. It can be done, but the results will not be pretty.[12]

Do pastors make statements about God? Certainly they do, as did the apostles and our church members. What then? How were Peter and Mathew, John or James, Simon, Thaddeaus, or Thomas—how were any of the disciples—sufficient for Christian ministry? What about Timothy or Titus? We have no indications that they were so trained. Of all those mentioned in the New Testament, perhaps only Luke, Paul, and Apollos would qualify for Christian ministry under this

---

[11] See the sources cited above.

[12] Emphasis added. Craig A. Carter, *Contemplating God with the Great Tradition: Recovering Trinitarian Classical Theism* (Grand Rapids: Baker Academic, 2021), 324.

standard.

Do you feel the problem? The best system we have for training pastors is a system that undermines our confidence in the Bible, fails to develop the most crucial qualifier for Christian ministry (Christian character), and requires students to leave the one institution the Bible credits with this task, the local church.[13] This system also systemically discriminates against those from a disadvantaged social background, those who are not academically inclined, people who are economically disadvantaged, and those who aren't from major population centres. This is not to mention the discrimination against people from non-Western nations, who are looked down upon because of their lack of formal theological education. This is not guess work; I have talked with these pastors and with those who are attempting to remedy these issues. It is not Jewish fishermen like Andrew, Peter, James, and John who are likely to be recognised and trained through ordination for ministry on this model; no, it will probably be intellectually inclined, educated middle or upper-class citizens or residents of major cities in Western nations who will be so trained. If we take the Bible seriously, this should be a problem. If we take Jesus's words seriously, that a great harvest is ready, needing only workers, this should trouble us (Matt 9:37-38). Something is broken, and merely attempting to change our seminary curriculums or boost enrolment is not sufficient. We need to ask serious questions about *why* our system looks this way. But before we do that, let's consider the problem from another perspective.

B. A Consensus

Maybe you haven't observed what I have observed, but if you have frequented Christian media at all, you surely have heard a similar report: Bible Colleges and Seminaries are in decline, and at the same

---

[13] See further J. Alexander Rutherford, *The Being of Churches: A Neo-Congregational Polity*, Teleioteti Technical Studies (Teleioteti, 2023), https://doi.org/10.6008/ eikd5738.

time, our need for pastors is rapidly growing. The academic dean at PLBC was already telling me that enrolments across Canada were dropping in 2010; recent years have not been kind. Several colleges in Surrey closed during this time, one of them merging with PLBC.[14] The principle and staff at Regent College were saying something similar in 2014 and have spoken frequently since then about the financial struggles the college experiences to stay afloat. Several Christianity Today articles have documented this trend in major American bible colleges and seminaries, which have considered downsizing or actually downsized to stay afloat.[15] The problem of viability facing these colleges is only increased by the declining enrolment rates that frequently make headlines. For example, in 2020, the Association of Theological Schools reported at 57% decline in enrolment among member institutions.[16] Between 2014-2018, a Christian and Missionary

---

14 For the general trend of college closure, see Bill Muehlenberg, "Evangelical Seminaries in Decline," Blog, Culture Watch, accessed February 2, 2024, https://billmuehlenberg.com/2022/05/18/evangelical-seminaries-in-decline/.

15 Christianity Today has document this for Gordon-Conwell, TEDS, and Fuller. Daniel Silliman, "Gordon-Conwell to Sell Main Campus, Move to Boston," News & Reporting, Christianity Today, May 17, 2022, https://www.christianitytoday.com/news/2022/may/gordon-conwell-sell-campus-financial-enrollment-struggle.html; Daniel Silliman, "Facing Financial Challenges, TEDS Cuts Faculty Positions," News & Reporting, Christianity Today, April 12, 2022, https://www.christianitytoday.com/news/2022/april/teds-financial-trouble-crisis-perrin-faculty-cuts.html; Megan Fowler, "Fuller Seminary Won't Leave Pasadena After All," News & Reporting, Christianity Today, October 31, 2019, https://www.christianitytoday.com/news/2019/october/fuller-seminary-pasadena-campus-cancel-move-pomona.html.

16 J.D. Payne, "An Overlooked Reason for Decline in Seminary Enrollment," *ChurchLeaders* (blog), July 21, 2023, https://churchleaders.com/outreach-missions/455242-an-overlooked-reason-for-decline-in-seminary-enrollment.html; Religion News Service, "Theological Schools Report Continued Drop in Master of Divinity Degrees," The Presbyterian Outlook, December 5, 2022,

Alliance affiliated college in Redding California observed nearly a 50% decline in attendance.[17] Not only are bible college and seminary enrolments down, but churches are closing or going without ministers of the Gospel. In Sydney, 20 Sydney Anglican parishes (as of January 2024) have no lead minister (presbyter); many of them are combined parishes because of the closure of previous parishes. This is down from 30 parishes in 2020.[18] That number "20" includes some parishes that have recently merged with another but not historical mergers (the Parish of Canterbury was once three parishes, Hurlstone Park, Canterbury, and Ashbury; the Parish of Riverwood-Punchbowl was once three parishes, Riverwood, Punchbowl, and Beverly Hills North). In the USA, as of 2019, 20% of Catholic parishes (3,363 of 17,007) are vacant, and 4500 Protestants churches closed that same year.[19] In 2018, 38 of 228 ELCA churches in Northwest Minnesota were in need of a pastor.[20] For the same denomination, 1 in 4 churches can no longer

---

https://pres-outlook.org/2022/12/theological-schools-report-continued-drop-in-master-of-divinity-degrees/.

17 Liam Adams, "Christian Colleges Are Changing to Survive. Is It Working?," News & Reporting, Christianity Today, September 9, 2020, https://www.christianitytoday.com/news/2020/september/enrollment-crisis-christian-college-cccu-evangelical-humani.html.

18 "Vacant Parish List," *Southern Cross*, March 2024, 27, https://issuu.com/sydneyanglicans/docs/sc24_02-03. For the 2020 numbers, see https://sydneyanglicans.net/news/where-are-all-the-senior-ministers.

19 Robert David Sullivan, "Parishes without Pastors Decline, but Only Because More Churches Have Closed," America Magazine, June 14, 2019, https://www.americamagazine.org/faith/2019/06/14/parishes-without-pastors-decline-only-because-more-churches-have-closed; Aaron Earls, "22 Vital Stats for Ministry in 2022 - Lifeway Research," Lifeway Research, January 5, 2022, https://lifewayresearch.com/2022/01/05/22-vital-stats-for-ministry-in-2022/.

20 Jean Hopfensperger, "Fewer People Are Entering the Seminary as Need Declines, Church Budgets Shrink," News & Reporting, Star Tribune, August 19, 2018, https://www.startribune.com/fewer-people-are-entering-the-seminary-as-need-declines-church-budgets-shrink/490381681/.

afford to pay a minister.[21] Like many other denominations, the ELCA is seeing more ministers retire than they are ordaining (3661 to 2241 in 2010-2018).[22]

The closure of churches and the famine of ministers is mirrored by the general drops in church attendance across the Western world, which has been well documented for many years.[23] Of those who do graduate and enter into ministry, another problem becomes intertwined with this: many are feeling burnt out and retiring early.[24] Off the top of my head, I personally know four ministers who have done so. In addition to my anecdotal experience of those who attend seminary or Bible College and left the faith entirely, embraced heterodox expressions of Christianity, or joined Catholic or Orthodox churches, social media is afire with stories of so-called "exevangelicals." I personally know at least one who was formerly a pastor and many more who received theological training, though I cannot find stats on the numbers.

C. Three Additional Fault Lines in Pastoral Ministry

So, many Evangelicals are deconstructing and leaving the faith; many pastors are retiring young; church attendance is generally declining; and

---

21 Ibid.

22 Ibid.

23 E.g. Liz Jakimow, "Is Australia Losing Religion: The State of the Church," Education, Australian Centre for Christianity and Culture, accessed February 2, 2024, https://about.csu.edu.au/community/accc/about/latest-news-assets/2023/is-australia-losing-religion-the-state-of-the-church.

24 Kate Shellnutt, "The Pastors Aren't All Right: 38% Consider Leaving Ministry," News & Reporting, Christianity Today, November 16, 2021, https://www.christianitytoday.com/news/2021/november/pastor-burnout-pandemic-barna-consider-leaving-ministry.html; Earls, "22 Vital Stats for Ministry in 2022 - Lifeway Research"; "Pastors Share Top Reasons They've Considered Quitting Ministry in the Past Year," Barna Group, April 27, 2022, https://www.barna.com/research/pastors-quitting-ministry/.

our seminaries are training fewer and fewer pastors as more and more retire, leaving churches without pastors. This is well documented and should be of serious concern to us. A question that should be explored is the relation between these trends, if any. Before we do that, consider with me briefly three other fault lines in the contemporary church.

First, as I observed during my studies, there is a growing identification of Evangelical Christian ministry with the academy; this began in the early days of the Evangelical movement and has recently grown more prominent.[25]

Second, there is evident moral decay within the pastorate, with many ministers destroying their families and churches over moral failings, such as pride, adultery, bullying, financial mismanagement, or child abuse. One thinks of spats of sex abuse scandals, the collapse of Mark Driscoll and Mars Hill Church in Seattle, the fall of various Pentecostal and Charismatic preachers in recent decades, the fall of James MacDonald, the recent sexual abuse allegations concerning the Southern Baptist Conference in the USA, the well document sexual abuse perpetrated by Catholic priests, the infidelity and fall from ministry of Art Azurdia and Tullian Tchividjian, etc. This list goes on endlessly; we cannot ignore it. We must look at the problem and grieve the abuses that have been perpetrated by men who have been ordained into ministry, who were supposed to model godly character to their

---

[25] Cf. Frame, "The Academic Captivity of Theology." See also the comments from Carter and Guthrie quoted above. Cf. *Biblical Higher Education.* Mark Noll has documented another movement within Evangelicalism, but Reformed Evangelicals have been particularly susceptible to the association with higher education, and Evangelicalism is known for starting many major higher education institutions in North America, such as Fuller Seminary, TEDS, and Gordon-Conwell. Frame, "The Captivity of Theology"; Carter, *Contemplating God*; Guthrie, "The Study of Holy Scripture and the Work of Christian Higher Education"; David S. Dockery and Christopher W. Morgan, eds., *Christian Higher Education: Faith, Teaching, and Learning in the Evangelical Tradition* (Wheaton: Crossway, 2018); Mark A. Noll, *The Scandal of the Evangelical Mind*, With New Preface and Afterword (Grand Rapids: Eerdmans, 2022).

congregations and shepherd them with all care and diligence.

Third, there is the professionalisation of ministry, which, despite the criticism that has repeatedly been raised against it, has continued to grow across the church.[26] 'Professionalisation' is the tendency to treat the church as analogous to other human institutions: this may include treating the pastorate like another career, with appropriate emotional distance from the people involved and regular role switching to climb the corporate ladder; it often includes taking business principles into the pastoral role, structuring the local church or denomination like a corporation and often replacing *pastoral* ministry with leadership; professionalisation also involves adapting a pragmatic approach to ministry, evaluating success on the basis of measurable outcomes and relying on human wisdom to ensure 'success' so defined.

What is the connection between all these seemingly disparate markers of crisis? Certainly there is no single connection that explains the problem entirely, but there is certainly a problem for which all of these prove to be symptoms. To put it simply, there is a failure of pastoral training in the Western Church. There is a failure of our pastoral training model that is having real-life impacts on the church. As has been observed, falling enrolments are linked to falling church attendance, yet there is a vicious cycle here: biblically speaking, a healthy pastorate is essential to a growing church, but where the pastorate fails, churches will fail, and college enrolment numbers will likewise fall. Enrolment numbers are further threatened by the barriers our current system of training puts before potential ministers. The costs of seminary training can be prohibitive, not to mention the dislocation from family and church and the heavy intellectual requirements of academic pastoral training. Without pastors, churches inevitably close, which then affects evangelisation and outreach in communities so affected. The low enrolment numbers are exacerbated by the number of students dropping out, abandoning the faith,

---

26 E.g. John Piper, *Brothers We Are Not Professionals A Plea to Pastors for Radical Ministry.*, Updated&Expanded (Nashville: B&H, 2013).

abandoning Evangelicalism, or importing heterodoxy into local churches. However, the numbers do not tell the full story: of those who make it into the pulpit, many will leave the ministry. When combined with the fact of moral failure and professionalisation, it seems that those who pass through the current pastoral training systems are not adequate as *pastors*, the very thing they are being trained for. This is confirmed by the observation that the academic bent of our seminaries and Bible colleges results in "pastors" who do not know how to pastor, that is, in ordained persons who know theology, know how to write, know how to speak publicly, but do not understand how to connect the Bible with the hearts and hands of their congregation.[27]

D. Conclusion

Do you feel this problem? Many lament the failures of our pastoral training institutions, yet I want to suggest that their proposed solutions often reinforce the root of the problem.[28] Several decades ago, John Frame identified a problem in our theology, decrying its captivity to academia, and reflected on the effects this has on our institutions.[29] Yet, since he wrote these essays, Evangelicals have only doubled down on the identification of theology with higher education. In recent years, prominent Evangelicals can and have claimed that to "make

[27] Cf. Paul David Tripp, *Dangerous Calling: Confronting the Unique Challenges of Pastoral Ministry*, 1st edition (Wheaton: Crossway, 2012); David Powlison, *The Pastor as Counselor: The Call for Soul Care* (Wheaton: Crossway, 2021); Martin Bucer, *Concerning the True Care of Souls*, trans. Peter Beale (Edinburgh: Banner of Truth Trust, 2009).

[28] E.g. Douglas A Sweeney, "A Call and Agenda for Pastor-Theologians," blog, The Gospel Coalition, June 16, 2017, https://www.thegospelcoalition.org/article/a-call-and-agenda-for-pastor-theologians/.

[29] John M. Frame, "Proposal for a New Seminary," *Journal of Pastoral Practice Winter 1978*, January 1, 1978, https://frame-poythress.org/proposal-for-a-new-seminary/; Frame, "The Academic Captivity of Theology"; Frame, "Seminaries and Academic Accreditation."

statements about God" or to study the Bible rightly, a student needs to be even more academically qualified then our current institutions are achieving—so much so that J.I. Packer, Bruce Ware, John Frame, and Wayne Grudem, among others, are not competent to "make statements about God."[30] I want to contend that this is *the* problem. One of the causes behind the plethora of problems I introduced above is a failure in the pastoral ministry caused by a failure to understand what a pastor is and to wrestle with training ministers in light of that.

Pastors have been identified with scholars and theologians, and 'theology' has been carefully defined in such a way that a fisherman or tax collector no longer qualifies for Christian ministry. By redefining the core task of pastors as 'teachers,' where teaching involves communicating this 'theology,' and redefining the competencies of pastoral ministry in line with this definition, the Western church has succeeded in producing generations of pastors ill-equipped for the reality of pastoral ministry and ill-equipped for the realities of the Christian life in a culture that is growing more and more hostile to the central tenets of the Christian faith. An ill-equipped pastorate has often, though by God's grace not always, resulted in unhealthy churches. The anecdotes with which I began this introduction certainly point in this direction, and the numbers agree.

The bulk of this book will seek to demonstrate this problem theologically. In Part 1, I will seek to show that many in the church have adopted a destructive epistemology and that this epistemology has distorted our understanding of pastoral ministry. In Part 2, I will seek to show how the Bible provides very different answers to the key problems this epistemology was introduced to address. In Part 3, we

---

30 Carter, *Contemplating God*, 298, 324; Guthrie, "The Study of Holy Scripture and the Work of Christian Higher Education," 83; James E. Dolezal, *All That Is in God: Evangelical Theology and the Challenge of Classical Christian Theism* (Grand Rapids: Reformation Heritage Books, 2017), 21–35, 71–73.

will then analyse how we could redefine pastoral training in light of the Bible's view of things.

—PART 1— ANALYZING THE FOUNDATIONS

DIAGNOSING THE PROBLEM 1: DRAWING NEW LINES[1]

> Do not move the ancient landmark that your fathers have set. – Prov 22:28 (ESV)

> So for the sake of your tradition you have made void the word of God. You hypocrites! Well did Isaiah prophesy of you, when he said: "This people honors me with their lips, but their heart is far from me; in vain do they worship me, teaching as doctrines the commandments of men." – Matthew 15:6-9 (ESV)

There was a thesis put forth in the late 19th century, which found a hearing throughout the 20th century, that the early church sold out to Greek Philosophy and replaced biblical, Hebrew categories for thinking about God and his world with pagan, Greek, philosophical categories. The response to this thesis has been comprehensive and voluminous, shedding much light on what was actually going on in the 2nd-6th centuries as early Christian thought developed. However, an

[1] This chapter is adapted from my essay, J. Alexander Rutherford, "Whose Fall? What Hellenism? Christianity's Fall into Hellenistic Philosophy Revisited," *The Teleioteti Journal for Christian Ministry* 1, no. 1 (2023): 1–40, https://doi.org/10.60080/cliw1201.

opposing error has emerged as an overreaction to this position. This overreaction, or what I will show to be an overreaction, takes the refutation of the so-called 'Hellenisation thesis' to mean that the relationship between the Early Church and Greek philosophy was not problematic. We are told that Christians who criticize the fathers in this regard are guilty of modernism and theological error.[2] The Fathers, we are told, engaged in "missionary theology," "taking concepts and breaking them apart by hammering them on the anvil of Scripture and then reforging them in the flame of truth until they were bent into a usable shape for proclaiming the gospel."[3] However, with John C. Peckham, I want to suggest this is a false dichotomy: we do not have to choose between the theories that the church sold out or that they were impeccable in their philosophical engagement. Showing that the early church engaged critically with ancient philosophy is sufficient to dismiss the 19th-century "Hellenization thesis" but not sufficient to dismiss every criticism that may be made about the role of philosophy in early Christian thought.[4]

In this chapter, I want to argue that the early church made a critical error in their engagement with pagan philosophy. The result of this error is the exaltation of learning over simplicity and the inclusion of extensive learning as a prerequisite to be theological teacher.[5] It is

---

[2] Paul L. Gavrilyuk, *The Suffering of the Impassible God: The Dialectics of Patristic Thought* (Oxford University Press, 2004), 21; Kevin J. Vanhoozer, *Remythologizing Theology: Divine Action, Passion, and Authorship*, Cambridge Studies in Christian Doctrine 18 (Cambridge, U.K.; New York: Cambridge University Press, 2010), 89.

[3] Vanhoozer, *Remythologizing Theology*, 90; Carter, *Contemplating God*, 216–17.

[4] John Peckham, *Divine Attributes: Knowing the Covenantal God of Scripture*, 2021, chap. 1.

[5] Careful readers of Patristic literature will observe that this was not the only trend; there was also a strong mystical tradition that placed a strong emphasis on radical living, asceticism, and good works. This mystical

neither an obvious error nor as significant an error as that of their opponents, who sold out to paganism, but it is an error, nevertheless. I will argue that by using the tools of ancient philosophy, even as critically as they did, Christians not only made minor mistakes (none of us are perfect in our "missionary theology," are we?) but, more significantly, also bought into crucial assumptions of that philosophy.[6] For the purposes of this book, the biggest problem that emerges from the embrace of the assumptions of philosophy is the identification of orthodoxy and right Christian theology with a philosophical model of the doctrine of God. This, in turn, means that leading theologians and pastors will be the intellectuals. Eventually, this will mean that to be orthodox and a Christian teacher, one will need to be educated and competent in philosophy. We are now witnessing this development among those who are calling for a *ressourcement* of the Early Church's theology.

The parable Iain McGilchrist used for his 2009 book, *The Master and the Emissary*, is fitting for the problem I am identifying,

> There was once a wise spiritual master, who was the ruler of a small but prosperous domain, and who was known for his selfless devotion to his people. As his people flourished and grew in number, the bounds of this small domain spread; and with it the need to trust implicitly the emissaries he sent to ensure the safety of its ever more distant parts. It was not just that it was impossible for him personally to order all that needed to be dealt with: as he wisely saw, he needed to keep his distance from, and remain ignorant of, such concerns. And so he nurtured and trained carefully his emissaries, in order that they could be trusted.

tradition has continued, especially in the East, but the dominant voices in the West, especially in Protestantism, have been those of the orthodox discussed in this chapter.

6 "Missionary theology" is Vanhoozer's description of what the Early Church was doing. Vanhoozer, *Remythologizing Theology*, 90.

> Eventually, however, his cleverest and most ambitious vizier, the one he most trusted to do his work, began to see himself as the master, and used his position to advance his own wealth. He saw his master's temperance and forbearance as weakness, not wisdom, and on his mission on the master's behalf, adopted his mantle as his own—the emissary became contemptuous of his master. And so it came about that the master was usurped, the people were duped, the domain became tyranny; and eventually it collapsed into ruins.[7]

Ours is likewise a story of the servant usurping its master, but in this case, we are dealing with Christian life and engagement—particularly in its intellectual dimensions. Theology did not begin as a Christian science; as early as Aristotle, the science of *theologia* is identified, "There must, then, be three theoretical philosophies, mathematics, physics, and what we may call theology [θεολογική, *theologike*], since it is obvious that if the divine is present anywhere, it is present in things of this sort."[8] This is not how "theology" is often used today (it is certainly not the way I use the term), but I have no objections to using the term for this science.[9] As Christians engaged with a world that itself

[7] Iain McGilchrist, *The Master and His Emissary: The Divided Brain and the Making of the Western World*, New expanded edition (New Haven: Yale University Press, 2019), 14, https://doi.org/10.12987/9780300247459.

[8] *Metaphysics* VI.I, 1026a in Aristotle, "Metaphysics," in *The Works of Aristotle*, ed. W. D. Rose and J. A. Smith, Logos Edition, vol. 8 (Oxford: The Clarendon Press, 1908).

[9] E.g. "I would suggest that we defined theology as 'the application of the Word of God by persons to all areas of life.' The meaning of this definition ought to be fairly clear, except for *application*. I would define *application* as 'teaching' in the New Testament sense (*didache, didaskalia*), a concept represented in some translations by *doctrine*. Teaching in the New Testament (and I think also in the Old) is the use of God's revelation to meet the spiritual needs of people, to promote godliness and spiritual heath." John M. Frame, *The Doctrine of the Knowledge of God*, A Theology of Lordship (Phillipsburg, NJ: P&R Publishing, 1987), 81.

had a *theologia* along with accompanying accounts of physics, metaphysics, and ontology, Christian intellectuals naturally engaged with their peers on the same level, seeking to show how the biblical teaching is neither anti-metaphysical nor anti-theological but is actually the appropriate end of metaphysics and *theologia;* it is true not only in the spiritual and phenomenal realms, but in every sphere of intellectual activity. In this way, philosophy (by which I mean that sphere of intellectual activity that is often associated with the Hellenisation thesis, such as metaphysics and *theologia*) is a tool in a broader Christian project of living life in submission to Christ. Not only is it a tool, but it is arguably a servant and secondary tool to a greater purpose and goal.

Christ's commission to his disciples was to "Go therefore and make disciples of all nations, baptizing them in the name of the Father and of the Son and of the Holy Spirit, teaching them to observe all that I have commanded you. And behold, I am with you always, to the end of the age." (Matt 28:19-20, ESV). The tools they were given to do so were the public reading of Scripture (e.g. 1 Tim 4:13), the teaching of the word and doctrine (e.g. Acts 2:42; 1 Tim 4:13; 2 Tim 3:16-17), self-less service to one another and the world (e.g. Gal 6:10), corporate life together (e.g. Eph 4:11-16), the Lord's supper (1 Cor 11:17-34), Baptism (Matt 28:19), etc. The primary activities given by the Lord for the church to accomplish his mission are contingent and particular activities, pertaining to individual events and persons; doctrine in Scripture focuses on the level of God's revealed self in space and time, not so much on the conceptual refinement and search for universal, necessary truths associated with metaphysics and *theologia.* However, nothing about Christ's commission suggests that philosophy is an illegitimate tool for thinking about God and his world, engaging in the works he has entrusted to the church, and for rationally commending the faith to others. However, philosophy is clearly not the commission of the church; it is not integral to its purpose, nor is it necessary for Christians to know, love, live for, and teach Christ and him crucified (1 Cor 2:1-5). In this sense, it is a tool and, therefore, a servant—a very useful one at that.

However, what if at some point or another (probably at many points) that tool metastasised from its position as a servant to the role of the master? What if this servant began to see itself as wiser and more efficient than its master and other servants? What if this servant staged a revolt and subtlety submitted every other servant to itself, perhaps—if at all possible—usurping the master itself? This is the grain of truth that I want to argue is present in the thesis of "Christianity's fall into Hellenistic philosophy." Instead of throwing itself uncritically into a mode of thought antithetical to the gospel—embracing a "Greek" way of thinking instead of a "Hebrew" one—I want to suggest that Christian thinkers and eventually much of the Church bought into the thesis of Plato's great dividing line, that the intelligible world is more valuable than the perceptible world (*Rep.* 509c-511a), that truth is not opinion (and the latter is the object of the senses), and (with Aristotle) that Wisdom—the knowledge of "causes and principles"—is the highest form of knowledge (e.g. *Meta* 980a-982a). The particularity of "Christ and him crucified" has given way to the claim that "primarily and principally, theological intelligence intends eternal and necessary truths, by the gift of God penetrating to their depths," deriving the practical therefrom.[10] In sum, metaphysics and *theologia*—knowledge as *scientia*—became the goal of Christian contemplation of God, the warp and woof of their God-talk, the form which was actualized in preaching and teaching, and even the goal of biblical exegesis. In the latter case, one thinks of Origen's account of exegesis in the *First Principles* (e.g. *Prin.* Pref. 8-10), but let's turn to a contemporary example to see this trajectory among those who vehemently deny the so-called 'Hellenisation thesis,'

The study of patristics has not been regarded as

---

[10] John Webster, "What Makes Theology Theological?" in God Without Measure: Working Papers in Christian Theology, vol. I, T&T Clark Theology (London; New York: Bloomsbury T&T Clark, 2016), 221.

> essential preparation either for systematic theologians or for *pastors*, and this creates problems in *understanding* and *passing on* classical *orthodoxy*. The decline in the study of Greek philosophy by theologians also renders them unable to comprehend what the fourth-century debates were all about.... Holding together classical theism and trinitarian theology requires tolerance for mystery and sustained attentiveness to the nuances of philosophical and theological debates of the fourth century. Classical theism without trinitarian theology gives us the god of the philosophers, that is, the remote and impersonal god of Deism, who does not speak or act and who, crucially, *cannot save us*.[11]
>
> No one can be an expert in everything, but statements about God constitute theology, and theology is a single activity. Anyone who wishes to do theology of any sort—from Old Testament exegesis to systematic theology—needs basic competence in all of the following areas: the history of philosophy and theology, biblical languages, biblical hermeneutics, biblical introduction, the history of biblical interpretation, biblical theology, and dogmatic theology. To ask that it be made easier is to ask the impossible; it cannot be less complicated than it is. Asking that theologians without competencies in all these areas be allowed to do theology is like demanding that a person with only high school biology be allowed to perform surgery. It can be done, but the result will not be pretty.[12]

Is it not evident how *scientia* has taken a central place? To even speak about God, we need to be academics of unparalleled calibre—to such depth that Bruce Ware and J.I. Packer never reached.[13] No longer are

---

[11] Emphasis added. Carter, *Contemplating God*, 29.

[12] Carter, 296.

[13] Carter, 298. Cf. Dolezal, *All That Is in God*, 21–34; Guthrie, "The Study of Holy Scripture and the Work of Christian Higher Education," 83.

fishermen filled with the Spirit sufficient to bring the Gospel to all nations, to speak the truth of God; no longer can a young man like Timothy pass on the good deposit he has received (1 Tim 4:12; 6:20; 2 Tim 2:1-7). No longer is the truth of God able to be uttered by the uneducated rocks or lived by young men and women (Luke 19:40; Ps 119:9-16).

How is it that the servant has become the master? This is, I believe, the true story of Christianity's "fall." It is not a fall into something totally other; Christians throughout the ages have been wise enough to avoid that ditch. Instead, it is the soft seduction of *scientia*, the fact that Christianity is indeed more cogent, more commendable, and eminently more reasonable than its peers that has led us to Carter's Elite Theism. In wielding the tool of Philosophy with great insight and prowess, filled with the Spirit and equipped with the written Word of the Creator himself, Christians have beaten their unbelieving peers at their own game, yet they have succeeded where the philosophers never did—in making that game the only game in town.

For the reader who still needs to be convinced that Christians used philosophical tools and did so critically, there are many resources available making this point. Paul Gavrilyuk and Andrew Radde-Gallwitz have made the case for Christian critical engagement with their sources in reference to impassibility and simplicity; in a later period, there are various efforts to mitigate the implications of metaphysics on the eternality of matter and the free creation of God, motivated by their adherence to Scripture.[14] One could argue that the

[14] Andrew Radde-Gallwitz, *Basil of Caesarea, Gregory of Nyssa, and the Transformation of Divine Simplicity*, Oxford Early Christian Studies (Oxford; New York: Oxford University Press, 2009), https://doi.org/10.1093/acprof:oso/9780199574117.001.0001; Gavrilyuk, *The Suffering of the Impassible God.* Grigory Benevich, "God's Logoi and Human Personhood in St Maximus the Confessor," Studi Sull'Oriente Cristiano 13, no. 1 (2009): 137–52; Maximos Constas, "Maximus the Confessor, Dionysius the Areopagite, and the Transformation of Christian Neoplatonism,"

reason tension exists in the Definition of Chalcedon, as several authors have argued, is because its authors were unwilling to accommodate the biblical teaching of the incarnation to their metaphysical frameworks, so they put together a statement that upheld both and, as a result, contained significant tension.[15] Nevertheless, I digress; this is not our project here.

Instead, I want us to first consider the council of Nicaea and its later interpretation in the context of the controversy over the Son's relationship to the Father. I want to consider, in particular, what tools

---

Analogia 2, no. 1 (2017): 1–12; Vladimir Cvetković, "'All in All' (1 Cor 15:28): Aspects of the Unity Between God and Creation According to St Maximus the Confessor," Analogia 2, no. 1 (2017): 13–28; Emma Brown Dewhurst, "How Can We Be Nothing?: The Concept of Non-Being in Athanasius and Maximus the Confessor," Analogia 2, no. 1 (2017): 29–34; Timur Shchukin, "Matter as a Universal: John Philoponus and Maximus the Confessor on the Eternity of the World," Scrinium 13, no. 1 (2017): 361–82, https://doi.org/10.1163/18177565-00131p23; Vladimir Cvetkovic, "Re-Interpreting Tradition: Maximus the Confessor on Creation in Ambigua Ad Ioannem," in Questioning the World. Greek Patristic and Byzantine Question and Answer Literature, ed. Bram Bemulder and Peter Van Deun, Lectio 11 (Turnhout, Belgium: Brepols, 2021), 147–80.

15 Arguing for tension or aporia are Jean-Yves Lacoste, "Homoousios et Homoousios: La Substance Entre Théologie et Philosophie," Recherches de Science Religieuse 98, no. 1 (January 2010): 85–100, https://doi.org/10.3917/rsr.101.0085; Johannes Zachhuber, *The Rise of Christian Theology and the End of Ancient Metaphysics: Patristic Philosophy from the Cappadocian Fathers to John of Damascus* (Oxford University Press, 2020), 103–11; Bruce Lindley McCormack, *The Humility of the Eternal Son: Reformed Kenoticism and the Repair of Chalcedon* (Cambridge University Press, 2021), https://doi.org/10.1017/9781009000123. My PhD thesis sought to identify if such a tension existed and, if so, what its contours were. James Rutherford, "Maximus the Confessor's Use of the Divine-Human Analogy and the Niceno-Chalcedonian Tradition," *Phronema* 38, no. 1 (Spring 2023); J. Alexander Rutherford, "Rightly Defining the Son of God: Examining the Definition of Chalcedon's Conceptual Apparatus" (Ph.D. Thesis, Sydney, NSW, Moore Theological College, 2023), https://moore.quartexcollections.com/Documents/Detail/rightly-defining-the-son-of-god-examining-the-definition-of-chalcedons-conceptual-apparatus/10.

were wielded in this struggle and the result they had on Christian ecclesiology at the end of the 4th century. Second, I want to consider how Nicaea was received at Chalcedon and the tools that were used in the debates over the incarnation from Ephesus I (431) to Chalcedon (451). Finally, I will bring together these threads and argue that Chalcedon reflected in writing an attitude towards orthodoxy that developed in the preceding century, an attitude that enshrined *scientia* as the measure of right faith and the mark of "in" and "out" among Christians, simultaneously making orthodoxy and Christian ministry a matter of *Scientia.*

A. Arius and the Significance of Nicaea

The 4th-century did not create an interest in Christian engagement with the Hellenistic intellectual tradition, nor did it signal a significant deviation from the use of philosophy in the 3rd century. As many have observed, Arius and many others were "Origenian" in their approach to such matters.[16] In his compelling treatment of Arius, Rowan Williams argues that in this sense, Arius was a "conservative," specifically because of his adherence to received tradition.[17] However traditional the metaphysic was through which Arius developed his theology, his bold statements of Christ's ignorance of and radical difference from the Father were sure to provoke his Alexandrian peers

---

16 E.g. Rowan Williams, Arius: Heresy and Tradition, 2. ed (London: SCM, 2001); Giulio Maspero, "Isoangelia in Gregory of Nyssa and Origen on the Background of Plotinus," in Papers Presented at the Seventeenth International Conference on Patristic Studies Held in Oxford 2015 Volume 10 Evagrius between Origen, the Cappadocians, and Neoplatonism, Studia Patristica 84 (Leuven: Peeters, 2017), 77–100; Ilaria Ramelli, "Gregory Nyssen's and Evagrius' Biographical and Theological Relations: Origen's Heritage and Neoplatonism," in Papers Presented at the Seventeenth International Conference on Patristic Studies Held in Oxford 2015 Volume 10 Evagrius between Origen, the Cappadocians, and Neoplatonism, Studia Patristica 84 (Leuven: Peeters, 2017), 165–231.

17 Williams, *Arius.*

and the bishop, Alexander (it didn't help that Arius seemed to be a popularizer in his approach to disseminating his teaching).[18] In response to Arius and the threat that the growing conflict in Alexandria posed to the unity of his Empire, Constantine convened the first ecumenical council at Nicaea (325) to address the growing conflict in the Alexandrian church. Nicaea did not end the controversy, which quickly expanded across many different fault lines as Christians (or so-called Christians, if you prefer) battled over which account of the Son's relationship to the Father would be secured. Cogent accounts of this period are plenty; I merely want to focus on two aspects of it.[19] First, Nicaea as a response to Arius's purported error and the reception of Nicaea in the second half of the 4th century.

i. The Response to Arius's Error

In Constantine, Rome had its first Christian emperor, yet Rodney Stark argues that he did not "Christianise" the empire but instead responded to the startling phenomenon of the previous centuries, namely, that Christianity—a largely persecuted religion—grew to the point where being a "Christian" Emperor was pragmatically ideal, however sincere Constantine's conversion may have been.[20] As the head of an Empire

---

18 E.g. M. L. West, "The Metre of Arius' 'Thalia,'" *JTS* 33.1 (1982): 98–105; Rowan D. Williams, "The Quest of the Historical Thalia," in *Arianism: Historical and Theological Reassessments: Papers from The Ninth International Conference on Patristic Studies*, ed. Robert C. Gregg, Reprint., Patristic Monograph Series V. 11 (2006: Wipf and Stock Publishers, 2006), 1–35; Philostorgius, *Epitome*, 2.2.

19 E.g. John Behr, *The Nicene Faith: Vol 2 of Formation of Christian Theology* (Crestwood, N.Y.: St Vladimir's Seminary Press, 2004); Lewis Ayres, *Nicaea and Its Legacy: An Approach to Fourth-Century Trinitarian Theology*, 1st ed. (Oxford: Oxford University Press, 2004), https://doi.org/10.1093/0198755066.001.0001; Frances M. Young, *From Nicaea to Chalcedon: A Guide to the Literature and Its Background*, 2nd ed. (London: SCM Press, 2010).

20 Rodney Stark, *The Rise of Christianity: A Sociologist Reconsiders History* (Princeton University Press, 1996).

with a large population of Christians, the inter-Christian theological debates could no longer be ignored; a serious split in the global Christian church would have serious ramifications for the Empire. At Nicaea, a document was produced as the answer to Arius' error, a "Creed" (σύμβολον, *sumbolon*) that would be acceptable to the majority of the bishops in the Empire but unacceptable to Arius. There is a broad agreement among scholars that the term ὁμοούσιος ("consubstantial") was introduced to achieve the latter purpose: it was a term that Arius would certainly not agree with.[21] There were good reasons for Arius not to agree: the term was associated with a 3rd-century heresy associated with Paul of Samosata and had significant materialist connotations that all parties were certain to deny.[22] However, the Creed was a concerted effort to delineate some as "in" and some as "out" in the global, Imperial church, and the term served this purpose. Nevertheless, the result was not so clear cut. Decades of debate ensued. Nevertheless, the means the council used to secure their goal are as important as its immediate result.

The Nicene Creed, with its anathemas, was an unassuming document: it contained clear Scriptural claims, "the Father almighty," "Son of God," "only-begotten," etc. However, the bishops recognized that repeating the statements of Scripture was not enough: Arius did this as well. They needed to fight at the level of concepts and ideas. On

---

[21] E.g. R. P. C. Hanson, *The Search for the Christian Doctrine of God: The Arian Controversy 318-381* (Edinburgh: T. & T. Clark, 1988), 202; Williams, *Arius*, 68–70; Behr, *The Nicene Faith: Vol 2 of Formation of Christian Theology*, 157.

[22] G. L. Prestige, *St Basil the Great and Apollinaris of Laodicea* (London: SPCK, 1956), 209; George Christopher Stead, *Divine Substance* (Oxford: Clarendon Press, 1977), 242–44, https://doi.org/10.1093/acprof:oso/9780198266303.001.0001; Hanson, *The Search*, 190–97; Williams, *Arius*, 134–35; John Behr, *The Way to Nicaea*, The Formation of Christian Theology, v. 1 (Crestwood, NY: St. Vladimir's Seminary Press, 2001), 187–88; Behr, *The Nicene Faith: Vol 2 of Formation of Christian Theology*, 137. Cf. Athanasius, *Syn.* 3; Basil of Caesarea, Ep. 361-363.

this level, the particular tools they used to fight Arius's error were those of Arius's own tradition—a tradition shared by many at Nicaea. They were the tools of Christian philosophy. Ὁμοούσιος (*homoousios*, "consubstantial") is an unambiguously metaphysical term, as are οὐσία (*ousia*) and ὑπόστασις (*hypostasis*) given in the anathemas (there, these terms are used synonymously).

ii. The Reception of Nicaea in the 4th Century

It is important to observe that the significance of Nicaea was not in 325 or 326 what it was in the last half of the 4th century. As many scholars have argued, the significance of Nicaea and its Creed, especially the word *homoousios*, was a gradual matter.[23] Gradual as it may have been, the fact is that *homoousios* along with the Creed became a watchword of the global, Imperial Church—of orthodoxy or the mainstream conciliar tradition—by the end of the 4th century. The major conciliar thinkers of this period came to use the term, giving it various degrees of significance, yet more importantly, they developed a shared account of the conciliar or orthodox Christian account of the Father, Son and Spirit in their diversity and unity. As we shall see, this account was thoroughly metaphysical.

With varying emphases, key conciliar thinkers of this period, such as Athanasius, Basil of Caesarea, Gregory of Nazianzus, and Gregory of Nyssa in the East and Hilary of Poitiers in the West developed similar accounts of the unity and plurality in the Godhead. The first three eastern fathers are particularly significant in light of Chalcedon, where they are the most commonly cited authorities for interpreting

---

23 E.g. Mark S. Smith, *The Idea of Nicaea in the Early Church Councils, AD 431-451* (Oxford: Oxford University Press, 2018), 7–28, https://doi.org/10.1093/oso/9780198835271.001.0001.

the Nicene Creed and its tradition.[24] Though they occasionally employed the term *homoousios*, the fathers mentioned above developed similar conceptual accounts of the Trinity using a diversity of terms and arguments. Focusing on the first three (this view is present but less prominent in Nyssa), they articulate a shared account where God the Father is the one true God from whom the other two receive identical essence as from a first principle (causal without temporal implications) and unbroken continuity of being. In other words, as a son is identical in essence to his father, so the Son is identical to the Father in essence and so properly spoken of as "God." The same is the case for the Spirit, who is likewise from the Father and rightly called "God" (though this was elaborated in the Constantinopolitan Creed of 381). The unity of the Father, Son, and Holy Spirit was not secured merely by essential identity, for this may imply that they were merely "collaterals" (ἀδελφά) who receive identity through a transcendent norm or antecedent substance or were three completely independent substances (Athanasius, *Syn* 51.1; Basil, *Ep.* 52.1). Instead, the Father, Son, and Spirit were alike in essence without deviation (as Basil would say) because they had the same substantial being (*Ep. 9.3, Ep. 361).* The one substance of the Godhead was God the Father: the Son and Spirit are "from" him in such a way that they share in his being, as a river flows from its source or a ray from the sun (Athanasius, *Dion.* 10:3; 18; *Dec.* 23).[25] There is an unbroken continuity of being between

---

[24] See James Alexander Rutherford, "Interpreting the Definition of Chalcedon" (Australia & New Zealand Association of Theological Studies Annual Conference, 2022, Sydney, June 2022), https://www.academia.edu/82687829/Interpreting_the_Definition_of_Chalcedon.

[25] Athanasius, *Dion.* 10.3; 18; *Dec. 23*. Cf. Lewis Ayres, "Athanasius' Initial Defense of the Term Homoousios: Rereading the De Decretis," *Journal of Early Christian Studies* 12, no. 3 (2004): 337–59, https://doi.org/10.1353/earl.2004.0035.

the three, rooted in the *monarchia* of the Father.[26] This was developed in Athanasius, Apollinaris, and others through an analogy with their account of the unity of the human substance rooted in its first member, Adam.[27] Though it is not identical with the philosophical models of their peers, this account of divine and human unity-in-plurality fits within the Neo-Platonic philosophical milieu of the 4th century.[28]

Now, this metaphysical framework for the unity-in-plurality of the Godhead was not developed without reason; no, these fathers were actively debating with those who were steeped in a similar tradition of philosophy and philosophical theology as themselves. The conciliar fathers and their opponents were using similar tools to fight their theological battle; this is clearly seen, for example, in Eunomius's account of the comprehensibility of God's essence and Basil's response, which sought to uphold genuine knowledge of God along with the incomprehensibility of God's essence.[29] Whatever the justification, the growing recognition of Nicaea at the end of the 4th century accompanied with the sophisticated accounts of God's unity-

---

26 Cf. John A. McGuckin, "'Perceiving Light from Light in Light' (Oration 31.2): The Trinitarian Theology of St. Gregory the Theologian," *Greek Orthdox Theological Review* 39, no. 1 (1994): 12 ftn. 6, 27, https://doi.org /10.7916/D8GF144P.

27 Athanasius, *Dion.* 10.3; *Dec.* 19-20, 23.1; *Syn* 42, 48, 51-53; *Ep. Serap.* 2.3; Basil, *Eun.* 1.20; *Ep.* 52.2; Apollinaris, *Basil's Epistle* 362 in Prestige, *St Basil the Great and Apollinaris of Laodicea.* Cf. Ayres, "Athanasius' Initial Defense of the Term Homoousios."

28 Cf. Johannes Zachhuber, "Derivative Genera in Apollinarius of Laodicea," in *Apollinaris Und Die Folgen*, Studien Und Texte Zu Antike Und Christentum 93 (Tübingen: Mohr Siebeck, 2015), 93–114.

29 See the first *Apology* in Eunomius, *The Extant Works*, trans. Richard Paul Vaggione, Oxford Early Christian Texts (Oxford; New York: Clarendon Press; Oxford University Press, 1987); Basil of Caesarea, *Against Eunomius*, trans. Mark DelCogliano and Andrew Radde-Gallwitz, The Fathers of the Church, v. 122 (Washington, DC: Catholic University of America Press, 2011). Cf. Radde-Gallwitz, *Basil of Caesarea, Gregory of Nyssa, and the Transformation of Divine Simplicity.*

in-plurality created an unparalleled ecclesiological situation moving into the 5th century, a situation that would be explicated and ratified at Chalcedon.

There are several accounts of a power struggle among Christians in this period, between a view of Christian authority rooted either in charismatic teachers and their schools or in the ecclesiastical hierarchy or between monastic groups and bishoprics.[30] With the first ecumenical council and the dawn of a Christian empire, there was a growing investment of power in councils, canonical law, and bishops.[31] In the 2nd and 3rd centuries, Clement of Alexandria and Origen developed sweeping syntheses of biblical, theological, and philosophical thought, accounts which would in later eyes be considered heretical (at least in Origen's case). However, there was significant latitude to do so at that time; this is not to say orthodoxy and right belief did not exist, but the canonical structures of the 4th and 5th centuries for defining a global orthodoxy did not yet exist, and—more significantly—the measures of orthodoxy employed prior to the 4th century were not as metaphysically robust as Nicaea came to be regarded. The rule of truth in Irenaeus, the early baptismal declarations, and the Apostles' Creed are not thin: they make

---

30 E.g. Williams, *Arius*; Michael Gaddis, *There Is No Crime for Those Who Have Christ: Religious Violence in the Christian Roman Empire*, The Transformation of the Classical Heritage 39 (Berkeley: University of California Press, 2005); Thomas Graumann, "Orthodoxy, Authority and the (Re-) Construction of the Past in Church Councils," in *Invention, Rewriting, Usurpation: Discursive Fights over Religious Traditions in Antiquity*, ed. Jörg Ulrich, Anders-Christian Jacobsen, and David Brakke, Early Christianity in the Context of Antiquity, v. 11 (Frankfurt am Main: Lang, 2012).

31 Cf. Patrick T. R. Gray, "'The Select Fathers': Canonizing the Patristic Past," in *Studia Patristica* (Louvain: Peeters, 1989), 21–36; Patrick T. R. Gray, "Covering the Nakedness of Noah: Reconstruction and Denial in the Age of Justinian," *Byzantinische Forschungen* 24 (1997): 193–205; David Wagschal, *Law and Legality in the Greek East: The Byzantine Canonical Tradition, 381-883* (Oxford University Press, 2015); Smith, *The Idea*; Thomas Graumann, *The Acts of the Early Church Councils: Production and Character* (Oxford University Press, 2021).

important claims about Christian beliefs and the centrality of Scripture. However, in none of these was a metaphysical account of these doctrines rendered normative.[32] As such, metaphysics could—for good or for ill—be explored with impunity by the so-called Alexandrian school. Though the phrase "one *ousia* (οὐσία) in three *hypostases* (ὑποστάσες)" is not of Cappadocian coinage, it certainly captures the spirit of conciliar Christianity at the end of the 4th century, pitted against the equally metaphysical accounts of the heterodox. For those engaged in the frontlines of the controversy, these terms are not mere placeholders nor ill-defined concepts but signifiers of a robust and articulate synthesis of biblical thought in philosophical modes, built through critical interaction with both the pagan philosophers and the heretics.

Roughly speaking, *ousia* signified the philosophical universal and *hypostasis* the particular. Universality was further delineated in terms of essence or the "account of being" (τὸν τοῦ εἶναι λόγον, *ton tou einai logon*) and fundamental reality; the particular was understood as the universal individuated through a particular property or properties (ἰδιώματα, *idiomata*).[33] Turning to the 5th century, this was not in debate. However, how the incarnation would be articulated and its

---

[32] Cf. Irenaeus, *Against Heresies*, 1.8.1; Cyprian, *Ep.* 69.2, 75.7, (NPNF numbering); *Demonstration of the Apostolic Preaching*, 6. Adriani Milli Rodrigues, "The Rule of Faith and Biblical Interpretation in Evangelical Theological Interpretation of Scripture," *Themelios* 43, no. 2 (August 2018): 257–70; J. N. D. Kelly, *Early Christian Creeds* (New York: Bloomsbury Academic, 2006), chap. 4; Wolfram Kinzig and Markus Vinzent, "Recent Research on the Origin of the Creed," *The Journal of Theological Studies* 50, no. 2 (October 1999): 534–59; Liuwe H. Westra, *The Apostles' Creed: Origin, History, and Some Early Commentaries*, Instrumenta Patristica et Mediaevalia 43 (Turnhout, Belgium: Brepols, 2002), 21–72.

[33] E.g. Basil, *Eun.* 2.4-5, 9, 28-29 (Greek). Cf. Basil, *Spir.*, 17.41; *Ep.* 189.8; *Ep.* 214.4; Gregory of Nazianzus, *Or.* 25; Athanasius, *Apologia de Fugua Sua* 13, cf. *C. Ar.* III, 18.1, 18.2, 32.4.

relationship to this Trinitarian ontology were.

B. The Council of Chalcedon

The first significant controversy concerning the union of humanity and divinity in Christ broke out in the late 4th century among the pro-Nicene conciliar parties, with Apollinaris articulating a one nature Christology of the Divine Word and Flesh and receiving a strong response from Gregory of Nyssa.[34] Given the heavily metaphysical account of Trinity forged in the prior decades, theological battles between truth and heresy were now being waged on the fraught battle grounds of metaphysics. It was out of his commitment to Nicene Orthodoxy that Nestorius first set out on troubled waters in the early 5th century. By denying the appropriateness of *Theotokos* (θεοτόκος, "Mother of God") as a title for Mary, he was not seeking to deny a true union of humanity and deity in the single Christ but to articulate (perhaps in a clumsy fashion, or perhaps with logical precision) an account of the *communicatio idiomatum* that would maintain the Nicene insistence on the Word's undeviating identity of essence with the Father (a view that would be endangered if "suffering" or other such non-divine attributes were predicated of the divine substance).[35]

---

[34] Cf. George D Dragas, "The Anti-Apollinarist Christology of St Gregory of Nyssa: A First Analysis," *The Greek Orthodox Theological Review* 42, no. 3–4 (1997): 299–314; Brian E. Daley, "Divine Transcendence and Human Transformation: Gregory of Nyssa's Anti-Apollinarian Christology," in *Rethinking Gregory of Nyssa*, ed. Sarah Coakley (Malden, MA: Blackwell, 2003), 67–76; Gregory of Nyssa, *Anti-Apollinarian Writings*, trans. Robin Orton, The Fathers of the Church, a New Translation, volume 131 (Washington, DC: The Catholic University of America Press, 2015).

[35] Cf. Nestorius, *2nd Reply to Cyril* in John A. McGuckin, *St. Cyril of Alexandria, The Christological Controversy: Its History, Theology, and Texts*, Supplements to Vigiliae Christianae 23 (Leiden: Brill, 1994), 365; *Quaternion* 17 in Michael Gaddis and Richard Price, *The Acts of the Council of Chalcedon*, 3 vols., *Translated Texts for Historians* (Liverpool: Liverpool University Press, 2005), vol. 1 p. 324; Nestorius, Sermons XII, XV (Fragments) in Nestorius,

Indeed, it is arguable that it was Nestorius' lack of metaphysical rigor that landed him with the condemnation of a heretic. A close reading of the *Bazaar* and his other treatises shows that his primary concern was not metaphysical but logical; *prosopon* (προσώπον) for him did not mean "individual" as it would at Chalcedon or the subjective self, as is sometimes attributed to him.[36] Instead, it was a primarily logical term: it was neither the existential nor ontological "I" but the grammatical one. It was denoted by names and corresponding properties. However, by maintaining the discussion at a logical level, Nestorius was able to preserve the fullness of the divine and human identities as well as their union via the discrete *prosopon* (προσώπον) and their unity, the Christ.[37] This, of course, begged significant metaphysical questions, which Cyril was quick to observe. There was no small amount of political and religious machinations involved at this point, yet Cyril perceived in Nestorius's account a serious metaphysical problem: if *prosopon* meant individual, as it would in Cyril's vocabulary, then the incarnation results in two "sons"—a human individual and a divine individual—in a merely moral union. Nestorius expressed frustration over Cyril's failure to interpret his intent, yet Cyril concern is completely understandable in a post-Nicene climate where the battle for orthodoxy was waged precisely on the battleground of metaphysics.

Similarly, when the Second Council of Ephesus (449 AD) was

Nestoriana: Die Fragmente Des Nestorius, ed. Friedrich Loofs (Halle: Max Niemeyer, 1905), 360; J. F. Bethune-Baker, *Nestorius and His Teaching: A Fresh Examination of the Evidence* (Cambridge: Cambridge University Press, 1908), 84; Nestorius, *The Bazaar of Heracleides: Newly Translated from the Syriac and Edited with an Introduction, Notes & Appendices*, trans. G. R. Driver and L. Hodgson (Oxford: Clarendon, 1925), 85–86, 262.

36 E.g. Charles M Stang, "The Two 'I's of Christ: Revisiting the Christological Controversy," *Anglican Theological Review* 94, no. 3 (2012): 529–47.

37 E.g. *Bazaar* p. 157, 179; *Sermon XII*, translated in Bethune-Baker, *Nestorius*, 84.

convened in response to the Constantinople Home Synod of 448, a metaphysical question was at the heart of the debate. Eutyches shows no sign of seeking to diminish either the humanity or divinity of Christ in his account; instead, he expressed indifference to metaphysical precision and an unwillingness to engage in the sort of conceptual delineation characterizing the Christology of those following the Formula of Reunion (see *The Acts of the Council of Chalcedon*, Session I.513-514, 527, 535, 542-544).[38] When offered terminology from the Dyophysite bishops with accompanying explanation, he unequivocally express willingness to accept this language (Session I.422). However, he refuses to anathematise those who will not adopt it (Session I.535, 542-544). Now, I am not seeking to defend Nestorius or Eutyches in these accounts, for the issues are far more complicated than what they said or didn't say theologically—often involving some level of political and ecclesiological ineptitude. However, the reasons that Eutyches and Nestorius were condemned was not for a denial of any biblical teaching or theological synthesis, such as the perfect deity and humanity of Christ Jesus and his perfect identity with the Father that does not amount to the multiplication of deities. So far as their theology is concerned, Nestorius was exiled for his inadequate account of metaphysics of the incarnation and Eutyches for his failure to engage with metaphysical depth the issues he entered into (perhaps he was unable to, as Pope Leo would have it).[39] This is the stage in which Emperor Marcian conveyed the council of Chalcedon in 451 AD (symbolically convened at Nicaea, though it was forced to move). Here, the issues surrounding Ephesus II were to be resolved and a unitive position on the Catholic faith was to be hammered out—

---

[38] Gaddis and Price, *The Acts of the Council of Chalcedon*. From here forward, *The Acts*.

[39] In the *Tome*, Leo calls him "very imprudent and very inexperienced." Cf. René Draguet, "La Christologie D'Eutychès D'après Les Actes Du Synode de Flavien (448)," *Byzantion* 6, no. 1 (1931): 456.

though not without initial objections from the bishops involved.[40]

That is, the bishops understood their role to be putting Dioscorus and those who allied with him at Ephesus II (which Pope Leo branded *latrocinium* ("The Robbers Synod")) on trial. This happened, and Dioscorus' condemnation was secured in Session I and II (according to the Greek *Acta* printed by Schwartz).[41] The imperial representatives soon made it clear that they had a more substantial agenda in mind. Though the ecclesiastical party expressed objections—"We will not produce a written exposition" (Session III.7-8; *The Acts* 2:11)—Session V demonstrates that they were eventually persuaded to produce a "definition" (*horos*, ὁρός) of the Faith. The bishops objected on the basis of Canon 7 from Ephesus I that prohibited producing any creeds or normative conciliar documents after Nicene (Session III.7); Nicaea was to be the sole standard. Ephesus I did not itself produce a creed, but it was connected with Nicaea in the minds of many of the bishops, together enshrining conciliar orthodoxy, hedged by the Creed and the canon, "Nicaea and Ephesus."[42] To get around Ephesus I, the Imperial party and its ecclesiological allies (particularly Anatolius of Constantinople) used the hereto relatively unknown Creed produced in Constantinople (381) against the so-called Pneumatomachians (those who wage war against the Spirit), showing that though

---

[40] Cf. G. E. M. De Ste. Croix, "The Council of Chalcedon with Additions by Michael Whitby," in *Christian Persecution, Martyrdom, and Orthodoxy*, ed. Michael Whitby and Joseph Streeter (Oxford; New York: Oxford University Press, 2006); Richard Price, "The Council of Chalcedon (451): A Narrative," in *Chalcedon in Context: Church Councils 400-700*, ed. Richard Price and Mary Whitby (Liverpool: Liverpool University Press, 2011), 70–91.

[41] The English numbering of Price and Gaddis' translation differ at this point, Dioscorus trial occurring in Session III. Eduard Schwartz, ed., *Acta Conciliorum Oecumenicorum II: Concilium Universale Chalcedonense*, 6 vols. (Berlin: Walter de Gruyter, 1914). Henceforth, ACO.

[42] Cf. Smith, *The Idea*, 172–85.

sufficient, Nicaea needed to be applied to new errors as they arose.[43] Thus, the Definition came to enshrine a view of Nicene pre-eminence received from Ephesus I while permitting further expansions or extensions of it to new errors:

> We therefore decree—we ourselves upholding the order and all the decrees of the faith of the holy synod formerly taking place at Ephesus, over which presided the most holy in memory Celestine of Rome and Cyril of Alexandria—on the one hand, that the exposition of the right and spotless faith by the 318 holy and blessed fathers at Nicaea, gathered together by the pious in memory Constantine who was then Emperor, shines forth preeminent and, on the other hand, that the decrees of the 150 holy fathers in Constantinople give support for the uprooting of heresies that then sprung up and the confirmation of the same universal and apostolic faith which is ours. (ACO V.31)[44]
>
> And, because of those who seek to destroy the mystery of the economy and shamelessly speak with frivolity to the effect that the one born from the virgin Mary was a mere man, [the council] accepted (ἐδέξατο, *edexato*) the conciliar letters of the blessed Cyril, who was shepherd of the church of Alexandria, both to Nestorius and to those of the Orient as being fitting for both the refutation of Nestorius' madness and the interpretation (ἑρμηνείαν, *hermeneian*) of the saving creed for those who with pious zeal seek understanding (ἔννοιαν, *ennoian*). To these is suitably attached (συνήρμοσεν, *sunermosen*) for the confirmation of sound doctrine also the epistle of the president of the great and senior Rome, the most blessed and holy

43 This is based on the first chapter of my PhD Thesis, "Rightly Defining the Son of God." Cf. Rutherford, "Interpreting the Definition of Chalcedon." Both build on the argument of Smith, *The Idea.*

44 My translation. See ACO 2.1.2, p. 127 lns 1-8 for the Greek text.

> Archbishop Leo, which he wrote to Archbishop Flavian (now among the saints) for the removal of the perversity of Eutyches since it agrees with the confession of the great Peter and is a universal pillar against those with false beliefs. (V.34)[45]

There is a "right and spotless faith" passed on from the apostles; following Ephesus I, the participants at Chalcedon recognise the Nicene Creed as the pre-eminent exposition of that faith, receiving support and confirmation from the Constantinopolitan Creed and Cyril's conciliar letters (2nd Letter to Nestorius and the Letter to John of Antioch) with the support of Leo's *Tome.* The Creed is to be interpreted through these three letters and, as the rest of the *Acta* demonstrate, a select number of fathers.[46] Chalcedon goes further in its adherence to Nicaea: not only is it pre-eminent, but it is the "unerring faith of the Fathers" (V.31). Subsuming Constantinople under Nicaea (both having just been read), the Definition then declares "Thus this wise and saving Creed of divine grace was sufficient for complete knowledge of and confirmation of godliness; for it both thoroughly teaches the complete matter [τὸ τέλειον, *to teleion*] concerning the Father, the Son, and the Holy Spirit, and it also presents the Lord's enanthropation [ἐνανθρώπησιν, *enanthropesin*, "becoming human"] of the Lord to those who receive it faithfully" (V.34). Thus, the one holy, apostolic, universal faith is the faith expressed by Nicaea and its conciliar tradition. As Nicaea had uttered anathemas on particular metaphysical concepts, the Definition follows suit, anathematising "those who, on the one hand, invent fables concerning the two natures of the Lord before the union and those who, on the other, imagine in vain one after the union." The shocking thing about this last anathema (directed at Eutyches, the former at Nestorius) is that in the discussion over the draft in Session V, Dioscorus with his

45 My translation. ACO 2.1.2, p. 129 lns 6-16.

46 Cf. Rutherford, "Interpreting the Definition of Chalcedon."

"one nature" theology was explicitly said not to have been found to be in theological error (Session V.13); however, at the insistence of the Imperial officials, "in two natures" was added in the place of the more ambiguous "from two natures" (Session V.17-22), and with this anathema, Dioscorus and sympathetic Cyrillians would now find themselves among those anathematised. The Definition concludes,

> Therefore, these things being formed in every way carefully and diligently, the holy and ecumenical synod has decreed [ὥρισεν, *horisen*] that it is not permissible for anyone to bring forth another faith [πίστιν, *pistin*] or, therefore, to write, compose, think, or teach otherwise.[47] But those who dare to set forth another faith or, therefore, to produce or teach or pass on another creed [σύμβολον, *sumbolon*] to those desiring to turn to the knowledge of the truth from Hellenism, from Judaism, or, therefore, from whatever sort of heresy, consequently these, whether they are bishop or clerics, bishops are to be estranged [ἀλλοτρίους εἶναι, *allotrious einai*] from the episcopate and clerics from their office [κλήρου, *klerou*], and if they be monks or laypersons, they are to anathematized. (V.34)[48]

The Definition, a carefully worded response to Nestorius and Eutyches with an eye to Apollinaris, built upon Ephesus I to enshrine Nicene Christianity as the true expression of the one holy, apostolic, and catholic faith. What is ratified is not a mere formulas or words, but an extensive conceptual apparatus that was used from Nicaea to Chalcedon to explain, defend, and develop what was said there. In the

[47] γοῦν (*goun*, "therefore") is postpositive, so its placement suggests that the latter three infinitives are to be grouped together, rather than the division of Gaddis and Price, *The Acts*.

[48] My translation.

Definition itself, the anathemas address particular ontological errors ("one nature" or "two individuals") and the densely argued expositions of the two-nature doctrine in Cyril and Leo's letters is given as the authoritative interpretation of this tradition. For words such as *homoousios* (ὁμοούσιος) and *hypostasis* (ὑπόστασις), which appear in these letters but are not developed, the officially published *Acta* (produced by Marcian in conjunction with Anatolius of Constantinople) repeatedly points to select fathers as the authoritative interpreters of Trinitarian dimensions of this tradition.[49]

C. The Rise of the Emissary

By the end of AD 451, something has happened. There has been a shift from the 1st century to the 5th century: the right, holy, catholic faith is now a necessarily metaphysical faith. Metaphysical speculation had long been a component of Christian intellectual engagement, yet it had now moved from the halls of philosophy, monasteries, and catechetical schools to the churches and bishoprics. To be a catholic bishop, cleric, monk, or layperson meant subscribing to a *theologia*, a developed metaphysic attending to the Christian reflection on God and his world. This is not to say metaphysics eclipsed reading and teaching from Scripture, nor that other forms of theological reflection ceased, only that the right faith was now necessarily a metaphysical faith. Attendant to this, a trend did emerge of expositions of the Fathers and their faith alongside expositions of Scripture (such as the various *Ambigua* produced by Maximus the Confessor), but that

[49] On the publication, see Gaddis and Price, *The Acts of the Council of Chalcedon*; Tommaso Mari, "The Latin Translations of the Acts of the Council of Chalcedon," *Greek, Roman & Byzantine Studies* 58, no. 1 (March 2018): 126–55; Tommaso Mari, "Greek, Latin, and More: Multilingualism at the Ecumenical Council of Chalcedon," *Journal of Latin Linguistics* 19, no. 1 (July 2020): 59–87, https://doi.org/10.1515/joll-2020-2003; Graumann, *The Acts of the Early Church Councils*.

development lies outside of our scope.[50]

As I indicated at the start of this chapter, I am not interested in reviving the classical Hellenization thesis: I see no reason for metaphysics to be opposed to the Bible, theology, or simple faith. Indeed, I want to argue that the Bible has metaphysical implications: it points us to a God active in this world over against atheism and physicalism, it indicates that all things depend on God's continued activity, etc. However, these are genuine "implications," for they are not worked out in a systematic or metaphysical manner. However, seeing metaphysics as a legitimate Christian endeavour—as one tool among many others—is a different beast than making a metaphysic a necessary condition for the orthodox, catholic, and apostolic faith.

D. Conclusion

In this chapter, I have argued that by the end of the council of Chalcedon in 451, a metaphysical system was granted the status of the measure of orthodoxy. Christians in the 4th-5th centuries did not simply roll over to Hellenistic philosophy; no, they critically engaged with it, built upon it with the tools given them in Scripture, and perhaps bested the pagans at their own game. However, in doing so, they began to wage the battles of Christian orthodoxy more and more on the battleground of ontology and metaphysics until those battlefields became the entire war—or so it seemed in the aftermath of Chalcedon. What was once a useful tool for the defence and elucidation of the Christian Faith became its key structure and provided much of its content. With that move made, it was easy enough for the Christian intellectual life at all levels, lay persons through clergy, to take on a particular philosophical bent: attention moved from the contingent and mutable events God accomplished in this world—God's covenanting and, above all, Christ and him crucified—to the

50 Cf. Gray, ""The Select Fathers.""

"universal, necessary truths" of *scientia*.[51] I am rightly reminded by a Catholic brother that many outside of the major cities and episcopal sees did not go down the metaphysical route I have described here, yet this still describes the dominant stream of ecclesial authority, which has exercised significant influence on present-day Protestantism.

[51] On the Biblical-theological role of covenant in early theology, see Ligon J Duncan III, "The Covenant Idea in Ante-Nicene Theology" (Ph.D. Thesis, Edinburgh, University of Edinburgh, 1995).

2

DIAGNOSING THE PROBLEM 2: EMBRACING THE ACADEMY

> Scholasticism can be identified as a form of rationalism in the former sense, particularly given the assumption of most scholastic efforts that rational forms must be used in the exposition of doctrine and that reason can be employed as a tool or instrument in the formulation of theology. – Richard A. Muller[1]

The account of the early church given above is a root of the later developments that contribute to the identification of the pastoral role with the academy, so this and the following chapter may appear disproportionately small compared to the last. However, this reflects the material we must cover to display the issues: with the material of Chapter 1 behind us, it will be much easier to deal with the developments in post-Reformation theology and in contemporary Evangelicalism.

In this chapter, I want to focus on Richard A. Muller's refutation of the 19th and 20th-century polemic against Post-Reformation

[1] Muller, *Prolegomena to Theology*, 139.

theology, often summarised as "Calvin against the Calvinists."[2] Though Muller's argument is commonly accepted, he makes a subtle concession that demonstrates, however faithful they were to their reforming predecessors, the so-called "Reformed Scholastics" made the same error as we identified above in the Early Church.

A. Calvin Against the Calvinists

In the "Calvin against the Calvinists" narrative, a significant development is portrayed from Calvin to his Reformed heirs. They, according to this narrative, developed a theology around a central dogma, predestination in particular; built around a central dogma, this theological system is a rationalising deduction, not a system built on the Scriptures. Theology in this era of Orthodoxy also became arid and rationalistic; rationalism in this pejorative sense was "the incorporation of a rationalist philosophy into Protestant theological system or, indeed, as the use of reason as the fundamental source and norm of truth."[3] Jack Rogers and Donald McKim, for example, conclude that,

> the followers of Luther and Calvin in the seventeenth century in Europe endeavored to systematize the work of their masters by casting it into an Aristotelian mold. Thus, a period of Protestant scholasticism was launched in the immediate post-Reformation period. This Protestant scholasticism rejected the Augustinian approach of faith leading to understanding and reverted to the Thomistic approach, which gave reason

---

[2] In addition to the above-cited volume, see Richard A. Muller, *The Unaccommodated Calvin: Studies in the Foundation of a Theological Tradition* (Oxford: Oxford University Press, 2001); Richard A. Muller, *After Calvin: Studies in the Development of a Theological Tradition* (Oxford: Oxford University Press, 2003), 63–102.

[3] Muller, *Prolegomena to Theology*, 139.

priority over faith.[4]

Brian Armstrong argues that the "orthodox Calvinists of the seventeenth century … showed themselves to be much more interested in metaphysics and systematization, and so were preserving elements of medieval scholasticism quite in contrast to the humanistically shaped thought of Calvin and Amyraut."[5] Armstrong suggests by the framing of his argument that it would be a concern for "Calvinists" to depart from the thought of John Calvin—whom, he observes, they rarely cite.[6]

Against the latter claim, Muller has shown that Calvin was far from the creator or standard for Reformed theology (latter called "Calvinism"); for example, Henrich Bullinger and Martin Bucer were influential Reformers.[7] However, his main argument seeks to show that there was indeed continuity between the Reformers and the Post-Reformed Orthodox. Scholastic method did not mark a significant break, for

> Neither Calvin's own theology nor the theology of various significant predecessors, such as Luther, Zwingli, and Bucer, or Reformed contemporaries, such as Vermigli and Musculus, can be understood apart from the positive impact of elements of the medieval scholastic background.[8]

---

[4] Jack B Rogers and Donald K McKim, *The Authority and Interpretation of the Bible: An Historical Approach* (Eugene, OR: Wipf and Stock Publishers, 1999), 187, cf. 147–261.

[5] Brian G. Armstrong, *Calvinism and the Amyraut Heresy: Protestant Scholasticism and Humanism in Seventeenth-Century France* (University of Wisconsin Press, 1969), xix.

[6] Armstrong, xvii–xix.

[7] For the following discussion, see Muller, *Prolegomena to Theology*, 27–148.

[8] Muller, *After Calvin*, 72; Muller, *The Unaccommodated Calvin*, 39–58.

Similarly, "humanism" and "scholasticism" are not mutually exclusive categories.[9] Furthermore, Muller argues, scholasticism as a method was not a full embrace of any philosophical paradigm: "it is not necessarily allied to any particular philosophical perspective, nor does it represent a systematic attachment to or concentration upon any particular doctrine or concept as a key to theological system."[10] Though scholasticism was a *reasoned* approach to theology, and so could be called "rationalism," it did not presuppose rationalist philosophy that "identified human reason as the prior and primary norm of all constructive intellectual endeavor."[11] Further, the reformers and their heirs did not structure their theological systems after a single, central dogma—certainly not predestination. Instead, theological systems often followed he *loci* method of Melanchthon, organising and elucidating theological *loci* or topics taken from the Scriptures.[12]

It would seem that Muller and others who have written on the topic, with careful attention not only to the original sources but also to the method by which we approach them, have succeeded in overthrowing the "Calvin against the Calvinists narrative." They have demonstrated that there was not a cataclysmic shift from Calvin to those after him and that Calvin's thought should not be treated as the measuring stick for Reformed or "Calvinist" thought. However, though they have overthrown *this* narrative, they have glossed over a related development. As in our treatment of the Early Church, exonerating the post-Reformed Orthodox theologians from the charges laid against them does not mean they are not guilty of anything, nor that there is no kernel of truth in the now overthrown narrative. Muller speaks positively of the development between the early reformers and their

[9] Muller, *After Calvin*, 72–73.

[10] Muller, *Prolegomena to Theology*, 37.

[11] Muller, 138.

[12] Muller, 59, 104–7, 178–80, 188, 209; Muller, *The Unaccommodated Calvin*, 127–30.

heirs we could call "institutionalisation." He suggests this is a good and necessary consequence of theology coming to maturity, but in doing so he fails to address the presuppositions held by the Reformed Orthodox and their Medieval predecessors that lead to his evaluation.

B. The Institutionalisation of Reformed Theology

Is institutionalisation a natural step in the maturation of Christianity and its churches? Is the academy the ideal home for orthodoxy and right teaching to be instilled in pastors? Can theology be treated as another academic discipline (even if it is, perhaps, the pre-eminent discipline)? Muller appears to presuppose a "yes" to these questions. "Scholasticism," the title often given to this period of Protestant thought, refers to "the academic life" and "the general method of training, applicable to virtually any discipline."[13] Muller criticises previous studies for failing to make a distinction between "the rationalizing tendency that is an integral part of the creation of a theological system and the rationalist philosophy of the seventeenth century that identified human reason as the prior and primary norm of all constructive intellectual endeavor."[14] The sole principle (*principium*) of theology was revelation, yet reason is given a significant role in developing theology from this principle.[15] Though Protestant scholasticism never "set the standards of scriptural revelation and rational proof on an equal par," it is still accurate to speak of "the rationalization and intellectualization of theology."[16] "The Protestant orthodox systems," Muller tells us, "searching out and defending 'right teaching,' had as their goal the formulation of a universally valid statement of Christian truth."[17] "System" here "simply indicates the

---

13 Muller, *Prolegomena to Theology*, 190.

14 Muller, 138.

15 Muller, 140.

16 Muller, 141.

17 Muller, 200.

basic body of doctrine in its proper organization."[18] The authors in the period Muller identifies as "early orthodox" (1565-1618, 1618-1640),

> shared the desire to create a theological system suited to the successful establishment of Protestantism as a church in its own right, catholic in its teaching, capable of being sustained intellectually against its adversaries, and sufficiently technical and methodologically consistent to stand among the other disciplines in the university.[19]

In Muller's estimation, the rise of Protestant Scholasticism does not reveal a doctrinal break with prior generations of Reformers but "the participation of theological faculties in the academic culture of the age," which he sees as a "positive development."[20] For Muller, "the success of the Reformation led to the establishment and institutionalization of its reforms and of the theology on which those reforms were based."[21] Muller states that,

> From the very beginning of Luther's protest, the university and university-trained theologians were at the centre of the movement. The process of establishment and institutionalization of the Reformation viewed in terms of the need to train new generations of Protestants in theology led to a reexamination of theology as an academic discipline.[22]

The academic theological method is not for scholars, therefore, as if these could be separated from pastors. No,

> The fully developed mode [i.e. a 'prolix and large …

[18] Muller, 202.

[19] Muller, 62.

[20] Muller, 63.

[21] Muller, 177.

[22] Muller, 177.

> scholasticall' treatment of the *loci communes*] is that which we use with reference to those who, by reason of further progress in heavenly doctrine (*in coelesti doctrina*), the Holy Spirit commonly called adults, developed ones.[23]

The study of theology, for the Reformed churches, was not "an academic matter"; instead, "the study of theology was an enterprise intended for all Christians—and the detailed academic study of the subject was to be the practical foundation for sound study on all levels."[24] The 16th century Reformer Andreas Hyperius, in his *De Theologo*, saw theology as a "spiritual or pious exercise," but this does not take away from the rigour of theological study. The list he gives of "the kinds of study 'necessary' to theological training" goes like this,

> grammar, logic, and rhetoric (the *trivium*), arithmetic, geometry, music, and astronomy (*the quadrivium*), philosophy, physics, ethics, politics, oeconomics, metaphysics, history, architecture, and agriculture, and above all Latin, Greek, and Hebrew."[25]

For Johann Heinrich Alsted, "the work of academic theology … is the activity that occupies the student in his study of divine things for the sake of teaching them to others."[26] In addition to demanding attention to piety, Gisbertus Voetius insisted on the "careful examination of students in doctrine, language skills, and philosophical tools."[27] Franz Burman indicated that the theology student "must also attend to the sound cultivation of the mind (*bona mentis cultura*) through the study of

---

23 Maccovius (d. 1644), *Loci communes,* I, quoted in Muller, 199.

24 Muller, 210. See Muller's discussion of Voetius and Witsius in Muller, *After Calvin*, 110–19.

25 Muller, *Prolegomena to Theology*, 210.

26 Muller, 211. Muller points to Alsted's *Praecognita,* II.i.

27 Muller, 213. Cf. Han Van Ruler, *The Crisis of Causality: Voetius and Descartes on God, Nature and Change* (Leiden: Brill, 1995), 1–35.

the liberal arts and sciences and through these studies learn the proper exercise of memory and judgment."[28]

Thus, during the Reformation and Post-Reformation period, a dominant form of theology (*the* form of theology by the High Orthodox period) was institutional and academic, employing a "scholastic" method. This theology wasn't for academics alone but was the maturation of catechetical theology taught to children; this was mature theology. To be able to do this theology properly, one had to be thoroughly trained in academic disciplines. Muller contends that this is a natural and good development of Reformed theology, necessary to see it established and to maintain orthodoxy among its churches. However, is Muller right to gloss over this methodological shift from Calvin and Luther as insignificant and insist that the method is detached from theology—from the content developed by that method?

C. The Presuppositions of Scholasticism

I want to contend that method is not as philosophically neutral as Muller suggests. Indeed, the particular method Muller discussed, scholastic method, moves theology in the same direction as Nicaea and Chalcedon, discussed above. If this sort of theology was accepted as *an* appropriate *academic* approach to the knowledge of God, we could perhaps disagree, yet our concerns would be minimal—for the academy can tolerate a wide variety of approaches to theology and other disciplines. However, by identifying the theology attained by the scholastic method as "mature" theology, as the sort of theology pastors teach, Reformed and Post-Reformed thinkers did the same thing as the 5th century: they made a tool acceptable for intellectual engagement with God's word and world the only game in town, or so I will argue. Thus, the methodological decision of these Reformers does indicate a

---

[28] Muller, *Prolegomena to Theology*, 213–14. Muller cites Burman's treatise, *De studio theologico*, I.6-10, 17.

significant departure from Calvin and Luther, among others. The choice of discursive theology versus systematic is not, therefore, as innocent as Muller suggest. This is not to suggest, of course, that second and third generation reformers ought to be measured by the standard of Calvin and Luther, or that either thinker ought to be put forth as a paradigm of Reformed Christianity. Instead, engaging with their thought will aid in our effort to show that the adoption of scholastic method *did* involve adopting theological and philosophical assumptions, assumptions that are ultimately problematic. It may be argued that Calvin and Luther agreed with (or at least would have agreed with) the assumptions evident in their scholastic heirs; this point may be admitted without trouble. It remains the case that the chosen genre and conventions of their discourse presuppose a different conceptual framework than the genre of later scholastics. It is possible that the framework undergirding their approach could be carried over into a form of systematic theology, as perhaps the final edition of Calvin's *Institutes* displays, yet it is nevertheless the case that the form of systematic theology adopted by other Reformers and the following generations betrays a different basis.

Writing of the "unsystematic theology" of Luther, Muller contends that it "belongs to an entirely different genre than the highly systematized theology of his successors."[29] It is difficult to separate the medium (the genre used) from the message, Muller admits, contrasting the discursive, often polemical, writings of Luther to the systems of the later orthodox,

> the former occasional, paradoxical, primarily exegetical or homiletical, and the latter deliberately systematic and argumentative, resting on exegesis but only infrequently stating a theological point in the form of

[29] Muller, 46.

an exegetical exposition.[30]

Muller observes that the earlier systematic efforts of the Reformers (e.g. Zwingli's *Commentarius*, Bullinger's *Compendium,* Calvin's *Institutes*) "are intended to be instructions in the basic teachings of Scripture, preparation for biblical study."[31] Stylistically, these workers are discursive; "The Passage of Reformed theology into the era of early orthodoxy can be charted in terms of the movement from basic, discursive instruction to a more sophisticated, dialectical model."[32] However, the form of systematization practiced by the orthodox presupposes beliefs not clearly found in the works of Calvin and Luther, presuppositions that seem incompatible with their chosen media. Consider, first, the mode of discursive communication, and then scholasticism.

The purpose of Calvin's *Institutes*, according to the prefatory "Epistle to the Readers," was

> to prepare and train students of theology for the study of the Sacred Volume, so that they might both have an easy introduction to it, and be able to proceed in it, with unfaltering step seeing I have endeavoured to give such a summary of religion in all its parts.

He indicates that he has structured the work so that the reader may discern what doctrines to search out in the Scriptures and how to consider those doctrines in relation to others ("to what head he ought to refer whatever is contained in it").[33] In the epistle to the last edition,

---

30 Muller, 46.

31 Muller, 61.

32 Muller, 61.

33 Epistle to the Reader, affixed to the Second edition. John Calvin, *Institutes of the Christian Religion*, trans. Henry Beveridge, Logos Digital Edition (Edinburgh: The Calvin Translation Society, 1845), Vol I, 27.

he adds "to prepare and train candidates for the sacred office."[34] For Calvin, the model of discursive and polemical communication was an adequate tool for the use of training Christian ministers. Though it employs a discursive model which Muller identifies with preparatory and catechetical instruction, namely, the sort of instruction appropriate for lay persons and children, Calvin finds this genre an appropriate tool for communicating a picture of the whole of Scripture with its principal doctrines to equip the student of theology to engage with God's word confidently.

This confidence in the sufficiency of such methodology is also displayed in the translator's preface to the 1587 English translation of Henry Bullinger's *Decades*, used to train pastors in England. Though he commends various works of other Reformers, including systematic common places, he judges,

> questionless, no writer yet in the hands of men can fit them better than master Bullinger in these his Decades; who in them amendeth much Calvin's obscurity with singular perspicuity, and Musculus's scholastical subtlety with great plainness and even popular felicity. And all those points of Christian doctrine, which are not to be found in one, but handled in all, Bullinger packet up all, and that in good order, in this one book of small quantity.[35]

Again, though scholastic treaties like Musculus' *Loci Communes Sacrae Theologiae* have a place, the translator judges the *Decades* to be adequate to communicate the Christian faith to pastors desperately in need of training.

---

[34] Calvin, Vol I, 31.

[35] H. I., "A Preface," in Heinrich Bullinger, *The Decades of Henry Bullinger* (Cambridge: Cambridge University Press, 1849), 8, http://archive.org/details/ decadesofhenrybu0000bull_n6r5.

At the very least, the discursive theology of Calvin and Bullinger (to whom we could add Luther) indicates their belief in the usefulness of contingent (that is, circumstantially shaped) theology, theology that is not necessarily communicated in a structure reflecting a universal reason nor communicated in a manner aiming towards universal truth. Rather, their presentation of theology reflects the authoritative Scriptures elucidated and applied through the shaping influences of their circumstances and reasoned thought. This was not only sufficient for catechetical purposes but useful for training ministers for the right handling of God's word in preaching and teaching.

The scholastic method presupposes different assumptions about these same issues. Muller indicates his belief that the development of scholasticism is both natural and positive. For example, the systematic writers (among which he includes Calvin), "are crucial both to the survival of the Reformation as a theological movement and as a form of the Christian Church and also to the gradual development of an 'orthodoxy,' a fully defined body of Church-doctrine belonging to the Reformed churches."[36]

> This positive development of the theology of the Reformation into a dogmatic system—or what could be equally well described as the radical adaptation of the traditional topics of dogmatic system to conform to the exegetical, anthropological, and soteriological insights of the Reformers—is the natural and perhaps ecclesially and culturally necessary result of the Reformer's need to train followers and successors in the faith.[37]

The success of the Reformation as a movement required, Muller maintains, "Protestant theologians create an orthodoxy, an institutionally viable, genuinely catholic body of right teaching resting

---

[36] Muller, *Prolegomena to Theology*, 56.

[37] Muller, 50–51.

upon, elaborating and defending the church's confessions."[38]

However, we must ask, why was scholasticism seen as a necessary movement for the adequate training of pastors and mature explication of faith in God? What assumptions lay beneath Muller's defence of the development of Protestant scholasticism, assumptions certainly shared by those who were themselves proponents of such a theology? Surely there are many, but several important philosophical points emerge, shared by Scholastics committed to Ramist platonic realism, Thomism, and the emerging rationalism associated with Descartes. With Muller, Scholastic theology agrees that "even a theology aware of its limitations intends to point toward timeless truth."[39] That is, even when it is treated as a discipline with a practical end, as with Ramism, Scholastic theology presupposes a rational connection grounding all theology in timeless truths, in the theological *principia* that are the causes of all theological phenomena.[40] Polanus writes that

> If God speaks not only of singular things (*res singulares*), but truly of universals pertaining to the right knowledge of himself; then it is necessary that there be theology. That which precedes is true; therefore also that which follows.[41]

That is, scholastic methodology pertains to universals, not particulars (to necessary and overarching truths, not contingent, temporal truths involving particular things). Muller explains,

> If knowledge is merely the perception of particulars, no relationships can exist and no overarching cohesion

---

38 Muller, 66.

39 Muller, 47.

40 Muller, 149–64; Simon J. G. Burton, *Ramism and the Reformation of Method: The Franciscan Legacy in Early Modernity*, Oxford Studies in Historical Theology (New York: Oxford University Press, 2024).

41 Polanus, *Syntagma*, I.ii. Quoted in Muller 163.

> of ideas can be expressed. For there to be theology, revelation must be revelation of true concepts, of universals, capable of providing a framework for knowledge.[42]

Scholasticism would appear to presuppose a form of realism concerning universals, dismissing conceptualism or nominalism.[43] Scholastic theology distinguished between earthly theology and its divine archetype, but theologians of various persuasions were convinced that the archetypical theology (*theologia archetypa*) is at least a portion of *scientia necessaria*, "that perfect knowledge by which God knows himself."[44] This commitment to necessary, eternal truth is presupposed in the scholastic method of tracing (whether deductively or inductively) causes and effects, that is, the eternal theological *principia* in God and their outworking in creation and redemption. So, scholasticism as a method still presupposes significant philosophical claims, namely, that there is a necessary connection discernible by logic between God's acts in the economy of Salvation and God in himself. It presupposes that behind the contingency of revealed theology (behind God's actions in the creation) are timeless, universal truths. Conceptualism (and Nominalism) are thus rejected, positions which give epistemological priority to the particularly over the universal.

Related to this assumption are two others. First, scholasticism appears to presuppose the epistemological priority of definition, or the belief that concepts like theology, God's attributes, and other points of theology can be defined by words and that there is a correct or false understanding of these things. That is, there is an assumption, associated with Greek and Medieval forms of realism concerning the universals, that the truth of theological claims relies on a linguistic correspondence between the definitions made of a thing and the reality

42 Muller, *Prolegomena to Theology*, 163.

43 Muller, 163.

44 Cocceius, *Aphorismi prolixiores*, I.3, quoted in Muller, 234.

of this thing, which is such that linguistic definition remains the most adequate human method to articulate that truth. As described by one modern author, language is a "map to the shape of natural reality"; linguistic distinctions mirror "real distinctions in the things about which we are speaking."[45] Second, it presupposes that as *scientia* ("knowledge") or *sapienta* ("wisdom"), theology has a place among the other academic disciplines; it needed to be "sufficiently technical and methodologically consistent to stand among the other disciplines in the university."[46] The chosen method assumes a whole paradigm of the interweaving of human knowledge as it echoes the Divine archetype, with the implication that the natural context for theology is the academy. The philosophical presupposition here is this: knowledge of God is the sort of thing appropriate to the intellectuals and philosophers, those who are willing and able to penetrate to universal, necessary truth. The changes in philosophy between the Reformer's discursive writing and the systems of the scholastics was not the result of "doctrinal change, but of the participation of theological faculties in the academic culture of the age."[47] That is, theological methodology was not driven by the Bible or theology itself but the academic culture.

We see, therefore, that scholasticism was not philosophically neutral, nor was it driven by a developing insight into the nature of God and his word. The assumptions beneath this method are not clear in Scripture; instead, like the 4th and 5th century, the development of "orthodoxy" required changes to theology that were increasingly academic and intellectual. Very soon, pastors and mature Christians were required to be schooled in academic, philosophical theology.

---

45 Dolezal, *All That Is in God*, 58–59.

46 Muller, *Prolegomena to Theology*, 62.

47 Muller, 63.

3

DIAGNOSING THE PROBLEM 3: EVANGELICALISM AND RECLAIMING THE MIND

> The scandal of the evangelical mind is that there is not much of an evangelical mind. – Mark Noll[1]

Evangelicalism is a varied entity, associated with different thinkers and movements following the Reformation. David Bebbington famously identified Evangelicalism with four qualities, 'Biblicism,' 'Crucicentrism,' 'Conversionism,' and 'Activism.'[2] Evangelicalism describes a great many churches and persons across Protestant history. However, in the USA, there was a period where Evangelicals rose to prominence in contrast with the Liberal churches and the Fundamentalist movement as it existed in the late 40s and 50s.[3] With the launch of Christianity Today (1956), the ministry of Billy Graham,

---

[1] Noll, *The Scandal of the Evangelical Mind*, 3.

[2] David W. Bebbington, *Evangelicalism in Modern Britain: A History from the 1730s to the 1980s* (London: Routledge, 2003), chap. 1.

[3] For trends in late 20th-century education within mainline Protestant institutions, developing on their own trajectories but reinforcing the Evangelical developments within the context of the renewed ecumenicism and Evangelical participation in the broader world of academia, see David H. Kelsey, *Between Athens and Berlin: The Theological Education Debate* (Grand Rapids: Eerdmans, 1993).

and the launch of Fuller College (1947)—among many other post-war developments—Evangelicalism moved out of the anti-cultural and (as many would charge) anti-intellectual perspectives of Fundamentalism into an outward-looking, socially active, evangelistic, and intellectual movement.[4] Though he calls for far greater intellectual development, Mark Noll identifies that "something of a revival of intellectual activity has been taking place among evangelical Protestants since World War II."[5] Noll wrote in 1994 with the concern that Evangelicals were not making an impact on the broader world of scholarship; though they believed in the Bible as God's very words, they failed to cultivate a serious life of the mind, in contrast with their Protestant forefathers and others farther back in history.[6] Whatever we may make of the contribution Evangelicals make to scholarly learning (and how we evaluate that given the radically counter-cultural perspective of the Bible), it is certainly the case that the Evangelical life of the mind blossomed in the early post-war period and has continued to do so through the 90s (when Noll wrote) until now.[7]

Evangelicals, especially of the Reformed persuasion, have invested heavily in developing a strong seminary culture and have published extensive amounts of literature on the Bible, biblical studies, philosophy, and theology. Noll's comment may suggest that Evangelicals have avoided the exaltation of the intellect and philosophy we identified with the early Church and the Reformed orthodox. However, despite the historical reluctance of Evangelicals to engage in the broader field of secular knowledge associated with the

---

[4] See Carl F. H. Henry, *The Uneasy Conscience of Modern Fundamentalism* (Grand Rapids: Eerdmans, 2003).

[5] Noll, *The Scandal of the Evangelical Mind*, 5.

[6] Noll, *The Scandal of the Evangelical Mind.*

[7] E.g. Stuart Piggin and Robert Dean Linder, *Attending to the National Soul: Evangelical Christians in Australian History 1914-2014*, The Fountain of Public Prosperity, Vol. II (Clayton, Victoria: Monash University Publishing, 2020), 299–324.

universities (a reluctance I believe has shifted since Noll wrote), Evangelicalism has developed a similar culture of scholarly pastors as we identified in the early Church and Reformed orthodoxy.

A. Reclaiming the Mind with Tradition and Integrationism

Though this culture developed in uniquely Evangelical ways, the renewed interest in the tradition over the last 20 or 30 years has led to the growing interest in Patristic and Medieval theology and philosophy, Latin, and Patristic Greek. This desire is certainly commendable; I have spent the last 8 or so years learning these languages and engaging with Patristic philosophy and theology, and I do not believe it has been a waste. With this renewed interest in tradition has come the desire to *ressource* or reclaim ancient orthodoxy: it is claimed that the Christian past has the answers to present problems and without serious engagement with the tradition, we cannot or will not be thoroughly Christian.[8] The divergence between modern Evangelicalism and Patristic theology, especially in the doctrines of God, the Trinity, and Christology, are trumpeted as examples of Evangelicalism gone awry—all because it has neglected the tradition.[9] In recent years,

[8] E.g. D. H. Williams, *Evangelicals and Tradition (Evangelical Ressourcement): The Formative Influence of the Early Church* (Grand Rapids: Baker, 2005); Hans Boersma, *Heavenly Participation: The Weaving of a Sacramental Tapestry* (Grand Rapids: Eerdmans, 2011); Hans Boersma, "Up the Mountain with the Fathers: Evangelical Ressourcement of Early Christian Doctrine," *Canadian Theological Review* 1, no. 1 (2012): 3–22.

[9] See the exchanges over impassibility and the other attributes, the debate over eternal begottenness as the distinguishing feature of the Son, the eternal functional subordination debate, and the debates over contemporary Trinitarian theology. E.g. John V Dahms, "The Subordination of the Son," *Journal of the Evangelical Theological Society* 37, no. 3 (September 1994): 351–64; Charles J Kelly, "Classical Theism and the Doctrine of the Trinity," *Religious Studies* 30, no. 1 (March 1994): 67–88; Gilbert Bilezikian, "Hermeneutical Bungee-Jumping: Subordination in the Godhead," *Journal of the Evangelical*

proponents of "Classical Theism" have charged fellow Evangelicals with the betrayal of their heritage; many Evangelicals have, supposedly, embraced a Modernist theology that is at odds with historic and biblical Christianity.[10] The claim made by this camp is that Christian pastors

---

Theological Society 40, no. 1 (March 1997): 57–68; Craig S. Keener, "Is Subordination within the Trinity Really Heresy? A Study of John 5:18 in Context," *Trinity Journal* 20, no. 1 (Spring 1999): 39; Stephen D. Kovach and Peter R. Schemm, "A Defense of the Doctrine of the Eternal Subordination of the Son," *Journal of the Evangelical Theological Society* 42, no. 3 (September 1999): 461; Karen Kilby, "Perichoresis and Projection: Problems with Social Doctrines of the Trinity," *New Blackfriars*, October 2000, http://theologyphilosophycentre.co.uk/papers/Kilby_TrinNBnew.pdf; Kevin Giles, *The Trinity & Subordinationism: The Doctrine of God and the Contemporary Gender Debate* (Downers Grove: InterVarsity Press, 2002); Christopher Cowan, "The Father and Son in the Fourth Gospel: Johannine Subordination Revisited," *Journal of the Evangelical Theological Society* 49, no. 1 (March 2006): 115–35; Millard J Erickson, *Who's Tampering with the Trinity? An Assessment of the Subordination Debate* (Grand Rapids: Kregel Academic & Professional, 2009); M. F. Bird and R. Shillaker, "Subordination in the Trinity and Gender Roles: A Response to Recent Discussion," *Trinity Journal* 29, no. 2 (2008): 267–83; Kevin Giles, "Response to Michael Bird and Robert Shillaker: The Son Is Not Eternally Subordinated in Authority to the Father," *Trinity Journal* 30, no. 2 (Fall 2009): 237–56; Keith E Johnson, "Trinitarian Agency and the Eternal Subordination of the Son: An Augustinian Perspective," *Themelios* 36, no. 1 (May 2011): 7–25; D. Glenn Butner, "Eternal Functional Subordination and the Problem of the Divine Will," *Journal of the Evangelical Theological Society* 58, no. 1 (March 2015): 131–49; Luke Stamps, "The New Evangelical Subordinationism? Perspectives on the Equality of God the Father and God the Son/The Eternal Generation of the Son: Maintaining Orthodoxy in Trinitarian Theology," *Journal of the Evangelical Theological Society* 59, no. 4 (December 2016): 874–81; Michael F. Bird and Robert Shillaker, "The Son Really, Really Is the Son: A Response to Kevin Giles," *Trinity Journal* 30, no. 2 (Fall 2009): 257–68.

[10] E.g. James E. Dolezal, *God without Parts: Divine Simplicity and the Metaphysics of God's Absoluteness* (Eugene, OR: Pickwick Publications, 2011); Steven J. Duby, *Divine Simplicity: A Dogmatic Account*, T&T Clark Studies in Systematic Theology, volume 30 (London; New York: Bloomsbury, 2016); Dolezal, *All That Is in God*; Matthew Barrett, *None Greater: The Undomesticated Attributes of God* (Grand Rapids: Baker Books, 2019); Carter, *Contemplating*

and scholars have not done their homework; they have not sat in the tradition long enough and engaged broadly enough to emerge from and stand above the Modern waters in which they swim.[11] Thus, this emphasis on tradition has led to antagonism towards the sort of clear, exegetical theology developed by Wayne Grudem and John Frame (among many others) and calls for serious dogmatic engagement as practised by the Reformed Orthodox.[12] This recent emphasis on serious dogmatic engagement could perhaps be traced back to the influence of Karl Barth and his disciples, yet when married with the *ressourcement* movement that developed among Catholic theologians in the mid-20th century, it has found a conservative hearing and has become a powerful force among Reformed theologians and Evangelicals more broadly.[13]

God; Steven J. Duby, *Jesus and the God of Classical Theism: Biblical Christology in Light of the Doctrine of God* (Grand Rapids: Baker, 2022).

[11] See the discussion in the introduction.

[12] Wayne A. Grudem, *Systematic Theology: An Introduction to Biblical Doctrine*, 2nd Ed. (Grand Rapids: Zondervan Academic, 2020); Frame, *The Doctrine of the Knowledge*; John M. Frame, *The Doctrine of God*, A Theology of Lordship (Phillipsburg, NJ: P&R Publishing, 2002); John M. Frame, *The Doctrine of the Christian Life*, A Theology of Lordship 4 (Phillipsburg, NJ: P&R Publishing, 2008); John M. Frame, *The Doctrine of the Word of God*, A Theology of Lordship (Phillipsburg, NJ: P&R Publishing, 2010).

[13] John Webster has been particularly influential in Reformed Circles, and Hasn Boersma offers an Evangelical account of the Catholic *ressourcement* movement. See Hans Boersma, *Nouvelle Théologie and Sacramental Ontology: A Return to Mystery* (Oxford; New York: Oxford University Press, 2009), https://doi.org/10.1093/acprof:oso/9780199229642.001.0001; John Webster, "Principles of Systematic Theology," in *The Domain of the Word: Scripture and Theological Reason*, 2013, 133–49; John Webster, "On the Theology of the Intellectual Life," in *God Without Measure: Working Papers in Christian Theology*, vol. II, II vols., T&T Clark Theology (London; New York: Bloomsbury T&T Clark, 2016), 141–56; Webster, "What Makes Theology Theological?"; Willem-Maarten Dekker, "John Webster's Retrieval of Classical Theology," *Journal of Reformed Theology* 12, no. 1 (2018): 59–63, https://doi.org/10.1163/15697312-01201004.

In many ways, this movement is pushing back on the Christian integrationism that developed within Evangelicalism, where scholars attempted to engage seriously with secular biblical studies, philosophy of religion, religious studies, and theology. Evangelicals attempted to make intellectual progress in the broader world of religious scholarship, waging war with the same methodologies and in the same academic journals and universities as their secular colleagues. Reflecting on the development of integrationism within Christian psychology, Eric Johnson describes the development of broader Evangelical integrationism,

> In order to receive advanced training in various disciplines, Christians began to reenter the academic realm (that had by [the mid 20th-century] been entirely taken over by modernism), and they discovered that much of the knowledge being taught was valid and useful, in spite of the fact that there could be no public reference to God or faith. Yet there was a nagging sense that faith should have some role to play in that knowledge. The concept of integration was formulated to help deal with the issue. The task of integration was based on a recognition of the "all-embracing truth of God" .... The Foundation of all truth is the fact that it is revealed by God. This revelation is found primarily in the Bible, but it is also manifested in the natural world, sot he Bible and nature can be called God's "two books." [Frank] Gaebelein offered his ideas about what integration might look like in a few different fields (mathematics, literature and music) and suggested that it involves studying the subject matter in light of what the Bible has to say about it, recognising that its beauty and complexity come from God, and engaging in its activity (e.g. musical performance) as service for Christ's sake. [14]

---

[14] Eric L. Johnson, *Foundations for Soul Care: A Christian Psychology Proposal*

Perhaps Evangelicals did not make the advances Noll would have liked, but there has certainly been an attempt to do so. Engaging with the voluminous literature involved in these disciplines has required more and more hyper-specialisation: to be able to make a meaningful contribution, one needs to focus so closely on a particular facet of their chosen discipline that they often lose sight of the bigger issues and all the other disciplines that relate to that facet. Moreover, engaging with secular scholarship requires the use of secular, "neutral" methodologies in academic work.[15]

However, scholars like Craig Carter have responded to this development, arguing that Christian scholars have become too narrow, engaging within the restricted world of their discipline and not broadly enough to do Christian scholarship well.[16] Moreover, those who insist on the need for *ressourcement* and a return to the tradition have argued that integrationism, by embracing secular methodologies, has lost a distinctly Christian approach (and therefore the right approach) to the Scriptures.[17]

(Downers Grove: IVP Academic, 2007), 87. Engaging with, Frank E. Gaebelein, *The Pattern of God's Truth: The Integration of Faith and Learning* (New York: BMH Books, 1985).

[15] The concept of neutrality has been heavily criticized within Christian circles and without. See, for example, Michael Polanyi, *Personal Knowledge: Towards a Post-Critical Philosophy*, First Harper Torchbook Edition (New York: Harper Torchbook, 1964); Michael Polanyi, *The Tacit Dimension* (Chicago; London: University of Chicago Press, 2009); Cornelius Van Til, *The Defense of the Faith*, ed. K. Scott Oliphint, 4th ed (Phillipsburg: P&R Pub, 2008); Frame, *The Doctrine of the Knowledge.*

[16] Carter, *Contemplating God*; Dolezal, *All That Is in God.*

[17] Daniel J. Treier, *Introducing Theological Interpretation of Scripture: Recovering a Christian Practice* (Grand Rapids: Baker Academic, 2008); Boersma, *Heavenly Participation*; Craig A. Carter, *Interpreting Scripture with the Great Tradition:*

Although the forces of integration and ressourcement appear to be opposing, they have nevertheless come together to demand that Christians be more educated and more intellectual. Whether it is the tools necessary for engaging in the secular fields of biblical and religious studies or the tools for serious engagement with the tradition, pastors must acquire an extensive range of academic tools to do their job properly.

B. Denominational Desire for an Educated Pastorate

These theological developments mean that the expectations laid on pastors are beginning to look more and more like those we identified in the last two chapters. This is evident when we look at the practices of major Western Protestant denominations. The largest Protestant denomination in the United States, the Southern Baptist Convention, does not practice ordination, so it does not require seminary education for ministry. However, its churches are free to hold this as a requirement, and it supports six theological seminaries as well as having a list of 50 related colleges and universities.[18] These seminaries have this mission:

> to prepare God-called men and women for vocational service in Baptist church and in other Christian ministries throughout the world through programs of spiritual development, theological studies, and

Recovering the Genius of Premodern Exegesis (Grand Rapids: Baker Academic, 2018); Don C. Collett, *Figural Reading and the Old Testament: Theology and Practice* (Grand Rapids: Baker Academic, 2020); Carter, *Contemplating God.* Cf. Johnson, *Foundations for Soul Care: A Christian Psychology Proposal*, 87–106.

18 "Colleges and Universities - SBC.Net," https://www.sbc.net/, accessed February 23, 2024, https://www.sbc.net/resources/directories/colleges-and-universities/; "Theological Seminaries - SBC.Net," https://www.sbc.net/, accessed February 23, 2024, https://www.sbc.net/resources/directories/theological-seminaries/.

practical preparation for ministry.[19]

So, despite not having seminary training as a requirement for service in an affiliated church, the SBC clearly supports an academically trained pastorate.

Other denominations explicitly require a higher education degree, often a Master of Divinity, for ordination. Deacons in the Sydney Anglican Diocese (an ordained ministry position equivalent to an assistant pastor in other denominations) are normally required to have completed a 4-year Bachelor of Divinity degree at Moore Theological College (a degree that has recently been converted into a combined undergraduate and postgraduate course).[20] The exception to this rule still requires at least 2 years of formal theological study in addition to experience; if someone wants to be ordained as a Presbyter (a priest or pastor), they are required to complete the 4-year degree.[21] Even a lay minister (someone licensed by the dioceses to preach) is required to have theological training. The Christian Reformed Church in North America requires a MDiv from an accredited seminary.[22] The Baptist Association of Western Australia requires theological study for accreditation.[23] When I first attended Bible College, even Pentecostal denominations had begun requiring a two-year theological degree

19 "Theological Seminaries - SBC.Net."

20 "Bachelor of Divinity (BD) – In Teach-Out," Moore Theological College, accessed February 23, 2024, https://moore.edu.au/courses/bachelor-of-divinity-bd/.

21 "Considering Ordination - Policy," Sydney Anglicans Ministry and Development, accessed February 23, 2024, https://www.mtd.org.au/considering-ordination/policy/.

22 "Paths to Ordination | Candidacy in the Christian Reformed Church," Christian Reformed Church, accessed February 23, 2024, https://www.crcna.org/candidacy/paths-ordination.

23 "Accreditation - BCWA," *Baptist Churches Western Australia*, October 31, 2021, https://www.baptistwa.asn.au/accreditation/.

before ordination.[24] There is a clear desire among Evangelical churches for an educated pastorate, for pastors who have received training in institutions of higher education. This alone echoes the institutionalising tendencies we observed early in the Protestant movement. However, considering the contemporary seminary demonstrates that the sort of education being received reinforces the same tendency to make academic theology and biblical studies an essential component of pastoral ministry.

C. The Hidden Curriculum of our Institutions

There are good things that could be said of our seminaries, but I hope to dig beneath the surface to explore problems that may not be readily apparent.[25] Because I am attempting to dig beneath the surface, the following considerations are not immediately pejorative; indeed, they may be good in their own right. Consider with me a modern seminary and the general atmosphere it fosters. When taken as a whole, the hidden curriculum or the message communicated by the medium and methods adopted by Evangelical seminaries is more insidious than a cursory glance at their curriculum reveals. Perry Shaw defines "hidden curriculum" as

> the potent sociological and psychological dimensions of education, which are usually caught rather than intentionally taught. The hidden curriculum are those pervasive environmental features of education that include such things as the nature of behaviors which

---

[24] For a list of the ordination requirements for various Protestant churches with a variety of theological outlooks, see "Ordination Process by Denomination," Union Theological Seminary, accessed February 23, 2024, https://utsnyc.edu/academics/career-paths/ordination-process/.

[25] This section is adapted, sometimes word for word, from my blog post J. Alexander Rutherford, "Authority Structures and Biblical Education – Teleioteti Articles," Teleioteti, April 14, 2021, https://www.teleioteti.ca/2021/04/14/authority-structures-and-biblical-education/.

> are encouraged, the type of relationships modeled, and the values emphasized in the learning community.[26]

The following observations are consistent with the three schools I have personally attended and the observations I have gathered from numerous other seminaries.

Evangelical seminaries look very different than universities and seminaries of the older sort, where status required students to call their teachers by their titles, such as Professor or Doctor. At Evangelical seminaries, faculty are often addressed by their first names, and they often build a successful rapport with their students, engaging in extracurricular activities and sharing a coffee. This coheres with the most influential pedagogical methods in modern education, which posture the teacher as a co-learner, examining the evidence alongside his or her students.[27] Through readings, writing assignments, and discussion, students are encouraged to arrive at their own conclusions, engage the data critically, and go where it leads. To pursue such education, students are usually required to travel some distance and so enter a new church environment. Some schools encourage their students to serve at multiple churches during their education (Moore College encourages students to attend at least two different churches for a 4-year degree). In addition, many students get internship-like positions in churches, where they are part of the leadership team and learn skills for church leadership.

There are reasons for all of these things; there are reasons for the informal quality of student-faculty relations, the structure of assignments and independent learning, the location of seminaries in major cities, and the requirement for internships or student ministry positions in multiple churches. Some of these reasons are very good.

---

26 Shaw, "Hidden Curriculum," 25–26.

27 See, for example, Parker J. Palmer, *To Know as We Are Known: Education as a Spiritual Journey* (New York: Harper Collins, 1993).

However, it is worth considering what they communicate when taken together as a whole.

When we look at this picture, issues emerge in terms of "authority structures." We could define authority used in this way as a relationship between persons where one person has obligations towards the other, where the person under authority ought to act in certain ways towards the person with authority. An authority structure describes a framework within which persons exist in subordinated relationships, with restrictions on the one in authority. That is, a structure implies both the relationship between the one in authority and their subordinates and between the one in authority and their superior, by whom their authority is restricted. Cases where there is explicit subordination and restriction we may call "vertical" relationships of authority. However, not all authority is vertical; there are situations where a horizontal relationship exists, where two persons who are each accountable to the same authority are empowered to keep one another accountable in their submission. We may call the vertical relationship "authority" and the horizontal "accountability," though both are relationships of authority in the above sense. compared with authority structures presented in the New Testament, the primary structures in which a seminary student finds themselves are horizontal.[28] A horizontal authority structure is a structure of mutual accountability; such structures exist among all Christians as they equally stand before God and under his word. However, the Bible prescribes both horizontal and vertical authority structures; vertically, all Christians stand under God's authority through the Bible, and non-ordained Christians stand under the authority of their local pastors (who are themselves under Christ's authority with unique responsibilities and accountabilities corresponding to their role).

Not only does the seminary setting primarily foster horizontal

[28] Cf. Rutherford, *The Being of Churches*; Rutherford, "Authority Structures and Biblical Education – Teleioteti Articles."

structures, but these may be best described as malformed structures. That is, the primary accountability a student has in their Christian maturation is peer-oriented: they are accountable to their teachers and fellow students in the college setting. In an internship, they are accountable as peers with their fellow leaders. I describe these relationships as "malformed" because they are artificially separated from the regular church life and the ideal circumstances for accountability. These relationships, occurring at the most formative point in a Christian leader's life, are fresh, without the depth of a life lived together. Furthermore, they are, for the most part, short-lived. These relationships are not regularly built within the context of the local church's inward and outward focus but within the artificial constraints of the college atmosphere. College professors are often godly individuals, and they may even be ordained, but however much "spiritual care" might be part of their portfolio, they are not "pastors" in the biblical sense. The seminary is not a local church and professors are not shepherds with authority invested by the risen Lord to speak prophetically into the lives of their sheep and help them grow through pastoral leadership.[29] Not only are students lacking the vital input of a long-term pastor, but their pastors and teachers will rarely take the posture of an authoritative teacher or pastor speaking concretely into the students' lives to shape them spiritually and theologically; often this is the case because the relationships are too short-lived and the number of students too numerous. Lastly, many of their student peers will be at a similar maturity level without the variety in experience and faith found in the local church.

The most significant absence is the elder's vertical authority structure over the parishioner, in which the former wields authority over the latter to see them grow spiritually and in their knowledge of Scripture.[30] Thus, the hidden curriculum regarding authority structures

---

29 See further Rutherford, *The Being of Churches.*

30 See ibid.

is that the learner is at the top of the pecking order, so far as human oversight goes. Pair this with two other factors in contemporary Christian education, and the result may very well be devastating. First, most of our students are raised in a generally anti-authoritarian culture, where age does not equal wisdom and where everybody is on an equal playing field, with a right to be heard. Indeed, the dominant force in the practical epistemology of the Western person is "emotivism," the dominance of desire.[31] The combination of a bias towards one's own intuition over external authority and the individualism of our culture, which is often militantly opposed to tradition and authority, orient the learner of theology towards themselves as the primary reference point for truth. Instead of being corrected in our seminaries, this is only reinforced by our seminaries' hidden curriculum. Second, our teaching hardly supports our claims to biblical clarity and sufficiency. Students are shown a vast range of data (itself ambiguous) necessary to interpret Scripture and are exposed to dozens of differing opinions from intelligent sources. Given the questions concerning the appropriate method and the complexities of actually employing that method, let alone moving from a right understanding of Scripture to the right application, it almost appears that the Bible has become our peer. It does not appear to be over us but beside us as we dialogue with it and dozens of other sources to arrive at a true or liveable position.[32] This is evident in the quotes I presented in the Introduction above and is everywhere (though perhaps less explicit) in the books regularly used within the seminary context.

N.T. Wright has repeatedly lamented the errors of prior generations resulting from their lack of insight into 1st-century Judaism

---

[31] See Alasdair C. MacIntyre, *After Virtue: A Study in Moral Theory*, 2nd ed (Notre Dame, Ind: University of Notre Dame Press, 1984).

[32] Cf. *The Gift of Knowing, The Gift of Reading – Part 1,* and *The Gift of Reading – Part 2* in Rutherford, *The Gift of Knowledge;* J. Alexander Rutherford, *The Gift of Revelation: A Biblical Perspective on the Bible*, God's Gifts for the Christian Life - Part 2: The Gift of Truth, I (Airdrie, AB: Teleioteti, 2021).

and the literature associated with what is often called 2nd-Temple Judaism; with the recovery of the Dead Sea Scrolls and several other 20th-century archaeological finds, we are better positioned than they were to understand the Bible.[33] Similarly, George Athas laments the myth of the so-called "400 silent years" and argues that Christians need to seriously engage with this period if they are to rightly understand the New and Old Testaments. He writes,

> Unfortunately, biblical scholars rarely venture outside the pages of canonical literature in their endeavor to understand it and the world in which it arose. There is a pragmatic consideration here: it is very difficult to master the many disparate fields it takes to come to grips with this literature and its contexts, and so biblical scholars tend to specialize. However, an unwanted fruit of this tendency is that the canonical literature gets treated as though it were hermetically sealed from the rest of the reality in which it arose.... There is, therefore, benefit in a large-scale analysis that integrates an understanding of how the biblical literature of the Second Temple period arose, what it meant in its original context, what the covenant people of God experienced in this period, and how the Old Testament leads in to the New. It is a daunting task that involves the close reading of biblical and nonbiblical literature; interpretation and evaluation of sources written in Hebrew, Aramaic, Persian, Greek, and Latin; consideration of political, cultural, religious, economic, and social history across five centuries; appraisal of archaeological excavations and artefacts that they unearth; sensitivity to the theological and philosophical developments among Jews, Samaritans,

[33] E.g. N.T. Wright, *The New Testament and the People of God*, Christian Origins and the Question of God 1 (Minneapolis: Fortress, 1992); N.T. Wright, *What Saint Paul Really Raid: Was Paul of Tarsus the Real Founder of Christianity?* (Grand Rapids; Cincinnati: Eerdmans; Forward Movement Publications, 1997); N.T. Wright, *Justification: God's Plan & Paul's Vision* (Downers Grove: IVP Academic, 2009).

> Persians, Greeks, and Romans; and doing all this with an eye on discerning the trajectories between the old covenant and the new.[34]

Though certainly a believer in the clarity of Scripture, John Stott casually echoes this posture toward Scripture in his definition of expository preaching, "To expound Scripture is to bring out of the text what is there and expose it to view. The expositor pries open what appears to be closed, makes plain what is obscure, unravels what is knotted and unfolds what is tightly packed."[35]

Our approach to biblical studies makes the Bible the subject of extensive academic investigation and repeatedly declares the insufficiency of simple reading to properly interpret the Bible.[36] We do not often say this explicitly, and our doctrines of sufficiency and clarity

---

[34] George Athas, *Bridging the Testaments: The History and Theology of God's People in the Second Temple Period* (Grand Rapids: Zondervan Academic, 2023), 12–13. Athas's claim that scholars are not doing this seems at odds with the dominant trends in secular and confessional biblical studies in the last 100 years. The dominant Evangelical approach, grammatical-historical exegesis, has intended to engage seriously with the historical context, much more so in Old Testament studies than in New Testament studies. The historical-critical methods have produced much literature on the ancient contexts, even if the methods used do not always produce valid conclusions. The New Perspective on Paul and related schools in New Testament studies have studied in great detail the Intertestamental Period and the literature associated with 2nd-Temple Judaism; proponents of the "old perspective" have also investigated these sources closely to offer contrasting conclusions. The quote from Guthrie in the Introduction also indicates the self-understanding of the task of biblical studies. My introduction to biblical studies was steeped in these presuppositions; much of my writing has been an attempt to reassert biblical clarity and sufficiency against these very trends. See, for example, Stephen Westerholm, *Perspectives Old and New on Paul: The "Lutheran" Paul and His Critics* (Grand Rapids: Eerdmans, 2004).

[35] John Stott, *Between Two Worlds* (Grand Rapids: Eerdmans, 2017), 92.

[36] Cf. J. Alexander Rutherford, *The Gift or Reading – Part 1 & Part 2* in *God's Gifts for the Christian Life – Part 1: The Gift of Knowledge.*

are supposed to deny it, yet this is the dominant message communicated by the curriculum of our seminaries and the books they produce or use.

D. Conclusion

If we look closely at the theological trends that have dominated Evangelical thought for several decades now, the requirements for ordination in Evangelical denominations, and the hidden curriculum of our institutions, a uniform picture emerges. From every side, pressure is applied towards an educated pastorate. The ressourcement and classical theist movements within theology push for a return to expansive classical learning, covering philosophy, history, Latin, and Patristic Greek. Proponents of integrationism call for interdisciplinary engagement with secular studies in all relevant fields. Denominations require prospective candidates to attend Bible college or seminary, and these institutions communicate that knowledge and skill is more important than character, that students are authorities unto themselves, and that pastoral ministry requires an academic skill set. The Evangelical church has gone down the same road as its Patristic and Reformed forefathers, embracing an intellectualised approach to theology and orthodoxy, thereby relegating the pastorate to the educated and intelligent. In the next chapter, we will analyse the assumptions driving these developments before turning, in Part 2, to consider how the Bible addresses them.

ANALYSING THE PROBLEM: PRESUPPOSITIONS OF CONTEMPORARY CHRISTIAN MINISTRY

In the last three chapters, we have recounted the parallel developments of intellectualised theology and an educated pastorate at three points in Church history. In the 4th and 5th centuries, the newly Imperial church used councils to define who and what theological positions would be in and out of the church. To do this, they used the tools of philosophy, articulating a conceptually robust account of God's Trinitarian one-in-threeness and Christ's incarnational two-in-oneness. For much of the church after Chalcedon, orthodoxy meant adhering to a rigorously philosophical theology. Similarly, as the Reformation transformed into established churches, theology became institutionalised. Like the Medieval church before it, the Reformers developed theology in the context of the academy and its disciplines and identified this intellectually rigorous and institutional theology as closest human equivalent to the knowledge God has in himself (in contrast with the catechetical theology of the young or spiritually immature) and the sort of theology necessary for pastors. Finally, in our own day, Evangelicals have, for various reasons, sought an educated pastorate. Various forces at work within contemporary Evangelicalism push for pastors to become more and more academically literate.

At each period in history, proponents of these developments did not think they were betraying any aspect of the Gospel or setting up any obstacles to its flourishing. No, at each moment, these movements have been thought to be right and necessary. For the early church, theology was already being debated in a philosophical register, but with the recognition of the church by the Roman Empire and an increasingly hierarchically ordered and unified global church, theological unity needed to be secured across the far reaches of the Empire. The flair-up with Arius showed the dangers of division; if the church divided, the Empire could very well divide, too. Arius, Eusebius, and others who thought similarly were arguing theology at a dense, philosophical level, so it appeared that only dense, philosophical ripostes could defeat them. Theology was already thickly philosophical in certain schools at this time, but the controversies required identifying this sort of theology with orthodoxy, or so it seemed at the time. Concepts of theology and orthodoxy closely tied together in the 4th and 5th centuries appear to necessitate the developments we traced in Chapter 1. These same views of orthodoxy and theology stand behind the institutionalisation of the church in the post-Reformation period. Likewise, the same view of orthodoxy and theology stands out in contemporary Evangelicalism, despite falling out of favour throughout the 19th and 20th centuries.

Breaking this down a bit, we can identify five facets of the developments we have traced in the last three chapters: 1) there is an identification of orthodoxy with creeds or confessions, with universalising statements of Christian faith; 2) there is an identification of God's own knowledge and the knowledge we have of God as necessary and universal, not contingent and particular; 3) consequently, there is an understanding of ordained ministry in terms of adhering to and teaching orthodox doctrine, requiring an immense amount of knowledge; 4) there is an understanding of the Bible as insufficient in itself as a measure of orthodoxy and insufficient for its own interpretation; and 5), as a consequence of these, there is an exaltation of the academy to the centre of Christian theological engagement and pastoral training. In this final chapter of Part 1, we will consider each of these facets; we will then consider how the Bible presents an alternative to each of these in Part 2.

A. Orthodoxy Is Defined by Adherence to Creeds and Confessions

What does it mean to be orthodox? The word itself signifies "right belief," and we usually use it to describe individuals or groups that believe rightly, namely, hold to the essential truths of the Christian faith. The opposite of being orthodox is being heterodox, believing something other than the true Christian faith, or heretical, leading or participating in a group that separates from the true Christian faith. We want to maintain, on biblical grounds, that there is right and wrong faith; there are beliefs that are genuinely Christian, and there are beliefs that deviate from the "sound doctrine" of the Gospel (1 Tim 1:10). However, acknowledging that there is such a thing as orthodoxy is easier than identifying the content of orthodoxy and measuring it. We see from the New Testament through the Early Church the importance of doing so, yet the New Testament teaching of the Apostles and the "rule of faith" urged by Irenaeus are distinctly different from the form and measure of orthodoxy that emerged in the 4th century.

Before the 325 AD (or to be more precise, the recognition of its importance in the second half of the 4th century), there were various measures used to pass on the orthodox faith. We see creeds used locally for baptism in the 3rd century, and sketches of the whole of Scripture called "rules of faith." However, a crisis emerged in the 4th century that required, in the eyes of the bishops and emperor, a new solution. We have traced this movement in the 1st chapter, so we will focus on the result of it here. At the end of the 5th century, a new conception of Orthodoxy had emerged, one that has continued into our day.

In the late 4th century, the Nicaean Creed was recognised as important for its ability to unite the various parties that upheld the true and full divinity of the Son over against subordinationism (the teaching that the Son was less divine or of a different sort than God the Father). It was also recognised for its ability to separate off the various factions that rejected the identity of the Son with the Father. At Ephesus I, a new development emerged: creeds other than Nicaea were forbidden.[1] Nicaea was to be the sole creed; if Ephesus I's canon 7 was not clear on what it meant for Nicaea to be the only permissible creed, Chalcedon was far more specific. Listen to Chalcedon's *Definition*,

> We therefore decree—we ourselves upholding the order and all the decrees of the faith of the holy synod formerly taking place at Ephesus, over which presided the most holy in memory Celestine of Rome and Cyril of Alexandria—on the one hand, that the exposition of the right and spotless faith by the 318 holy and blessed fathers at Nicaea, gathered together by the pious in memory Constantine who was then Emperor, shines forth preeminent and, on the other hand, that the decrees of the 150 holy fathers in Constantinople give support for the uprooting of heresies that then sprung up and the confirmation of the same universal and apostolic faith which is ours.
>
> … Thus this wise and saving Creed of divine grace was sufficient for complete knowledge of and confirmation of godliness; for it both thoroughly teaches the complete matter concerning the Father, the Son, and the Holy Spirit, and it also presents the Lord's *enanthropation* [i.e. "becoming human"] to those who receive it faithfully.
>
> … this now present holy, great, and ecumenical synod, teaching thoroughly the immovability of the proclamation previously given, sets forth firstly that

[1] See Chapter 1 and Smith, *The Idea*; Rutherford, "Rightly Defining."

> the faith of the 318 holy fathers is to remain inviolate. Because of those who made war against the Holy Spirit, [the council] confirms [the teaching of Constantinople vis-à-vis the Spirit]." (ACO V.31, 34; 2.1.2, 127 lns 1-8; 128 lns 15-18; 128, ln 24 – 129, ln 6)[2]

At this period in history, it was clear; if you could not pledge full adherence to the Nicaean Creed, you were not orthodox. The Nicene Creed was the preeminent "exposition of the right and spotless faith." This Creed is not only wise but is salvific and "sufficient for complete knowledge of and confirmation of godliness." Rightly received, it contains the "complete matter" concerning the Father, Son, and Spirit as well as the incarnation. The Council of Chalcedon proceeds to recognize that this Creed is "immovable" and "inviolate."

Though it may at times need further exposition or application, as demonstrated by the Constantinopolitan Creed (381 AD) and the Definition of Chalcedon (451 AD), the Nicene Creed was *the* standard of orthodoxy. Thus, by 451 AD, there was a view of orthodoxy as something that can be captured in universal theological statements applicable across all times and places; this theology can not only be expressed in propositions (statements of truth), but in propositions that are communicable across the Empire and from that time onward. Not only was it deemed necessary for orthodoxy to go beyond the words of Scripture, which is necessary to communicate the Bible across cultures and languages, but it also appeared necessary for orthodoxy to contain more conceptually than the Bible's teaching. This might not be immediately evident, so let's revisit the Nicene Creed and then the interpretation of this Creed that was accepted by the end of the 4th century.

The Nicene Creed (325 AD) according to the Definition of

---

2 This is my translation, from my PhD thesis, Rutherford, "Rightly Defining."

Chalcedon reads as follows,[3]

> We believe in one God, Father almighty, maker of heaven and earth, of things both visible and invisible; in one Lord, Jesus Christ, the only-begotten Son of God, begotten from the Father before all ages, true God from true God, begotten not made, consubstantial [ὁμοούσιον, *homoousion*] with the Father, through whom all things came to be, who on account of us humans and on account of our salvation came down, was incarnated [σαρκωθέντα, *sarkothenta*], became human [ἐνανθρωπήσαντα, *enanthropesanta*], suffered, rose again on the third day, ascended into heaven, and is coming to judge the living and the dead; and in the Holy Spirit.
>
> But those who say 'there was a time when he was not,' 'before he was begotten he was not,' that from things that were not he came to be, or who assert that the Son of God is from a different reality [ὑποστάσεως, *hupostaseos*] or substance [οὐσίας], subject to turning [τρεπτὸν, *trepton*], or subject to change [ἀλλοιωτὸν, *alloioton*], persons such as this the Catholic and Apostolic church anathematises.[4]

Without a doubt, "consubstantial" was a term with strong philosophical pedigree; it was highly suspect given its associations with Paul of Samosata in the 3rd century, who had been deposed by a council at Antioch. Those who received the Nicene Creed were quick to give this term alternate meaning, as we will consider shortly, but it was

---

[3] It should be observed that there was flexibility in the wording of the Creed even in the Acts of Chalcedon; Sessions I and III have different wording than Session V (the *Definition*). Richard Price and Michael Gaddis, trans., *The Acts of the Council of Chalcedon*, vol. 2, Translated Texts for Historians (Liverpool: Liverpool University Press, 2005), 191–94.

[4] This translation is from my PhD Thesis, Rutherford, "Rightly Defining."

almost invariably used with dense conceptual meaning, meaning not readily deduced from the Scriptures. The use of the term was deemed necessary to exclude Arius, for it was presumed that he would never agree to this term (given its problematic conceptual heritage). Moreover, whatever one's take on the term "begotten" (which has a legion of defenders among Evangelical theologians today), it's meaning here is a conceptual elaboration upon the teaching of Scripture. The Early Church was quick to deny that Jesus was made, that he had a beginning of any sort; however, they identified begottenness as an essential component of a father-son relationship, so the Son must have been begotten from the Father. They could have, perhaps, relied on the term μονογενῆς (*mongenes*, see its use in the creed), which is heavily debated in contemporary literature, or passages like Psalm 2:7 and Hebrews 1:5 where God is said to beget the Messiah, but they drew this concept of sonship into a broader network of meaning. Athanasius writes,

> what is naturally begotten from any one and does not accrue to him from without, that in the nature of things is a son, and that is what the name implies. Is then the Son's generation one of human affections? … in no wise.… As then men create not as God creates, as their being is not such as God's being, so men's generation is one way, and the Son is from the Father in another (*De Dec.* III.10-11 [NPNF 2.4]).

"Begottenness" was seen, despite the significant disanalogies with human begetting, as the critical link between Father and Son, signifying both identity (a son is what his father is) and continuous being (in an earthly relationship, a portion of the father's substance is communicated to the son, but in the Divine relationship, there is no partitioning or loss, so the whole of the Father's substance is communicated to the Son and is shared with him) (*De Dec.* V.20). Whether or not this account of begottenness is true is not important for our discussion, only that it is a conceptual elaboration based on the analogy of human parents from the Bible's claim that Jesus is 1) God's

Son and 2) he is only-begotten, uniquely God's son. In addition, the Creed also anathematises those who would teach that the Son is from a different "substance" or "reality" than the Father; though it appears right to deny the claim the Creed is denying, there is a level of conceptual elaboration here upon the unity of Father and Son declared in Scripture, conceptual elaboration that is false or perhaps nonsensical within philosophical frameworks that reject the concepts of "substance" as it was treated in this period. The Creed moves beyond merely using different words for the orthodox faith to mandating as part of orthodoxy the concepts associated with *homousios* (ὁμοούσιος, "consubstantial"), *gennetos* (γεννητός, "begotten"), and *ousia* (οὐσία, substance), concepts which are neither explicitly given in Scripture nor necessary deductions therefrom. Perhaps those drafting the Creed did not intend to have such conceptual implications but merely intended for the presence of the word *homoousios* to be repugnant to Arius and like-minded bishops, as is often claimed.[5] However, by the end of the 4th century, the received interpretation of the Creed involved lengthy elaborations of these terms and the conceptual framework they involve.[6]

For Athanasius, these three terms were all related to the twin ideas of substantial unity (i.e. the Son's being was the Father's) and essential identity (i.e. the Son was what the Father was). Similar claims were made by other interpreters of Nicaea like Apollinaris (before his Christology got him in trouble), Basil of Caesarea, and Gregory of Nyssa. Each term was keyed to a broader explanation of the Creator and the created order and their connection. To follow Nicaea was to accept a dense philosophical paradigm that explained God's oneness and threeness without falling into the errors that various anti-Nicene parties charged against the Creed. It wasn't enough to proclaim that

[5] Cf. Hanson, *The Search*, 202; Williams, *Arius*, 68–70; Behr, *The Nicene Faith: Vol 2 of Formation of Christian Theology*, 157.

[6] See further, Rutherford, "Rightly Defining."

Father and Son were *homoousios*, for various interpretations of this phrase where unacceptable (either that the Father and Son were ontological co-laterals, requiring a 4th entity, the Divinity, by which they were both identified as God, or that the Father and the Son were both made of the same stuff), neither was merely proclaiming the Son *begotten* enough, for this claim could not mean that the Son was a creation likely the rest of creation (cf. Athanasius, *De Dec.* III.7).

The establishment of *Nicaean* orthodoxy was simultaneously the declaration that orthodoxy must be measured by something other than Scripture, that this "other" could be codified in universal truth statements, and that orthodoxy was not merely the teaching of Scripture but theology, a meditation upon and elaboration of the teaching of Scripture. This sense of orthodoxy was taken up in the Reformation period, as we saw. The establishment of the Reformed churches was thought to require the institutionalisation and scholastic theology that characterised the period after the Reformation. There have been periods in recent history where a different sense of orthodoxy and theology connected with it appeared to be adopted, where diversity of philosophical and conceptual articulation was permissible so long as claims of Scripture were maintained, where Creeds like Nicaea were treated as guides to the sort of language we could use but not conceptual parameters for right Christian faith. Whether these developments are good is certainly debatable; at least in some circles, they have been accompanied by serious deviations from the biblical teaching and historic Christian faith. However, in contemporary Evangelicalism, there has been pushback against this more flexible definition of orthodoxy and a return to the equation of orthodoxy with a philosophically dense, theologically elaborate faith. When defined in this way, to be a teacher of orthodoxy requires a depth of knowledge and significant intellectual abilities. If this is what orthodoxy means, then the claims of Carter and others make sense. This idea of orthodoxy is closely associated with important presuppositions about the knowledge of God.

B. The Highest Form of the Knowledge of God is Universal and Necessary

What is theology? You may respond with a definition for *theologising*, the action performed, but what is the "theology"? If by theology we mean statements of truth, what sort of statements are meant?[7] Perhaps we could also approach the question from another direction: what does it mean to *know* God? Is our knowledge of God composed of theoretically quantifiable statements about God? This seems to be the implications of the discussion of theology within Classical Theism, and this follows the classic discussion of knowledge in Plato and Aristotle. Classically, 'knowledge' referred to certain, demonstrable or necessary knowledge contemplated by the mind, not the sense data derived from immediate experience. Something that may be true or false is opinion; only that which is always true is "knowledge."

When we talk about theology and knowing God in the three periods we have discussed, these are associated with not only true statements but statements that are necessarily true. For this reason, "theology" aims at "eternal and necessary truths" about God and the world in relation to him.[8] If theology pertains to eternal and necessary truths, then the sort of conceptual elaboration witnessed at Nicaea, a "second exegesis," as Carter calls it, is necessary to move from God's self-testimony in Scripture to theology proper. God's revelation in Scripture is not necessary or certain in the philosophical sense (though it is certainly reliable and true), for it is communicated in the flexible garb of culture and is almost entirely devoted to 'contingency,' to things that could have been otherwise, namely, historical events, characters, and responses. This is why we saw the Reformed orthodox use Scripture to identify the topics of theology *(loci)*, but these *loci* were developed theologically from *principia* or causal principles from which

---

[7] E.g. Carter, *Contemplating God*, 296.

[8] Webster, "What Makes Theology Theological?," 221.

all the effects of God's actions in history could be traced.

These *prinicipia* are not demonstrable axioms like in,

> It is not necessary for the habit of a science so to comprehend its object as to have a perfect knowledge of whatever belongs to it. It is sufficient if it knows many things concerning it and can draw deductions from its principles. Therefore, a science need not necessarily be equal to its subject by an exact and arithmetical equality.[9]

However, they are universal truths, not contextualised in this or that circumstance, and are necessary aspects of God's character.

> The common saying—"science is not of particulars, but of universals"—must be received with limitation... if theology treats of such (as of Adam, Noah and others), it does this not principally, but only to unfold the origin of things or for an example of life and a testimony to divine providence (and therefore on account of general causes). ... God can with great propriety be reckoned among universals for he is universal in causation, since he is the universal cause of all things also in predication; not indeed directly, but indirectly for though all things are not God, they are nevertheless of God, or to or from him. Accordingly every relation of universality is not wanting in this part in the subject of theology.[10]

God's knowledge, revelation and expression of knowledge in Scripture could be traced back to a principle of knowledge or a general cause—

---

[9] Francis Turretin, *Institutes of Elenctic Theology*, ed. James T. Dennison, Jr., trans. George Musgrave Giger, vol. 1 (Phillipsburg, NJ: P&R Publishing, 1992), T.1, Q.5 p. 17, http://archive.org/details/institutesofelen0001turr.

[10] Turretin, 1:T.1, Q.5, pp. 17–18.

an attribute of *omniscience*—in God himself.

Sometimes a distinction is drawn between *theologia*, who God is in himself, and *oikonomia*, God as revealed in creation (these are related to the so-called "imminent" and "economic" Trinity).[11] Of this distinction in the fathers, Vladimir Lossky writes,

> Economy is the work of the will, while Trinitarian being belongs to the transcendent nature of God. This is the basis of the distinction between οἰκονομία [*oikonomia*] and θεολογία [*theologia*], which goes back to the fourth and perhaps even to the third century and which remains common to most of the Greek Fathers and to all of the Byzantine tradition.[12]

Similarly, the *Catechism of the Catholic Church* states, in section 236,

> The Fathers of the Church distinguish between theology (theologia) and economy (oikonomia). "Theology" refers to the mystery of God's inmost life within the Blessed Trinity and "economy" to all the works by which God reveals himself and communicates his life. Through the oikonomia the theologia is revealed to us; but conversely, the theologia illuminates the whole oikonomia. God's works reveal who he is in himself; the mystery of his inmost being enlightens our understanding of all his works. So it is, analogously, among human persons. A

---

[11] See Markus Mühling's entry, "Immanent/Economic Trinity," though John Behr highlights the distinction between these two sets of terminology. Markus Mühling, "Immanent/Economic Trinity," in *Religion Past and Present* (Brill, April 1, 2011), https://referenceworks.brillonline.com/entries/religion-past-and-present/immanenteconomic-trinity-SIM_10307; Behr, *The Nicene Faith: Vol 2 of Formation of Christian Theology*, 477.

[12] Vladimir Lossky, *In the Image and Likeness of God* (Crestwood, NY: St. Vladimir's Seminary Press, 1974), 15, http://archive.org/details/inimagelikenesso0000loss.

> person discloses himself in his actions, and the better we know a person, the better we understand his actions.[13]

Lewis Ayres describes these terms in Basil of Caesarea like this,

> Basil generally uses θεολογία [*theologia*] of a mode of insight into the nature of God at that comes as a result of an ability to see beyond material reality, or beyond the material-sounding phraseology of some scriptural passages. Οἰκονομία [*oikonomia*] is used to describe a wide range of acts of ordering of events and behaviour: in the case of divine ordering Basil can speak of an οἰκονομία in creation and an οἰκονομία in the work of redemption through the incarnation. In this latter case Basil speaks of God's οἰκονομία as the ordering of the incarnation so that it would appropriately accomplish its purpose.[14]

There is a necessary connection of cause to effect between these, yet we do not perceive God in himself in his self-revelation in history, the revelation we find in Scripture. No, it takes reasoning to move from effect to cause. At Nicaea, there is a movement from the revelation of the unity of the Logos and God in Scripture as well as the Father-Son relationship to the elaboration of the concepts of *consubstantiality, substance,* and *begottenness* to describe what must be true of God for this revelation to be true.

It is not that God's revelation in the *oikonomia* is not true, but it does not constitute doctrine or theology. Theology pertains to necessary, universal statements about God communicated through his self-

---

13 Liberia Editrice Vaticana, "Catechism of the Catholic Church," Vatican, accessed March 8, 2024, https://www.vatican.va/archive/ENG0015/__P17.HTM.

14 Ayres, *Nicaea and Its Legacy*, 220.

condescension in Scripture, through his accommodations to the limitations and means of human communication.

If *theology* and *doctrine* mean truth statements such as this, and orthodoxy pertains to right doctrine or theology, then orthodoxy must express such truths, namely, it must be more than what Scripture says; it must express that eternal reality about God we discover through reasoned meditation on Scripture (see Chapter 2). This is the sort of theology that undergirds the developments we traced in the last three chapters. This sort of theology requires philosophical precision and intellectual rigour, even when it is oriented towards "practice," as many Reformed theologians would have it. It is one thing to know God in the *oikonomia*, but it is another to approach (in as much as human knowledge is able to do so) God as he is in himself through theology. The latter form is a better, more mature understanding of God.

C. Pastors Are Teachers

Given these presuppositions, we would expect that in the 6th century and following, clergy would be expected to be highly educated and able to pass on the received orthodoxy and teach others in the knowledge of God. By the 3rd century, the extant writings of Eastern and Western bishops demonstrate that key members of the clergy were highly educated and serious thinkers. This was not incidental to their role but was critical to the depiction of Bishops and clergy as defenders of the faith, taking up the pen and mounting erudite arguments to uphold right Christian doctrine against errors. The medieval era certainly attests to this. In the periods we have been tracing, the texts from post-Reformation Protestantism demonstrate that the role of pastor or ordained minister in the church was associated with the form of orthodoxy and knowledge identified above. The data from contemporary Evangelicalism attests to the same fact. The presupposition behind the contemporary and ancient practices of ministerial training is that teaching and defending theology in the sense discussed above are critical to the role of a minister of the Gospel.

If ministers are responsible for teaching, upholding, and defending this sort of theology, they will need to develop the knowledge and skills necessary to do so. This requires significant time and intellectual ability, which are best expressed in the traditional academic institution. There is, thus, a close connection between the meaning of orthodoxy and theology and our practice of training pastors. Moreover, if this theology is central to the role of a minister, then those who are unable for various reasons to develop the knowledge and skills required to do this sort of theology, whether for want of ability or access to resources to do so, are not sufficient for ministry. If this theology is truly necessary for the right passing on of the Christian faith and a mature understanding of God and, therefore, a mature Christian life, then only those who themselves possess this theology are competent to teach others and model mature godliness. Thus, the real situation of pastoral training and ministry discussed in the Introduction, the theological controversies of the 4th and 5th centuries, and the theological developments in Reformed Orthodoxy and contemporary Evangelicalism are intimately connected with the presuppositions concerning orthodoxy and theology espoused in those same periods.

D. The Bible Is the Source of Theology

The Bible is highly practical in its instructions and moving in its narratives and poetry, yet if the distinction between the *oikonimia* and *theologia* is accurate and if the knowledge of God is really one rational step removed from the contingent features of biblical revelation, then right understanding of God and his ways is not manifest in this immediate perception of Scripture. Instead, the Bible is the foremost, if not the sole, *principia* of theology; it is the source of the principles from which the theological *loci* are developed (as well as the source of the *loci* themselves). The Bible is, thus, intimately connected with and entirely necessary for theology. However, there is a step of reasoning, a 'second exegesis,' introduced between what Scripture says and the knowledge of God. Truly knowing God and a mature faith are not yielded by the understanding of the Scriptures in its various forms of communication but by reflecting upon the principles yielded by the Bible and identifying the universal, necessary truths about God revealed through these principles.

The view of the Bible as a source of theology is based upon the view of theology and orthodoxy identified in Sections A and B above and reinforces the requirements for ministers discussed in C. Consider the weaving together of these themes in the discussion of preaching found in the *Westminster Directory of Public Worship*,

> It is presupposed (according to the Rules for Ordination) that the Minister of Christ is in some good measure gifted for so weighty a service by his skill in the Original Languages, and in such Arts and Sciences as are handmaids unto Divinity, by his knowledge in the whole body of Theology, but most of all in the Holy Scriptures, having his sense and heart excited in them above the common sort of Believers, and by the illumination of God's Spirit, and other gifts of edification, which, (together with reading and studying of the Word) he ought still to seek by Prayer, and a humble heart, resolving to admit and receive any truth not yet attained, when ever God shall make it known unto him. All which he is to make use of and approve in his private preparations before he delivers in public what he has provided….
>
> Ordinarily, the subject of his Sermon is to be some Text of Scripture, holding forth some principle or head of Religion, or suitable to some special occasion emergent; or he may go on in some Chapter, Psalm, or Book of the Scripture, as he shall see fit.[15]

---

[15] Westminster Assembly (1643-1652), *A Directory for the Publique Worship of God throughout the Three Kingdoms of England, Scotland, and Ireland: Together with an Ordinance of Parliament for the Taking Away of the Book of Common-Prayer and for Establishing and Observing of This Present Directory throughout the Kingdom of England and Dominion of Wales: With Propositions Concerning Church-Government and*

Perhaps this view of the Bible as a *source* or *principia* for theology is seen in the primacy of symbolism in the Orthodox and Catholic liturgical traditions, which view ritual and icon as things that help us behold and encounter God, that is, where the Bible, icons, and ritual help us see through the contingency of this world to the God who stands behind it all. Despite the emphasis on the Bible as a source of theology seen in the Westminster *Directions for Preaching*, the Anglican *Book of Homilies*, and the doctrinal preaching practised by the English Puritans and others, the Reformed liturgies were saturated in the written word.

However, within Evangelicalism, the centrality of preaching in the service has, at times, highlighting this presupposition. In the school of preaching that focuses on the text's "big idea," or the singular meaning (conceived in the form of a proposition, a statement of truth), the focus of the service has been on drawing forth doctrinal or moral meaning from the text, rather than the text itself.[16] John Frame identifies the issue as inventing a third thing, "meaning" understood as a singular proposition, which stands between the congregation and the Bible, a "meaning" which requires skilled excavation to uncover and convey.[17]

E. The Academy Has a Central Place within the Church

In the Late Patristic era, with some antecedents in the theological schools of the 2nd and 3rd centuries (which were not exclusively

---

Ordination of Ministers (London: Printed by T.R. and E.M. for the Company of Stationers, 1651), 19–20, http://archive.org/details/directoryfo00west.

16 E.g. Haddon W. Robinson, *Biblical Preaching*, 2nd ed. (Grand Rapids: Baker Academic, 2001); "The Chicago Statement on Biblical Inerrancy" (ICBI), accessed April 16, 2014, http://library.dts.edu/Pages/TL/Special/ICBI_1.pdf. Cf. J. Alexander Rutherford, *The Gift of Reading – Part 2*, in Rutherford, *The Gift of Knowledge*.

17 Frame, *The Doctrine of the Knowledge*, 98.

identified with clergy members), the rise of monasteries and their rigorous patterns of devotion and study began to institutionalise the training of clergy and the development of theology, but for our purposes, the primary evidence for this presupposition and its link the prior ones is found in the period after the Reformation and in contemporary Evangelicalism.[18] The form of orthodoxy and corresponding theology adopted was built in interaction with and employing resources from philosophy and the arts more generally, which would become key components of the curriculum of the universities. By the time of the Reformation and in the period afterwards, the university was awarded a crucial and central place in the task of theologising and training teachers for the church.[19] In the contemporary Evangelical world, pastors are expected to be trained in seminaries, bible colleges, or universities, and theology is seen as an academic discipline that is developed in academic journals, scholarly monographs, and academic conferences. As a place of training for pastors, academia has held a central place for hundreds of years. The academy in its various forms has also been the place of serious theological engagement, from which have come the commentaries and books used by pastors to inform their preaching and discipleship.

The priority of the academy follows from the highly specialised form of theology identified above, with its corresponding view of the Bible and the expectations it places upon teachers. In contemporary Evangelicalism, this trend has converged with a seemingly opposing trend emerging from the discipline of Biblical Studies. Here, the Bible is treated as a historical artifact that requires immense learning to understand. Though the cause is different, the result is the same: the academy is necessary to prepare ministers to unearth the meaning of

[18] On the role of schools, charismatic teachers, and learned bishops, see Williams, *Arius*; Behr, *The Way to Nicaea*; Gaddis, *There Is No Crime*.

[19] In addition to the discussion above, see the account of Voetius's conflict with Descartes and the role of theology among the sciences and in the university identified there in Van Ruler, *The Crisis of Causality*.

the Bible and present it to God's people. Either development alone is enough to place significant emphasis upon the academy in the formation of ministers, the development of theology, and the reflection upon the meaning and significance of Scripture. Evangelicalism seems to be pushing back against the academicisation of biblical studies in the direction of theological interpretation, but this does not remove the need for the academy, for the sort of theology involved requires immense learning (as we saw above).

If all institutions of Christian academic engagement were suddenly removed, the loss would be catastrophic to the contemporary models of training ministers and theology. Not only would ministers be missing the resources they use to do their work, but ministers would no longer have a place to train, and theology would no longer have a place within which it could be developed against the various trends that threaten the fidelity of the church and its theological witness. The presuppositions identified above require the exaltation of the academy to its central place in the Christian world and are simultaneously fostered by that exaltation. Where pastoral training is located in academic institutions, it will inevitably be shaped by the presuppositions of those institutions, by their hidden curriculum; it will begin to look more and more like the structure within which it is developed.

F. Conclusion

These five presuppositions are amply attested in the sources we have traced in Chapters 1-3. Our analysis of the early church, the Reformation, and Evangelicalism supports the claim made in the introduction that the current crises in pastoral ministry, namely, the lack of ministers being trained and quality of those ministers who are trained as ministers, are closely tied to our practices in training them. The views of theology espoused by our theologians and the structures of our institutions are mutually reinforcing and together restrict the body of potential candidates for ministry and create an atmosphere less conducive to spiritual development as intellectual development. Many would warn us, of course, of dividing these from one another. "Say what you will, do what you will," B.B. Warfield told the students at Princton Theological Seminary in 1911, "the ministry is a 'learned profession'; and the man without learning, no matter with what gifts he may be endowed, is unfit for its duties." He will go on to argue that learning, though valuable, is not sufficient:

> aptness to teach alone does not make a minister, nor is it his primary qualification. It is only one of a long list of requirements which Paul lays down as necessary to meet in him who aspires to this high office. And all the rest concern, not his intellectual, but his spiritual fitness. A minister must be learned, on pain of being utterly incompetent for his work. But before and above being learned, a minister must be godly.[20]

If Warfield is correct, then the difficulties of training ministers in the method we are employing are no less difficulties, but perhaps they are necessary ones. If learning of the sort identified by the Reformation, taught in 20th-century Princeton Seminary, and maintained by contemporary Evangelicals, if that learning is necessary for ministry, then the theological college or seminary is certainly an ideal model for preparing ministers for the Gospel. There are probably improvements that could be made to accommodate students of various backgrounds, the use of a mixed curriculum (digital and in person) to train students in remote areas could perhaps alleviate some issues, and the sort of in-church pastoral training done by MTS could certainly be adopted more broadly, but the fundamental issues concerning the intellectual demands of the task and the corresponding resources necessary to engage in the study and uphold an institution facilitating that study are

[20] "The Religious Life of Theological Students," *B. B. Warfield*, February 25, 2011, https://bbwarfield.com/works/sermons-and-addresses/the-religious-life-of-theological-students/.

difficulties that emerge from the way things are.

But what if Warfield is wrong? What if Paul's "able to teach" does not require the extensive learning perpetuated by the traditions we have considered? What if such learning is unhelpful or even detrimental to the pastoral task (which is my own conviction)? Perhaps you are not (yet) willing to go that far, but what if someone can be competent for pastoral ministry without this sort of learning, without higher education? In that case, it may be argued that learning has a genuine contribution to make to the ministry of the local church and that some Gospel ministers should be equipped to engage in this sort of theology, however, there would also be room for pastors of a different sort, who are not so trained. In Part 2, I intend to argue for the former claim, that when weighed against the Bible's teaching, the sort of learned theology that evolves naturally out of Chalcedonian orthodoxy is incompatible with the Bible's own description of pastoral ministry and the knowledge of God. However, like the approach to theology I seek to critique, my approach involves certain philosophical assumptions. I am convinced these assumptions are rooted in Scripture, yet it would be foolish to claim certainty for them. However, I think the biblical testimony *is* sufficient to uphold the second claim that the sort of learned theology we have discussed thus far is not *necessary* for pastoral ministry. I will proceed, therefore, by attempting to show that lesser claim from the clear teaching of the Bible; then, bringing that into engagement with the broader witness of Scripture, I will attempt to show the greater claim as well.

—PART 2— REBUILDING THE FOUNDATIONS

5

WHAT IS ORTHODOXY?

> This people honors me with their lips,
> but their heart is far from me;
> in vain do they worship me,
> teaching as doctrines the commandments of men. –
> Matthew 15:8-9 (ESV)

From the beginning of this book, I have laid out my conclusion that the efforts we haven taken to reform Christian ministry through more rigorous training, statements of orthodoxy like Nicaea and Chalcedon, and the seminary system are counterproductive, that these efforts are mutually reinforcing and are mutually corrosive to Christian ministry. From Chapter 1, I have framed this as an issue of priority: from the 4th century until today, a useful tool in the Christian's toolbox has metastasised itself into the very definition of Christian ministry. I have a broader concern that the way that tool has been conceived is itself problematic, which has exacerbated the problem. However, if we fix the issue of priority, many of the problems resulting will be mended. In this and the following chapters, I will attempt to renew the biblical foundations for Christian ministry and the training of ministers in place of the five presuppositions I identified in Chapter 4. I will attempt, first, to demonstrate that the biblical account of orthodoxy, the knowledge of God, pastoral ministry, the Bible, and the place of the academy shows that philosophical theology, namely, the sort of conceptually elaborate theology developed in the wake of Nicaea, is not *necessary* for any of these things. I will attempt, second, to show that this sort of theology is counterproductive to the biblical account of these things.

In this chapter, we will consider the biblical foundation for understanding orthodoxy. Closely linked to the question of orthodoxy is our view of tradition. As I have argued in other places, I believe the tradition of the church is a gift to us and ought not to be neglected, yet I will maintain that the Bible claims to be *sufficient* for orthodoxy, indeed, I will claim that it forbids establishing a standard of orthodoxy other than Scripture and does so as strongly as Ephesus I forbid any other standard than Nicaea. I will claim that this is not a naïve position but that it does require us to think differently than we have about manner by which we *maintain* orthodoxy. I will offer some short remarks on the positive use of creeds and confessions, but I direct the reader to other books, especially my book *The Trinity and the Bible,* for a further discussion of that matter.[1] What follows is adapted from Chapter 20 of *The Trinity*, though I have focused on the conclusions made there about orthodoxy and not the broader engagement with the tradition and the use of creeds and confessions.

A. Orthodoxy in the Bible

For some, the Christianity of the ecumenical creeds or their brightest interpreters is "orthodoxy"; it is heterodox to diverge from the creeds or even their interpreters. On a lesser level, creeds and confessions serve as the gatekeepers for participation in many Protestant denominations. However, though we ought to maintain the value of creeds and confessions and the importance of the Christian tradition, of the historical work of God's Spirit in his people, the Bible does not

---

[1] See J. Alexander Rutherford, *The Trinity and the Bible: How All Scripture Testifies to One God in Three Persons*, Teleioteti Technical Studies 3 (Campbell River, BC: Teleioteti, 2022), chap. 20.

allow us to make such things measures of who is in and out of God's people—of "orthodoxy" or the right doctrine necessary to confess the true Gospel and receive the saving grace of God. The historical creeds require something in addition to Scripture for orthodoxy, which Scripture will not allow, and for this very reason fail to uphold the purity and unity of Christ's Church.

The Bible (as we will see) does not allow us to grant human doctrines the same status as God's word, namely, to grant human doctrine the role of declaring who is in and who is out of God's kingdom. Scripture also insists on excluding false teachers and maintaining "healthy doctrine" (e.g. 1 Tim 1:3-11). Protestants have traditionally presented Scripture and Scripture alone (though perhaps not Scripture by itself) as the standard of right or wrong faith, of orthodoxy.[2] However, the fragmentation of Protestantism after the Reformation has led many to turn back towards the tradition or ecclesiological structures of the Catholic or Eastern Church. Many are asking, how can *sola scriptura* be an adequate principle of orthodoxy when this is what has resulted?[3]

In answer to this, I will argue that the Bible presents right doctrine and right practice, *orthodoxy* and *orthopraxis*, as intertwined. Belief has implications for actions and vice versa, and the Bible never relegates questions of who is in or out to questions of belief alone. Therefore, if by orthodoxy we mean that by which someone is judged in or out of Christ's Church, we must consider belief and practice together. By its very nature, then, orthodoxy cannot be measured by a statement of

---

[2] Vanhoozer argues that the Reformers held to *sola scripture,* not *solo scriptura:* Scripture alone is the authority, but its authority is that of God expressed through the administration of his work on earth, including the present and past church. Kevin J. Vanhoozer, *Biblical Authority after Babel: Retrieving the Solas in the Spirit of Mere Protestant Christianity* (Grand Rapids: Brazos, 2016).

[3] E.g. Boersma, *Heavenly Participation.*

faith. I will argue the Bible presents itself as a sufficient standard of the right faith and right character by which orthodoxy can be adjudged.

However, several issues emerge when we consider the "belief" pole of orthodoxy. Firstly, God's Word alone is the perfect and sufficient guide for life and godliness (1 Tim 3:16-17; 2 Pet 1:3); secondly, the application of God's Word by his people is authoritative (e.g. Heb 13:17). That is, though God's Word is sufficient so that all we do may be pleasing before God and it alone is ultimately authoritative, the Bible does not balk at assigning a mediating authority to God's people.[4] Yet, thirdly, God's people are barred, I will argue, from setting up any human teaching in the place of God's Word, as a standard of or necessary component of godliness. The tension between these three things may not be immediately evident, yet it emerges when we think about it a bit more closely.

The Bible teaches the Trinity, yet the Bible does not explicitly state that it is wrong to believe that the Son is "god" in a different sense than the Father is "god," such as Arius taught. Our immediate intuition is that it does speak to Arius' error, yet it does not explicitly address the terminology, framework, or specific propositions he developed. So, our extension of the biblical teaching of the Trinity to refute Arius' error seems to be justified, yet if we declare this error to be unchristian and a dangerous false teaching, are we violating the biblical prohibition on adding anything to the Word of God? In favour of the judgement against Arius, the Bible in numerous places instructs pastors and teachers to speak authoritatively to God's people from his Word and to make judgments on situations beyond what the Scriptures directly address (e.g. Deut 17:8-13, 18:19; 1 Tim 4:11, 5:7, 6:2; Heb 13:17). Thus, the application of the Word of God by the people of God shares in the authority of God's very words; to disobey those who speak

[4] On the Bible's sufficiency and authority, see my books *The Gift of Knowledge* and *The Gift of Revelation*. On the mediating authority of God's people, see Rutherford, *The Being of Churches*.

God's word rightly is to disobey God. Therefore, there is a sort of extension of God's word that receives God's approval, that is not the invention of human doctrines, yet there is another sort that is wrong, the elevation of human teaching to the place of God's word. We will first look at what is prohibited, and then consider what is permitted, finding normative right-belief (to be differentiated from the broader sense of orthodoxy as who is in and out) in that latter category of the biblical teaching and the justified extensions of that teaching.

i. Inventing Human Doctrine

> This people honors me with their lips,
> but their heart is far from me;
> in vain do they worship me,
> teaching as doctrines the commandments of men.
> (Matt 15:8-9, ESV)

In Matthew 15, Jesus confronts the teachers of Israel over their treatment of God's Law. They ask him why his disciples do not follow the traditions of the elders; he responds with a criticism of their traditions as a whole and particularly the way their tradition was used to justify their violation of God's law. It is important to observe that Jesus does not condemn only the error these teachers were making, namely, abrogating God's Law with human tradition, but he addresses the more general error of elevating human commands to the status of doctrine.

The particular teaching with which Jesus is concerned is the use of religious gifts to override God's command to honour mother and father (Exod 20:12). Instead of honouring their parents, the pharisees and scribes were taking what should have been given to their parents and giving it to God, telling their parents, "What you would have gained from me is given to God" (Matt 15:5, ESV). These gifts were not commanded in Scripture; they were a human tradition. Yet, in fulfilling this tradition, those giving the gifts violated God's very commands. Against this use of tradition, Jesus cites Isaiah's condemnation of the false worshipper, whose lips "honour me, but his heart is far from me" (Isa 29:13). Their error, in Isaiah's day as in Jesus's time, was to build right living and right thinking not on the word of God but on the teachings of human beings.

"Doctrine" is perhaps not the best translation of διδασκαλία (*didaskalia*) in this context. "Doctrine" is often used in terms of not only right-thinking but a certain type of right-thinking; it is often used for the abstract, universal truths of philosophy and theology. That Jesus rose from the dead is not so much "doctrine" these days as is the significance of the resurrection. If that is what comes to mind when the word is used, then "doctrine" is not the best word to use in this context. In Isaiah, the phrase is "their fear of me" (יִרְאָתָם אֹתִי; *yir'atam 'oti*).

The fear of the Lord in the Old Testament encompasses both right thinking and right doing in relation to God; it is the proper posture of love, submission, and right knowledge of God accompanied by the appropriate actions. Διδασκαλία (*didaskalia*) generically means a "teaching"; in the New Testament, it is used for what we believe about God and his actions in the world and our proper response to them (e.g. Col 2:22; 1 Tim 1:10, 4:1-6). The problem is that the Jewish teachers in Jesus's day and their predecessors in Isaiah's day were filling in "the fear of the Lord" with human teaching, not with the teaching of the Bible. However, God cares about how we think about him and act in response to him; he cares enough to give us sufficient teaching concerning life and godliness (2 Pet 1:3), a sufficient word so that "the person who follows God [ὁ τοῦ θεοῦ ἄνθρωπος; *ho tou theou anthropos*] may be adequate [ἄρτιος; *artios*], equipped for every good work" (1 Tim 3:17, my translation).[5] We deny the sufficiency of God's Word

[5] Alternatively, "the man of God," which would refer to a male specially appointed for ministry, such as an elder, apostle, or prophet; however, I think

and the wisdom of his commands when we feel the need to supplement what God has said with our own inventions. If the Bible is sufficient for the fear of the Lord, how then would God take our efforts to hedge in the biblical teaching with added material? When we claim that you need to do this or that or believe this or that to be a Christian, to follow God rightly and truly—to fear the Lord—and the content we are claiming is not taught by the Bible, this is the sort of innovation condemned by God. If our "orthodoxy" involves such additions, then we would hear from God these same words, "in vain do you worship me!" However, if this is the case, what do we do with the rightful extension of God's word that we find attested to throughout Scripture? What is the line between human invention and rightful biblical application?

ii. The Application of the Word of God

A problem confronts us immediately at this point, for the Bible was written for us through the circumstances of others. It does not address what to do in the contemporary world in direct terms, yet it says enough that we may live rightly before God today as Christians were able to in the 1st century. This is the claim of 2 Timothy 3:16-17, among other places. The language Paul uses here is that of entire sufficiency: Scripture is not given so that the person following God might be incomplete and equipped for some good works, but complete and equipped for every good work: the Bible is entirely sufficient for life and godliness. God "has granted to us," Peter writes, "all things that pertain to life and godliness" (2 Pet 1:3, ESV).

However, if we identify orthodoxy as solely the *words* of Scripture, then no application beyond the narrow situations condemned in the

---

"the person of God" is more appropriate for the context. "Of God" could have many connotations, I chose "follow" because it is similarly broad in its connotations and "person of God" sounds too ambiguous and unnatural to my ear.

Bible would be justified—not even the translation of the Scriptures in English. So when we identify "orthodoxy" or right belief with God's word, we are not identifying it with the bare letter but with the application of the word. This is a pattern we find throughout Scripture: in the Old Testament, for example, the exceedingly broad Ten Commandments are complemented by the casuistry, or case-laws, which give concrete circumstances where this or that law applies. Between these two, the abstract command "you shall not kill unlawfully" (Exod 20:13)[6] and the concrete examples, e.g. if a man falls off your roof through negligence you are guilty of that commandment (Deut 22:8), innumerable circumstances are caught.[7]

The Bible is sufficient for all human life, that we may live godly and obedient lives before our God. The Bible's sufficiency is expressed not only in the words on the page but the innumerable applications it has to our lives. It is through this extension, through right application, that we understand the Old Testament to have been written for Christians throughout the ages (1 Cor 10:11). Right belief is then encompassed by all that Scripture says and all that it rightly applies to. Two issues arise with this identification. First, none of us adequately adhere to the full teaching of the Bible: we all sin, so we transgress God's commands, and we err in our understanding; we are also limited in our life circumstances, so we will not exhaust the innumerable implications the Scriptures have for our beliefs. Thus, orthodoxy in the sense of 'right belief' is identical with the entire witness of Scripture, but 'orthodoxy' as that which we use to judge someone to be in or out of Christ's church cannot be identical with the entire witness of Scripture. If it were, none of us would be "in." We must, therefore, inquire to what extent we must believe what the Bible teaches to be "in." Second, if orthodoxy in the first sense is identified with the entire witness of

6 My translation. "Kill" is too broad and "murder" too narrow for what is intended.

7 See my *The Gift of Reading – Part 1* (2021), *The Gift of Reading – Part 2* (2021) (both in *The Gift of Knowledge*), and *The Gift of Revelation* (2022).

Scripture and in the second sense with some subset thereof, we must guard against making applications of applications, or "second-order" reflection, a standard of "orthodoxy." That is, we can and must distinguish different ways the Bible applies. I want to first address the second issue (not making second order applications a standard of orthodoxy) before revisiting the first, namely, the extent of right belief necessary to be "in" God's kingdom.

Though there are innumerable points between them, we can juxtapose two sorts of applications, those that are directly connected to Scripture and those that are distant from it. For example, the Bible does not directly teach that killing someone with a car while driving drunk is a violation of the commandment "you shall not kill unlawfully," yet we have good reason to apply the text in this case. Though there are some acts of killing that are not unlawful according to this command (e.g. various cases in war), in this case, the driver has both violated civil law (which God has commanded us to obey, e.g. Rom 13:1-7) and committed negligence as in the case of the one who does not fence in their roof (Deut 22:8). From the case laws in Scripture, we adduce that "kill" in this command encompasses death via negligence; through common sense and contemporary law, we conclude that drunk driving is a case of negligence. This is "direct" in the sense that the application made falls within the scope of that command as interpreted within the analogies Scripture provides. It is tangibly different from the sort of application that involves a mediating principle to fill the gap of Scriptural analogies.

Take our doctrine of God, for example. The Bible teaches that God is unchanging, perfect, and different from us. No example of these qualities in Scripture states explicitly that God does not experience substantial change (in his "essence"), subjective change (in his "experience"), change in states of knowledge (from knowing it will be to knowing it has been), or changes in non-substantial predicates (e.g. he did this or that). Now, if we assume that essentialism is correct, that everything, including God, has an essence, then being perfect and unchanging must mean that God's essence does not change (he can never become not-God). If we assume that subjective experience is undesirable, then God's perfection must exclude such experience. If a change in non-substantial predicates (e.g. colour, size, activity) indicates imperfection and creatureliness, then God as the perfect Creator cannot undergo such change. However, Scripture does not identify the change or imperfection involved in each of these cases as something inappropriate to God. In each case, there is some mediating principle involved that moves from the Bible's teaching to the conclusion. If every principle were itself taught in the Bible, then such conclusions would be warranted as part of orthodoxy, yet in all these cases, the principles involved are not derived from the Bible. They involve the application of the Bible to a question or problem produced through reasonable reflection upon the world. Such reflection is good and right and ought to be done in interaction with the Bible, yet the applications derived therefrom are separated by several orders from Scripture.[8]

The Bible does not regard such reflection as "doctrine" in the sense of the right fear of the Lord. This, again, does not make such thinking bad, but it should caution us against making it the standard of who is in or who is out, what is false teaching or not. In addition to the argument from silence (i.e. that Bible does not warrant this), we can also point to the positive teaching that the Bible is sufficient for us to live right before God and worship him properly. That *we* are to live and think rightly encompasses the application of the Bible to our circumstances, yet it does not warrant us to extend beyond that. The Bible cautions us from elevating human doctrine to the status of the fear of the Lord.

Finally, the Bible teaches us that we are all fallen and sinful and that this extends to our thinking as much as our doing. We not only act

---

[8] See Rutherford, "Of Metaphysics"; J. Alexander Rutherford, *The Gift of Seeing: A Biblical Perspective on Ontology*, God's Gifts for the Christian Life Part 1 - The Gift of Knowledge, III (Airdrie, AB: Teleioteti, 2021).

wrongly but we think wrongly because of sin. Thus, we ought to be cautious in assuming that our second-order conclusions and the non-biblical assumptions that we use to arrive at them are sufficiently secure to declare such conclusions the measure of orthodoxy.

iii. Godly Ecumenicism

This leaves us in an uncomfortable place, for the Bible leaves many things unsaid. If we accept that the Bible and the justified application thereof is sufficient for the belief aspect of orthodoxy, we open ourselves to great diversity in the Christian faith. First, we still have not identified to what extent someone must believe the full witness of Scripture to be "in," and second, at the level of second-order thinking, we are going to face much disagreement (and this is not necessarily a bad thing). There will be even greater diversity in the way we think about the Bible's application to the bigger themes of philosophy and living.

a. The Scope of Right Belief

When I first attended Bible College, I had a very narrow view of orthodoxy. I was utterly convinced that the beliefs I grew up with were the correct ones and that to disagree with these beliefs was to be a heretic. By God's grace, I was quickly dissuaded of this sort of thinking, but I maintained a relatively strict view of orthodoxy, primarily restricted to the Reformed Protestant tradition, for many years. However, the more I studied and read, the more I encountered disagreements among my own school of thinking, discovered persuasive, biblical arguments from all over the theological map, and encountered people with evidently genuine faith yet shallow or wrong theology (at least as I perceived it). At the end of four years studying the early church alongside Roman Catholic and Eastern Orthodox clergy and scholars, I was starkly aware of our differences and convicted of the critical doctrines of the Reformation, yet I was simultaneously conscious that these were brothers and sisters in Christ.

As I searched the Scriptures, I could not find a clear indication that the theology of these men and women, theology I disagreed with for solid biblical reasons, disqualified them from the Kingdom of God. There appear to be several critical areas of belief the Bible discusses as essential, but the numerous examples of people who were counted among the people of God show that these areas are far less than the full extent of biblical truth.

The Bible primarily focuses on *bad character* as the evidence of false faith and being outside of the people of God; this does not suggest that right belief does not matter but that it is hard to identify exactly what set of beliefs disqualifies someone from the kingdom or what beliefs qualify them. Therefore, because God identifies correct belief with right practice, bad practice is the surest evidence of being outside the people of God. This is not so because right belief does not matter but because the clearest evidence of wrong belief is not what someone says or writes but how they act,

> Beware of false prophets, who come to you in sheep's clothing but inwardly are ravenous wolves. You will recognize them by their fruits. Are grapes gathered from thornbushes, or figs from thistles? So, every healthy tree bears good fruit, but the diseased tree bears bad fruit. A healthy tree cannot bear bad fruit, nor can a diseased tree bear good fruit. Every tree that does not bear good fruit is cut down and thrown into the fire. Thus you will recognize them by their fruits. (Matt 7:15-20 ESV, cf. Matt 3:7-10, Gal 5:16-26).

Perhaps you have met men and women in the church who could tick all the theological boxes but demonstrated from the way they lived that they were outside the people of God. Sometimes, it is those most passionate about the truth that reveal themselves to be wolves; God certainly cares about correct belief, yet the fundamental virtue he calls from his people is love, love that hopes all things and believes all things, love that is humble and open to correction, love that is not quick to create divisions and disfellowship from others (John 13:34-35; 1 John 2:7-17; 1 Cor 13:1-13). Despite their flaws, Paul himself was eager to call the Corinthians fellow saints (1 Cor 1:1-3), and Christ himself is hesitant to reject the churches to whom he writes in Revelation 1-3, churches full of all sorts of errors (Rev 2:4-7, 4-16, 20-23; 3:1-5, 15-18).

In addition to these churches, we have Jesus's words to the robber on the cross; we are not sure what this man believed about the Messiah, his kingdom, salvation, or numerous other issues, yet Jesus unequivocally affirmed the validity of this man's faith (Luke 23:43). Philip is willing to baptise the Ethiopian man after their conversation (Acts 8:26-40), and numerous others are baptised after professing a simple faith in the proclamation of the Gospel (16:11-15, 25-40). Problems presented themselves because of this, as seen in the confusions of the Corinthian, Roman, and Galatian churches (among others), yet the early church did not forbid baptism for or declare to be outside the church those who seized onto the Gospel with an initial faith. Numerous examples show that the scope of correct belief necessary to be in the family of God is not the whole of truth given in Scripture, nor a significant portion thereof. Not forgetting the essential element of character, which we will address shortly, the positive beliefs that seem consistent with genuine saving faith are discussed in Romans 10 and Galatians 1.

Paul puts it very simply,

> if you confess with your mouth that Jesus is Lord and believe in your heart that God raised him from the dead, you will be saved… for everyone who calls on the name of the lord will be saved. (Rom 10:9, 13)

In Galatians, he speaks strongly against those who would mislead the congregations in Galatia,

> if we or an angel from heaven should preach to you a

> gospel contrary to the one we preached to you, let him be accursed. As we have said before, so now I say again: If anyone is preaching to you a gospel contrary to the one you received, let him be accursed. (Gal 1:8-9)

We can understand the depth of these confessions from John's 1st epistle, where he writes that those opposed to Christ reject Jesus as the Messiah (1 John 2:22) and reject the Father and the Son (22-23). John in his 1st epistle and Paul in the epistle to the Galatians are addressing false teachers, so presumably, these false claims reveal a *false teacher*. Yet, this does not necessarily mean that a congregation member is an unbeliever if they err in their beliefs about the Gospel.

In Romans, Paul indicates the content of saving faith: someone must depend on Christ for salvation, follow him, and believe in his salvific crucifixion and resurrection. The crucifixion is obviously implied in the belief in the resurrection, and verse 13 indicates that the sort of faith that saves is the one that seeks salvation from Christ. The confession that Jesus is Lord is, minimally, an expression of allegiance to the king; in the context of Romans and the rest of the New Testament, it is simultaneously an acknowledgement of the identity of Jesus as God.[9] Paul corrects numerous beliefs in his letter to the Romans, presupposing the entire time that his readers are genuine Christians, even though they need correction on numerous points (similarly in Galatians). Perhaps we may include a belief in God's revelation of himself and the Gospel in Scripture to these essential beliefs because of Paul's insistence that this faith only comes through "the word of Christ" (Rom 10:17, ESV), his use of the Scriptures explicitly to ground his claims about the Gospel (Rom 10:5-13) and the necessity of the Scriptures to supply meaning to the words "Lord," "Christ," "resurrection," and "salvation." Jesus is not any "Lord" but

---

[9] See Rutherford, *The Trinity and the Bible: How All Scripture Testifies to One God in Three Persons*.

the Lord of Scripture, and he is the Messiah anticipated by the Jewish people on the basis of God's testimony in the Old Testament. His "resurrection" is the physical resurrection attested to in the Old and New Testaments, and "salvation" is only that salvation attested to in Scripture.

John helps us see that the confession of Jesus as Lord must simultaneously be a confession of the Father, so a basic Trinitarianism is implicit in saving faith, a belief in the Lordship of Jesus who calls God his Father. Of course, maturing faith will flush that out and cannot exclude the divinity of God's Spirit and his presence with us. In Galatians, Paul argues firmly against those who would teach a Gospel contrary to the one the Galatians had received. In the rest of the Gospel, he unpacks numerous issues with the false teaching the Galatians have received, especially the extension of the Gospel to the nations as the nations and not as members of the Old Covenant and the centrality of faith in Christ to receive a favourable judgment on the final day. Paul focuses specifically on the *teaching* of the Gospel, so I would conclude that saving faith for someone who is not a teacher is characterised by knowledge and response consistent with the necessity of faith and the need to cast themselves upon Christ, as Paul writes in Romans 10, not necessarily the details of the mechanics involved.

However, a teacher is held to a higher standard (Jam 3:1), and they must know the Scriptures well enough to teach them. In Galatians, Paul identifies errors around the Gospel and its meaning as critically important errors, errors that lead to a curse on those who commit them. However, reflecting on his encounter with Peter ("Cephas"), Paul identifies a breach in Peter's understanding of or practice of the Gospel without implying that Peter was not a believer. So, even here, a violation of the Gospel does not immediately disqualify a teacher if they display broader conformity to the biblical testimony and a reproachable spirit (Gal 2:11-14). It would seem, therefore, that discerning what Gospel-oriented mistakes and false beliefs disqualify a person from the faith or ministry is necessarily a contextual one, requiring knowledge of character and the evidence of the person's response to correction; only such a contextualised process could discern the non-disqualifying error of Cephas from the disqualifying errors of those who "preach to you a gospel contrary to the one we preached to you" (Gal 1:8, ESV).

It would appear, therefore, that the basic scope of belief necessary to be counted "in" is a foundation of beliefs consistent with and expressed in saving faith directed towards Jesus our Lord and Messiah. However, we saw that this is difficult to pin down and judging even this foundation requires a judgment of character and an understanding of context. We will shortly consider the role of character and practice in making a judgment of orthodoxy, but before doing so, one more matter concerning second-order thought is necessary.

b. Second-Order Thought Remains Normed not Norming

Though we have differentiated the relatively immediate applications of Scripture to our lives from second-order thinking that involves tentative, speculative intermediary principles, we must nevertheless avoid the error of pretending that second-order thinking is sequestered in its own world and untouched by the Bible's teaching. This is the sort of error that imagines that what we dream up in our philosophies and sciences is unaccountable to the Bible because it is not the study of the Bible, preaching, or theology (those things that ostensibly have Scripture as their primary subject matter). This is an error because the Bible has immediate application across innumerable areas of life, some that we may wish could be separated as second-order. Integrating the Bible's doctrines of immutability and perfection with Aristotelian physics and metaphysics has led some Christians to conclude that God is not actually active in the World: he is distant, unmoved, timeless, and unaffected by anything in the created world. However, this stands at odds with the biblical testimony to a God who is perfect and whose perfect plan unfolds without flaw, yet who engages with his creatures, talks with them, loves them, commits himself to them, and acts on their behalf.[10]

The direct application of Scripture in this regard is that our philosophy is wrong if it postulates that God cannot do such things. If our science arrives at a conclusion that invalidates the biblical teaching concerning miracles, a historical Adam, a global flood, or God's personal involvement in creation, here also, the Bible has something to say.[11] In such cases, principles drawn from outside of the Bible are often used to cast doubt on the Bible's teaching or explain why it cannot affect our conclusion. Brothers and sisters, we cannot let this be our approach to such matters. The Bible does speak to many of these things.

If we are to take the Bible itself as our standard of orthodoxy, we need to flush out a bit further the role of context and character.

B. Orthodoxy and Contextuality

If God wants his people to be united, as is evident throughout Scripture (consider John 17 and Ephesians 2-3, for example), then why is the Bible ambiguous on so many things? For example, why does it not give us an answer to the "worship wars"—telling us what sorts of songs and instruments are acceptable? It does not command us to use certain buildings and not others, to have two leaders in the church or ten (yet it does tell us to have more than one), or to have the Lord's supper every week or monthly. The Bible is specific about many other things that we wish it were not specific about, yet there are a good many practical issues about which the Bible is silent. This, I believe,

---

[10] See my *The Gift of Seeing*, in Rutherford, *The Gift of Knowledge*; Rutherford, "Of Metaphysics."

[11] Cf. Vern S. Poythress, *Redeeming Science: A God-Centered Approach* (Wheaton: Crossway Books, 2006).

serves an important purpose.[12]

The Bible fosters a healthy diversity, a unity that is based not on external conformity but on right faith and right worship. The Christian church is made up of males and females, the Greek world and everyone else, Jews and the nations. God in his word has laid out many things that confront our cultures and challenge us to change our views of what it means to be men and women, how we are to live as spouses, parents, and children—ways that will fit comfortably in some cultures and stand out boldly in others—yet in as many ways as it confronts and affirms our culture, it also gives space for us to express our faith in different ways. The *adiaphora* or "things indifferent" are many, and this makes us uncomfortable.

We would like God to tell us that praising him with an organ alone is ungodly or that drums are of the Devil, yet he does not do so. He does not tell us exactly how he relates to time, how and to what extent he allows himself to be affected by creatures and to what extent he transcends us: there are some things said clearly on these matters, but other things are left silent. There is much room for us to engage in second-order reflection on God and his ways, and there is much room for us to embody the Gospel in different ways in Canada, Australia, Uganda, or Thailand. We have the freedom to translate the Bible in different ways and are not told that only this or that translation principle is perfect. We are not given one model of preaching or teaching, the appropriate length of a sermon, what a minister should wear when they lead a worship service, how often we should meet together in a week or month and how many times missing a corporate gathering is sinful—though we are told that churches should gather (Heb 10:24-25). We are not actually told that God's people must gather on the Lord's Day, on Sunday, though that is certainly appropriate and has been regular Christian practice from the 1st century until today. Yet, if we live in a country where God's people are best able to gather on

---

12 See further, Rutherford, *The Being of Churches.*

Friday instead, we have no biblical teaching that would say that is ungodly and wrong.

The Bible speaks to a great many things, and we tread a dangerous line when we use the Bible's ambiguities in some areas to ignore God's teaching in others. Yet, in pursuit of the right beliefs, we cannot stretch "orthodoxy" to encompass the grey area where God has granted us freedom. 5th-century Christology is an area that I believe attests to this danger, of making our second-order reflections normative. The Bible tells us that God came as a man, Jesus Christ our Lord. It teaches us many things about what it means for Jesus to be God and to be human. Yet the Bible does not fill in much more than this. It does not tell us the logic of the compatibility of humanity or deity or the ontology (the real-world makeup of humanity and divinity) that justifies the claim that one person is God and is human. In the 5th century, this became an area of significant debate.

Christians who agreed on the essential claims that Jesus is truly God and like the Father in every way except that he is the Father and Jesus is the Son, who agreed that Jesus was like us in every way except that he was also God in every way and born of a virgin, Christians who agreed on these two claims disagreed in dozens of ways on how these claims could be reconciled. A particular difficulty emerged because the interpretation of the Trinity in the 4th century didn't quite work with the facts of the incarnation; trying to reconcile the 4th-century solution to the Trinity with the incarnation led to solutions that were inadequate in various ways.

There are layers to this conflict that we cannot explore here, including the character of those involved, yet as measured by the Bible, all those who we call "heretics" in this century, namely, Nestorius and Eutyches, agreed on the same points of the biblical teaching as the "orthodox," Cyril and Leo among others. On this point, there is no biblical reason to say one or the other was not a true follower of Jesus. However, the fallout of different sides branding the others a heretic continues to this day; though the Western churches (namely, Protestants and Roman Catholics) are largely in agreement with each other, the Eastern churches are divided along the same lines as they were in the 5th century, with the Orthodox, Miaphysite, and Nestorian traditions continuing independently today. If we are to take the Bible as our sole standard of orthodoxy, we must be ready to live with an uncomfortable level of diversity. We may analyse, reflect upon, and formulate ideas and philosophies from the biblical testimony, but we cannot make these ideas and philosophies the measure of right and wrong faith, of being a Christian or an unbeliever.

C. Enforcing this Orthodoxy

Thus far, I have suggested that character is fundamental to a biblical account of "orthodoxy," or determining who is in and out. It is there that we will now turn. We can define character as a person's posture towards God and his word, as the habits displayed in behaviour that reveal a pattern of conduct towards God, his word, and his world. The Bible is seriously concerned with right character, perhaps more than it is concerned with right belief (for the reasons given above, that right character is the best demonstration of right beliefs). Jesus uses the image of a tree to describe his followers: someone who follows Christ and loves God will produce good fruit demonstrating a right heart, that is, they will have a true or good character (the heart with its concomitant manifestations) (Matt 17:15-23). This is obviously a key theme in the Psalms and Proverbs (e.g. Psalm 1, 19). In the New Testament epistles, the primary qualifications for pastoral ministry are character qualifications, such as sobriety, purity, truthfulness, humility, faithfulness, etc. (1 Tim 3:1-7; Titus 1:6-9; 1 Pet 5:1-5). When false teachers are discussed—which is often—their character is the key diagnostic of their error and is as dangerous as their doctrine (2 Pet 2:1-22; Jude 3-16). 2 Peter makes the particular connection between bad character and the distortion of Scripture, speaking of Paul's letters,

> There are some things in them that are hard to understand, which the ignorant and unstable twist to their own destruction, as they do the other Scriptures.

> You therefore, beloved, knowing this beforehand, take care that you are not carried away with the error of lawless people and lose your own stability. (2 Pet 3:16-17, ESV)

It is because these people are already unstable and immoral ("lawless") that they twist Scripture to their destruction. Bad character has implications for doctrine, and the reverse is certainly true.

We can imagine two extremes that show the necessity of both right doctrine and good character. Someone may have impeccable character but not believe a word of the Bible; they are not a Christian (1 John 2:18-25). Someone may have impeccable doctrine and yet reprehensible character; they are, once again, not a Christian (Matt 17:15-23). Thus, right belief and right character are both markers of who is in and who is out, of "orthodoxy." In his first letter, the apostle John identifies both character claims and belief claims that demonstrate someone is outside the people of God: if they continue in sin, hate their brother, or love the world and the things in the world, they are not born of God; similarly, if they deny that Jesus is the Messiah or deny the Father and claim the Son is not from God. One or the other is sufficient to disqualify someone, but together they demonstrate someone to be unchristian, even antichristian.

D. Conclusion

Given the history of orthodoxy from 325 AD until the present, the centrality and unavoidability of character in determining whether someone is in or out leaves us in an uncomfortable position. No list of doctrines will be sufficient a measure of orthodoxy, for no list can verify character. Only careful attention to an individual in their circumstances, with attention to belief and practice, evidencing character, will suffice to demonstrate orthodoxy or heterodoxy. Such attention will only be found through long-term observation of a person's corporate and private life, the sort that is found in long-term and intimate, familial relationships such as Scripture prescribes for the local church. To remove someone from such relationships is not only destructive to the forming of character (as I will argue in Part 3) but also detrimental to the effort to discern character. Long-term involvement in a specific church body would seem to be the ideal context within which to discern if someone has the character sufficient for ministry.

This does not mean that the ancient creeds and more modern confessions have no function or use, only that they are not sufficient or even necessary to determine someone's orthodoxy. The Creeds attest to biblical beliefs in a specific period of time, so they point to our fellowship with a community across time that has confessed the same essential truths about God and the Gospel, even if our contexts have changed the philosophical frameworks and language we use to express these beliefs. Confessions and articles of faith can foster common understanding among denominations, congregations, church groups, and parachurch organisations. However, there remain dangers here. If our confessions are too restrictive, we may withhold resources and fellowship from those with whom partnership centred on a shared commitment to the Gospel could produce outcomes conducive to God's purposes in and through the church. We may also put too much trust in our confessions as part of a process of vetting the adequacy of future ministers; the Bible's emphasis on character suggests that whatever role confessions may have in such a process, we must not give them too much weight. Far more important is an accurate assessment of a candidate's character.

6

WHAT IS THE KNOWLEDGE OF GOD?

> [18]For the wrath of God is revealed from heaven upon all the ungodliness and righteousness of humans, who hold the truth unrighteously. [19]For the knowledge of God is evident among them, for God has made it evident among them. [20]For his invisible attributes have been seen with mental comprehension from the creation of the world by created things, both his eternal power and his divinity, in order that they would be without excuse. [21]For although they knew God, they did not glorify him as God or give thanks, but they became foolish in their reasoning, and their foolish hearts became dark. [22]Claiming themselves to be wise, they became foolish [23]and exchanged the glory of the incorruptible God for images in the likeness of corruptible humans, birds, quadrupeds, and reptiles. – Romans 1:18-23[1]

In the first part of this book, we considered the development of orthodox theology and what it identified as the knowledge of God.

[1] My translation. This chapter is based on Chapter 19 of my book, *The Trinity and the Bible.*

The developments in the early church are more complicated than our short discussion permitted us to explore, and much happened in the time between Chalcedon and the Reformation. Nevertheless, it is evident that by the Reformation, knowledge of God is best considered as universal, necessary statements about God as he is in himself, not contingent (that is, unnecessary, changeable) things, such as his actions in history. Among Evangelicals, this position has perhaps been expressed most poignantly by Craig Carter when he identified extensive academic knowledge as the prerequisite for speaking truthfully about God (see the Introduction and Chapter 3). However, if this sort of knowledge is not necessary for orthodoxy, nor is it part of the requirements for pastoral ministry, then we are left with a significant question. If a pastor is to know God pre-eminently, at least in comparison to other Christians, then what is the content of that knowledge if it is not universal, necessary truths such as characterise Patristic, Reformed, and some Evangelical theology?

In this chapter, I want to argue that the knowledge of God in the Bible is primarily the knowledge of a *person*. Within this paradigm, discussions of God's attributes and other traditional topics of theology have an essentially pedagogical function: they help people come to know God as he is revealed in Scripture. In my book *The Gift of Knowledge,* I discuss several dimensions of human knowledge, but the knowledge of persons is one that I think is severely undervalued, especially in its applicability to the question at hand. The knowledge of persons is, very simply, the sort of knowledge we have of other people, even of ourselves. For example, if you think about the knowledge you have of your best friend, you will very quickly realise that it cannot be fully resolved into propositions (i.e. subject + predicate claim: "James Rutherford was writing"). Now, to say that it does not resolve into propositions does not mean that it has no propositional content: this would be a ludicrous claim. If you knew nothing propositional about your mother, brother, or best friend—if you did not know their names (e.g. "my mother is named Carolyn"), anything about their appearance, no facts about them—then any claim you made to know them would be immediately treated as a farce.[2] However, no matter how many propositions you can list, none of this is equivalent to your knowledge of your best friend: your knowledge includes propositions but is more than propositional.

Indeed, one of the most frustrating things about this knowledge is that it is mostly inexpressible yet involved in all interpersonal interactions. Though my mother-in-law probably knows more propositions about my wife, Nicole, than I do, I know Nicole better than her mother. This knowledge is a product of numerous interactions between Nicole and me. I have listened and observed what she does and how she responds; I have watched her grow in numerous ways. My knowledge of Nicole includes who she once was but incorporates an element of growth: I do not act towards her as I did when we were first married nine years ago, yet I remember what she was like then. My knowledge of Nicole allows me to anticipate her response to things I say and anticipate how she will react in certain circumstances. This knowledge allows me to surprise her with gifts and to counsel her amid despair. This ineffable but clearly real knowledge is what I mean by "knowledge of persons." It is knowledge I have gained through observation and through the effects of Nicole's interiority, her "self," seen in what she does. This knowledge incorporates both interiority, what cannot be seen, and exteriority, her physical presence and features. It is knowledge gained through effects, yet it is genuine knowledge of the one who affects things. It is knowledge of the visible and invisible, of a person's "invisible attributes," to borrow Paul's phrase in Romans 1:20.

If God is a person, a subjective self that acts and is acted upon (however much we qualify that latter claim), does not the paradigm of person-knowledge seem to offer a promising avenue to consider our knowledge of God? Indeed, the tensions between knowing and being

[2] Cf. Ronald H. Nash, *The Word of God and the Mind of Man* (Grand Rapids: Zondervan, 1982).

on the edge of the unknown (incomprehensibility) receive vivid content: this is a description of all interpersonal relationships—though magnified to an inestimable degree in the case of God. I genuinely know Nicole, yet I have not stopped and will never stop growing in my knowledge of her. Part of that is because she is constantly changing, but it is more than that. Consider what it would mean to know someone completely. Would it not mean knowing them so thoroughly that we knew everything propositional about them and could anticipate their response to every single circumstance they faced, thus gaining a true and fully orbed portrait of that inner self manifest in their life? Such is knowledge only God has. So, my knowledge of Nicole is simultaneously true and incomplete; it is perfect in as much as it is true and imperfect in as much as it is limited.

Consider God through this paradigm. God has truly revealed himself in word and deed. We know what we are to expect of him: he will fulfil his promises. We know that he desires mercy, not sacrifice, and he will freely forgive us through his Son, Jesus Christ. We know that he loved us so much that he sent his Son while we were yet enemies to die for us and to ransom us from our sins. This knowledge is propositional, yet it is more than that. As Martin Kähler once argued, the Bible paints a portrait of Jesus.[3] Is this not the case for the whole Trinity? We encounter the living God in Scripture and walk away with a picture of a person, a glimpse of his interiority. We can anticipate how God will act; we can depend on him and begin to commune with him according to the portrait painted in Scripture. This is much like a long-distance relationship in a bygone age, where correspondence was delayed by distance and performed through writing. Through the exchange of letters, one could gain genuine knowledge of the other person (though perhaps it was limited compared to interactive and in-person communication). Our knowledge of God is thus genuine and personal. Yet, as with all personal knowledge, it is not exhaustive. I

---

[3] Martin Kähler, *The So-Called Historical Jesus and the Historic, Biblical Christ* (Vancouver: Regent College Pub., 1998).

know God is faithful and that I can trust him; I know that he will work all things together for good.

However, despite what I have known of God, I could not have anticipated him taking the life of my unborn son, Asher, in the 28th week of pregnancy. I truly believe that the Lord gives and takes away (Job 1:21), so this was not out of his control; it is my great comfort that God is truly in control. I could not anticipate how his faithfulness and goodness would look in these circumstances, that he would permit such a thing and that he would not give life miraculously back as he once did for Lazarus. However, that I could not anticipate the course of events surrounding Asher's death nor how God would act towards Nicole, Aliyah, and me in the following months did not invalidate my original knowledge of God; it only expanded it. As I clung fast to the personal God in whom I trust, my understanding of his power and goodness was expanded amid grief as, in innumerable ways, he acted to comfort the three of us and to transform, strengthen, and sustain us.

I do not know God perfectly, and I am growing in my knowledge daily, yet there is a stable core to this knowledge. My understanding of the God I meet in the Bible is ever added to but does not become other than it is. In this way, God is immutable: the same God who acted to send his Son to the Cross for my sake and raise him from the dead is the same God who acts each day in my life. This is the same God, "yesterday, today, and forever" (Heb 11:8). This paradigm makes sense of the tension between knowing and unknowing, between resting in our knowledge of God as we stand on the precipice of the unknown. I know of no other paradigm that succeeds in these regards. In addition, this paradigm allows us to make sense of the knowledge of God Paul talks about in Romans 1:18-32.

A. The Knowledge of God in Romans 1:18-32

Though many Christians, especially of the Reformed persuasion, agree that all unbelievers have knowledge of God, what "knowledge of God" could mean with reference to an unbeliever is a difficult issue. The key text in consideration is Romans 1:18-32. What is clear is that in this text, Paul intends to teach that all people know God in some sense and, for this reason, are liable to judgment. However, it is evident that unbelievers deny such knowledge: few unbelievers are willing to admit they have any beliefs concerning God except that he may exist or does not exist. What, then, are we to make of this knowledge? To suggest that it is unconscious does not fit any account of "knowledge" nor Paul's point.[4] The same can be said of the view that they "suppress" it: to suppress the truth of God implies that they have knowledge of God which is then "suppressed." What is meant by "suppressed" is vague (sometimes taking on Freudian tones of "repression")[5] but may be best interpreted as "consciously restrained." However, interpreted in this way, what is meant is still not clear. How can you consciously restrain what is unconscious, what is not acknowledged at all? This is not consistent with the denial of such belief among unbelievers. Instead, unbelievers regularly deny knowing any "God," and many would deny positive knowledge of the Christian God.[6] In what sense, then, do unbelievers know God? Our paradigm of person-knowledge introduced above goes a long way to resolving this problem. I will proceed by making several observations on the text and then drawing a summary.

---

[4] There are clearly tacit beliefs in a person's worldview, but tacit belief is not what we would usually call "knowledge." Knowledge involves belief but also the consciousness of that belief, whether consciousness is in the present or in memory. Cf. Polanyi, *The Tacit Dimension*.

[5] Frame makes this observation. Frame, *The Doctrine of the Knowledge*, 52.

[6] That is, they have knowledge *about* the God of Christianity but deny that this knowledge accurately represents the nature of reality.

i. Who hold the truth unrighteously (1:18b)

The phrase ἐν ἀδικίᾳ κατεχόντων (*en adikia katechonton*) is often translated "who by their unrighteousness suppress" (ESV), often substantiated with an appeal to the present context and the meaning of κατέχω (*katecho*) in 2 Thessalonians 2:6-7 and Philemon 13.[7] Yet, once again, what does it mean for the unbeliever to "suppress" the truth? Certainly, they do not allow the truth (whatever 'truth' refers to in this context) to shape their lives, but it is not even clear how they possess the truth, so how can they hinder it? Furthermore, there is no clear text in the Bible where this word means "suppress." In Philemon, the word means "hold/possess" as in all other biblical uses, though the context has a specific manner of "holding" in view, namely, keeping Onesimus with him. This is clearly a contextual instance of a sense "keep/hold/possess." The two instances in 2 Thessalonians 2:6-7 are also unclear. Morris suggests the translation "hold back" (appealing to Phlm 13) with "hold firm" (cf. 1 Thess 5:21) as a plausible option.[8] However, if Philemon 13 does not mean "hold back," then "hold firm" is the default option and fits the context as much as "hold back."[9] Such an idea fits well if Paul intends something like the vision of Satan held by chains in Revelation (Rev 20:1-3). This corresponds to the other 13 uses of the verb, which mean "hold/possess/keep." Without evidence for the sense "hold back" in the New Testament—let alone "suppress," which would appear to be an extension of the meaning "hold back"—"hold" or "possess" would be the evident meaning for

---

[7] E.g. Douglas J. Moo, *The Epistle to the Romans*, NICNT (Grand Rapids: Eerdmans, 1996), 103.

[8] Leon Morris, *The First and Second Epistles to the Thessalonians* (Grand Rapids: Eerdmans, 1991), 128.

[9] Now, both senses are nearly identical. However, "hold back" has the added nuance of "restraint" which may be present in an event where someone is "held firm," yet it is not clear that κατέχω is ever used to invoke such connotations.

Romans 1:18, if it fits the context.

Indeed, this makes great sense here, resulting in the translation "who hold the truth unrighteously" (my translation, cf. KJV). This would mean that the unbeliever has the truth but does not have it in a righteous manner. This coheres well with the biblical picture of knowledge, for truth brings moral obligation so that knowledge can be unrighteous (disobedient) or righteous (obedient).[10] The unbeliever has the truth, but their possession of it does not suit what it is. We still must identify what it means for the unbeliever to "hold truth," yet the problem of explaining how the unbeliever consciously withholds or suppresses the truth without acknowledging positive belief in God is removed.

ii. Have been seen with mental comprehension (1:20a)

The phrase νοούμενα καθορᾶται (*noumena kathoratai*) could be translated as "being seen with mental comprehension" or "perceived with the understanding." The phrase (lit. "being understood, are seen") employs a relatively rare word for physical perception in the LXX (cf. Exod 10:5; Num 24:2; Deut 26:15), used only here in the New Testament, καθοράω (*kathorao*). This word is used along with a standard word for understanding or comprehension, νοέω (*noeo*), which is used specifically for mental acts. This suggests an interpretation such as that proposed by BDAG, "perceived with the mind's eye."[11] It does not denote something seen *in the creation* or (directly) arrived at by reason but something perceived mentally. It does not, of course, preclude an experiential component, but this

---

[10] Moo, *The Epistle to the Romans*, 102–3; Frame, *The Doctrine of the Knowledge*, 108–9.

[11] Frederick W. Danker, *A Greek-English Lexicon of the New Testament and Other Early Christian Literature*, 3rd ed. (Chicago: University of Chicago Press, 2000), s.v. ποίημα.

phrase focuses on the mind. If all people possess this knowledge, this suggests it is not experiential, for many people have significant physical and mental handicaps that may prevent deriving knowledge from experience. It is also not clearly rational, for there is no mention of an active process by which potential knowledge is grasped and many people are unable to mentally deduce the existence and nature of God from reason.[12] Because the phrase refers to mental comprehension rather than physical perception, I think τοῖς ποιήμασιν (*tois poiemasin*) does not mean "in the created things" but "by the created things." Both are acceptable interpretations of the Greek dative case.

iii. Although they knew God (1:21a)

Now we are in a place to consider the meaning of "although they knew God" (γνόντες τὸν θεὸν; *gnontes ton theon*). Nowhere in this passage is a content-knowledge statement ("know Person A to be B," "know that Person A did B") unambiguously used. However, personal knowledge statements are used ("know Person A"). The statement in verses 19-20, that God's "invisibles" (ἀόρατα; *aorata*) are clearly perceived (namely, eternal power and divine nature) could imply either direct content-knowledge ("they know that God has eternal power and divinity") or an aspect of personal knowledge ("they know God who has eternal power and divinity"). That is, when a knowing verb receives a personal or analogously personal object (i.e. an object or objectified concept: "the way of righteousness," "human heart," "will of the master," "times"), person-knowledge is in view.

In the biblical sense, "to know person A" does not mean to know something specific but to have a relation of some familiarity with Person A. Such a relationship could be hostile (e.g. Ps 138:6) or

[12] Cf. Jeffery D. Johnson, *The Failure of Natural Theology: A Critical Appraisal of the Philosophical Theology of Thomas Aquinas*, New Studies in Theology (Free Grace Press, 2021), 8–32.

familial, from which the idiom for sexual intercourse emerges ("he knew his wife"). Such a statement does not mean "A knows B about C," though the context may specify a content statement (Deut 9:2, Ezek 28:19); it means something more than but not less than propositional knowledge. An example sometimes used is that of a president: a history buff may have much propositional or content knowledge of George Bush Sr. but having not met him, may not know him in the personal sense.[13] ("May not" is an important limitation, for there is a sense in which rigorous study of a subject may yield a certain personal knowledge.) The gardener at the white house, on the other hand, may have relatively little content-knowledge of George Bush Sr. and yet *know him* better than the history buff. It is this later sense of knowledge that I call person-knowledge and is sometimes found in the biblical use of a verb of knowledge with a concrete object or, occasionally, a complex concept ("the way of righteousness"), but it is used especially with a person.

Turning to Romans, γνόντες τὸν θεὸν (*gnontes ton theon*) would seem to be a case of person-knowledge, given that it has a concrete, personal subject, and no specific content-knowledge (even "invisibles" and "eternal power and divinity," though they could be ideas making up content-knowledge, are ambiguous and an aspect of, not identified with, the knowledge of God). It must be emphasised that personal knowledge is not *content-less* but not necessarily *content-explicit.* That is, the gardener never has to cognise the beliefs "George Bush Sr. is the president of the USA," "George Bush Sr. lives at the white house," "George Bush Sr. is kind," etc. to have personal knowledge of George Bush Sr. and know these things implicitly. When asked, he may answer correctly to questions concerning the character of the president without having previously formulated his opinions. As observed above, person-knowledge is not proposition-less but cannot be resolved into propositions. Moreover, we could distinguish

[13] I cannot trace the source from which I am borrowing this illustration.

propositional knowledge as the explicit knowledge of certain things (e.g. "the gas constant R is 8.314") and propositional knowledge as an implication of person-knowledge. In the former case, what is known is a proposition; in the latter, what is known is a person and that knowledge can be expressed in a proposition, such is the case of the gardener who may never have thought "George Bush Sr. is kind" but can say so and affirm its veracity when asked. This contrast between content-knowledge, which involves belief in a particular proposition, and person-knowledge, which minimally involves implicit content-knowledge, gives us better categories for interpreting what is going on in Romans 1:18-32.

Person-knowledge is such that it can be implicit (I may know, in some limited sense, the bus driver I see daily and talk to occasionally without ever identifying this as knowledge or thinking intentionally about the man) and can be misidentified. This last point is very important. For content-knowledge, misidentification falsifies the knowledge: if George Bush Sr. was president in the 1990s and George W. Bush was president in the 2000s, it would be false to say that "George Bush was president in the 1990s" while referring to George W. Bush. However, we can conceivably have genuine person-knowledge that is misidentified, leading to false content-knowledge. For example, if Baby A and Baby B were swapped at birth. The parent of Baby A would acquire person-knowledge of Baby B but misidentify Baby B as Baby A. They may believe that Baby B was born at a certain time, to certain parents, with certain biological origins and certain genetic proclivities, etc. and be wrong about all these things. Nevertheless, they may have genuine person-knowledge. Furthermore, if they attribute their person-knowledge of Baby B to Baby A, they are wrong while possessing genuine person-knowledge.[14]

---

[14] Tragically, I have drawn this analogy from real events, e.g. https://www.cbc.ca/radio/thecurrent/the-current-for-jan-15-2020-1.5427568/it-tore-me-in-pieces-men-switched-at-birth-regret-never-

Applying this analysis to unbelieving knowledge of God, we can make sense of the significant statements and implications Paul makes in this passage. Unbelievers know God even if they have no propositional beliefs concerning him—or even a negative belief (i.e. "Yahweh does not exist" or "he is not god"). I explore this to a greater extent in my books *The Gift of Knowledge* and *The Trinity and the Bible*, but we can summarise that if we are all born with person-knowledge of God, then we have sufficient conditions to recognise the creation as his handiwork and give him the glory due his name and to interpret our behaviour in light of him and so make positive or negative moral evaluations. This is the content Paul gives to the knowledge of which he speaks in Romans 1. This knowledge is enough to convict us of unbelief and moral failing. This knowledge is expressed in action, yet under the guidance of sin, this knowledge of God is applied to the creation, as in the case of the swapped babies. Though unbelievers know God to be in this or that way (to be eternal, beneficent, powerful, good, etc.) and reflexively interpret the creation and their lives in light of this knowledge (rightly identifying good or bad, assuming the creation to be inherently ordered, etc.), they give glory to created things instead of God, deifying nature as all-powerful, good, eternal, etc. Thus, person-knowledge allows us to explain our knowledge of God and its limitations as well as the unbeliever's knowledge of God and its corruption.[15]

iv. Implications

Several significant implications may be drawn from this. First, because this epistemological sin involves miss-association, the unbeliever will err in knowledge in two ways. 1) They will fail to associate everything they learn and know with God. 2) They will attribute their knowledge of God to created things—whether idols, demons, creatures, humans,

meeting-biological-parents-1.5427574.

[15] See *God's Gifts for the Christian Life – Part 1: The Gift of Knowledge*.

etc.—implying misapplied content-knowledge (e.g. the created order is eternal; fate determines all things). The unbeliever has what they need to make the proper identification, yet in unrighteousness they make this exchange, leaving them liable.

Second, this epistemological exchange will be pervasive, infecting all areas of human life—for in every area, humans are commanded to submit to God and further his glory. We can expect a mixture of error and truth in all human thought, for there is the knowledge of God (truth) misapplied to the creature (falsehood). God will be tamed into a creature, such as when Ludwig Feuerbach proclaimed "god" to be the idealisation of all that humanity is and could be.[16] Nature itself might be made into god, as Carl Sagan exemplified:

> In its encounter with Nature, science invariably elicits a sense of reverence and awe. The very act of understanding is a celebration of joining, merging, even if on a very modest scale, with the magnificence of the Cosmos.[17]

In intellectual effort, attributes of God will be attributed to the creature, such as when Aristotle made matter to be eternal.

Third, the best way to know God is to become acquainted with his actions, that is, to spend time with him and learn more about him. When I first met Nicole, my wife, I wanted to know her more. To do this, I did not give her a list of questions or interrogate her; instead, I spent time with her. I served alongside her at our college and in churches. I spent time with her and her family, and we did activities together. During our relationship, I have learned more about her as I

---

[16] Ludwig Feuerbach, *The Essence of Christianity*, trans. George Eliot (Amherst, New York: Prometheus Books, 2010), https://doi.org/10.1017/CBO9781139136563.

[17] Carl Sagan, *The Demon-Haunted World: Science as a Candle in the Dark*, 1st Ed (New York: Ballantine Books, 1997).

have seen how she lives and interacts with people. Even a century ago, writing letters was a way to get to know someone; through written correspondence, people could grow intimate relationships. Whether in person or writing, developing person-knowledge requires time and involves witnessing (whether directly or through various media) the way someone acts and what they say. This fact was not alien to the ancients; when two parties in the Ancient Near East were to enter a formal relationship, their agreement often contained a written preamble introducing both parties and the history of the relationship.[18] Laying out a pattern of historical behaviour gave a basis of knowledge for both parties to enter into an agreement. To a much greater extent, the document of the covenant God made with his people, Israel, contains such an introduction.[19]

The first part of the Torah or Pentateuch introduces Israel to their God and his history of interactions with ancestors. By showing them God's consistency and character, they were given a basis of knowledge for their commitment; they knew that God could fulfil the promises he was making and deliver on the curses threatened. They would also know that God was worthy of their commitment above all the idols of the surrounding nations. For us, who are under the covenant instituted by Jesus, the entire Old Testament serves as a covenant introduction, showing us the common plight and state of humanity, the character of God, and the history that led to and necessitated the New Covenant. Narrative and epistle, historical accounts of events and personal communication, are entirely adequate, even necessary, means for

---

18 Meredith G. Kline, *Treaty of the Great King: The Covenant Structure of Deuteronomy; Studies and Commentary* (Grand Rapids: Eerdmans, 1963); Dennis J. McCarthy, *Treaty and Covenant: A Study in Form in the Ancient Oriental Documents and in the Old Testament* (Pontifical Biblical Institute, 1963).

19 Meredith G. Kline, *The Structure of Biblical Authority*, Rev. ed (Grand Rapids: Eerdmans, 1975); Miles Van Pelt, *A Biblical-Theological Introduction to the Old Testament: The Gospel Promised*, ed. Miles Van Pelt (Wheaton: Crossway, 2016), Introduction.

communicating person-knowledge, even though they are terribly inefficient at delivering *theology* in the scholastic sense. If the knowledge of God is primarily person-knowledge, as we have argued, then the best way for a minister to acquire this knowledge is to read the Scriptures, spend time in prayer, meditate on the glory of God perceived in his creation (Ps. 19), and spend time with God's people, who, being made in his image and conformed to that image in his Son, are mirrors of his character.

A fourth implication of this conclusion is that academic or scholastic theology may actually be a hindrance to properly knowing God. In a moment, we will consider the positive role that propositional accounts of God and systematic theology may have, yet there is a real danger here. First, scholastic theology is a hindrance when it tells the minister of God's word and the people of God that their time is better spent in theological reasoning and understanding the theological tradition than reading the word of God and spending time in the local church, God's appointed means of self-revelation. Second, scholastic theology is a hindrance because it dismisses God's chosen medium for communication as insufficient or inefficient for the purpose for which God has delivered it; in its place, it would erect a speculative and obtuse genre requiring vast learning to master. Third, scholastic theology is a hindrance because it engages in "destructive analysis," to employ a term used by Michael Polanyi. Reflecting on the complex phenomena of human knowledge, Polanyi writes,

> We can see how an unbridled lucidity can destroy our understanding of complex matters. Scrutinize closely the particulars of a comprehensive entity and their meaning is effaced, our conception of the entity is destroyed. Such cases are well known. Repeat a word several times, attending carefully to the motion of your tongue and lips, and to the sound you make, and soon the word will sound hollow and eventually lose its meaning. By concentrating attention on his fingers, a pianist can temporarily paralyze his movement. We can

> make ourselves lose sight of a pattern or physiognomy by examining its several parts under sufficient magnification. …
>
> But my examples show clearly that, in general, an explicit integration cannot replace its tacit counterpart. The skill of a driver cannot be replaced by a thorough schooling in the theory of the motorcar; the knowledge I have of my own body differs altogether form the knowledge of its physiology; and the rules of rhyming and prosody do not tell me what a poem told me, without any knowledge of its rules[20]

Analysing a complex entity, like a body or an event, argues Polanyi, can reveal a sort of knowledge, even beneficial knowledge. However, doing so does not replace the original perception of the whole. Zooming in on the details destroys the original perception, though not always irredeemably. Analysing the parts of a car or the movements and judgments involved in driving cannot substitute for the ability to drive, something we do intuitively. Similarly, though there is a role for discussions of God's attributes, this sort of analytic knowledge is no substitute for person-knowledge of God, especially if the goal is to know and love God and invite others into that relationship, just as interviewing my wife and assémbling a list of characteristics and facts about her is no substitute for the knowledge I have of her.

B. Propositional Truth about God and the Traditional Attributes

Though I have argued that person-knowledge of God is pre-eminent in Scripture, the Bible evidently communicates propositional or content-knowledge about God. Not only do the prophets and epistles make such claims, but the narrative of God's creation and Redemption of Israel also contains innumerable propositions, e.g. God created all things; Yahweh is the one true God; there is none like Yahweh; God

[20] Polanyi, *The Tacit Dimension*, 19–20.

is knowable; God saved his people from slavery in Egypt; etc. We must maintain that the Bible makes truth claims. Consistent with our argument above, we must notice that such propositions are implications of the narrative God has given us about his actions in history and are insufficient as a substitute for them; these truth claims are necessary implications but, as such, are subordinate to the narratives.[21] The way God has told us about these things communicates more than just bare propositions. Nevertheless, it is appropriate to identify these claims as proper implications of God's communication. Furthermore, the Bible is not only a narrative but also makes direct claims about God, such that he is light, holy, and love (1 John 1:5; 2:20; 1 John 4:7-8). Propositional statements about God have numerous functions within the bible and outside of it. Such propositions become important when we engage in apologetics and want to show the veracity of the narratives from which we derive knowledge of our God. That is, God has shared his history so that we might know him; this history must be true to accomplish its purpose.

This is an important difference between the *parabolic stories* Jesus used in his ministry and *historical narratives*. As a story, a parable is often an "extended metaphor or simile."[22] It is a teaching tool, a story that is meant to illustrate or reinforce a claim; the same claim could be illustrated with numerous parables or without a parable at all because the claim is not uniquely suited to parabolic form. A true event could be used parabolically, yet the truth of the event is incidental to its literary function, namely, to convey emotional import, provoke a response, or illustrate a claim being made. The claim itself is not

---

21 Though there are numerous aspects of the project I would like to critique, N.T. Wright makes numerous similar observations of the narrative context for theological discussion in Paul's letters. See, for example, Wright, *The New Testament.*

22 D. A. Carson, "Matthew," in *The Expositor's Bible Commentary: Matthew–Mark (Revised Edition)*, ed. Tremper Longman III and David E. Garland, vol. 9 (Grand Rapids: Zondervan, 2010), 349.

proven by the parable but rests on some other foundation for its veracity. Perhaps the parable brings the claim to bear on common experience, provoking an "a-ha" response: the parable did not provide proof for the claim but brought it close enough to a person's experience so that they will accept it as common sense. In other cases, the claim rests on the speaker's authority for its veracity. Historical narratives are different because their veracity rests on the truthfulness of the accounts they give.[23]

If someone is accused of committing adultery, the conclusion that they have a compromised character and are immoral is true only if the accusation is correct. Similarly, if one country cites an attack of a foreign nation as the reason to go to war, this reasoning is only valid if the attack actually happened as it was said to have happened. If it were, instead, a false-flag operation, then this would not be a convincing reason. Similarly, when God cites his track record of upholding his promises, this only communicates his faithfulness if that track record were true (e.g. Exod 3:6); if God had a habit of breaking his promises, his track record would show him to be lying. The death and resurrection of Jesus Christ have numerous implications, as the apostles make clear, but these are only valid if these events really happened. If not, "then our preaching is in vain … your faith is futile and you are still in your sins" (1 Cor 15:14, 17). So, person-knowledge of God communicated through historical narrative relies on the validity of the implied truth claims.

Isolating the truth claims made by a narrative allows those claims to be integrated with broader historical discussion, logic and reason, and the analysis of the natural sciences. Making claims about God based on his self-revelation in Scripture also serves a significant communicative purpose, namely, to summarise the broad testimony of God in history: to say "God is love" presupposes a pattern of God's

---

[23] See V. Philips Long, *The Art of Biblical History*, Foundations of Contemporary Interpretation, v. 5 (Grand Rapids: Zondervan, 1994).

self-revelation in history, both receiving its meaning from this pattern and helping us see an aspect of similarity that emerges from the juxtaposition of diverse events. Propositional content-knowledge thus has a role and is a genuine component of God's revelation in Scripture, but it often serves a role other than communicating the knowledge of God. When it does function to do so, it is inextricably tied to God's historical actions. It makes explicit what may be possessed implicitly as person-knowledge.

Often, these truth claims have factored into the discipline of systematic or dogmatic theology, which has been conceived in various manners across church history. It has often been thought that the historical events recounted in the Bible have a necessary or ontological connection to God in history such that they correspond to an ontological ground in God himself; understood in this way, knowledge of God in the economy of creation (in the ways he has acted in history) is subordinate to God as he is in himself, *theologia*. This claim is usually understood to mean that God has definable attributes that are true or false, attributes that describe the way God actually is. The view I have described bears a superficial resemblance to this view since I claim that God's actions in history reveal something about him, thereby claiming an ontological ground for God's actions in himself. This resemblance is only superficial, for character cannot be resolved into definitions and is itself undefinable.

C. Character and the Attributes of God

In the period leading up to the Reformation, there were two significant positions on the relationship between God's economic activity and *theologia*, or God as he is in himself. This corresponds to different accounts of the attributes of God or the meaning of terms like 'love' and 'omnipotent' (all-powerful) when attributed to God.[24] On the one

---

[24] See the discussion of the Medieval antecedents and the Reformed views

hand, various positions accepted that these attributes were properties or real aspects of God, that is, discrete, meaningful components of his being. Because of the doctrine of divine simplicity, namely, the claim that God could not be composed of parts, the assertion of properties in God was maintained in numerous ways. It was held that there was a necessary, ontological connection between God's actions in the economy of creation and in God himself. Thus, the Father-Son relationship enjoyed by the incarnate Christ and God the Father is grounded in a necessary reality of God, namely, that the second person of the Trinity was eternally begotten or received his being and identity from God the Father. An economic effect (for example, the Fatherhood of God and the sonship of Jesus) is grounded in what Thomas Aquinas called a "real relation" within God.

The alternate position held that the connection between God and his economic activities was entirely contingent and, therefore, revealed nothing about God beyond the fact that God acted in that way (in essence, there is nothing stable in God to know). That is to say, God is bound by no necessity and is free to will whatever he wills; something is 'good' if God wills it, but God does not will something because of any intrinsic 'goodness' it possesses. Goodness is defined solely by God's will, nothing else. Therefore, God's attributes are merely names we use to describe God's activities but do not reveal anything about him; 'love' merely describes things God has done, but because it does not have an anchor in who God is, there is no guarantee that this pattern will continue in the future. In the contemporary West, many Muslims are proponents of this radical view of divine freedom or 'voluntarism.' I want to argue for a genuine revelatory and stable connection between God's revelation in history and who he is without falling into the extremes of the rationalising *oeconomia-theologia*

---

of divine attributes in Richard A. Muller, *The Divine Essence and Attributes*, Post-Reformation Reformed Dogmatics: The Rise and Development of Reformed Orthodoxy, ca. 1520 to ca. 1725, Vol. 3 (Grand Rapids: Baker, 2003), 21–364.

distinction nor nominalism and voluntarism.

I want to accept that the connection between what God does in history and who he is is *volitional* and, therefore, contingent. We are not given a picture of a world that had to be created or even created in this way; God chose to create a world with marvellous complexity and, in a sense, superfluousness—rich in colours and aesthetic beauty that are not necessary in any significant sense.[25] We can conceive of a creation that is far sparser and more conservative yet still functional. Moreover, we want to reject the idea that there is an immediate ontological connection between God's actions and his eternal reality. That is, if 'love' is something God possesses, something distinct within himself, then 'love' causes God to do what he does and, more significantly, God is dependent on this property (among others) to be what he is.[26] Theologians across the history of the church have rejected this possibility because it makes God like his creatures, limited and dependent on something other than himself. However, rejecting distinct properties in God and accepting the volitional nature of creation does not mean rejecting God's genuine self-revelation. Over against radical voluntarism and nominalism, I want to maintain that volition is itself causally grounded. The cause of all personal volition is what I am calling "character."[27]

Character is simultaneously a simple and complex concept. It is ontologically simple because it cannot be broken up into parts, but it is thick or complex in the way it governs volition. Character is the

---

25 Cf. M. B. Foster, "The Christian Doctrine of Creation and the Rise of Modern Natural Science," *Mind* 43, no. 172 (1934): 446–68.

26 See Plato's *Euthyphro*.

27 John Frame gets at something similar when he writes, "Our standard of love is not something in God, alongside other things, but God himself. And to find what eternity is, we should not search among abstract 'eternal objects' like numbers and the properties of creatures; rather, we should look to God himself." Frame, *Doctrine of God*, 388.

interior cause of all personal action. If someone does something consciously, character has a role in this act, whether through wilful action or habit. Character is the ontological cause of every action a person does. Though the effects of character can be measured and articulated in propositions, it is not itself propositional or definable. Our knowledge of character is fundamentally tacit: it is real, yet slippery. We know it and respond to it, but our knowledge is demonstrated in familiarity and intuition, not a catalogue of facts. If character is ontologically simple, it may be asked how an abstract proposition can be true for a person.

What does it mean to say "God is love" if all God's actions are contingent or volitional, though this volition is grounded in character? That is, there does not seem to be enough conceptual thickness to make "love" simultaneously true and meaningful. However, we can make some headway here. "Love" in this proposition refers to a concept, and that concept supposits for or refers to a network of related actions. Attributes are not something God fundamentally possess but a way of describing his character manifest in his actions; they are a fact of revelation, not God "in himself." As God acts in history, he has given us language to describe patterns of his behaviour and ours. "Love" is one such pattern. So "God is love" is true because "love" accurately describes God's character manifest in the creation. "Love" is meaningful because it refers, archetypically, to God's actions and, ectypically, to ours.

There is a difficulty here: does this not make 'love' identical to 'character' and, therefore, all attributes tautological ('justice' and 'love' referring to the exact same thing)? I do not think it does. It seems hard to deny that all of God's actions are loving in some sense: Hell, for example, is God acting for the love of justice, his own holiness, and the righteous. However, some things seem more loving or, perhaps, more apt to be called 'love.'[28] As all humans are related to Adam, but we restrict 'family' to a small group of humans with a shared heritage and family resemblance, so particular actions share family resemblances that justify our grouping them more closely together than other things that remain related, but to a lesser extent.[29] So, though our concept of love could be stretched to encompass all of God's actions, it naturally fits a smaller subset or fits them more aptly.[30] If we suppose that language is a gift to us and that God ordained some patterns as appropriately revelatory (as suggested by the writing of Scripture), then we can say that though all of God's actions manifest his character in its entirety, we relate certain actions together with certain of our actions and call this "love," or rather, God has taught us to call this love. Defined in this way, there is no one-to-one correspondence between God's character and the attributes we use to describe God, so there may be variability in both what terms we use for God and how we use them (what they include and exclude).[31]

Speaking about God in this way was God's idea and helps us

---

28 I take this to be the meaning of John Frame's comment on the attributes: "Does God's simplicity, then, mean that his eternity is the same as his love, or that his knowledge and justice are identical? The attributes do differ in perspective and emphasis, but they ultimately coalesce." Frame, 388.

29 "Family resemblances" is an analogy Ludwig Wittgenstein uses to describe the relationship between various items referred to with universal terms. George Berkeley speaks of "proportions" and "resemblances" among those things for which we use universal language. See George Berkeley, *Alciphron* 7.12, 14; *The Principles of Human Knowledge*, §§89, 101; Ludwig Wittgenstein, *Preliminary Studies for the "Philosophical Investigations," Generally Known as the Blue and Brown Books* (Oxford: Blackwell, 1958), 17, 19, 35; Ludwig Wittgenstein, *Philosophical Investigations*, trans. G. E. M. Anscombe (New York: Macmillan, 1958), http://archive.org/details/philosophical investigations_201911.

30 See Rutherford, "Of Metaphysics and Theology," and my forthcoming paper, "Towards a Conceptualist Christology" (JETS, 2025)

31 Cf. Vern S. Poythress, *Symphonic Theology: The Validity of Multiple Perspectives in Theology* (Grand Rapids: Academie Books, 1987).

understand him by drawing together his revelatory activity in like sets. We can discuss them, teach them to each other, and refute errors concerning these sets. So, knowing the attributes is not better than person-knowledge of God; instead, these are two ways of looking at the same thing, one explicit and one implicit. The attributes are, in a sense, subjective and language variable, but that does not remove their usefulness. Because they ultimately receive their meaning from events and persons for which they supposit or to which they refer, the attributes depend on personal knowledge of God as revealed in his historical activity.

D. Conclusion

In the first part of this book, we saw that significant theological trends extending into the present focused on universal and necessary truth as the highest and most mature knowledge of God. However, this view runs into several issues when it comes to Scripture. It cannot explain how God claims that everyone knows him, though they possess that knowledge unrighteously, nor does it make sense of the pervasive claims of Scripture that God's people, young and old, know him (e.g. Jer 31:34) and the focus on God's acts in history as the primary revelations of this knowledge. In this chapter, we have argued that the Bible presents the knowledge of God as, foremost, person-knowledge, knowledge like that we have of persons. This conclusion does not mean that the propositions and truth claims about God we find in systematic theology and throughout Scripture have no use, which is obviously not the case. However, it does show that we cannot prioritise explicit knowledge (truth claims) over tacit or implicit knowledge (person-knowledge); the connection between person-knowledge and historical events and the narrative form of texts argues against the prioritisation of universal and necessary claims in theology. We argued that a focus on the latter sort of claims (if we grant that such claims are meaningful) can produce numerous problems. However, we argued for an alternate foundation for truth claims about God that fits well with God's narrative revelation and the priority of personal knowledge.

On this model, the relationship between God's actions in history and God as he is in himself is both contingent, rooted in his will and possible to be other than it is, and necessary, for God's will is rooted in his unchanging character. Because God's character is undefinable (it cannot be propositionally expressed) and is revealed in action, truth claims about God will always be based on contingent circumstances and will not be ontologically necessary. However, this knowledge is a firm and certain revelation of God.[32]

[32] I am, perhaps, stressing the differences between my account and the scholastic one without giving equal weight to their many similarities. I do so because it is in the differences that the problems I am identifying emerge.

7

WHAT IS PASTORAL MINISTRY?

> I myself will tend my sheep and have them lie down, declares the Sovereign LORD. I will search for the lost and bring back the strays. I will bind up the injured and strengthen the weak, but the sleek and the strong I will destroy. I will shepherd the flock with justice. – Ezekiel 34:15-16 (NIV)

In this part of the book, we seek to revisit the foundations upon which our understanding of pastoral ministry and training is built. I argued in Part 1 that prominent elements in Church history, especially Reformed Protestantism and its Evangelical heirs, stressed the identification of pastors or ministers of the Gospel as *teachers*. In the previous chapters, we first revisited the concept of orthodoxy. We argued that, biblically speaking, orthodoxy is to be judged primarily on the basis of character as the clearest manifestation of right belief and right practice, though certain beliefs do characterise orthodoxy. We then argued that the knowledge of God in Scripture is pre-eminently person-knowledge. In this chapter, we will consider the biblical account of pastoral ministry. I will argue that pastoral ministry, which is synonymous with eldership and oversight in the New Testament, is likewise primarily character-oriented in its qualifications and relational in its goals.[1] There is a significant element of *teaching* involved in this role, but I will argue that there is no evidence for this teaching to be doctrinal in the way we discussed in Chapter 4. Instead, we will argue that teaching primarily refers to the proper proclamation of the Gospel and application of the Scriptures to the lives of those in a minister's congregation. We will argue first for the identification of pastors, elders, and overseers in the New Testament before analysing the nature of Christian ministry. As in my book, *The Being of Churches*, I conclude that the diaconate pertains to service in the church and not primary leadership, soul care, or teaching, so I will not discuss further the nature of deacons.[2] What follows is adapted from that book.

A. Identifying Pastoral Ministers in the New Testament

In Church history, there have been several positions concerning the lead role(s) in the church. The most common positions distinguish either between ruling and teaching elders, a position found in many presbyterian or congregational churches and echoed in some episcopalian churches in the role of warden (called elders by some elders), or between elders (presbyters or 'priests') and bishops.[3] In the first case, two offices are maintained in the church, elders (πρεσβύτης, *presbutes*) and deacons (διάκονος, *diakonos*), but the former office is divided into two categories, ruling and teaching elders. In this model,

[1] Cf. Rutherford, *The Being of Churches,* chs. I, III, IV, V.

[2] Rutherford, *The Being of Churches*, 118–20.

[3] 'Priest' is an English term derived, like 'presbyter,' from πρεσβύτης (*presbutes*, "elder"), which is transliterated from the Greek word we translate "elder." However, the use of this term for πρεσβύτης fails to distinguish the two different roles that are designated "priest" when it is translated as such, the Old Testament cultic officers and the rulers of the congregations, elders. Thus, presbyter or elder is to be preferred to refer to the ruling role and "priest" to the cultic role; this echoes contemporary English usage.

all elders rule or lead, but only some teach. The ruling elders are often unpaid lay elders (a term used in Baptist churches), and the teaching elders are pastors or paid staff.

Episcopalian denominations, such as Catholic, Eastern, Anglican, and many Pentecostal groups, attribute the role of overseer or bishop (επισκόπος, *episkopos*) to clergy who stand over several congregations. The term may also be used, as it was in the 2nd century and later, for the "monarchical bishop," or the elder who led the team of elders (the "presbytery," πρεσβυτέριον, *presbuterion*)—the first among equals (*primus inter pares*).[4] In both cases, the bishop is both bishop and elder, though the elders are only elders. As the church grew out of persecution in the 3rd and 4th centuries, a hierarchy developed among the bishops, with provincial bishops (archbishops) over local bishops.

We will argue that neither of these distinctions is correct. In the New Testament, overseers or bishops are identical to elders, and all elders are expected to teach.[5]

i. Elders and Bishops Are the Same

The reasons for holding that elders and bishops are the same in the Bible are two: nowhere are they distinguished clearly from one another, and they are frequently identified with one another. When Paul speaks to the elders of Ephesus, he instructs them to watch themselves and

---

[4] For a contemporary example of this usage, see David T. Harvey, *The Plurality Principle: How to Build and Maintain a Thriving Church Leadership Team* (Wheaton: Crossway, 2021).

[5] For a more treatment of these positions and their grounding in the Old Testament or natural law, see *The Being of Churches*. Though there are differences between Strauch's work and the account given here, *Biblical Eldership* remains a great resource for thinking through the biblical account of elder-overseers. Alexander Strauch, *Biblical Eldership: An Urgent Call to Restore Biblical Church Leadership*, Rev. and expanded (Littleton, CO: Lewis and Roth Publishers, 1995).

their flock carefully; they have been made *overseers* of the flock (Acts 20:28). Here, the plural elders are also a plurality of overseers; there is not a single overseer among them. In Philippians 1:1, Paul speaks of "overseers and deacons"; again, there is a plurality of overseers, and they are in the same place we would expect "elders." 1 Timothy 3 similarly describes overseer as a role alongside deacon. In Titus 1, Paul begins describing the qualities of an elder, which are similar to the description he gives in 1 Timothy 3 (where he speaks of "overseers"), then he describes the reason an elder must be qualified in this way, "for an overseer, as God's steward, must be above reproach" (Titus 1:5-7). Finally, in 1 Peter 5, speaking to elders, Peter instructs them to "shepherd the flock of God that is among you, exercising oversight (επίσκοπεω)"; here, he uses the verbal form of the noun translated overseer (επισκόπος) to describe the role of an elder. Thus, we nowhere find the roles distinguished; their qualifications are described similarly (1 Tim 3:1-7; 2 Tim 2:1-2; Titus 1:5-9; 1 Pet 5:1-4); the terms are used interchangeably (e.g. Titus 1:5-7); and they both perform roles of pastoring, teaching, and oversight or rule. So, I take the view that "elder" and "overseer" are two ways of describing the primary leadership role in a local congregation.[6]

The evidence from the early church does not overturn this conclusion. The writings of the so-called apostolic fathers attest to different understandings of the relationship between the roles of bishop and elders. Writing in the 4th century, Jerome suggests that later (relative to Paul's letters, apparently), "one presbyter was chosen to preside over the rest"; "this was done to remedy schism and to prevent each individual from rending the church of Christ by drawing it to himself." Jerome suggests this arose in Alexandria under Mark the

---

[6] This view is not modern; it is found in the Apostolic Fathers, and in the 4th century, Jerome makes this claim, citing Philippians 1:1, Acts 20:28, Titus 1:5-7, and 1 Peter 5:1-2, "For when the apostle clearly teaches that presbyters [i.e. elders] are the same as bishops…" Letter CXLVI, "To Evangelus," §1 (NPNF 2.6, pg. 288).

Evangelist (i.e., the writer of the Gospel).[7]

For similar reasons, I see no reason to distinguish between ruling and teaching elders. All elders are expected to exercise oversight and to lead (1 Tim 3:1-7; Titus 1:5-9; Acts 20:28), and all of them are expected to teach (1 Tim 3:2; 2 Tim 2:1-2; Titus 1:9). In 1 Timothy 5:17, Paul indicates that elders who do their job well are worthy of a twofold honour, usually interpreted as honour and remuneration; this is especially true for those who labour in preaching and teaching. Given that all elders are to be able to teach and that this is part of their rule and oversight, this should not be interpreted as indicating a subset of elders, ruling elders and ruling elders who teach. Instead, it suggests a division of labour; though all elders are to teach, it makes sense for some elders to specialise in this task. Because specialising in teaching and preaching is particularly time-consuming, the honour of remuneration seems particularly appropriate for these elders.

B. The Nature of Pastoral Ministry

Having identified elders with overseers, we can draw on the passages that use either term to understand the nature of eldership or pastoral ministry. We will do so in two ways, first considering the qualifications of elders and then their duties. Together, the qualifications and duties of eldership given in Scripture demonstrate that teaching is not the most important task performed and what teaching is performed is not theological in the sense we discussed in Chapter 4.

i. The Qualifications of an Elder

The primary qualifications for an elder are character, supplemented with several other important considerations. Elders are to be exemplary in character, above reproach (1 Tim 3:2; 1 Pet 5:3). Though

---

7 Letter CXLVI, "To Evangelus," §1 (NPNF 2.6, pg. 288), cf. CXXV, "To Rusticus" §15 (NPNF 2.6, pg. 248).

no Christian is perfectly sinless (1 John 1:8), elders are to live repentant, humble lives characterised by obedience to Christ. Their behaviour is not the sort that will lead the flock astray or open the congregation to charges of immorality from either members or outsiders. They are to be well regarded by everyone, both inside and outside the church (1 Tim 3:7). Though their obedience to Christ might earn them the world's condemnation, elders are to ensure that in every other way, they are faithful, humble citizens, walking in righteousness and obedient to God-ordained authorities (Rom 13:1-7). They must be sober, gentle, humble, devoted husbands, good fathers, and slow to anger (1 Tim 3:1-7; Titus 1:5-9).[8] They must not consider themselves better than those they lead but lead as servants (Matt 20:25-28; 1 Pet 5:1-4); they must not be greedy or quarrelsome (1 Tim 3:1-3; Titus 1:7; 1 Pet 5:2), and they must be eager to welcome strangers into their house, to care and provide for those who come along their path (1 Tim 3:2; Titus 1:8).

The expectations of an elder are so steep because Christ entrusts them with such great authority. When they fall, as we have seen far too often in recent history, Christ's redeeming work suffers greatly. Christians are terribly hurt and fall back into sin, Christ's name is shamed among unbelievers, and doors are closed for Gospel ministry. Paul instructs Timothy to appoint elders slowly, with great care, lest such consequences follow (1 Tim 5:22). Elders will not be perfect but must demonstrate humility and repentance, owning their sin proactively, not waiting for it to be revealed by others. They must continually grow in holiness; self-righteousness and spiritual pride are cancers that will destroy the leader, their families, and the churches they lead.

Because elders are imperfect and have great authority, the principle

[8] On my answer to the issue of whether women may be pastors or elders, see *The Being of Churches*, especially pp. 120-122, 153-172.

of plurality is important.[9] An elder is never a lone wolf; they always share their authority with equals to whom they are accountable for their ministry and personal lives. They must keep a close watch on themselves and each other as much as they do the flock (Acts 20:28). This is also why we must not make a *primus inter pares*, a first among the elders. Christ is the head of the Church and each church; therefore, no man can stand above his co-elders (Eph 1:22; 4:15; 5:23). Each is equally accountable to one another and to Christ, their head. As mentioned above, this does not mean there is no division of labour among a team of elders, but a division of labour cannot become a stratification of authority. We have no mandate for this from Christ, our Lord.

In addition to character qualifications, elders must be "able to teach" (1 Tim 3:2; 2 Tim 2:2; Titus 1:9). Other than the ability to manage one's household, and so the church (1 Tim 3:4-5), this is the only skill required of elders in the Bible. They do not even have to excel at teaching; they only need *to be able* to do so. Paul is scant on the details in this context but does not set the bar terribly high. This confronts the contemporary attitude towards church leadership, where only the best and brightest are sought, and they must demonstrate an extensive skill set before being ordained. The mere ability to teach aligns with Jesus's own choice of leaders for his church, namely, fishermen and tax collectors—hardly an inspiring and excellent group. An elder must also not be a recent convert (1 Tim 3:6), though they do not necessarily need to be old (1 Tim 4:12; 2 Tim 2:22).

---

[9] Though he defends the principle of first among equals, David Harvey's account of the plurality of eldership is still helpful. Harvey, *The Plurality Principle*. Cf. J. Alexander Rutherford, "Review of The Plurality Principle – Teleioteti Book Reviews," Teleioteti, 2021, https://www.teleioteti.ca/2021/07/06/review-of-the-plurality-principle/.

ii. The Duties of an Elder

The duties of an elder may be gathered under three principal heads: to rule the church, to offer pastoral care, and to teach. On the other hand, ruling, caring, and teaching could all be seen as different aspects of the one duty, namely, to shepherd the flock over which they have been placed. Let us consider each of these in turn.

a. Ruling

In the Old Testament, elders primarily had the role of community leaders. In Numbers 11, God chose 70 of the elders of the people, who are also "officials," to share the burden of leadership with Moses (11:16, 17). In Josh 7:6, the elders join Joshua in mourning. In the New Testament, the local church elders have an analogous role.

Paul attributes to the elders the role of ruling or leading (προΐστημι) the churches in 1 Timothy 3:4. We are not given many details into what their elders' rule looks like, yet it appears to include maintaining the orderly conduct of worship, leading the congregational gatherings, and ensuring the congregation is taken care of, growing in spiritual maturity (Eph 4:11-14; 1 Cor 14). They are also to lead the saints in the works of service, by example and equipping them to do this work (Eph 4:11-14; 1 Tim 1:1-4; 1 Pet 5:3). Perhaps we could also include within ruling ordaining other elders (1 Tim 4:14; 1 Tim 5:22).

The New Testament gives little detail about what this ought to look like. However, we can surmise from the analogy Paul gives in 1 Timothy 3 that just as every family will need to be led uniquely so that its purpose is achieved before God, so every local church will also need to be led in such a way that its purpose is achieved. The elders are responsible for providing this rule. Using the analogy of a shepherd, the elders ensure that the entire flock is orderly and moving towards its goal, the kingdom's growth and maturity in Christ.

b. Offering Pastoral Care

If the elders' rule sets the path, ensuring appropriate organisation and structural support for the growth and life of a congregation, pastoral care is the elders' specific leadership of the individual sheep entrusted to them. Elders are to pay close attention to their sheep so that they might shepherd them (Acts 20:28). "Shepherd" is a rich metaphor used throughout Scripture, especially for God's care and provision for his sheep (Ezek 34:1-31). As under-shepherds of Christ the chief shepherd (1 Pet 5:3-4), elders are Christ's instruments to exercise his shepherding care for the Church.

As a shepherd provides for the health of his sheep and protects them, the elders are to be concerned for their congregation's spiritual and physical health. They use the tools of pastoral care and teaching to address the spiritual health of individual sheep while also using their authority in the church and their teaching to protect against false teachers who would destroy the sheep. The aim of their ministry "is love that issues from a pure heart and a good conscience and a sincere faith" (1 Tim 1:5). The image of a shepherd is not that of a cold, distant CEO who manages a complex bureaucracy but of intimate, relational care. Shepherds are "keeping watch over [our] souls, as those who will have to give an account" (Heb 13:17).

We see an example of this shepherding care in the lives of both Jesus and Paul, who engage in meaningful relationships with those under their care, relate with them personally, and can speak firmly and lovingly into the different situations of their lives. Paul's letters are dripping with love for the congregations under his care, expressed in earnest prayer and joyful thanksgiving over them. To be a shepherd is to be personally invested in the sheep. Think of Paul's interaction with the different churches; take the Thessalonians as an example,

> But now that Timothy has come to us from you, and has brought us the good news of your faith and love

> and reported that you always remember us kindly and long to see us, as we long to see you—for this reason, brothers, in all our distress and affliction we have been comforted about you through your faith. For now we live, if you are standing fast in the Lord. For what thanksgiving can we return to God for you, for all the joy that we feel for your sake before our God, as we pray most earnestly night and day that we may see you face to face and supply what is lacking in your faith? (1 Thess 3:6-10, ESV)

Paul rejoices in the churches' successes (e.g. Phil 4:10) and is burdened by their failures and suffering (e.g. 2 Cor 2:1-4; 11:28-29; 12:11-21).

As shepherds, elders are to minister God's word to the sheep with all patience and gentleness (1 Tim 6:11; 2 Tim 4:23-26), exemplifying Godly character in these relationships (1 Tim 4:12;.2 Pet 5:2-3). With authority given them by God (2 Cor 10:8, 13:10; Titus 2:15; Heb 13:17), elders provide specific instruction to those in need (e.g. 1 Cor 5:1-5; Philemon; Heb 2:1-4), adjudicate disputes (1 Cor 6:1-8; Phil 4:2-3; 1 Tim 5:19), rebuke and admonish those who are in sin (1 Tim 5:20; Titus 1:13-14), and encourage and restore those who are grieving and downtrodden (Gal 6:1-5; 1 Thess 2:11-12; 3:1-3; 2 Tim 3:16-4:5). As with anyone in the congregation, Elders may on occasion receive prophecies, authoritative words from God applying his Scriptures to the specific circumstances of a person's life, but their regular communication is invested with God's authority corresponding to their role, so they must be vigilant in their communication to speak appropriately and wisely in all circumstances. Though it is closely related to ruling and teaching, the aspects of shepherding I have discussed in this section are often performed in private, with families, in small groups, or one-on-one. Teaching, on the other hand, is the elders' public, word-based ministry.

c. Teaching and Preaching

Several times in the New Testament, it is said that elder-overseers must be "able to teach" (διδακτικός, *didaktikos;* 1 Tim 3:2; 2 Tim 2:24). Though our translations do not show it, the meaning of this word needs to be discussed (used only twice in the NT). As summarised by Paul Himes, the only other 1st-century uses of this word (in Philo) are incompatible with the context of Paul's letters to Timothy.[10] The Early Church understood the word to mean either teachableness or to be characterised by or able to teach.[11] One or two instances in Origen may mean being *skilled,* but this is not the only possible interpretation, and "skilled" does not fit the context of Paul's letters.[12] Benjamin Merkle rightly points out that the word cannot mean "teachable" in 2 Timothy 2:24, where it describes the ability of the "Lord's servant" to instruct opponents (see 2 Tim 2:25).[13] "Characterised by teaching" is itself ambiguous; Himes argues that it indicates experience in teaching.[14] It could also mean capable of teaching (not to be confused with "skilled at" or "proficient at teaching"). However, in the context of both letters, this ability ought to be demonstrated, so it is assumed that they will have a demonstrated capacity to teach.

Teaching is thus an essential component of their ministry. So far as I can determine, διδάσκω (*didasko*), the word we translate as "teach," is slightly more restricted than our English word "teach," at least when used in the context of Jesus and the Apostles's ministries. It nearly always refers to a public act of speaking, occasionally accompanied by

---

10 In Philo, the word characterises a subject as taught, i.e. "x is *taught* to Abraham."

11 Paul A Himes, "Rethinking the Translation of Διδακτικός in 1 Timothy 3.2 and 2 Timothy 2.24," *The Bible Translator* 68, no. 2 (August 2017): 194–96, https://doi.org/10.1177/2051677017715676.

12 Himes, 198–200.

13 Benjamin L Merkle, "Are the Qualifications for Elders or Overseers Negotiable?," *Bibliotheca Sacra* 171, no. 682 (April 2014): 181 n. 25.

14 Himes, "Rethinking the Translation of Διδακτικός in 1 Timothy 3.2 and 2 Timothy 2.24," 201–4.

the word κηρύσσω (*kerusso*), to speak publicly (e.g. Acts 28:31). The contrast between learning quietly and teaching in 1 Timothy 2:11-12 also suggests that "teaching" here is a public act, specifically in the gathered church (cf. 1 Cor 14:27-28, 33-35). Some instances are ambiguous, and Acts 20:20 distinguishes between Paul's teachings in public places and from house to house, but this may reflect a contrast between public places like the Areopagus or Hall of Tyrannus (Acts 17:16-34, 19:9) and the more intimate setting of house churches or small gatherings (Acts 12:12-17; 20:7-12).[15] Alternatively, this could reflect the more intimate ministry of the word we described as pastoral care, as John Calvin and Richard Baxter would have it.[16] However, in most instances, "teaching" is a public act of word ministry, explaining and applying the scriptures. They will not only explain the Scriptures but also publicly reprove, rebuke, and encourage in church gatherings (2 Tim 4:1-5). This is what I intend when I say "teaching" is a duty of the elders.

Teaching in this sense is a specific *mode* of the public proclamation of Scripture, a type of public speaking, κηρύσσω.[17] Teaching in the New Testament is almost invariably associated with the unique authority expressed by God's appointed messengers. Both teaching and prophecy are presented in the New Testament as acts of public proclamation of God's word (though prophecy is broader than teaching), but they differ in the basis for this proclamation. Teaching is rooted in the authority Christ has granted to an elder-overseer, so elder-overseers are told to speak with all authority (1 Tim 4:11, 6:1-3;

---

[15] Mikeal C. Parsons, *Acts*, Paideia Commentaries on The New Testament (Grand Rapids: Baker Academic, 2008), 291.

[16] Richard Baxter, *The Reformed Pastor: Updated and Abridged*, ed. Tim Cooper (Wheaton: Crossway, 2021); John Calvin, *Commentary upon the Acts of the Apostles*, trans. Henry Beveridge (Bellingham: Logos Bible Software, 2010), 2:244.

[17] *The Being of Churches*, IV.E

Titus 2:15), and we are told to listen to them (Heb 13:17). Prophecy, on the other hand, is rooted in a particular act of the Holy Spirit: the authority of the proclamation is not rooted in an abiding authority possessed by the speaker but in the origin of their utterance, as a word from the Spirit.[18] Therefore, prophecy is to be judged to discern whether or not it is from the Holy Spirit (1 Cor 14:29; 1 John 4:1). Because teaching and prophecy are two different modes of the public proclamation of God's Word, there is a danger in reducing the entire proclamation ministry of the church into "preaching," thereby eliding the significant difference in the basis of prophecy and teaching.

One component of this teaching function will be to equip the saints for the work of ministry (Eph 4:11-12). As elders address the congregation from Scripture, they will point them to the work God has entrusted to them. They must not only convict of sin and lead the saints to desire to do God's work but also equip them to do that work.

In none of the New Testament discussions or examples of 'teaching' does it resemble the account of teaching given by theologians. Teaching, in the Bible, often has as its content contingent communication, namely, the application of Scripture in the form of rebukes or commands and providing accounts of God's work in history. This teaching is addressed to the specific circumstances of the hearers. Indeed, we have no examples of teaching as identifying universal, necessary truths and developing doctrine based on reasoning from necessary truths about God. We can give many examples of teaching that is contingent communication. In Matthew 28:20, Jesus tells the disciples to *teach* future disciples to obey his commands. Jesus is frequently said to teach, and the few examples we have of his teaching in the Sermon on the Mount and the Olivet Discourse, alongside the parables and other discourses, are contextualised teaching about God, his will, future events, and the appropriate response to Jesus's claims. The disciples are said to have been teaching

[18] See *The Being of Churches*, III.A-B, IV.E; *The Gift of Revelation*, III.6.C.

that "the Christ is Jesus" (Acts 5:42), and some men from Judea were said to teach, "Unless you are circumcised according to the custom of Moses, you cannot be saved" (Acts 15:1). In Romans 2, teaching revolves around moral instruction relating to the Law; in 1 Corinthians 11:14, nature is said to teach that long hair is disgraceful for a man. 'Teach' is often used in 1 Timothy for what Paul is writing to Timothy: for example, Paul writes, "Teach and urge these things" (1 Tim 6:2) with reference to the previous section of the letter. 1 Timothy 6:3 aligns teaching with godliness, and 2 Timothy 4:3 indicates that false teaching suits the passions of those who desire it. Hebrews speaks of teaching concerning the "basic principles of the oracles of God" (5:12, ESV); he will soon move on to "maturity," leaving behind the "elementary doctrine of Christ" (6:1, ESV). The author has thus far considered Christ's deity and priestly role, seeking to persuade the Hebrews to persevere in the faith they have received and not depart from it. The rest of the book continues to unpack the completed work of Christ in contrast with the Old Covenant, all with a continued call to perseverance.

In all these instances, 'teaching' is oriented to the Scriptures and historical events with application to the audience's circumstances. Teaching and doctrine do not appear to be something behind Scripture or derived from it but the proper proclamation and application of Scriptures to the various circumstances the people of God face. To be able to teach, therefore, requires someone to have the ability to understand the Scriptures in order to apply them to the lives of their congregation, to provide teaching, reproof, correction, and training in righteousness (2 Tim 3:16). Although 'teaching' refers primarily to the public ministry of the elder, what content of teaching is nearly identical to the elder's private ministry; teaching is a generalisation of the same act found in private ministry, apply the word of God to specific circumstances.

Understood in this way, and accepting the Bible's own claim to be clear, "able to teach" does not require extensive learning on the part of an elder. Indeed, someone could be illiterate and still be a pastor. That is, some people have memorised the entire Bible; if someone did this and could meditate on the meaning of the Scriptures and communicate them clearly to the lives and circumstances of their congregation, they would appear to "be able to teach." Moreover, given modern technology, someone could study and reflect upon the Scriptures using audio Bibles. Literacy is desirable because God has given us the Bible in a literary form. However, nothing in Paul's requirement "able to teach" requires this, and God has granted us significant tools for illiterate men and women to study his Word.

We must, therefore, disagree with B. B. Warfield's contention that "the ministry is a 'learned profession.'" He told his students at Princeton that "the man without learning, no matter with what other gifts he may be endowed, is unfit for its duties." He argues this from the claim that a minister be "apt to teach" (as his translation has it); "teaching implies knowledge," Warfield insists.[19] We must agree with him that being "able to teach" requires a minister to have knowledge, to know God and his Word. Certainly, a minister must have more knowledge than the average person in his church. Nevertheless, nothing about these claims requires a minister to be "learned." Indeed, a person may have knowledge without a college education and know God and his Word without being able to read. This is confirmed by the examples we are given in the Bible.

Paul, Luke, and Apollos had some measure of learning, but it certainly was not anything like what the graduate of a contemporary seminary will have received at the end of their degree. It is doubtful these men would have qualified if the expectations of Craig Carter and George Guthrie were applied to them (see the Introduction above). Moreover, those Jesus chose for ministry were not educated like these men; Jesus himself was a builder, and his disciples were fishermen, tax collectors, or had similar professions. Timothy and Titus were young

---

[19] "The Religious Life of Theological Students."

when chosen for ministry, and we are not given details about their formal qualifications. Nevertheless, all these men were considered fit for Christian ministry and "able to teach."

C. Conclusions

From both the qualifications for pastoral ministry and the role of a pastor detailed in the New Testament, we find that character and relational skills are more significant for a successful minister than breadth or depth of learning. The primary qualifications of a minister are character-related, which makes sense given the immense responsibility a minister carries. Ministers are not only an example for the congregation to follow, but they are also given great authority from Jesus, authority which, if wielded carelessly or maliciously, may cause significant harm to the flock. The Bible frequently warns of wolves who enter the congregation to take advantage of the sheep and gain something at the cost of the sheep (Ezek 34:1-10; John 10:11-13; Matt 7:15-20; Acts 20:29-30). Wolves are so dangerous because they are given trust and even authority but do not have the character appropriate for what they have been given; they abuse their authority and are domineering (1 Pet 5:3), and they break trust, leading the flock to harm (Ezek 34:1-10). Christ is clear: such people will face severe judgement (Matt 18:6). For their own sake and the congregation, the worst thing they can be given is the platform and privileges of ministry. Therefore, a minister must have character appropriate to the position given them by Christ. This lines up well with our conclusions concerning orthodoxy in the previous chapters. A minister is not entirely different from a believer; they are not held to an altogether different standard. No, a minister is further down the same line as every other believer; they are to be more mature than other believers in the same characteristics God wants all his people to express.

In addition to character, a minister requires relational skills. They need to be able to maintain trust, hold a conversation, and listen well so they can offer effective pastoral care. Many aspects of character identified in the New Testament are closely tied to relational competency; someone who is patient, humble, slow to anger, and abounding in love will be more relationally competent than someone without such character. A minister must also be able to teach, but this requires a thorough knowledge of the Bible and God. Based on the pattern given in Scripture, such knowledge does not require extensive education. So, according to the qualifications for and nature of pastoral ministry identified in the Bible, a candidate for ministry needs character, knowledge of the Bible, and relational competency. Therefore, ministry training ought to seek to identify and develop these areas. A problem immediately emerges because character and relational competency are things higher education does not discern or develop well. Perhaps it is good at developing a knowledge of the Bible and God as he is revealed there, but our discussion of the knowledge of God points in a different direction. However, we have yet to consider what the Bible is, which we will now do; we will then consider the academy's place in the Christian life.

WHAT IS THE BIBLE?

> How can a young person stay on the path of purity?
> By living according to your word.
> I seek you with all my heart;
> do not let me stray from your commands.
> I have hidden your word in my heart
> that I might not sin against you.
> Praise be to you, LORD;
> teach me your decrees.
> With my lips I recount
> all the laws that come from your mouth.
> I rejoice in following your statutes
> as one rejoices in great riches.
> I meditate on your precepts
> and consider your ways.
> I delight in your decrees;
> I will not neglect your word. – Psalm 119:9-16 (NIV)

I do not know if it has clicked for you yet, but the first moment I realised something was wrong with our current education model happened in a class on biblical interpretation. I was eagerly learning the biblical languages and reading the Bible as much as I could, but I became more and more unsettled as I read books on biblical interpretation and practised the techniques I was being taught in class. I had access to a decent library and much time on my hands, so I could wade through commentaries and journal articles and wrestle with translating and interpreting passages. It became clear to me just how much work it would take to interpret the Bible if doing so actually involved excavating its ancient context and reconstructing its meaning before applying it to my culture—not to mention navigating the complexities of language and imagery I was taught to expect.[1] If this were true, I would need far more than a 4-year bachelor's degree to be capable of understanding and teaching the Bible.

A. The Bible's Clarity and Modern Scholarship

Approaching the end of my first degree, I felt the weight of what George Guthrie describes as the task of biblical studies,

> The process of learning, at its most basic, involves a deep study of the text of Scripture itself, and for the scholar, a deep study of Scripture calls for the hard work of biblical studies research.... To begin with, we must be able to engage the biblical languages with competence, as well as modern languages that facilitate our dialogue with others in the field. The study of the history of the ancient Near East and the Roman Empire, as well as a wide variety of cultural backgrounds, is mandatory. Since we are dealing with texts in a world of other texts, the ability to access and analyze ancient Near Eastern literature for Old Testament scholars or Second Temple Jewish literature and Greco-Roman literature for those studying the New Testament is mandatory, and increasingly, various aspects of modern linguistic theory play a part in our

[1] The textbook we used described interpretation as a journey between two cities, where the text was understood in its original city before being taken over the interpretive bridge into the receiver's city. J. Scott Duvall and J. Daniel Hays, *Grasping God's Word: A Hands-on Approach to Reading, Interpreting, and Applying the Bible*, 3rd ed (Grand Rapids: Zondervan, 2012).

> work as well. To understand and enter into dialogue with others in the field, we also must have some familiarity with the dizzying array of "criticisms," both higher and lower, in the history of investigating the biblical literature. Further, since texts are always interpreted, we need an awareness of what is going on in the areas of philosophical hermeneutics and biblical theology. On top of all this, we must keep up with developments in our own areas of focus—and bibliography has become daunting in almost all specializations.[2]

In his book *Exegetical Fallacies,* D.A. Carson was calling for a cool detachment from the Scriptures, a necessary "distanciation" so that we would not accidentally import our present assumptions into the ancient text.[3] Biblical studies continues to make claims like this, as seen in quote from George Athas given above.[4] This emphasis on the historical difficulties of exegesis has received significant pushback from proponents of Theological Exegesis, yet these authors would have us master an even more difficult history of discussion and toolbox of skills. We saw the approach to the Bible in the Reformation and among Evangelicals, but listen to the summary given by Craig Carter once more,

> No one can be an expert in everything, but statements about God constitute theology, and theology is a single activity. Anyone who wishes to do theology of any sort—from Old Testament exegesis to systematic theology—needs basic competence in all of the following areas: the history of philosophy and theology, biblical languages, biblical hermeneutics,

---

[2] Guthrie, "The Study of Holy Scripture and the Work of Christian Higher Education," 83.

[3] D. A. Carson, *Exegetical Fallacies* (Grand Rapids: Baker Books, 1996).

[4] Athas, *Bridging the Testaments*. Cf. Wright, *The New Testament*; Wright, *What Saint Paul Really Said*; Wright, *Justification.*

> biblical introduction, the history of biblical interpretation, biblical theology, and dogmatic theology. To ask that it be made easier is to ask the impossible; it cannot be less complicated than it is. Asking that theologians without competencies in all these areas be allowed to do theology is like demanding that a person with only high school biology be allowed to perform surgery. It can be done, but the result will not be pretty.[5]

Repeatedly, from a dozen different perspectives, this was the message I heard: biblical interpretation is very difficult. It requires immense knowledge and learning and a massive library of resources to consult. But this could not be the case! Over and over again, I heard the voice of God speaking in Scripture and through those who studied these Scriptures. Moreover, God calls pastors from the impoverished areas of the US, the Australian Outback, Africa, Latin America, and Asia to be his servants, to teach his word—pastors who do not often have access to this education or these resources. The answer cannot be to build seminaries and provide libraries in these places, for the obstacles to the use of these tools, if provided, are immense (not to mention that this would only work for pastors located in major cities).[6] Moreover, God has called pastors to himself for thousands of years without access to such learning. God expected people across the

---

[5] Carter, *Contemplating God*, 296. Cf. Treier, *Introducing Theological Interpretation of Scripture*; Ephraim Radner, *Time and the Word: Figural Reading of the Christian Scriptures* (Grand Rapids: Eerdmans, 2016); Carter, *Interpreting Scripture with the Great Tradition*; Collett, *Figural Reading and the Old Testament*; Boersma, *Heavenly Participation.*

[6] In his otherwise fantastic book, Conrad Mbewe identifies the local church as the place where ministers are "screened" and "prepared" for Bible college but argues that Bible colleges are needed to strengthen the Church in Africa. Conrad Mbewe, *God's Design for the Church: A Guide for African Pastors and Ministry Leaders* (Wheaton: Crossway, 2020), 167–73.

gentile world from the 1st century until now to understand his word communicated by Paul and to preach to others without access to the Dead Sea Scrolls and an intuitive grasp of 1st-century Judaism ('Second temple Judaism').

God expected Peter and the Apostles to accurately teach the Law and the Prophets without access to ancient Ugaritic and Canaanite texts and the details of their pantheon and divine council, worship of the storm god, Leviathan mythology, and numerous other aspects of ANE religion and cosmology—knowledge from hundreds even a thousand years before the 1st century. Throughout history, God has called pastors and deemed them able to teach without this knowledge, these libraries, and these skills.

He wants to give his people across the world pastors, but these authors' expectations present the Bible as inaccessible to most Christians from the 1st century until now. They communicate this despite the Bible's clear words to the contrary. Listen to our God describe his Word through the prophets, "Your word is a lamp for my feet, a light on my path" (Psalm 119:105, NIV). The Word of God is something that illuminates, not something in need of illumination. This is the resounding message of the Bible; it is God's gift to illuminate our way in a dark and murky world, not something that contributes to that murkiness:

> In a word: if Scripture is obscure or equivocal, why need it have been brought down to us by act of God? Surely we have enough obscurity and uncertainty within ourselves, without our obscurity and uncertainty and darkness being augmented from heaven! And how then shall the apostle's word stand: "All Scripture is given by inspiration of God, and is profitable for doctrine, for reproof, for correction?" (2 Tim. 3:16).[7]

[7] Martin Luther, *The Bondage of the Will*, ed. J. I Packer and O. R Johnston

The Psalmist writing 119 judges the Bible sufficient to train a young person to maintain a pure life (vv. 9-16), and God expects parents to teach it to their children (Deut 6:4-9). God instructs Joshua to meditate on the Law day and night, carefully obeying its instructions (presumably, he would understand it) (Josh 1:7-9). God's word always accomplishes his purpose (Isaiah 55:10-11), and his purpose for the Bible is to fully equip his people for every work pleasing to him (2 Tim 3:16-17). It must be fit for this purpose, so it must be understandable.[8] As Benedict Pictet (d. AD 1724) put it,

> … either God could not reveal himself more plainly to men, or he would not. No one will assert the former, and the latter is most absurd; for who could believe that God our heavenly Father has been unwilling to reveal his will to his children, when it is necessary to do so, in order that men might more easily obey it?[9]

God wanted his Scriptures to be understood by his people across the ages; he certainly could have accomplished this purpose. The Old Testament was written as much for us as it was for the ancient people of Israel, "These things happened to them as examples and were written down as warnings for us, on whom the culmination of the ages has come" (1 Cor 10:11, NIV; cf. Rom 4:23-24, 15:4; 1 Cor 9:9-10;

(Grand Rapids: Fleming H. Revell, 2003), 128.

[8] Cf. J. Alexander Rutherford, *The Gift of Reading - Part 1: Reading the Bible in Submission to God*, God's Gifts for the Christian Life - Part 1: The Gift of Knowledge 2a (Vancouver: Teleioteti, 2019); J. Alexander Rutherford, *The Gift of Reading - Part 2: A Biblical Perspective on Hermeneutics*, God's Gifts for the Christian Life - Part 1 2b (Vancouver: Teleioteti, 2019); Rutherford, *The Gift of Revelation: A Biblical Perspective on the Bible.*

[9] Mark D. Thompson, "The Clarity of Scripture," The Gospel Coalition, accessed August 18, 2020, https://www.thegospelcoalition.org/essay/the-clarity-of-scripture/. Cf. Mark D. Thompson, *A Clear and Present Word: The Clarity of Scripture*, New Studies in Biblical Theology 21 (Downers Grove: IVP Academic, 2006).

Psalm 102:18).

Having wrestled with the Scriptures my entire adult life, I cannot accept the conclusions of the scholars: God has given his word to be clear and accessible to his people, an enduring covenant testimony to who he is and what he expects from his people. To be understood is the whole reason God has given his Scriptures, and God does not fail when he sets himself to a task. The scathing rebuke attributed to Søren Kierkegaard captures the state of the matter well,

> The matter is quite simple. The Bible is very easy to understand. But we Christians are a bunch of scheming swindlers. We pretend to be unable to understand it because we know very well that the minute we understand we are obliged to act accordingly. Take any words in the New Testament and forget everything except pledging yourself to act accordingly. My God, you will say, if I do that my whole life will be ruined. How would I ever get on in the world?
>
> Herein lies the real place of Christian scholarship. Christian scholarship is the Church's prodigious invention to defend itself against the Bible, to ensure that we can continue to be good Christians without the Bible coming too close. Oh, priceless scholarship, what would we do without you? Dreadful it is to fall into the hands of the living God. Yes, it is even dreadful to be alone with the New Testament.
>
> I open the New Testament and read: "If you want to be perfect, then sell all your goods and give to the poor and come follow me." Good God, if we were to actually do this, all the capitalists, the officeholders, and the entrepreneurs, the whole society in fact, would be almost beggars! We would be sunk if it were not for Christian scholarship! Praise be to everyone who works to consolidate the reputation of Christian scholarship, which helps to restrain the New Testament, this confounded book which would one, two, three, run us all down if it got loose (that is, if Christian scholarship

did not restrain it).[10]

We could, of course, critique elements of Kierkegaard's own approach to the Scripture, but the claims that God has granted the Scriptures to be read by his people (and, I would add, in the context of his people gathered) and that the demands of the scholars prevent this from being realised is apt. Numerous objections are raised at this point: it may be theologically accurate to claim the Bible is "clear," but how do we reconcile that with the actual reading of Scripture? Answering that question is beyond the scope of this book, but I have attempted to answer it in several books I have written.[11] In the rest of this chapter, I want to argue that the Bible is a covenant document, shedding much light on its purpose for God's people.

B. The Bible is a Covenant Document[12]

> Not that we are sufficient in ourselves to claim anything as coming from us, but our sufficiency is from God, who has made us sufficient to be ministers of a new covenant, not of the letter but of the Spirit. For the letter kills, but the Spirit gives life.... For to this day, when they read the old covenant, that same veil remains

---

[10] Søren Kierkegaard, *Provocations: Spiritual Writings of Kierkegaard*, ed. Charles E. Moore (Maryknoll, NY: Orbis, 2002), 201–2, http://archive.org/details/provocationsspir0000kier.

[11] The entire series, *God's Gifts for the Christian Life*, is oriented to this question, but see in particular, Rutherford, *The Gift of Reading - Part 1*; Rutherford, *The Gift of Reading - Part 2*; Rutherford, *The Gift of Revelation: A Biblical Perspective on the Bible.* See also the introductions and sections on method and interpretation in J. Alexander Rutherford, *The Book of Habakkuk: An Exegetical-Theological Commentary on the Hebrew Text*, A Teleioteti Old Testament Commentary 1 (Vancouver, BC: Teleioteti, 2019); Rutherford, *The Trinity and the Bible: How All Scripture Testifies to One God in Three Persons*; Rutherford, *The Being of Churches.*

[12] This section is adapted from my book Rutherford, *The Gift of Revelation: A Biblical Perspective on the Bible.*

> unlifted, because only through Christ is it taken away. Yes, to this day whenever Moses is read a veil lies over their hearts. But when one turns to the Lord, the veil is removed. – 2 Corinthians 3:5-6, 14-16

It is probably not evident to many of us today what type of book the Bible is. It is clearly not a novel or work of fiction, yet it does not fit into our conventional non-fiction categories. Many of the world's religious texts take on conventions of myth or philosophy, yet these do not adequately describe the Bible. We can identify parts of Scripture: there are epistles, narratives, legislation, and poetry. But what is the Bible? I suspect we usually assume it to be a disparate collection of historical documents God has chosen to preserve. In one sense, this is correct, yet the Bible is more than this; it is truly a book, a single piece of literature. In many ways, it has no parallels in the ancient world, but in another significant sense, it does. In his book *The Structure of Biblical Authority,* Meredith Kline argued that the Bible, beginning with the Torah and encompassing the whole, closely resembles an Ancient Near Eastern covenant, specifically a suzerainty treaty (by which a powerful entity enters into an agreement with a less powerful entity).[13] This insight is profound because when we look at the Bible, this is how it repeatedly describes itself. Even the titles we take for granted to describe the portions of the Bible assume this. "Old Testament" and "New Testament" literally mean "Old Covenant" and "New Covenant" (*testatmentum* being the Latin word used to translate the Hebrew and Greek words בְּרִית, *berit*, and διαθήκη, *diatheke*, a "covenant").

Nowhere do the New or Old Testaments speak of themselves as completed books. However, the Old Testament speaks of the Torah as a completed unit, and the New Testament speaks of the Old Testament as a completed unit. In both cases, the term "covenant" or

[13] Kline, *The Structure of Biblical Authority.*

covenant language is used to describe them. After God delivers his people from Egypt and establishes a covenant with them, Moses writes the accompanying legislation (the reiteration and expansion of the Ten Commandments, along with other legislation such as ritual feasts, Exodus 20-23; cf. 24:4) in "the book of the covenant" (24:7). In the following chapters, the Lord gives more words which Moses then writes (cf. Deut 31:9). With more and more layers of detail, God's words are recorded in "the book of the covenant." This phrase does not appear again until 2 Kings 23:2; however, the synonymous phrase "the book of Law" or simply the Law (Deut 4:8, 44; 17:8; 31:9; 8:34, 23:6, 28:58, 31:9, 31:26; Josh 1:7-8, 8:31-32, 23:6; 2 Kings 14:6, 22:8, 11) becomes the default reference to this legislation and then the whole Pentateuch, or *Torah*, "the Law." So, the "Law" is not a generic piece of socio-political legislation but the constitution of a covenant between God and Israel. Genesis through Deuteronomy becomes known as the Law throughout the Old and New Testaments (e.g. Matt 12:5, 22:36-40; Luke 2:22-23, 24:44; 1 Cor 14:34).[14] In the New Testament, "Law" can summarise the Torah or the entire Old Testament (e.g. Matt 5:18; Luke 16:17; John 10:34, 12:34, 15:25; 1 Cor 14:21). Often, "Law" is used to refer to the Old Testament covenant structure, to the relationship mediated between God and man by the Torah legislation (e.g. John 1:17; Gal 3:17; Rom 7; Heb 7:11-12, 19, 28; 8:4; 9:19-22). So, minimally, the Torah is considered a covenant document. What do we make of the rest of the "Old Testament?"

The next instance where we are told of writing in the Bible tells us that Joshua added words of covenant renewal to "the Book of the Law of God" (Joshua 24:26). So even in the time after the official "Law" was completed, there continued to be expansions to the covenant constitution. Meredith Kline argues that the content we find throughout the Old Testament (and, in fact, the New) parallels the

---

[14] If 1 Cor 14:34 is a reference to creation (cf. 1 Cor 11:14), then this refers to Genesis; otherwise, it may be a case of "the Law" referring to the entire Old Testament.

content of the Torah. The Torah is full of legislation, but it also has narratives and exhortatory material. That is, it not only gives "thus saith the Lord" type commands but also records who God is, what he has done, and how his people have acted within the Covenant. This material illustrates the Law, clarifies its curses and blessings, and recounts the history of both parties of the covenant. Other material is explanatory; the case laws illustrate the legislation so that it may be applied; there are also many speeches from Moses in which he instructs and clarifies what obedience to the Torah ought to look like. Looking beyond the Torah, we find the same sort of material throughout the Old Testament; with an eye to this foundational document, the rest of the Old Testament expands upon and exhorts based on the Law and records a history of the parties who had covenanted together, recording God's faithfulness to his promises and Israel's unfaithfulness. The rest of the Old Testament thus expands upon the initial document, providing God's specific words to his people, interpreting their actions and calling them to obedience in light of the Covenant he had established. From the perspective of the New Testament, this entire package, namely, the foundational Law and God's continuing interpretive words, is the "Old Covenant." Paul says as much in 2 Corinthians 3:14 (cf. 3:6), and the rest of the New Testament authors can repeatedly refer to the whole thing as "the Law" (in addition to the texts cited above, perhaps Matthew 12:5).[15] In some cases, these may be instances of synecdoche, where a part refers to the whole, such that "Law" or "Law and prophets" may refer to a traditionally threefold document. However, this is not always the case; the whole document is sometimes considered the covenant legislation, "Law."

The language of "Law" points us to its nature as a covenant

[15] In this verse, the reference to "temple" may indicate that the author intends 1 Chronicles 9:32 instead of Numbers 28:9-10.

document from God.[16] Further precision is given when the foundation "Law" is distinguished from the later words of the Prophets. We find Jesus echoing the early Jewish practice of dividing the Old Testament three ways when he calls it the "Law, Prophets, and the Psalms" (Luke 24:44).[17]

The point is this: the Torah is identified as the Law or the book of the covenant. The rest of the Old Testament is then included under that banner; it all pertains to the Old Covenant. By analogy, with the coming of the New Covenant, we ought to expect a New Covenant document (cf. 2 Cor 3:6). Peter and Paul both call other parts of the New Testament "Scripture" (2 Pet 3:15-16, 1 Tim 5:18), and the New Testament epistles quote or allude to the Gospels in a manner very similar to the Old Testaments use of the Torah (cf. 1 Corinthians 7).[18] The New Testament gives every sign of being the New Covenant document corresponding to the Old Covenant. Because of the foundational nature of the Old Covenant to the New, the Old Testament takes on a role somewhat like Genesis in the Torah. The Old Testament provides the covenant preamble, explaining the reasons for, conditions of, and presuppositions for the institution of the New Covenant. It is indispensable to it, even if, in some ways, it is superseded by what follows.

---

[16] The broader use of Law to refer to a covenant may explain Paul's "law of Christ" (1 Cor 9:21; Gal 6:2) and James's "law of liberty" and "royal law," seemingly alluding to the New Covenant Scriptures or the Gospels (James 1:19-27, 2:8, 12). The Gospels then are a new "Law," not in the legalistic sense but in the sense of the foundations for the covenant.

[17] For the Jewish practice, cf. David G. Dunbar, "The Biblical Canon," in *Hermeneutics, Authority, and Canon*, ed. D. A. Carson and John D. Woodbridge (Grand Rapids: Academie Books, 1986); Roger T. Beckwith, *The Old Testament Canon of the New Testament Church and Its Background in Early Judaism* (Grand Rapids: Eerdmans, 1986).

[18] Paul's repeated claim that he speaks something, not the Lord, does not undermine his claims to authority but distinguishes what he offers as an inspired teaching and what he is basing on Jesus' teaching.

Meredith Kline has observed that the New Testament has the same pattern of legislation, narrative, and exhortatory material displayed in the Torah and Old Testament and a similar threefold structure (Torah/Gospels; Prophets/Acts; Writings/Epistles).

One last piece of evidence ties the whole package together nicely. In Revelation, we not only find the end of all things recounted, but we also find a carefully crafted answer to the initial problems of Genesis that required God's redemptive plan through his covenants culminating in Christ. Revelation mirrors the content of the first book, bringing the whole Bible and human history to a perfect conclusion. It also ends with a particular covenant formula, the curse upon anyone who would add to or remove from the document (Rev 22:18-19). Such a formula is typical of ancient covenant documents; it is only found elsewhere in the Bible in Deuteronomy 4:2 and 12:32, where it places a curse on anyone who would change God's Old Covenant document. Though in its context, it appropriately concludes the book of Revelation and its prophecy, it also brings the whole Bible to a close in a way remarkably fitting for a covenant document. One cannot help but see God's hand of providence in this finish. The covenant is now finished. Everything has been given. Let the one who would add or take away from it be cursed.

So, the Bible is a covenant constitution. If the Bible is intended to govern a covenant, to lead its people in their relationship with God under a Covenant, then its purpose, the goal of its teachings and stories are those of the Covenant it governs. Thus, we find that the purpose of the Bible is the same as the purpose of a covenant.

i. The Purpose of the Bible

The Bible legislates two covenants (and recounts several more). Significant overlap exists in the purpose of these covenants, so the Bible is unified. Yet, there are considerable differences, which explains why applying the Old Covenant to the New is difficult (see *The Gift of*

Reading – Part 1).[19]

To understand their shared purpose, we need to zoom out and catch the whole scope of God's creation. It all starts with the beginning, with God's creation. A careful reading of the Genesis creation account reveals that humanity is the pinnacle of God's creation. Why are we so important? We are told that men and women were created "in the image" and "likeness" of God (1:26-27) and given a commission. Our first parents were commanded,

> Be fruitful and multiply and fill the earth and subdue it, and have dominion over the fish of the sea and over the birds of the heavens and over every living thing that moves on the earth. (Gen 1:28)

Being in God's likeness and having a commission are not so dissimilar. To be made in the image and likeness of God not only means that we resemble him in what we are but that we resemble him (or ought to resemble him) in what we do. As God is building a kingdom and filling it, so we are also commissioned to build a kingdom by taking control of, ruling, and filling the creation. However, this kingdom was not the autonomous kingdom of humanity: the first humans were to do so as those in the image and likeness of God. So, by their rule, they would represent God. The rule entrusted to humanity was that of vice-regents, ruling on behalf of the true king.

Many (rightly, I believe) find a covenant in these early pages, but this is not the covenant legislated by the Old or New Testament.[20] As the creation story unfolds, we see that humans failed in this covenant. Adam and Eve did not follow God with all their hearts; they did not

---

[19] See also my study guide on Habakkuk, *Believe the Unbelievable* (Vancouver: Teleioteti, 2018).

[20] E.g. Peter J. Gentry and Stephen J. Wellum, *God's Kingdom through God's Covenants: A Concise Biblical Theology*, 2015, 69–93; Peter J. Gentry and Stephen J. Wellum, *Kingdom through Covenant: A Biblical-Theological Understanding of the Covenants*, 2nd Ed. (Wheaton: Crossway, 2018), chap. 6.

work to establish his kingdom. Instead, they listened to the serpent. They accepted his questioning of God's authority and rejected God's rule. By rejecting God's rule, they established a kingdom, but it was not the kingdom they were called to build. Their children became kingdom builders but built their own kingdoms under their god, Satan (cf. 2 Cor 4:4). God cursed the serpent, and he cursed humanity; in the very spheres where they were to serve him, multiplying and subduing the earth, they would face opposition (Gen 3:14-19). More than that, cut off from the Garden, they would die (Gen 2:15-17, 3:22-24). However, in the midst of the curse, God gives hope; his purpose for creation would not be thwarted. Instead, we find the promise of victory over the serpent:

> I will put enmity between you and the woman,
> and between your offspring and her offspring;
> he shall bruise your head,
> and you shall bruise his heel. (Gen 3:15)

God's purpose for creation was to institute his kingdom within it under the rule of humanity, the pinnacle of his creation. In the fallen world, this would somehow be accomplished through the woman's offspring; he would crush the head of the serpent.

It is not immediately clear how this would be accomplished, but as the Bible's narrative unfolds, it becomes more and more evident. It is apparent in the early chapters of Genesis that the kingdom of Satan is flourishing, with only a tiny presence of God's kingdom. Even after the flood, Satan's kingdom is united around the tower of Babel, yet God scatters them and thwarts their efforts. Hope is associated with Noah's son Shem; afterwards, it is focused on the line of Terah (Gen 9:26-27; 11:10-32). It is in Terah's son Abram that God's plan to crush the serpent and inaugurate his kingdom is seen. Changing his name to Abraham, God enters a covenant with him, promising to bring forth kings from his line and to multiply him greatly (17:6-8). In fact, through Abraham, all the nations of the earth would find themselves blessed (12:2-3). By the end of Genesis, this promise is focused on the sons of

Israel (Gen 50:22-26, cf. Gen 15:1-21).

In Exodus, the story picks up here, with the sons of Israel enslaved in Egypt. God will bring them up out of Egypt and make a covenant with them, the covenant which the Old Testament governs. Therefore, the Old Covenant is directly related to God's purpose to bless all the nations through Abraham and, in so doing, to crush the head of the Serpent and institute his kingdom on earth.

The Old Covenant legislated a religious-political society, a nation whose entire life revolved around God. The society was meant to be radically different from their neighbours and radically committed to their God; they were to be holy as he was holy. From the clothing they wore (Lev 19:19; Deut 22:9-11) to the food they ate (Lev 11:11-47), they were to image God and his character. More than this, they were a nation of kings and priests (Exod 19:6), entrusted with stewarding the land and mediating God to their neighbours. God also made provisions for a king who would rule as his vice-regent (Deuteronomy 17). However, throughout the Torah, we are frequently reminded that Israel lacked what they needed to fulfil their purpose; they needed hearts committed to God but lacked them (Deut 5:29; 10:16; 29:4; 30:6-14 [in Hebrew]).[21] The prophets record the fulfilment of Deuteronomy's prophecies concerning the apostasy of Israel (Deuteronomy 29, 32). Time after time, God's people rejected him for false gods and rejected his authority over them. They failed to subdue the land, let alone rule as representatives of God. Moreover, they frequently built Satan's kingdom; they worshipped idols and encouraged debauchery instead of building God's kingdom. Though God intended this kingdom to be a blessing to the nations, glimpsed faintly in the lives of David (e.g. 2 Sam 8:18, 15:18) and Solomon (1 King 10:1-13), Jonah's failures as a prophet parabolically indict Israel

---

[21] See my books *Prevenient Grace, The Gift of Reading – Part 2,* or *The Gift of Knowledge* for a translation of Deut 30:1-14 that catches the sense of vv. 10-14.

for their failure to do so (Jonah).

However, God's purpose did not end with the Old Covenant. In Deuteronomy 30, he promised a day when he would write his law—his covenant—on the hearts of his people, enabling them to fulfil its purpose. This promise is echoed in Jeremiah 31:31-40, Isaiah 54:13, and Ezekiel 36:22-37:28 (among other places). God would make a new covenant, an everlasting covenant of peace. In this covenant, God's purposes would be fulfilled. Most significantly, this new covenant was associated with God's Messiah. The Messiah would be a suffering servant who would accomplish God's purposes (Isaiah 53:1-54:17) and a Davidic son who would rule over God's kingdom (2 Samuel 7:11-16), who would even be God himself (Isaiah 7:14; 8:5-18; 9:1-7; 53:1). Through Jesus's death and resurrection, the most significant moment in the history of God's redemption occurred: the serpent had struck the heel of the woman's offspring, yet he rose from the dead, crushing the serpent. Jesus ascended to the throne of his Father and was exalted above all. All authority has been given to the Son; dominion is his. However, the world remains in the throes of Satan's rebellion; Satan and his kingdom have been crushed but have not yet perished. The fulfilment of God's purpose has been guaranteed, yet it has not yet been achieved.

This is where the Church enters the picture. As the body of Christ, the Church has been charged with participating in Christ's fulfilment of God's purpose (Eph 1:7-10, 15-23). Through our feet, Jesus is crushing the serpent (Rom 16:20). Jesus has suffered, but we labour "to fill up what was lacking in Christ's sufferings" (Col 1:24); Christ has been given all dominion, but we are entrusted with multiplying his kingdom, expanding it to the ends of the earth. The Church does not do this through military expansion, political action, or other similar means. Instead, they make disciples and teach them to obey their Lord:

> All authority in heaven and on earth has been given to me. Go therefore and make disciples of all nations,

> baptizing them in the name of the Father and of the Son and of the Holy Spirit, teaching them to observe all that I have commanded you. And behold, I am with you always, to the end of the age. (Matthew 28:18-20)

The New Covenant made in Jesus's blood (Luke 20:22) secures our salvation, and it provides the gift of the Holy Spirit, who fulfils the promise of a faithful heart and empowerment for ministry (Deut 30:6-14; Joel 2:28-29; Gal 3:1-9; 1 Cor 12:1-11). It also consecrates us as a royal priesthood under Christ (1 Pet 2:4-12; Rev 1:5-7) with the task of expanding his kingdom rule on earth through preaching the Gospel and equipping the saints. If this is the purpose of the covenant, then the Bible is given to guide us in this matter and ensure that the purpose of the covenant is fulfilled. As Paul puts it in 2 Timothy 3:16-17, "All Scripture is breathed out by God and profitable for teaching, for reproof, for correction, and for training in righteousness, that the man of God may be complete, equipped for every good work."

In *The Gift of Reading – Part 1*, I suggested three "purposes" within this purpose: the Bible brings us to faith, reveals God to us, and equips us for life before him. We can consider the way the content of the Bible is oriented to this purpose in its three dimensions by considering its contents as legislation, interpretation, and exhortation. The choice of this threefold division is not completely arbitrary, for it has its roots in the Jewish view of the Old Testament in the 1st century and prior. The Hebrew Bible is often divided into three sections: the Law, Prophets, and the Writings. There is good evidence that this threefold division dates to the later centuries BC. A fragment in the Qumran scrolls, for example, refers to the Law, the Prophets, and David.[22] "David" is probably an allusion to the Psalms, the first book of the Writings. We see the same threefold division in Josephus (1st Cent AD), Philo (1st Cent AD), and the Greek prologue to Ecclesiasticus (~3rd Cent BC), which identified the third division as "the other

---

[22] 4QMMT Fragment C, 11.10-11.

books."[23] With strong evidence for this threefold concept of the Old Testament canon in the 1st century and earlier, it becomes clear what Jesus is referring to when he speaks of "the Law, the prophets, and the Psalms" (Luke 24:44). Though this trifold division may be merely an organisational scheme, Miles Van Pelt argues persuasively that the books of each section share a similar perspective on the covenant. He summarises them as "The Covenant," "Covenant life," and "Covenant living."[24]

Moving from description to function, from what they are to what they do, we could identify the Torah as Covenant legislation, the Prophets as an interpretation of covenant history, and the Writings as an exhortation for Covenant living. Though each section of the Old Testament (and, as Van Pelt and Meredith Kline argue, the New Testament also) reflects one of these functions, there is a sense in which every passage in Scripture functions to legislate (indicate what is right or wrong, true or false), to interpret the past, present, and future in light of God's purpose, and to exhort the believer to act.[25] For example, the command "do not murder" has an explicit legislative function; it is sinful in the eyes of God to commit murder. It also is interpretive, for in light of it, every murderous act is seen to be sinful and rebellion against God; it is also part of a distinct historical event and attests to God's personal action in human history, telling us about

---

23 Josephus, *Against Apion* bk. 1, par. 38. and Philo's *The Contemplative Life*, par. 25. Beckwith provides more evidence from the *Talmud* and *Tosefta*. Beckwith, *The Old Testament Canon of the New Testament Church and Its Background in Early Judaism*, 112–13, 117; Stephen G. Dempster, "Canons on the Right and Canons on the Left: Finding a Resolution in the Canon Debate," *Journal of the Evangelical Theological Society* 52, no. 1 (March 2009): 59–64.

24 Van Pelt, *A Biblical-Theological Introduction to the Old Testament: The Gospel Promised*, 23–41.

25 Kline, *The Structure of Biblical Authority*; Miles Van Pelt, "Structure of the Christian Bible," Education, Biblical Training, accessed August 29, 2017, https://www.biblicaltraining.org/library/structure-christian-bible/biblical-theology/van-pelt-blomberg-schreiner.

God and his actions towards humanity. Finally, when seen with the eyes of faith, this command is exhortatory; it does not merely give us information ("it is wrong to murder"), but as a word from our Covenant God, it impels us to put away all murderous rage, anger, and hostility towards those made in God's image (cf. Matt 5:21-26).[26]

ii. The Bible as Legislation – Law

As we saw above, the Torah is explicitly seen as "the Law." It testifies that it was written as the book of the covenant or the Law. The Torah is filled with explicit legislative material, laws concerning religious and ritual practice, social structures, and government. The most similar part of the New Testament is the Gospels, which Paul and James are willing to identify as a sort of Law (1 Cor 9:21; Gal 6:2; James 1:19-27, 2:8, 12). The Torah and the Gospels are more than mere legislation; they both contain narratives concerning the founding of the Covenant and other events. However, the narratives of the Torah are not independent of the legislation; they have explanatory functions. That is, narratives not only tell stories, but they teach with stories. An author chooses what stories to include and how to tell them for specific purposes.[27] Jesus's ministry is revelatory of his person and is recounted in order to indicate the fulfilment of Old Testament prophecies and types but may at times serve to illustrate the parables and teachings he gives about life under the New Covenant.

In the Old Testament, the Law is framed in the context of curses

---

[26] John Frame made a similar observation about the threefold nature of each text in *The Doctrine of the Word of God.* He identifies the three functions of Scripture as normative, situational, and existential, according to his particular epistemological and ethical theory. Frame, *Doctrine of the Word.*

[27] Cf. Long, *The Art of Biblical History*; John H. Sailhamer, *The Pentateuch as Narrative* (Grand Rapids: Zondervan, 1992).

for disobedience and blessings for obedience (Deut 27:9-28:68). Not only would covenant obedience ensure the temporal prosperity of the Israelite kingdom, but it would also ensure that its people enjoyed a right relationship with God, identified as "life" (Lev 18:1-5).[28] In the New Covenant, curses are reserved for those who have transgressed the other covenants (e.g. Matt 11:20-24; Matt 25:41-46). Considering broader New Testament theology, Christ has born the curse in our place and guaranteed God's blessing for us—though the latter is interpreted as a blessing in the world to come and life with God now, not material blessings now (Rom 4:1-12; Gal 3:10-14). The New Covenant is presented in terms of blessing but not in a straightforward claim, "do this, and you will be blessed." Instead, the life of those who are blessed with every promise of God in Christ (1 Cor 1:16) looks like this:

> Blessed are the poor in spirit, for theirs is the kingdom of heaven.
> Blessed are those who mourn, for they shall be comforted.
> Blessed are the meek, for they shall inherit the earth.
> Blessed are those who hunger and thirst for righteousness, for they shall be satisfied.
> Blessed are the merciful, for they shall receive mercy.
> Blessed are the pure in heart, for they shall see God.
> Blessed are the peacemakers, for they shall be called sons of God.
> Blessed are those who are persecuted for righteousness' sake, for theirs is the kingdom of heaven.
> Blessed are you when others revile you and persecute you and utter all kinds of evil against you falsely on my account. Rejoice and be glad, for your reward is great in heaven, for so they persecuted the prophets who

---

[28] See my comments on Habakkuk 2:4 in *Habakkuk: An Exegetical-Theological Commentary* (2019).

were before you. (Matthew 5:3-12)

Some commentators have observed that the combination of "going up on the mountain" and "sitting" (Matt 5:1) is reminiscent of Moses "going up on the mountain" and "remaining" or "sitting" (ישב) on the mountain to receive the Law (Deut 9:9). Moreover, the narrative of Matthew leading to this point echoes the narratives of Exodus through Deuteronomy, with Jesus coming forth from Egypt (Matt 2:13-15; cf. Hos 11:1, Exod 4:22-23, 12:33-42), passing through the waters (Matt 3:13-17; cf. Exodus 14, 1 Cor 10:1-5), being tested in the wilderness (Matt 4:1-11; e.g. Deut 8:2-20), and then arriving at a mountain (Matt 5:1; Deut 9:6-12). This is followed by a direct discussion of the Ten Commandments (Matt 5:17-48; Exod 20:1-17). Now, the language used for "blessing" is not the that of a covenant blessing (בְּרָכָה, εὐλογία, *eulogia*) but of the state that results from receiving that blessing (אַשְׁרֵי, *'ashrey*, μαρκάριος, *makarios*; cf. Psalm 1). Nevertheless, the combination of "blessing" language with these allusions and the general perspective of the Gospels as the foundation of the New Covenant invites the comparison between the Sermon on the Mount and the Law delivered through Moses. The whole sermon has a similar function to legislate life under the New Covenant. The Beatitudes, like the Ten Commandments, are not the whole of the Law but programmatic for what life under their respective covenants would look like. Legislation consists of commands and statements about ethical norms governing behaviour; in a Covenant context, these are accompanied by the framework of their purpose, the rewards for obedience, and (where relevant) the curses for disobedience. In the Torah and the Gospels, we find this legislation amidst the narrative concerning the founding of the covenant. As this is a covenant from God, these narratives reveal much about the Lord with whom we enter a covenant.

In the Torah, we get glimpses of the behaviour of those with whom God enters the covenant. The last chapters of Deuteronomy foretell

Israel's failure under this covenant; earlier chapters reveal that Israel failed almost immediately (such as the incident with the golden calf, Exodus 32). Similarly, in the Gospels we witness the doubts and unbelief of Christ's chosen apostles and his disciples (Matt 16:5-12, 21-23; 26:30-46, 47-56; Mark 10:35-44; John 6:60-71). However, whereas in Deuteronomy, Moses prophesied Israel's failure because they had not yet been given obedient hearts (Deut 29:1-30:14, 31:16-32:52),[29] we see in the Gospels the gift of the Spirit fulfilled (Luke 24:49; John 1:12; 3:1-15; 6:1-59; 20:22; cf. Acts 2:1-13). The whole scope of Israel's history until the coming of the New Covenant was prophesied in the Torah (Deuteronomy 29, 31:16-32:47); its failure was a result of the corrupted hearts of those with whom God had entered a covenant. Even as he entered the covenant, God stated, "I know what they are inclined to do even today, before I have brought them into the land that I swore to give" (Deut 31:21). The New Covenant was guaranteed to be different, for not only had Jesus accomplished all things, received his throne (Matt 28:18-20; John 17:4; 19:28-30), and promised to be with his people (Matt 28:20), but he also gave them the long-awaited Spirit, who would ensure that all of God's people would know and love him (John 3:34; 7:37-39; 14:15-17; 15:26; 16:12-15; Luke 24:49). With the closing of the giving of the covenant, what remains to be seen is the result; how will God's purpose play out through these covenant relationships?

iii. The Bible as Interpretation – History

The Prophets in the Old Testament provide a thoroughly theological interpretation of Israel's history. The so-called "former prophets," Joshua through Kings, provide a theological interpretation of Israel's covenant life. Sadly, as prophesied in Deuteronomy, the Old Covenant is broken from the very beginning. In Joshua, despite God's promises,

---

[29] See the first chapter and first appendix of my book, *Prevenient Grace: An Investigation into Arminianism*, 2nd Revised Ed., Teleioteti Technical Studies 2 (Vancouver: Teleioteti, 2020).

Israel fails to follow through with their task (Josh 15:63). Very quickly, they descend into chaos, doing "what was right in their own eyes" (Judg 17:6, 21:25). In Samuel, the people first reject God's rule for a king of their own choosing (1 Sam 8:1-22); when God establishes his own choice for king, that king quickly demonstrates his fallibility (2 Sam 11:1-20:22).[30] Kings portrays the utter failure of Israel and its kings to uphold their covenant up to the final deportation to Babylon, the climax of the curses recounted in Deuteronomy (see Deut 29:27-30:1). The latter prophets, from Isaiah to the Book of the Twelve (Hosea – Malachi), zoom in on this period and the years afterwards (extending to the post-exilic period when Israel returned to the land), giving specific words of God directed towards the people and rulers of Israel and Judah. They offer the same perspective as the former prophets: Israel had failed its covenant obligations, yet God would one day bring restoration. Throughout the Prophets, three themes or words from God are unpacked. There is *indictment*, God's declaration of sin—sometimes in a formalised covenant lawsuit (in Hebrew, the word ריב [to bring a charge, a charge/lawsuit] indicates a formal charge and is found throughout the Prophets [165 times]). An indictment is accompanied by a declaration of *judgment* and often an account of its fulfilment. The Prophets do not stop there, however; they also contain promises of renewal or *restoration*, often in the language of Deuteronomy 30: God will return Israel to the land, give them renewed hearts so they can be faithful, bring complete cleansing from their sin, and bless them with his covenant blessings (e.g. Jeremiah 31; Isaiah 53-54; Ezekiel 36-37).

When we turn to the New Testament, we find a comparable covenant history in the Acts of the Apostles. However, there is a significant difference. Whereas in the *Nevi'im* or The Prophets, Israel failed their covenant obligations, the Acts recount God's Spirit

---

30 See my book J. Alexander Rutherford, *God's Kingdom through His Priest-King: An Analysis of the Book of Samuel in Light of the Davidic Covenant*, Teleioteti Technical Studies 1 (Vancouver: Teleioteti, 2019).

working through his people, ensuring the success of the New Covenant. The Prophets continually look forward to the day that God would pour out his Spirit, empowering all his people for right living before him and with gifts for ministry. Acts begins with the fulfilment of this promise; God's Spirit is poured out visibly and powerfully, enabling Peter and the other Apostles to powerfully proclaim the Gospel (1:1-4:22). God's Spirit is not only poured out on the Jewish disciples but also on the Samaritans and the Gentiles (8:14-24, 10:34-48). This indicated not only the fulfilment of the Old Testament promises (cf. Joel 2:28-29) but also the fulfilment of Jesus's words to his apostles, "You will receive power when the Holy Spirit has come upon you, and you will be my witnesses in Jerusalem and in all Judea and Samaria, and to the end of the earth" (Acts 1:8). Peter's ministry to Cornelius and his family indicates the beginning of the fulfilment of "to the ends of the earth," but the narrative of Acts continues the story, concluding with Paul's ministry in Rome (Acts 28).

The Holy Spirit is the game changer; what Israel was lacking has now been fulfilled, and Acts recounts the success of the New Covenant from its inception. However, the narrative does not cover the entire New Covenant era, for it has continued for 2000 years and will continue until Jesus returns. It does, however, indicate the trajectory of this covenant: through the Spirit's work, God's purpose under this Covenant is guaranteed to succeed.

iv. The Bible as Exhortation – Practice

The last sections of the Covenants, the *Ketuvi'im* or Writings (Psalms – 2 Chronicles) and the Epistles (Romans – Revelation), are neither legislation (the framework of God's promises towards and expectations for his people) nor Covenant history. Instead, they contain various forms of literature we could summarise as exhortation; the Psalms, wisdom literature, theological histories, Epistles, and so-called apocalyptic books are intended to exhort faithfulness to God and instruct his people how to live faithfully in a complicated World.

This is easily shown from books like Proverbs, Ecclesiastes, many of the Psalms, and the New Testament epistles. But what about the lament and imprecatory Psalms, Lamentations, Job, Ruth, Esther, Chronicles, and Ezra-Nehemiah? Even Daniel and Revelation?

God is not ignorant of the struggles of the Christian life; he knows the complications of life in a fallen world, the frequent experience of injustice and pain. He recognises these struggles; through certain Psalms and the book of Lamentations (and elsewhere), he has given his people a grammar for dealing with them. Christians and the Jews before them have not been called to stoic silence amid suffering; in light of Christ, we are exhorted to rejoice in the midst of suffering (Rom 5:1-4; Jam 1:2-4), but God recognises that it is often a journey to move through suffering to praise. This is the role of lament, to express despair and suffering to God in order to move towards trust in the midst of it. The lament psalms, Job's lament in Job 3, and the book of Lamentations guide the Christian in expressing their pain and moving towards God instead of becoming embittered towards him.[31] Imprecatory psalms have a different function: they give Christians a grammar for dealing with injustice. It may be easy to forgive others when they are willing to repent and seek reconciliation, but what do we do when injustice is perpetuated? When the one who has sinned continues in their sin without any remorse or desire to reconcile? What do we do when injustice continues unabated? The imprecatory Psalms are those Psalms that call on God to fulfil judgment and bring justice; they model in poetry what Paul describes in Romans 12,

> Repay no one evil for evil, but give thought to do what is honorable in the sight of all. If possible, so far as it depends on you, live peaceably with all. Beloved, never avenge yourselves, but leave it to the wrath of God, for

[31] Mark Vroegrop has written several great resources on this subject, Mark Vroegop, "Dare to Hope in God: How to Lament Well," Desiring God, April 6, 2019, https://www.desiringgod.org/articles/dare-to-hope-in-god; Mark Vroegop, *Dark Clouds, Deep Mercy*, 2019.

> it is written, "Vengeance is mine, I will repay, says the Lord." To the contrary, "if your enemy is hungry, feed him; if he is thirsty, give him something to drink; for by so doing you will heap burning coals on his head." Do not be overcome by evil, but overcome evil with good. (Rom 12:17-21)

Paul calls Christians to entrust judgment God and to live in light of his perfect justice; imprecatory Psalms are the impassioned cry of the believer for that justice to be realised,

> You know my reproach,
>   and my shame and my dishonor;
>   my foes are all known to you.
> Reproaches have broken my heart,
>   so that I am in despair.
> I looked for pity, but there was none,
>   and for comforters, but I found none.
> They gave me poison for food,
>   and for my thirst they gave me sour wine to drink.
> Let their own table before them become a snare;
>   and when they are at peace, let it become a trap.
> Let their eyes be darkened, so that they cannot see,
>   and make their loins tremble continually.
> Pour out your indignation upon them,
>   and let your burning anger overtake them.
> May their camp be a desolation;
>   let no one dwell in their tents.
> For they persecute him whom you have struck down,
>   and they recount the pain of those you have wounded.
> Add to them punishment upon punishment;
>   may they have no acquittal from you.
> Let them be blotted out of the book of the living;
>   let them not be enrolled among the righteous.
> But I am afflicted and in pain;
>   let your salvation, O God, set me on high! (Psalm 69:19-29)

Job, on the other hand, is an intense mediation on the believer's faith in God despite intense suffering. It repudiates a simplistic connection between sin and suffering. Instead, it calls the one who would trust God to trust him despite their circumstances. They are called to trust that his ways are inscrutable and trustworthy even when wisdom fails to grasp his depths (cf. Job 28). The narratives of the Writings move from instructing through song and teaching to showing the believer what right living before God ought to look like or illustrating the subtle ways God works. Ruth, for example, picks up on the woman who embodies wisdom in Proverbs 31 and exemplifies the fear of God in the lives of the Moabitess Ruth and the Israelite Boaz, both described as "worthy" (חַיִל, cf. Proverbs 31:10, Ruth 2:1, 3:11).

What about Daniel and Revelation? Surely these intense prophecies do not fit this pattern![32] Despite the speculation surrounding these books, a good argument can be made that they are intensely practical. In one sense, they address the whole sweep of human history, from their present circumstances to the climactic inauguration of Christ's kingdom on earth (see Dan 7:1-28). In another sense, they address every point in between, for both books describe a sweeping cosmic conflict between the kingdom of man under the rule of Satan and the kingdom of God. They both point to the ultimate victory of Jesus over Satan. The point in both books is the call to endurance. In light of God's current work and assured victory, we can and must persevere through all sorts of trials. As John puts it repeatedly,

> be faithful unto death, and I will give you the crown of life.... The one who conquers will not be hurt by the second death. (Rev 2:10-11; cf. 2:7, 3:5, 3:10-13; 13:10;

[32] These books are usually called "Apocalyptic," but Revelation identifies itself as a prophecy (Rev 1:3). The former title often obscures the similarities between these books and the Latter Prophets (Isaiah through Malachi). I discuss this issue further in *The Gift of Reading – Part 2*.

14:12; 21:7)

C. Conclusion

For contemporary Evangelicals, the Bible is the object of intense scholarly and critical engagement; anything less is insufficient to understand the Scriptures and speak truthfully about God. For the Scholastics and Reformed Orthodox and many in the Early Church, the Bible provided the data from which "theology" could be attained through a rigorous rational process. In both cases, the knowledge of God and his will in Scripture is one step removed from the actual reading of Scripture. Perhaps a simple reading of Scripture was permissible, yet maturity was associated with this deeper reading, with one of several exegetical methods, a "second exegesis," or theological interpretation. However, this does not match how the Bible describes itself. The Bible is a covenant document God intends to legislate his New Covenant with all people who follow his Son. This document is intended to entirely equip God's people to live in a manner wholly pleasing to him. This is a goal God has sought to achieve from the beginnings of the covenant in the 2nd Millennium BC until today. Through the public reading, singing, and teaching of Scripture, along with private reading and meditation, God has made it accessible to his people, young and old. It equips them to discern God's will, identify truth and falsehood, and persevere in a hostile world until Christ returns. By God's design, the Bible is perfectly suited to correct the corruption of our knowledge of God caused by the Fall, re-introducing us to the God we have known unrighteously. It is also perfectly suited to encourage, rebuke, and train us in righteousness. Though there is room for serious intellectual wrestling with the implications of the Scripture and the claims it makes, the Bible's testimony about itself and the knowledge of God it meditates (as well as who qualifies for pastoral ministry) indicate that it achieves its purposes without incredible feats of learning, even apart from literacy (e.g. Rev 1:3).[33]

[33] Cf. J. Alexander Rutherford, "Church in an Oral World – Teleioteti Articles," Teleioteti, April 30, 2024, https://www.teleioteti.ca/2024/04/30/church-in-an-oral-world/.

9

WHAT IS THE PLACE OF ACADEMICS IN THE CHRISTIAN LIFE?

> I propose first that we dump the academic model once and for all – degrees, accreditation, tenure, the works. This is not to say that classroom-type instruction is of no value in ministerial training; on the contrary, it is probably indispensable in some areas, e.g. biblical languages. Nor would I allege that the system of grades, hours and degrees measures nothing of importance to theological education. – John Frame[1]

In Chapter 4.E, I argued that the views of theology and orthodoxy developed in the Early Church as they reflected on the Nicaean Creed, the early Protestant churches, and contemporary Evangelicalism have led to a view of the academy as central to the Church. The academy was the ideal context to train ministers of the Gospel, to develop resources to equip those ministers, and to further our knowledge of God, his word, and his world. In the preceding four chapters, I have argued that the Bible presents a different view of orthodoxy, the knowledge of God, pastoral ministry, and the Bible than the presuppositions undergirding the eminency of the academy. The

[1] Frame, "Proposal for a New Seminary."

foundations we have considered in the last four chapters make this view of academia untenable. From four different angles, we have seen that theology and ministry are ill-suited to the halls of the academy. They are the possessions of all God's people with their various gifts and abilities. Though we have not argued this point yet, the nature of orthodoxy, knowledge of God, pastoral ministry, and the Bible put forth in Scripture make the local church the ideal place for good theology to be developed, good character discerned and developed, and ministry training to be conducted.[2] We will argue this in the next part of this book. However, what is clear at this point is that the place given to the academy in contemporary Evangelicalism is not only unbiblical but also untenable.

A. The Problem with the Academic Model

We have considered the intrinsic disadvantages of the academic model in the introduction and Chapter 3 (especially Section C). However, if the Bible mandated or supported the models of orthodoxy, theology, and ministry that came to pre-eminence during the Early Church, Reformation, and now in Evangelicalism, then these disadvantages would be a necessary part of doing theological education in a broken world, lamentable certainly, but is some sense inescapable. However, in the last three chapters, we have seen that the Bible puts forth a different model of orthodoxy, knowledge of God, and the Bible. This model is not fostered within an academic context that focuses on intellectual excellence and requires dislocation from the primary faith-forming relationships God has granted to his people, the local church. The implication of this is that the academic system is unbiblical. This system puts obstacles before ministry candidates and thereby exacerbates the present crisis of ministry; it also emphasises a view of God and Orthodoxy that is at best secondary in Scripture, thereby failing to uphold the primary measure of orthodoxy in Scripture

---

[2] Rutherford, *The Being of Churches.*

(character) and the primary nature of our knowledge of God (person-knowledge). By its very nature, the academic system does this. The academic model is thereby also untenable as a solution to the present crises in ministry. The academic model 1) is unable to develop and identify the very things necessary for a holy and successful pastorate, godliness; 2) it promotes hyper-intellectualisation and reinforces the assumptions that the knowledge of God is an intellectual endeavour and that the Bible is difficult to understand; 3) it pre-selects against numerous people who would be biblically qualified for ministry and tends to bias the intellectually accomplished, prosperous, and independent—virtues that are not necessarily coterminous with godliness. If the academic model is unnecessary (given its absence from Scripture and its excellence in things the Bible does not prioritise) and inefficient for the task we have assigned it, the question remains: What is the place of academic study and achievement in the Christian life and Christian ministry?

I am highly sympathetic to John Frame's contention that we should completely do away with the academic model for ministerial training. However, if we entirely, or almost entirely, eradicate the academic model for ministerial training, does this mean that we should completely withdraw from academic-style intellectual engagement? This is a point upon which I am not so convinced. There seems to be some benefit in the intensive intellectual engagement with Scripture, philosophy, history, and our knowledge of God. Such engagement is well fostered in environments conducive to serious study, equipped with the resources for such study, and capable of training people with the skills to do such study. However, once disassociated from ministerial training, Christian academic institutions in their present form are not sustainable (they are already struggling financially while receiving numerous ministry candidates and denominational and individual contributions). I suggest that participation in secular institutions and research centres attached to local churches or church groups provide opportunities to foster the positive intellectual engagement possible in our current systems. In this chapter, I will first argue for some benefit in serious Christian intellectual efforts; then, I will discuss the possible context for these efforts if ministerial training were partially or entirely removed from the academic context.

B. Intellectual Effort Is of Some Benefit

We have seen that intellectual effort is not central to pastoral ministry nor a necessary component of knowing God or interpreting Scripture; nevertheless, the benefit of serious Christian intellectual effort is apparent. Not every pastor needs to be able to analyse trends in our present culture and identify the dangers these trends hold for the church, yet this sort of analysis is invaluable as we think about caring for a flock constantly pressured to follow our culture. Not every pastor needs to know the biblical languages (though I will argue this is invaluable to the pastoral task; see §12.c.iv below), but we need some people with the skills to translate the Bible into contemporary languages and produce resources for translating and original language study of the Bible. Books that offer a Christian analysis of contemporary philosophy and biblical insight into the pressing problems of thought in our schools, workplaces, and universities are likewise invaluable. It also takes knowledge, research skills, and time to translate or present historical Christian thought and texts for a present audience. These are just a few areas where serious intellectual effort pays off for the work to which Christ has called his church.

It does our churches well to be acquainted with the tradition from which we have come and to be familiar with God's work across time, and it does our churches well to refute intellectual objections that the world places before our flock. There is great danger in making commentaries and the tradition necessary to the teaching and care of a pastor, but that does not negate their value. Especially in the West where our culture is vastly different than the Bible's and we tend to be overeducated in the world and undereducated in the Bible, commentaries and historical resources often confront our ignorance of God's will in Scripture. For the pastor in a Thai village, God can do this without an extensive library or even literacy, for God has done so for thousands of years. However, the fact that God can use non-literary means does not mean that he will not use literate means in our highly literate society. Our society brings unique challenges that are sometimes aided by serious intellectual effort. So, we can acknowledge that God does not need academic means or literary methods to achieve his work, but in societies so equipped, he can and does use these means. However, if we stop training ministers in academic institutions, these institutions will be unsustainable. I do not believe this potential outcome means we should maintain the status quo. However, it is not clear to me that this is the only possible outcome. If we were to lose Christian academic institutions as we now know them, there seem to be several viable alternatives to promote serious intellectual engagement with God's word and his world. First, there remains the opportunity for Christians to engage in the public sphere through secular universities and liberal arts colleges; second, there is the possibility of fostering research within local churches or denominations.

C. Christian Intellectual Engagement in the Public Sphere

Many Christians already work in secular universities and engage with scholars from many faith backgrounds in areas pertinent to theology, such as biblical studies, philosophy, philosophy of religion, sociology of religion, and Christian theology. This has sometimes given Christians a platform to develop genuinely Christian ideas and communicate God's grace and truth to the unbelieving world. However, a significant danger emerges when Christians engage intellectually with God's world in a "neutral" or supposedly objective way. When non-Christian scholars engage with the Bible, theology, and related disciplines, they do so with presuppositions about the objects of their study incompatible with the Christian faith.

That is, it is well established in numerous fields of study that it is impossible to come at any intellectual endeavour with a blank slate or without a pre-understanding of the matter and an underlying framework by which value judgements are made (everyone has an understanding of truth, for example, which shapes every endeavour they perform).[3]

Michael Polanyi argued in the mid-20th century that scientific theories provide an overarching interpretive paradigm that filters new data, dismissing incongruities and interpreting the data that coheres with the paradigm; it is not possible to move from one paradigm to another through gradual steps because a paradigm is all-encompassing, it is that by which we see the world. Developments in understanding occur in leaps, as one way of seeing the world is replaced by another. Thomas Kuhn appropriated this model in a less ontologically grounded way (for Polanyi, the developments gave us genuine insight into the world), calling these developments "paradigm shifts."[4]

Within theology, Cornelius Van Til argued that the Christian doctrine of God necessitated a particular approach to the world as created and pre-interpreted by God, utterly dependent upon him and oriented to him as its fundamental explanation. Without this theological framework, the world could not make sense, yet non-Christian thought sustains itself by retaining elements of biblical

---

[3] In addition to the resources cited below, see also Rudolf Bultmann, *New Testament and Mythology and Other Basic Writings*, trans. Schubert Miles Ogden (Philadelphia: Fortress Press, 1989); Esther L. Meek, *Loving to Know: Introducing Covenant Epistemology* (Eugene, OR: Cascade Books, 2011); Christopher Watkin, *Thinking through Creation: Genesis 1 and 2 as Tools of Cultural Critique* (Phillipsburg, NJ: P&R Publishing, 2017); Christopher Watkin, *Biblical Critical Theory: How the Bible's Unfolding Story Makes Sense of Modern Life and Culture* (Grand Rapids: Zondervan Academic, 2022).

[4] Polanyi, *Personal Knowledge*; Polanyi, *The Tacit Dimension*; Thomas S. Kuhn, *The Structure of Scientific Revolutions*, Fourth edition (Chicago; London: The University of Chicago Press, 2012); Martin X. Moleski, "Polanyi vs. Kuhn: Worldviews Apart," *Tradition and Discovery: The Polanyi Society Periodical* 33, no. 2 (2006): 8–24, https://doi.org/10.5840/traddisc2006/200733219.

theology while jettisoning its grounding in God. There is a genuinely Christian approach to knowing the world and radically different non-Christian approaches; these share common ground in the unjustified use of Christian presuppositions in the latter.[5] John Frame has developed Van Til's insight in interaction with contemporary philosophy and theology, arguing that God and his revelation in Scripture is the Christian's ultimate authority, which cannot be established by anything outside of itself. However, our presupposition of this authority can be supported by the way it makes sense of the world and shows other views to be false (thus, though ultimate authorities cannot be argued for from other authorities, they can be argued for on appeals to the world and other views as interpreted from that perspective, becoming a "wide" rather than a "narrow" circular argument).[6]

This is similar to the argument made by C.S. Lewis in *Miracles*, where he argues that the modern mind is prejudiced at a worldview level against the possibilities of miracles:

> Seeing is not believing. For this reason, the question whether miracles occur can never be answered simply by experience. Every event which might claim to be a miracle is, in the last resort, something presented to our sense, something seen, heard, touched, smelled, or tasted. And our senses are not infallible. If anything extraordinary seems to have happened, we can always say that we have been victims of an illusion. If we hold a philosophy which excludes the supernatural, this is

---

5 Van Til, *The Defense of the Faith*; Cornelius Van Til, *A Christian Theory of Knowledge* (Phillipsburg: Presbyterian and Reformed, 1969); John M. Frame, *Cornelius Van Til: An Analysis of His Thought* (Phillipsburg, NJ: P&R Publishing, 1995).

6 Frame, *The Doctrine of the Knowledge*; John M. Frame, *Apologetics: A Justification of Christian Belief*, ed. Joseph E. Torres, Second edition (Phillipsburg, NJ: P&R Publishing, 2015).

what we always shall say.[7]

Similarly, late 20th-century works in sociology have developed the idea of "plausibility structures" or "social imaginaries," which are (among other things) frameworks by which all future data is understood to be plausible or otherwise: data is not given a "fair hearing" but is always pre-understood by the subject, evaluated intuitively before being explicitly engaged.[8] These interactions with the phenomena of human knowledge echo similar insights from psychologists on our mind's construction of the world before we explicitly engage with it. From these different disciplines, we understand that the world is pre-interpreted at a tacit or pre-conscious level.[9]

Do you see the problem? Secular studies will approach the Bible as something other than it is, the written word of God, and will take a

---

[7] *Miracles* in C. S Lewis, *The Complete C.S. Lewis Signature Classics* (New York: HarperOne, 2007), 303.

[8] Peter L Berger, *The Sacred Canopy: Elements of a Sociological Theory of Religion* (New York: Doubleday, 1967), chaps. 1–2; Rikk E. Watts, *Isaiah's New Exodus in Mark*, Biblical Studies Library (Grand Rapids: Baker Books, 2000), chap. 2; Charles Taylor, *Modern Social Imaginaries*, Public Planet Books (Durham: Duke University Press, 2004), chap. 2, https://doi.org/10.1215/9780822385806; Carl R. Trueman, *The Rise and Triumph of the Modern Self: Cultural Amnesia, Expressive Individualism, and the Road to Sexual Revolution* (Wheaton: Crossway, 2020), chaps. 1–2.

[9] Merleau Ponty, *Merleau Ponty Phenomenology Of Perception*, trans. Colin Smith (London: Routledge & Kegan Paul, 1962), http://archive.org/details/merleaupontyphenomenologyofperception; Maurice Merleau-Ponty, "The Primacy of Perception and Its Philosophical Consequences," in *The Primacy of Perception: And Other Essays on Phenomenological Psychology, the Philosophy of Art, History, and Politics*, trans. James M. Edie (Evanston, IL: Northwestern University Press, 1964), 3–11; Maurice Merleau-Ponty, *Consciousness and the Acquisition of Language*, trans. Hugh J. Silverman (Evanston, IL: Northwestern University Press, 1973); McGilchrist, *The Master and His Emissary.*

similar approach to historical phenomena, the miraculous, and the present phenomena of the Christian experience. There is a Christian interpretation of these things that presupposes not only the possibility but the actuality of God's activity in history and in the present through his church. In some institutions, this Christian approach to things is tolerated, but in others, it is discriminated against as incompatible with scholarship. However, it is secular study that is incompatible with scholarship, for it presupposes an ordered world without confessing the only possible source of that order and attempts to interpret the world without the primary categories by which it makes sense, e.g. as the good creation of a triune God.[10] This does not mean we have nothing to learn from supposedly secular studies; no, because unbelievers "hold the truth unrighteously" (Rom 1:18, my translation), they perceive much that is true about God's creation and even God himself without giving the glory due unto God (Rom 1:21). However, it means that it is difficult to engage in genuinely Christian intellectual activity within the public sphere.[11]

To do so is possible, but it is not for the faint of heart. The world may engage with the Bible, but they are not our allies, for they do so under the direction of their god (2 Cor 4:4), who seeks to wreck God's church.[12] We are warned against being "unequally yoked with unbelievers," so we must not rush into partnership with the unbelievers in our intellectual endeavours (2 Cor 6:14-7:1). A clear

---

[10] See, for example, Cornelius Van Til, *Essays on Christian Education* (Phillipsburg: Presbyterian and Reformed, 1979); Poythress, *Redeeming Science*; Vern S. Poythress, *Logic: A God-Centered Approach to the Foundation of Western Thought*, Electronic (Wheaton: Crossway, 2013); Frame, *Apologetics*; E. R. Geehan, ed., *Jerusalem and Athens: Critical Discussions on the Theology and Apologetics of Cornelius Van Til* (Presbyterian and Reformed, 1971).

[11] Cf. Eric Johnson's proposal for a Christian psychology, Johnson, *Foundations for Soul Care: A Christian Psychology Proposal.*

[12] See J. Alexander Rutherford, "Towards a Biblical Theology of Satan's Kingdom," *Teleioteti Journal for Christian Ministry* 01, no. 01 (June 15, 2023): 42–52.

example of this is biblical studies, where Christians, Muslims, Jews, and atheists all engage with the Bible. With this jumble of plausibility structures coming together, the Bible is separated from common experience by many layers of scholarly fog. As I have dealt with in my book *The Trinity and the Bible*, it is a foregone conclusion in contemporary scholarship that ancient Israel were either polytheists, henotheists, or monotheists (or rather, there was a movement from a form of animism through polytheism towards a monotheism that acknowledged the existence of other gods but denied they were like Yahweh) and that the Old Testament is not Trinitarian. However, Christians for nearly 1600 years taught that the whole Bible was entirely Trinitarian; the Triune God is the God known to Adam, Noah, Abraham, and their descendants. The conclusion that this is an untenable reading of the Old Testament does not come from the Old Testament data itself (which I have argued is entirely compatible with the view that the whole Bible is Trinitarian) but from a set of assumptions developed in the period after the Reformation about the evolution of religion, a biblical theology of progress revelation, and an emphasis on objective historical analysis of texts and interpreting them in their (reconstructed) historical context.[13]

Mainstream universities may be places where Christians can engage intellectually with God and his world, but they face numerous obstacles if they are to do so in a Christian manner. It would undoubtedly be easier in some fields (perhaps philosophy), but some challenges remain. Nevertheless, some Christians find their calling in doing so and have successfully upheld their convictions and produced edifying literature in that context.

Another option for this sort of public intellectual engagement is theological study in the context of a liberal arts college. More common in North America than overseas, liberal arts colleges are often

---

[13] Rutherford, *The Trinity and the Bible: How All Scripture Testifies to One God in Three Persons.*

confessional institutions that offer courses equivalent to secular universities. Though they have not always navigated the integration of confessional Christianity successfully, a theological program in a liberal arts college could permit intellectual engagement without the need to train ministers within the same program. However, as evidenced by the essay cited above from George Guthrie, which deals with biblical studies in such a context, such institutions need to give serious attention to what Christian intellectual study looks on Christian presuppositions, where the Bible is not inaccessible and distant from us but God's present and active word to us.[14] Liberal arts colleges and secular universities offer two pathways for serious Christian intellectual engagement with God's word and world within the conventional academic paradigm. However, there is another pathway for this form of engagement outside of that paradigm.

D. Christian Intellectual Engagement in Church

Several parachurch organisations support research centres devoted to serious Christian research independent of academic institutions.[15] The same dangers present themselves in these endeavours as in Christian intellectual engagement within secular or confessional academic institutions, namely, the problem of research with the assumptions and methods of the secular academy rather than from a genuinely Christian basis. One way to anchor this work in the paradigm of knowledge, orthodoxy, and ministry identified above would be to intentionally locate such research in the context of the local church. Many churches already give to their denominational seminaries, as do individuals; these funds support not only the training of ministers but also the development of resources for Christian ministry and thought. If

---

[14] See Dockery and Morgan, *Christian Higher Education*; Guthrie, "The Study of Holy Scripture and the Work of Christian Higher Education."

[15] E.g. The Centre for Pastor-Theologians, The Tim Keller Institute, The Institute for Creation Research, The Discovery Institute, The Christian Psychology Institute, etc.

ministry training were moved out of the academy, some of that money would need to be given to new training contexts, such as ministry apprenticeships. However, these training alternatives would be significantly cheaper than maintaining a seminary's faculty, facilities, and staff (not to mention student fees). So, the need for Christian research and resources could be put forth as an object of investment. Instead of building centres or giving to parachurch organisations, I envision churches, groups of churches, or denominations giving to support researchers to do their research within local churches. These researchers may be ministers or lay persons. In cities with substantial research libraries, housing and cost of living support could be given to a researcher for a time, or the person could be hired as a staff member (perhaps a pastor with a specific role of research, writing, and teaching). In contexts where such libraries are unavailable, churches could invest in building digital or physical libraries or support the researcher to travel to access these resources.

Locating the work of Christian intellectual engagement in the context of the local church has, I believe, several benefits to locating it in academic institutions or parachurch organisations. In contrast with academic institutions, a researcher working in the context of the local church is free to be thoroughly Christian in their intellectual pursuits, thinking as a Christian for God's people and God's world as he has created it. In contrast with academic institutions and parachurch organisations, the local church is the context ordained by God in Scripture for Christian teaching, discerning and developing character (and, therefore, orthodoxy), and promoting God's purposes on earth. The church is thus the natural home for any genuinely Christian activity and is furnished with structures to ensure researchers are accountable in their lives and thoughts to the Word of God and the churches they are charged with serving.

E. Conclusion

I have argued in this chapter that academics or serious Christian intellectual engagement with God's word and his world has a place in Christian living and ministry. It is not a significant or even necessary component of pastoral ministry nor exclusive to ministers, yet it offers some benefit to God's churches. Given the unsustainability of bible colleges and seminaries if preparation and training for ministry are removed from their portfolio, we considered alternate contexts for performing this work. It was suggested, with some caution, that secular universities and liberal arts colleges are contexts where serious intellectual engagement can happen, though it may be challenging to do so in a genuinely Christian manner. Parachurch research centres and fellowships were also identified as potential contexts for this work, as was the local church. I argued that the local church is uniquely suited for this work despite the challenges in offering the physical resources necessary for serious research (though digital access to resources is rapidly removing even this barrier).

This leaves us in an interesting place: I have suggested thus far (and will argue in the following part of the book) that the local church is the ideal context to train ministers, and I have now suggested that the local church is also an ideal context to promote serious Christian intellectual activity. The paradox is this: the combination of academic pursuit and ministry as embodied in the academy appeared to be the source of the problems in the first place, but now we have ended with academic pursuit and ministry once again united. However, context is everything. The problem in the first case is that pastoral ministry subordinated to academic pursuits is not pastoral ministry at all: the work of pastoral ministry cannot be disassociated from the local church and the structures God has developed there, nor can pastoral ministry be developed on an epistemological and ontological foundation that prioritises academic achievement and intellect over character and the knowing God through his word.

However, the opposite is not the case: subordinating academic pursuits to ministry or locating academic pursuits in the context of the local church is not destructive to these pursuits; indeed, it may be conducive to them. The problem is that we have come to view intellectual engagement as something separated from what we do in the local church and something other than the everyday Christian experience, and we have disassociated our intellectual engagement with Scripture from the Christian's regular interaction with Scripture. We have either done this, or we have tried to make the church a miniature academic institution and have been left with anaemic, dying churches devoid of genuine knowledge and love of God and his people. Sitting under the word of God preached, engaging in relationships with other Christians, humbling ourselves in service, being forced to do more than just research, and doing our research for ends that will further God's church on earth are all things that will produce stronger, genuinely Christian intellectual activity, not hinder it.

It would be hard for biblical scholars and theologians to say what they say in the church. Telling a congregation they cannot speak truthfully about God because they do not have a PhD or understand the Bible because they do not have a university degree will get you fired very quickly. This is tacitly confessed by the very different tone taken in George Guthrie's work to help lay people read the Scriptures compared to the article he wrote on biblical studies.[16] God has given pastors and teachers so that the people of God might grow together into the full maturity of adulthood: this is the end of all Christian teaching and shepherding, and, I would argue, the entire Christian life (Eph 4:1-16). We are to seek the growth and perseverance of one another in the local church and that all our neighbours who do not yet know Jesus would be incorporated into his body and welcomed into his eternal kingdom. This is the aim of all our love for neighbours, our sacrificial service, hospitality, evangelism, and care. We are to love God and our neighbour as ourselves, meaning we will care for their physical

---

[16] Guthrie, "The Study of Holy Scripture and the Work of Christian Higher Education"; George H. Guthrie, "George H Guthrie: Helping You Read the Bible Better," George H Guthrie, July 29, 2023, https://georgehguthrie.com.

and emotional needs while not neglecting their spiritual needs (Deut 6:5; Matt 22:34-40; Luke 10:25-37). We can and must do good to everyone, especially the household of faith (Gal 6:10). If we do not pray for and act for the salvation of those we serve, our service is less than the love we are called to. The local church is the ideal place to see these things accomplished.

—PART 3—
TOWARDS A NEW STRUCTURE

10

MOVING FROM WHAT TO HOW: WHAT DOES IT MEAN TO TRAIN MINISTERS OF THE GOSPEL?

> This is why I left you in Crete, so that you might put what remained into order, and appoint elders in every town as I directed you— if anyone is above reproach, the husband of one wife, and his children are believers and not open to the charge of debauchery or insubordination. For an overseer, as God's steward, must be above reproach. He must not be arrogant or quick-tempered or a drunkard or violent or greedy for gain, but hospitable, a lover of good, self-controlled, upright, holy, and disciplined. He must hold firm to the trustworthy word as taught, so that he may be able to give instruction in sound doctrine and also to rebuke those who contradict it. – Titus 1:5-9 (ESV)

In the introduction to this book, I argued that our current system for training pastors is failing and, as a result, our churches and pastors are suffering. I suggested that a flawed view of ministry and theology undergirds our current model of pastoral training and was responsible for many aspects of the present crisis.

In Part 1, we traced the development and expression of this view of pastoral ministry and theology through the Early Church, Reformation, and 20th-21st century Evangelicalism. We concluded by analysing five presuppositions shaping this view of ministry and theology. These presuppositions were 1) Orthodoxy defined as adherence to statements of theological beliefs developed from reflection upon the content of Scripture, 2) the knowledge of God (or at least its highest form) defined as universal and necessary truth, 3) pastoral ministry identified with teaching, 4) the Bible understood as the source and principle of theology, and 5) the academy given a central place within the Church.

In Part 2, we then critiqued each of these presuppositions from the Bible and biblical reflection, offering five basic biblical presuppositions with some further reflection upon these presuppositions. These presuppositions were 1) Orthodoxy (understood as the measure of who is in and out of God's people) is a combination of right belief and right character, yet right character is the primary measure of orthodoxy because character reveals belief, but the profession of right belief is not an adequate measure of right character. 2) The knowledge of God is primarily tacit or implicit person-knowledge (on analogy with our knowledge of human persons), and explicit discussion of God's actions and attributes relies on God's self-revelation in history for their meaning (therefore, they defy universalising definition). 3) Pastoral ministry is primarily people work, "shepherding," and teaching extends this pastoral care into the public sphere. This often looks like a concrete application of the Scriptures to people's lives and thinking. 4) The Bible is a covenant document that God has given to legislate his people under the New Covenant, and as such, it is clear and sufficient to accomplish this purpose. 5) There is some benefit to serious Christian intellectual engagement with God's word and world; the local church is the ideal but not exclusive context for this engagement.

The first set of presuppositions undergirds the academic model of pastoral training used in our seminaries and bible colleges; we now must ask what form of pastoral training best suits the alternate presuppositions concerning ministry and theology we have identified in Scripture. This is what we will do here in Part 3. I will try to elucidate a model or structure for pastoral training through reflection on the presuppositions identified in Part 2 and the explicit teachings of Scripture. Our discussion in Part 2 allows us to begin by taking a step back and asking, given the nature of pastoral ministry, what are we trying to achieve in "pastoral training"? If we know our goal, we can determine the best way to achieve that goal. In this chapter, I argue that the New Testament does not prescribe a pastoral training plan because it focuses on discerning the qualifications for and call to ministry and then ordination. The New Testament presupposes that the competency and qualifications for ministry occur naturally in the Christian life and focuses on identifying and installing persons with these qualities.

I argued in Chapter 7.B.ii that the primary qualifications for pastoral ministry are character and mature knowledge. A pastoral candidate is, therefore, someone qualified in character, called to ministry, and who demonstrates maturity in knowledge and the ability to communicate it. I will argue in this chapter that the Bible does not require that these qualities be developed further before ordination but does model training in the competencies required for ministry. I will argue that two options for pastoral training result from the qualifications the Bible gives for ministry. Because the subjective desire for ministry or the 'call' to ministry is critical to the training of pastors in addition to their demonstrated qualifications, we will discuss calling alongside training and its relationship to ordination.

I will then argue that pastors are primarily charged with identifying, ordaining, and training pastors. The following two chapters will further explore how we may identify and train in godliness and teaching.

A. Calling, Ordination, Training

The contemporary model of pastoral ministry makes training a prerequisite for ordination and the practice of ministry; often theological education—if not a bachelor's or master's degree, or even a doctorate—is required to be ordained (see the Introduction above). The qualifications for pastoral ministry are seen to be something different than the qualities developed during the regular Christian life: something needs to be added to qualify a person for ministry. However, this is not the pattern we discover in Scripture.

Instead, the qualifications we identified above are precisely those of a mature Christian. In theory, any mature Christian may qualify for pastoral ministry. However, entering ministry does not happen automatically; a qualified person must be ordained (they must receive an external commission) and, prior to this, choose to pursue pastoral ministry. The pursuit of pastoral ministry is often described as receiving a 'call' from God, though Paul describes it as an "aspiration" (1 Timothy 3:1).[1] Once someone is recognised as qualified and aspires to be a pastor, the Bible (I will argue) does not require further training to enter the pastorate but does envision a lifelong development of ministry competencies.

Therefore, pastoral training is not necessary for ordination, nor does it have an end. Instead, pastoral training describes a life-long process of growing in character and competency within pastoral service; this context is the primary difference between pastoral training and regular discipleship. Without an explicit mandate from God, we may envision two possible scenarios for pastoral training. First, candidates who qualify for ministry may receive on-the-job training; they would be identified, ordained, and then trained. Second, qualified candidates may receive training and then be ordained. In this case,

---

[1] In *The Path to Being a Pastor*, Bobby Jamieson argues that the language of a subjective 'call' should be replaced with 'aspiration.' This is more appropriate to the language of 1 Timothy 3:1 and the posture of humility God calls for his people. Bobby Jamieson, *The Path to Being a Pastor* (Wheaton: Crossway, 2021), chap. 1.

someone may express their desire for ministry but not yet demonstrate character and competency. In this scenario, a pastor may give them a red light or offer to train them further to develop character and competency. To explore training further, we will consider calling, the place of ordination, and then the goal and context of training.

i. Calling

In one sense, being called as a minister is an entirely objective act of God before the creation of the world to identify, equip, and raise up qualified persons to enter ordained ministry.[2] God told Jeremiah that he was appointed a prophet before he was even born (Jer 1:5), and Paul likewise identifies his apostleship as coming from God's action (Rom 1:1; 2 Cor 1:1; Gal 1:1). However, God's prior choice of ministers to serve him is realised in history through the internal aspiration for or acceptance of ministry and the external identification and ordination of a person for ministry. In the Gospels, the call to apostleship came from Jesus: the apostles were called to their ministry by the Saviour and entered that call by following him—long before they understood the cost of following him (John 1:35-51). Paul's call to apostleship similarly began with a word from God (Acts 9:1-19).[3] Similarly, Paul commanded Titus to appoint elders in every town of

---

[2] What follows is applicable in many ways to the role of *deacon* as it is for *eldership*, but we are primarily concerned with eldership in this book.

[3] Historically, the language of 'call' expresses something like a divine invitation which is then accepted. However, more recent studies have observed that the language of 'calling' in Romans and elsewhere is rather "[Somone] is called to be something." God has declared Paul to be an apostle, and this calling was realised through the events by which God established him in that role. Similarly, God, through the Holy Spirit, appoints and equips men and women for the work of ministry, which is realised in time through the subjective aspiration for ministry, the development of fitting character, and through ordination. See Vivian W. Cheung, "Called 'My People' by God's Sovereign Grace: A Study of the Calling Motif in Romans" (PhD Thesis, Sydney, NSW, Moore Theological College, 2023).

Crete, identifying them based on their qualifications for ministry (Titus 1:5-9). Here, Titus identified and appointed elders; he wasn't instructed to invite those who desired ministry.

However, Paul does commend the desire to enter pastoral ministry, "if anyone aspires to the office of overseer, he desires a noble task" (1 Tim 3:1, ESV). So, there may be an internal desire to pursue ministry, though to actually enter ministry, the candidate must be qualified (1 Tim 3:2-7). This internal aspect of calling is echoed in 1 Peter 5:2, where Peter indicates that elders must shepherd willingly and not be forced into the role. In 1 Corinthians 16:15, we are told of the household of Stephanas, who "charged themselves with the service of the saints" (my translation; εἰς διακονίαν τοῖς ἁγίοις ἔταξαν ἑαυτούς, *eis diakonian tois hagiois etaxan eautous*). Though τάσσω (*tasso*) here is often translated as "devoted" (e.g. ESV, NASB, NET, NIV), the word usually means to arrange something or appoint someone or something.[4] Therefore, Stephanas and some in his household had put themselves forward for a ministry position; we know a ministry position is intended because Paul charges the Corinthians to "submit to such people." Perhaps Stephanas put himself forward as a deacon, for Paul speaks of "service" to the saints and speaks of "every fellow worker and laborer" (ESV; παντὶ τῷ συνεργοῦντι καὶ κοπιῶντι, *panti to sunergounti kai kopionti*), words associated with physical labour (e.g. Eph 4:28, 2 Tim 2:6; cf. Acts 6:1-6). Whatever the exact role, Stephanas and members of his household put themselves forward for the role of service, a role with some authority; this does not imply that their self-appointment was sufficient for them to receive authority, for the pattern across Scripture is always that authority is given from God through his appointed agents. However, the wording used by Paul suggests that the critical factor in receiving a serving role in the church was their act of putting themselves forward. They had an internal call

---

[4] See Danker, *BDAG*, s.v. τάσσω.

first, apparently.

Calling or aspiration is not a sufficient condition to enter pastoral ministry, but it would appear to be a necessary one; a person, no matter their qualifications, must first desire or feel the need to pursue ministry and be ready to suffer the burden of the role before being ordained or receiving training. The internal call, whether the conviction from God as Jeremiah felt (Jer 20:9) or the aspiration of which Paul speaks (1 Tim 3:1), needs to be assessed by those with the authority to ordain the person to ministry, which I have argued elsewhere is local church pastors (see below).[5] Desiring pastoral ministry, or even a feeling of compulsion towards ministry, is insufficient to qualify someone; this desire needs to be recognised and evaluated by God's people. At this point, the Bible does not give us precise instructions on how to proceed, nor do our conclusions about the nature of ministry require a specific pathway; instead, several options could be pursued. In contemporary practice, we move directly to training in preparation for ordination, but the Bible actually suggests that it may be appropriate to move first to ordination and then training. Because this is the more counterintuitive option, we will consider this first and then discuss what exactly pastoral training looks like on the foundation we have laid.

ii. Ordination

Two issues are involved in the claim that it may be appropriate to ordain first and then train: 1) the nature of ordination and 2) the relationship between qualification for ministry and ordination. First, regarding ordination, I am presuming that God requires ministers to be ordained and that the people with the authority to do this are pastors (to be specific, pastors lead congregations to appoint their leaders). In my book *The Being of Churches*, I argue that the power for identifying and commissioning leaders is shared by the laity and

[5] Rutherford, *The Being of Churches*, chap. 3.

officers of a church: the laity put forth and attest to the character of prospective ministers by electing them, although the process of electing leaders is open to construal (III.A.2.a), and the officers have the power from Christ to ordain new officers (III.A.3.b). Ordination is the consummation of the installation of a new officer, whereby leaders invest "visible and spiritual authority and power" in the new officer before the congregation. Through ordination, the "authority that the congregation perceives to reside in the elder is transferred to the new leader," and "the Spirit fills the leader with ministerial authority from Christ for the work they have been entrusted, along with the power to see it accomplished" (Num 8:9-14; 27:18-23; Duet 34:9; Acts 6:6; 8:17; 9:17; 19:6; 1 Tim 4:14, 5:22; 2 Tim 1:6; cf. Matt 9:18; 19:13, 15; Mark 5:23; 6:5; 7:32; 8:23; Luke 4:40; 13:13; Acts 8:17; 9:12, 17; 19:6; 28:8).[6]

Second, regarding qualification and ordination, regular congregation members will possess the qualifications described in the New Testament; some may be ordained based on these qualifications before being trained in the specifics of pastoral ministry. Looking over the list of qualifications in 1 Timothy 3 and Titus 1, nothing Paul requires is beyond what God asks of any Christian, except perhaps "being able to teach." However, as we have considered, "able teach" does not identify a specific skill set but sufficient maturity in Christian knowledge to teach others; it is merely quantitatively, not qualitatively, different from the knowledge and ability characterising the average Christian. For example, in Hebrews, the author suggests that if the congregation had grown in their faith rather than hesitating and being slow to hear, by now, they "ought to be teachers" (Heb 5:12); as it is, they still need basic instructions (5:12-14). Contrary to contemporary practice, there is no special qualification to begin pastoral ministry other than characteristics shared by many in a healthy congregation and public institution in a role through ordination. Perhaps this is

[6] Rutherford, *The Being of Churches*, 100–101.

because the primary difference between pastors and regular congregation members is the authority by which they perform their duties, or perhaps it is assumed that the unique skills and practices performed by a pastor can be learned on the job; either way, ordination often precedes training for the role of pastor.[7]

For instance, Paul instructs Titus to appoint elders in every town, and then he provides qualifications for who may be appointed. Paul does not identify a process of preparation but appears to assume that such persons will be found in the congregation and that Titus should proceed to appoint them (Titus 1:5-9). Similarly, Paul and Barnabas are said to have appointed elders in every church in a specific region, without any mention of training them (nor does it appear they had the time to train them) (Acts 14:23). In 1 Timothy 3, Paul does speak of the need for prospective candidates (in this case, for the diaconate) to be tested (δοκιμαζέσθωσαν, *dokimazesthosan*), but this requires the demonstration of qualifications not of training for the role. In Acts 6, seven qualified men were chosen for works of service and ordained, after which they began their work (Acts 6:1-7). In Jesus's ministry, he first called the apostles to follow him and trained them on the job, gradually giving them more and more authority (and this even before the pouring out of the Holy Spirit, which all of God's people now have).

There is no indication of an identification-train-ordain model in the New Testament. Joshua is perhaps an Old Testament example of such a model. Joshua served Moses for a long time and learned before he was granted some of Moses' authority to help lead the congregation, and then he finally was installed as the primary leader of God's people (Exod 24:13; Num 27:18; Deut 1:38; Deut 31:3-7; Josh 1:1-9). However, before Numbers 27:18, Joshua is described as a servant to

[7] On the authority of church officers, see Rutherford, *The Being of Churches*, chap. 3.

Moses and is not singled out for specific attention such that we would presume he was being prepared to take over for Moses. Nevertheless, in the New Testament, we do not find an identification-train-ordain model but an identification-ordain-train model.

If ordination follows identification, then any training received will occur in the context of active ministry. We can support this by the pastoral epistles, where Paul instructs Timothy and Titus on critical aspects of their ministry *while they are already performing this ministry*. Much of our understanding of God's will for pastors and the churches they lead is found in Paul's instructions given to those already leading churches. They evidently needed to grow and learn about this role, but they did so while performing it. Similarly, Paul exhorts elders about their role in Acts (Acts 20:17-37). Paul was called by the Lord on the road to Damascus (Acts 9:1-6) and received the Holy Spirit through Ananias (9:17-19). He then began his Gospel ministry, either in Damascus immediately after his encounter (Acts 9:19-22) or in Arabia and then back in Damascus (Gal 1:17; Acts 9:19-22).[8] If it is correct that some of the time Paul spent in Arabia was in meditation and reflection, as is often claimed (perhaps at Mount Sinai, cf. Gal 4:24-25), it remains the case that he did not receive any teaching or training from people before he began his ministry (Gal 1:11-24, cf. 1 Cor 15:3-11). This has important implications for the timing of pastoral training, the goal of pastoral training, and the context of pastoral training.

iii. Training

God does not command us to train pastors after they are ordained, though this appears to be a regular pattern in Scripture, nor does he forbid us from training pastoral candidates prior to ordination, so we have significant flexibility to identify, ordain, and train candidates for ministry. We should expect that training will be needed, as Jesus trained

[8] Cf. Douglas J. Moo, *Galatians*, Baker Exegetical Commentary on the New Testament (Grand Rapids: Baker Academic, 2013), 106–7.

the Apostles and Paul trained Timothy and Titus (and surely other elders as well), but training is not a prerequisite for entering Christian ministry. Therefore, the timing of training permitted by Scripture has significant implications for the goal of pastoral training.

a. The Goal of Pastoral Training

If training may follow ordination, then we do not train pastors so that they are eligible for ordination, nor do we train them so they are able to do the work of ministry. Instead, I propose we train ministers or ministry candidates (as we ourselves continue to be trained) so they are able to perform their work in a manner pleasing to God, grow in holiness, remain above reproach, and finish the race well. That is, training is about excellence and perseverance added to the basic competency that all Christians ought to have. Thus, in a significant sense, ministry training is the continuation of regular church discipleship in the context of pastoral ministry. However, this context requires some changes.

In Ephesians, Paul tells us that God has given various gifted or ordained people to the church "to equip the saints for the work of ministry" with the goal of a fully mature body of Christ on earth (Eph 4:11-16). All the saints are to be equipped for the work of ministry or service (ἔργον διακονίας, *ergon diakonias*) with this end, so a mature Christian ought to already be equipped to serve the body towards maturity. The difference is that every saint is not expected to equip others (though we have numerous examples of them doing so, e.g. 1 Cor 16:12), but pastor-teachers are expected to do so. Yet, in most cases, being able to equip others for the "work of ministry" does not require an entirely different skill set but merely to excel at this work, as a good electrician can model this work to others without training to be a teacher. God has given us the Scriptures so that we may be entirely equipped for "every good work," that is, so that all we do may be pleasing to God (2 Tim 3:16-17); to achieve this end, God has given us teachers and shepherds. Ministers are not free from the need to be shepherded towards this end. So, ministry training seeks to realise the multifaceted function of Scripture towards this end in the minister's life.

Many things remain the same for ministers as in regular discipleship: ministers ought to continue to be accountable to others, put their sin to death, and grow in righteousness and works of service, yet as ordained ministers, they face additional threats and bear new responsibilities that require special attention. James warns teachers of the added responsibility they bear as teachers (3:1), and Paul instructs the Ephesian elders to "pay careful attention to yourselves" (Acts 20:28, ESV) and Timothy to "keep a close watch on yourself and on the teaching" (1 Tim 4:16, ESV). This is essential for the salvation of the teacher and their hearers (1 Tim 4:16). Because Christ has given them great power, they will face the temptation to be domineering or lead others astray for their own gain (1 Tim 3:8; Titus 1:7; 1 Pet 5:2-3). The easy path for a minister is to "itch" the ears of their congregations, so a minister must be prepared to "endure suffering" and be "sober-minded" in fulfilling their ministry, not falling to the temptation of the easy route (2 Tim 4:1-5, ESV). For all Christians, following Christ requires perseverance (Rev 1:9; 2:7, 11, 17, 26; 3:5, 12. 21; 13:13, 14:12), and it is all too easy "[suffer] shipwreck with regard to the faith" (1 Tim 1:19-20, NIV). This danger is more severe for ministers because in doing so, they stand also to destroy those who imitate them (1 Cor 4:16, 11:11; 1 Tim 4:16).

The goals and tools for pastoral training are not utterly dissimilar to those of regular discipleship, yet the need for continued training is heightened by the added adversity facing a Gospel minister. Gospel ministers need help and care to persevere in their ministry, which is a critical goal of pastoral training. In addition to growing in holiness and endurance so the minister may honour God throughout their life, the minister must also grow in the abilities to perform the "work of ministry" and equip others to perform that work. I propose that we could define **regular discipleship** as *training the saints in righteousness and* *equipping them for the works of service in the context of the local church so that they would endure to receive a crown of glory on the final day and hear "well done good and faithful servant," having stewarded well the gifts God has given them for the building up of his body* (Matt 25:14-30, 31-40; 28:18-20; Eph 4:11-16; Gal 6:9-10; Rev 1:9; 2:7, 11, 17, 26; 3:5, 12. 21; 13:13, 14:12). We may then define **pastoral training** as *training Gospel ministers (or potential ministers) in righteousness and equipping them for works of service and to teach others so that they would endure to receive a crown of glory on the final day and hear "well done good and faithful servant," having stewarded well the gifts God has given them for the building up of his body.* The critical difference between these definitions is the expectation that a minister will not only be righteous and able to do works of service but also to disciple and equip others, as well as the cost of failing to do this training well. The cost of failing to train ministers in this way is more significant than for a non-ordained Christian because the failure of a leader has the potential to cause far more damage, wrecking not only the leader's faith but also the faith of those who listen to them (Acts 20:28; 1 Tim 4:16). So Paul instructs Timothy, "Do not be hasty in the laying on of hands, and do not share in the sins of others" (1 Tim 5:22, NIV). If this is the goal (or, at least, a biblically defensible goal) for pastoral training, then significant implications follow for the context of pastoral training, implications already present in our discussion of the timing of pastoral training.

b. The Context of Pastoral Training

As seen above, the primary examples we are given in Scripture for pastoral training are examples where training *follows* ordination; this is highly illuminating for our thinking about pastoral training. If training occurs in the context of ordained ministry, two things follow: first, the ideal context for pastoral training is in the local church; second, churches are expected to have or will regularly have a multiplicity of leaders, for there are those who are being trained and those who are training. A church will have relatively inexperienced and relatively experienced leaders. It is commonly held (and I have argued this in *The*

Being of Churches) that ordination has reference to a specific church: a minister is not ordained as a minister in general but as a minister for a specific group. A shepherd without a sheep is no shepherd at all. So, if training follows ordination, then training will happen in the context of a minister's service to the church he pastors. To be trained in this context will require a pastor or pastors farther along the path who can train that minister. Churches that do this will naturally have many elders or pastors. A plurality of elders offers significant advantages given the goal of pastoral training: in a context of a plurality (if there is not just a trainee and trainer but a group of elders and one or more trainees), pastors are less likely to develop a platform of inscrutable authority where they are treated with unrivalled authority in the local church and stand, in effect, above accountability.[9] From the goal of pastoral training identified above, sharing as it does much continuity with regular discipleship, it is also apparent that the local church is the ideal context for pastoral training.

Within the current model of pastoral training, it may make sense for academics to train pastors in many ways, for part of the pastoral task requires extensive knowledge and skills found pre-eminently in the academy. However, in our argument thus far, we have seen that pastoral ministry involves skills and knowledge formed within the course of regular Christian discipleship in the local church. Though pastors are not the only ones who will disciple believers in the local church, they have the unique roles of directing that discipleship, ensuring its quality, and equipping those under their authority to do this work. Given the continuity of discipleship and pastoral training and the significance of discipleship in the pastor's role, it seems natural and ideal for pastors to be the ones training pastors, and the local church appears to be the primary context for doing so. Thus, given the possible timing of training after ordination and the goal of pastoral training as something similar to regular local church discipleship, the

[9] See Rutherford, *The Being of Churches*.

local church is the ideal context for pastoral training. If it remains unclear that pastors are ideally situated to perform pastoral training, we will consider this point at greater length. As intuitive as this seems to some of us, this is not the current pattern of pastoral training in most contexts, so we need to belabour the point.

B. Pastors Are to Train Pastors

Our current pastoral training models presuppose that scholars and academics are those God entrusted with training the next generation of Gospel teachers and church leaders. To be sure, there are exceptions, but those with academic qualifications and in academic positions stand out as the primary trainers for our pastors. I have thus far argued that the nature of pastoral ministry, the timing for pastoral training in the Bible, and the goal of pastoral training all point to pastors as those entrusted by God with training the next generation of pastors. To this, we can add the Bible's witness to this matter and some considerations when we depart from the pastors-training-pastors model.

i. The Biblical Charge

The model of pastoral training in the book of Acts, if we can infer that training occurred, is church planting led by the apostles. However, as specially commissioned disciples who have witnessed the risen Christ and are charged with establishing his church, the apostles are not presented as having an enduring role. Along with the Old Testament prophets, the apostles laid a foundation (Eph 2:20). From Paul's ministry, it becomes clear that the apostles, as itinerant and global Church leaders, planted local congregations for which they trained and commissioned leaders (Acts 14:23). These leaders (elders or overseers) were then charged with raising up leaders in their communities. We see this charge in several places, particularly in the Pastoral Epistles (1 Timothy – Titus).

In 1 Timothy, we find a detailed account of the qualities that characterise an elder or overseer in the local church (1 Tim 3:1-7). As this letter is directed to Timothy, who functions more like an elder than an apostle (if he is not an elder himself), and this description is given in the context of considering those who would "aspire" to "the office of overseer" (1 Tim 3:1, ESV), it would seem that this was given so that Timothy and his fellow elders could identify and train future leaders. That Paul intends Timothy to do just this is seen in later chapters. After telling Timothy that an elder/overseer is worthy of a wage and outlining the principle of two or three witnesses in the context of a charge against an elder (1 Tim 5:17-21), Paul then says, "Do not be hasty in the laying on of hands" (5:22). "Laying on of hands" refers to the commissioning of future leaders, as is clear from the context. The passage moves from the value of an elder's role to the care in treating an accusation and then concludes with a warning: Be careful, therefore, when you lay on hands, lest you do so carelessly and are implicated in the devastation of a church leader's sin (a reality all too familiar for us today). We see the association of "laying on of hands" and the appointment or commission of leaders in several passages, confirming this interpretation (Acts 6:6; 13:3; 1 Tim 4:14; 2 Tim 1:6). Thus, Paul desires Timothy and his fellow elders to commission new leaders.

In 2 Timothy 2:2, this is made more explicit: Timothy is to "entrust to faithful men" what he received from Paul, men "who will be able to teach others also." This dual requirement of faithfulness and the ability to teach echoes Paul's requirements for an elder in 1 Timothy 3:1-7 and Titus 1:6-9 (cf. 2 Tim 2:22-26; 1 Pet 5:1-5). When we turn to Titus, we find the same thing. Indeed, Paul left Titus in Crete both to put things in order and to "appoint elders in every town as I directed you" (Titus 1:5). Titus functions as an elder (Titus 2:1, 7, 15), but his charge is more extensive than Timothy's; he is given the task to appoint elders throughout the island of Crete. Nevertheless, the pattern is still local elders appointing local elders. The instructions for the sort of person Titus is to appoint in Titus 1:6-9 echo the list Paul gave Timothy in 1

Timothy 3:1-7. Thus, the primary training model in Scripture involves those in authority over local churches, whether as apostles or elders, identifying and raising up the next generation of church leaders. This model is frequently overturned in contemporary practice, so it is worth asking what will happen when we overturn this elders-appointing-elders system.

ii. What We May Lose When We Abandon Such an Approach

Perhaps the most significant loss is the accountability built into this system. On the one hand, because elders in a local area appoint elders in a local area, they are in the ideal place to discern the character necessary for an aspiring elder. On the other hand, because they are responsible for identifying, training, and working with those they train, elders are responsible for failures and must proceed with the utmost care—lest, through the hasty laying on of hands, they get caught up in the sins of others (1 Tim 5:22). When this training is outsourced to other elders or perhaps non-elders, the organic relationship between those being trained and the trainer is broken; no longer is the trainer responsible from start to finish. I think it is self-evident that long-term relationships are necessary to identify someone's character and that the greatest spiritual development happens in the context of such relationships; the model for which Paul calls implies exactly these relationships (see Chapters 3 and 7 above). When training is outsourced, these essential relationships are broken.

In addition, this model of leaders training leaders shifts the implicit focus of our resources and strategy. If training is to be performed by local leaders in local churches, the resources that would otherwise go towards supporting independent faculty and infrastructure will be directed to the local church. Local churches will need to have sufficient resources to do this training, but there will not be as many parachurch organisations vying for these resources.

iii. The Impact on Strategy

Turning to strategy, our ministry recruitment strategy, our understanding of the trajectory of training, and our understanding of church growth will change based on our view of ministerial training. Currently, we give a limited amount of training to those in our spheres of influence before sending them off to college. During their college education, a future minister usually gets a student position at multiple churches before being hired for an assistant role. Some may then pursue a senior minister position (this reflects the context here in Sydney but has clear parallels elsewhere). For recruitment, the local church does not necessarily play a key role; parachurch ministries, such as college outreach, are generally more effective. The trajectory involves identifying someone who is interested and has the potential to grow into a leader, then sending them to a college; after graduation, finding a position often looks like any other job.

Imagine if our training model followed what we identified in the Bible. Because training depends on each local church's capacities, recruitment must be a lot more focused. It must first be asked if anyone in the congregation should be trained for church leadership. If the answer is no, a church can ask how it can better build disciples so that some may be fit for ministry and ask, perhaps, if they are selling the desirability of such a position well enough (1 Tim 3:1). They may also work together with other local churches: perhaps a neighbouring congregation has an abundance of candidates but not enough training capacity. If Gospel ministry depends on healthy leaders being available, and it is the job of local churches to train them, then each church must actively seek to do so. They cannot wait for an appropriate candidate.

Pastors, this is part of your job. Models of ministry where most responsibilities are divided between lay leaders and a senior minister may struggle to train leaders in addition to the regular duties of church life, but this is part of a minister's job description. It is much more tenable on a plurality-of-elders model.

Nevertheless, having an in-house training program will change the nature of a minister's trajectory. Especially on a plurality-of-elders model, competent, trained men will often need to step into a leadership position within that specific local church. Even in an episcopalian or single-leader model, each leader would be wise to plan their succession; having someone trained under their leadership offers an easy pathway to succession. On a multi-service or site church model, there will be a continual need for campus/service pastors as a church grows, which a training program may provide.[10] On a church planting model (where a church sends out church plants regularly as they grow), there will be a continual need for trained elders to lead a new church, which a training program can provide. In each of these contexts, a training program based in the local church means that a new elder in each situation will already be familiar to and have built a relationship with their future congregation. It is conceivable that a church may train more leaders than their eldership, church planting, or campuses require, making it necessary to send trained leaders out. The options on this front are many, such as international missions or serving in a local church that needs leadership.

The possibilities for such a program are more than I can outline here, but the dynamic differs considerably from the contemporary model. The emphasis is continually local and, in many cases, relational. If we flip this around, we can see what we lose when we outsource pastoral training. No longer are future ministers for a congregation trained there; those who go away for college rarely return. Elders often must start from scratch building relationships with their flock, which affects the sensitivity and effectiveness of all aspects of ministry. Leaders are usually trained in cultural and intellectual contexts significantly different from where they will eventually serve. We will end here, but numerous practical benefits result from this model of pastors training pastors in the local church, even apart from the

---

[10] I personally find this model unsatisfactory, as I argue in *The Being of Churches*.

significant biblical warrant for this model.

C. Conclusion

In this chapter, we have covered several issues concerning training Gospel ministers. Significant themes from our discussion are the pattern of ordination followed by training, the continuity of regular discipleship and pastoral training, the importance of the local church for such training, and the role of pastors in training pastors. These themes offer exciting directions for training pastors but also highlight the distance between our current models of pastoral training and the patterns God has seen fit to give us in Scripture. Notably, ordination often precedes training, for this indicates that regular church discipleship ought to mature Christians to the point where they are ready for pastoral ministry. The close connection between discipleship and pastoral ministry suggests that our problems with pastoral ministry are not merely problems with ministry and ministry training but also problems with *discipleship*.

On the one hand, we can see how we have softened those aspects of pastoral ministry that the Bible identifies as most difficult, namely, being relational and the call to be holy, and made aspects of pastoral ministry that are not even considered in the Bible difficult, such as academic competency and intelligence. On the other hand, when we focus on the competencies the Bible does give for pastoral ministry, we will probably still struggle to identify persons in our congregation who are fit for ministry. This indicates an underlying problem with our discipleship, for God in Scripture indicates in numerous places that Christians discipled well can be competent for ministry.

To better train pastors, we must be better at making disciples. The following two chapters will consider how we can do both of these better by considering what is involved in the primary competencies for ministry, godliness and the ability to teach. We will see that both of these are rooted in solid discipleship, for a disciple of Christ will know him and his word, obey him, have the knowledge that is the basis for teaching, and have corresponding godliness. In each chapter, we will discuss to a greater extent than we have thus far what godliness and teaching are, how we can identify these qualities in people, and how we can help develop these qualities.

11

HOW DO WE IDENTIFY AND TRAIN IN GODLINESS?

> Let the word of Christ dwell in you richly, teaching and admonishing one another in all wisdom, singing psalms and hymns and spiritual songs, with thankfulness in your hearts to God. And whatever you do, in word or deed, do everything in the name of the Lord Jesus, giving thanks to God the Father through him. – Colossians 3:16-17 (ESV)

Our churches lack godly leaders because of a more general failure of discipleship; this is the conclusion we drew at the end of the last chapter. If there is firm continuity between regular discipleship and pastoral training, and if regular discipleship ought to produce people competent for Christian ministry, then a lack of qualified people desiring the role indicates a failure of the discipleship. Now, we must acknowledge that part of the failure is what we traced in the first part of the book, namely, unbiblical (and unrealistic) expectations concerning the nature of pastoral ministry and its qualifications. However, once we have replaced this model with one that focuses on character or godliness and the ability to teach, we still struggle to identify suitable candidates. To be sure, part of this struggle is our failure to commend the value and worth of pursuing ministry, but it is also a failure to develop mature Christians in our congregations. It is a failure to disciple men and women so that they know the Bible thoroughly, love God, and pursue him with all their heart, living a life that models his character in the love of God and their neighbours. If we want to train pastors, we must first make disciples of our congregations; this is what God has called us to do. If we cannot do this well (Matt 28:16-20; Eph 4:7-16), how will we train pastors to do so? In this chapter and the following chapter, we will consider how we can make disciples of Christ and, in that context, identify and train some of these disciples to be Gospel ministers. In this chapter, we will consider character or godliness; in the next chapter, we will consider the ability to teach. Before we do this, we must acknowledge the challenges awaiting us.

God in Scripture does not give us a method we can apply in every circumstance to produce mature Christians. When we survey the New Testament, we find that helping men and women grow in godliness and knowledge is difficult and often unrewarding. In Jesus's ministry, he was confronted by stubbornness and confusion by his disciples—and one of the Twelve betrayed him. Even among those closest to Jesus, a wolf was found. The apostles were sometimes divided among themselves (Acts 15:36-41; Gal 2:11-14). Paul warned the Ephesians elders to whom he ministered of wolves arising among them (Acts 20:29-31). Peter, in his 2nd Epistle, and Jude wrote against false teachers who have infiltrated the churches. The Corinthian church entertained a distorted spirituality and pride, along with immoral behaviour (e.g. 1 Cor 5:1-13), and the churches to whom John wrote may have denied a physical incarnation (1 John 1:1-10; 2:18-27; 4:1- 6). The Romans were divided along Jew-Gentile lines, and the six of the seven churches to whom Jesus writes in Revelation had wavered to different degrees in their faith and obedience to Christ (Revelation 1-3). No church community in the 1st century was perfect, so we should not expect ours to be.

However, God calls ministers of his Gospel to perform the difficult work of leading God's flock into "mature adulthood" (Eph 4:13). We trust that God will produce fruit from our labours, as clumsy as our efforts may sometimes be. God has built his church through the work of imperfect people across the ages, so we engage in the work of discipleship and training pastors with the assurance that God will make disciples, raise up pastors, and preserve his church until the final day.

A. What is Godliness?

I speak of 'godliness' in this chapter because 'character' may be used for a person's general disposition—good or bad. Thus, by 'godliness,' I intend *right* character. Godliness is Christian maturity; it is being like Jesus in word, thought, and deed. In Scripture, we find godliness as an attitude, state, and pattern of activity. There is an attitude, state, and pattern of activity characteristic of those who have been filled with the Holy Spirit and are identified with Christ. To some degree, this threefold godliness is present even in a new believer and will be perfected in the resurrection of life when we are glorified and made to partake of the divine nature (2 Pet 1:4).

i. Godliness as an Attitude

As an attitude, godliness is *repentant*. A follower of Christ will hate their sin and progressively renounce it in word and deed. Jesus proclaimed a message of repentance (Mark 1:15), and John reiterates this as an essential criterion of genuine faith: "Everyone who abides in [Jesus] does not sin; every sinner neither sees him nor knows him." John draws a strong antithesis, but he acknowledged already that genuine Christians still sin (1:10-2:2). His point is clear enough: unbelievers and false teachers are characterised by sin, whereas Christians are characterised by their obedience to Christ and pursuit of Christ, of putting off sin and obeying Christ's commands (2:1-6). There is a godly grief over sin that produces repentance, and this leads to salvation (2 Cor 7:9-10); there is a worldly grief over sin that does not renounce that sin and turn from it, instead merely lamenting its consequences (Heb 12:17; 2 Cor 7:10). Worldly grief leads to death (2 Cor 7:10).

ii. Godliness as a State

As a state, godliness is characterised by death to sin and the Devil and union with Christ (Rom 6:1-14; Gal 2:20; 6:14; Eph 2:1-10). This union is not visibly perceived, but it is a work of the Spirit producing genuine faith in our hearts (John 3:1-15). Our faith declares this union to be true of us; this invisible union is visibly re-enacted and demonstrated through baptism (e.g. Rom 6:1-14).[1] This is the stable core of godliness, the root and foundation of repentance and right living; to be godly requires a death to sin and union with Christ, and true godliness demonstrates this to be the case. On this basis, Christians who fall into grave sin may still be reckoned "saints," God's holy people (e.g. 1 Cor 1:1-3).

iii. Godliness as a Pattern of Activity

As a pattern of activity, godliness is manifest in love for God and love for one's neighbours. Jesus confirms the judgment of the Jewish teacher that these are the most important commandments in Scripture (Mark 12:30-31), and the rest of Scripture unpacks these commands in numerous dimensions.

a. Love for God

Love for God requires complete devotion to God (Deut 6:4-5), including the refusal to acknowledge that anything or anyone is like God or shares his power and rule (Exod 20:2), a refusal to attribute worship or characteristics of God to created things or worship God in an unauthorised way (Exod 20:4-6; Rom 1:18-32),[2] honouring God in word and commitments (Exod 20:7), and honouring God through obedience to his commands, prioritising his ways, and remembering his faithfulness (Exod 20:8-11). In the New Testament, love for God

---

[1] See Rutherford, *The Being of Churches.*

[2] On "unauthorised," see the introduction of ibid.

is primarily manifest as entire devotion to Jesus Christ demonstrated in following him and obeying his commands (Matt 28:18-20; Luke 18:18-23). Love for Christ is manifest in radical commitment to his church as it seeks to expand his kingdom on earth (e.g. Matt 6:33, 12:46-50; Mark 10:28-31; John 15:1-17; 1 John 2:7-11; Eph 1:22-23; 4:11-16, 25-32; Gal 6:10).[3] There is, therefore, no firm distinction between the love for God and the love for neighbour, for refusing to love ones neighbour is failure to love God (e.g. Gen 9:5-6), especially in the case of the church, which is Christ's body and the "fullness of him who fills all in all" (Eph 1:23, ESV).

b. Love for Neighbour

The love for neighbour manifests in refraining from harmful behaviour towards others and acting positively for their betterment at a cost to oneself (e.g. Exod 20:12-17; Luke 10:25-37). Bridging the love of God and the love of neighbour is a set of dispositions which will characterise those filled with God's Holy Spirit, including love but also a range of attitudes and postures towards God, present circumstances, and other people that manifest in trust and commitment to Christ, hope in the future he promises, and likeness to him, or faith, hope, and love (Gal 5:22-24; 1 Cor 13:13). The Bibles gives numerous lists and expositions of what this looks like in particular circumstances, but "love" is ultimately presented as a pattern of behaviour God demonstrates towards his creatures which we are to imitate (John 3:16-17; 15:12-13; Eph 5:1-2; 1 John 4:7-12). As directed towards God, love is loyalty, commitment, honour, and obedience as towards a loving father, creator, and king. As directed towards other humans, love is the selfless sacrifice of oneself to see other people built up, taken care of, and reconciled to Christ (e.g. Matt 25:34-40; 1 Cor 13:1-13; 2 Cor 5:16-21; 12:19-21; Eph 4:15-16, 25-32; 1 John 3:16-18). Godliness is being like God, and so fundamentally, godliness is about knowing God (Rom

[3] See ibid.

1:18-32; 2 Cor 3:16-18).

When it comes to pastoral ministry, there are specific aspects of godliness that God calls us to watch for. Godliness is, generally, composed of an attitude, state, and pattern of behaviour that identify followers of Christ and towards which discipleship seeks to lead believers. As Christians mature, they are expected to grow in godliness, and the church, under pastoral oversight, aims to facilitate this growth. Christian leaders are intended to be examples of godliness, so they are expected to excel in love for God and their neighbour (e.g. 1 Cor 4:16; 11:1; Phil 3:17; 2 Thess 3:7-9; 1 Tim 4:12); through Paul, God gives specific characteristics that demonstrate the mature character of a potential leader (see Ch. 7).

B. Identifying Godliness

By God's grace, we know what to look for in identifying the measure of godliness appropriate for a Christian leader. However, knowing *what* to look for is only part of identifying or recognising the godliness appropriate for ministry. Paul calls for a testing of character (1 Tim 3:10), but he does not specify how we may do so. Knowing *how* to identify godliness is an acute problem in the contemporary church and training models. It is easy through social media to manufacture a façade of godliness, but there is an appearance of godliness without its power (2 Tim 3:5). If we only meet someone during a Sunday gathering, it is difficult to determine the quality and depth of their faith; it is easy to be tricked by the right words and participation in the church's life that there is genuine character, yet many such people are later discovered to abuse their families, commit adultery, actively view pornography, or engage in numerous other sinful activities.

Similarly, superficial participation in a small group can easily convey a false portrait of godliness—with a demonstration of Bible knowledge, measured vulnerability in prayer requests, and care shown through praying for others. All sin will be revealed someday, but some sin only appears later (1 Tim 5:24). Superficial and short-lived relationships are powerful tools to build a façade of godliness. Given enough time, people will get to know you and secrets come out. However, if relationships are maintained for short periods, it is possible to build a false perception of a person based on their apparent eagerness and public presence. Only as people participate in one another's lives will they begin to see the rough edges.

As trust is built, family members will begin to confide in others their genuine struggles and the fractures that exist beneath the surface of their lives or marriages. Given enough time, an accurate estimation of someone's character is possible, but our current church cultures and training programs do not foster the long-term relationships necessary to truly discern someone's character. I know of a church where one member was a long-time leader of the congregation, yet looking over many years of ministry, it was apparent that he cared more about his perception of truth than the love and unity of the church; this led to repeated divisive actions. It is doubtful whether this would have been apparent when he was first identified and installed as a leader. Similarly, I discipled a young man for a time who was eager to learn theology, listened regularly to good teachers, and wanted to serve in the church. However, after a few years, he was swept up in end-time speculation (cf. 1 Tim 1:4-5) and began withdrawing from active church participation. He grew more hostile towards the leadership and actively sowed division. In hindsight, this man's approach to God and the church was highly shaped by a preoccupation with eschatology and dogmatic commitment to a single position; if events had not then raised this pattern of behaviour to the surface, it would not have been so clear that he was "quarrelsome" (1 Tim 3:3) and divisive (Titus 3:10-11). To be clear, the theological inclinations of the men in these cases were not the issue but the way these inclinations manifested in behaviour that invited division among the congregation (Titus 3:10-11) and insubordination against God-appointed leaders (Heb 13:17).

It is common for pastors and church members to regularly switch churches (in Sydney, five years is a period of time that comes up often).[4] In my experience, four years is just enough time to really begin to know people and build the sorts of relationships that reveal character, but this is when things get uncomfortable. When you start to trust people and be trusted, relationships get complicated. People notice when you are lying or concealing something and are bold enough to confront you, and you begin to have serious and deep conversations with people about their lives and relationships—which can be exhausting. I know that it was only in the context of friendships developed over a three or four-year period that I was able to confess sins of pride and lack of judgment that I had ignored, sins that demonstrated a lack of wisdom and insight into my own heart; these sins would have given a yellow light, proceed with caution, for my pursuit of ministry, demonstrating that I was not yet qualified for the role to which I aspired. However, this sin was not apparent on the outside and (to my shame) took far too long to come out. I know of another person (actually several people) who aspired to Christian ministry; in the process, cracks started to appear in their beliefs and understanding of what ministry entailed, but this was not enough for them or those around them to identify the issues.[5] It was only over years of close friendship that it became apparent that the issue was a lack of genuine faith; this was not an issue that would have become clear through a questionnaire or a couple of years of service in the

---

[4] This practice is adopted from the world of business. I believe a particular book has disseminated the practice among pastors, but I do not recall which book. See Liz Ryan, "Ten Reasons Successful People Change Jobs More Often," Forbes, 2016, https://www.forbes.com/sites/lizryan/2016/10/28/ten-reasons-successful-people-change-jobs-more-often/; Garrett Parker, "Why You Should Never Stay at a Job For Too Long," Money Inc, September 1, 2016, https://moneyinc.com/why-you-should-never-stay-at-a-job-for-too-long/.

[5] See also this article, Jess Kurz, "When the Pastor Baptizes His Wife," The Gospel Coalition, February 17, 2021, https://www.thegospelcoalition.org/article/when-the-pastor-baptizes-his-wife/.

church.

In many pastoral training programs, students are expected to serve at multiple different churches during the training process; though this has the benefit of exposing them to different styles of church and congregations, it also cuts off and prevents deep relationships from forming. The tendency of young adults to move away from their home church to seek independence or to move for studies can also break the long-term relationships developed in their home congregation. Universities in Australia and North America are huge recruitment centres for ministry, but because of the transitory nature of university churches and Christian programs, the relationships developed in these programs are once against short and generally shallow.

There are exceptions to these trends; we occasionally meet people with whom we develop immediate, close, deep friendships. We may divulge much of our lives to people we have only known briefly. Yet, a problem remains: "The heart is deceitful above all things," Jeremiah reminds us (17:9). We cannot count on people's words—even honest words—as an accurate assessment of character, for we are often terrible judges of our own character. One way to get around artificial or unaware self-assessments is to observe how someone acts when they are not putting on a show, when they are with people they trust and let their guard down. Maybe this is at home over a family dinner, during a party with friends, on vacation, or in the workplace. When people develop familiarity with circumstances and with people, they will let their guard down; this is critical to seeing who they really are. However, developing relationships where this may happen takes time, time we do not often give our work or church relationships. A spouse may be a reliable judge of their spouse's character; however, if the husband is an abusive and controlling man, the wife may not be willing to offer an honest assessment or may be manipulated into thinking that he is a good man. Relationships are complicated, and the connection between godliness and behaviour is complex, yet Jesus assures us that our actions will reveal the state of our hearts (Matt 7:15-20); we need to have patience to persevere in relationships so we can make an accurate assessment.

The duration and shallowness of relationships are not the only obstacles we face in accurately identifying character. In addition to circumstantial factors like these, we also face relational barriers to accurately assessing these things. It was once standard practice for pastors to know everyone in their flock and to intentionally evaluate their faith and growth; this was an essential aspect of pastoral care in the early church and was retrieved during the Reformation after the neglect of pastoral care in the late medieval church.[6] Many pastors today fail to know their sheep, so they do not have an accurate assessment of their spiritual state. Compounding the problem of a lack of attention to pastoral care and investment in the lives of their sheep, many pastors lack the relational skill do accurately assess character. Perhaps the most critical skill for pastoral care is listening, actively engaging with what someone is saying and inviting them to continue without prematurely interposing advice or analysis. In addition to being able to actively listen, we need to demonstrate in our posture, tone, and actions that we are safe to talk to and willing to listen. Together, actively listening and building rapport get us beyond superficial conversation, but these alone will not move us beyond how someone perceives themselves to be doing. Whether due to a lack of self-awareness, impatience, or something else, we are not often the most reliable witnesses to our own state. Sometimes, to accurately assess how we are doing, we need gentle coaxing; we need someone to patiently ask the right questions and lead us to reflect at a deeper level.

There are, therefore, barriers that face assessing genuine godliness in our contemporary culture, where superficial and transitory

---

[6] See Gregory the Great, *The Book of Pastoral Rule*, St. Vladimir's Seminary Press "Popular Patristics" Series, no. 34 (Crestwood, NY: St. Vladimir's Seminary Press, 2007); Bucer, *Concerning the True Care of Souls*; Baxter, *The Reformed Pastor*.

relationships abound, and authentic, caring relationships are few. These barriers are not insurmountable, but we need to acknowledge them if we are to overcome them. Making an accurate assessment of someone's godliness takes long-term and close observation in a setting where trust is high; this can be aided through good pastoral care skills.

To put this in other terms, godliness is best identified through active participation in the life of a healthy church where individuals are involved in one another's lives, hospitality is encouraged, genuine vulnerability is demonstrated, weakness is neither discouraged nor hidden, love abounds, and pastoral care is practised.[7] These are all aspects of the church that the New Testament demonstrates and commands: Christians are supposed to love strangers and open their homes to others (e.g. 2 – 3 John). Christians are supposed to care for one another, meet each other's needs, and be involved in each other's lives like family (Mark 10:29-31; Acts 2:42-47, 4:32-37; Rom 12:10; 1 Cor 12:24-26; Gal 5:13-15; Eph 2:19-22).[8] Christians are to acknowledge that God works in weakness and recognise that God often works through the weakest members of his people (1 Corinthians 1-10; 12:1-31; 2 Corinthians 10-12). Ministers are to shepherd the sheep God has given them (Acts 20:28, cf. Ezek 34:1-24).[9] If we are going to accurately assess the state of God's flock, we need to foster long-term relationships in the context of the local church and develop cultures of genuine pastoral care. Within this context, we are to look for specific characteristics as a measure of godliness suiting Christian ministry.

There is nothing expected of ministers that God does not expect of his people, except perhaps the ability to teach (though Heb 5:12), but

---

[7] Cf. Mbewe, *God's Design for the Church*, 168.

[8] See Rutherford, *The Being of Churches*.

[9] Gregory the Great, *The Book of Pastoral Rule*; Bucer, *Concerning the True Care of Souls*; Baxter, *The Reformed Pastor*; Powlison, *The Pastor as Counselor*; Rutherford, *The Being of Churches*.

God identifies specific areas that diagnose suitability for ministry. Perhaps these are chosen because pastors are particularly vulnerable to these vices—because these sins are not only likely to cause the greatest falls but are also areas of particular temptation for those entrusted with power. First, a minister must be above reproach (1 Tim 3:1, Titus 1:6) and well thought of by outsiders (1 Tim 3:7). There must be no public sins that haunt the minister and stand to open the minister, and through him, the church, to the Devil's traps. However, the lack of public sin or behaviour that would leave the minister open to the accusation of sin (e.g. sexual sin "must not even be named among you," Eph 5:3, ESV) is insufficient to qualify them. If they are married, they must be committed to their marriage and free from sexual immorality; the need for this qualification is obvious in light of the rampant sexual failings evident among pastors in the last several centuries (and not unknown during the Reformation and Medieval churches).[10] We can presume that for an unmarried person, they are to demonstrate the sort of behaviour conducive to a committed and holy marriage, so pornography, masturbation, and indulging in lust (let alone extramarital sex) would disqualify them (cf. 2 Pet 2:14). In 1 Timothy 3:3, Titus 1:7, and 1 Peter 5:2, greed is explicitly mentioned (cf. Ezek 34:2, 8, 10; 2 Pet 2:3, 14; Jude 12): a candidate for ministry must not be seeking gain through ministry greedy for money. With the authority entrusted to them by Christ, there is the opportunity for a pastor to abuse his position for selfish gain. Pastoral candidates are to demonstrate love for the stranger ("hospitality"), involving both care for their physical needs and the generosity and kindness shown them

---

[10] Some people believe this means divorcees are ineligible for ministry. In favour of this, they may cite 1 Timothy 5:9, for women would not be guilty of polyandry in the 1st century. However, if being a "one-man woman" or "one-woman man" means faithfulness and commitment to one's spouse, then faithfulness is intended alongside polygamy, and this applies appropriately to both sexes. There is slim evidence that this passage is meant to disqualify divorcees or widows, especially in the case of widows, for a young widow (1 Tim 5:14) is expected to remarry but may become an eligible widow later in life. See Strauch, *Biblical Eldership*, 189–92.

regardless of their social standing or spiritual state (e.g. Matthew 5:43-48; 9:10-13; 25:34-40; 1 Cor 5:9-13; Heb 13:1-3; James 2:1-7, 15-17; 3 John 5-8). Of the remaining qualities, many will only be exposed in the process of doing life together, witnessing someone's behaviour towards their family, in stressful circumstances, or outside formal gatherings like a Sunday gathering (where people tend to be on their best behaviour). "Not quarrelsome" is a critical quality for maintaining the unity of Christ's people, for a pastor will engage with many people with whom they disagree during the course of their ministry. In diagnosing this quality, we ask, do they seek conflict? What are they willing to sacrifice to uphold the unity of faith? Alexander Strauch writes of this virtue, "Fighting paralyzes and kills many local churches. It may be the single, most distressing problem Christian leaders face."[11] This is echoed in the many instances in the New Testament letters where sowing discord, divisiveness, being prone to quarrel, and the love of argument are decried (Phil 2:14; 1 Tim 1:4; 2:8; 6:3-5; 2 Tim 2:14, 23-25; Titus 3:2, 9; Jude 16, 17-19). Instead, a pastor must be gentle, kind, and patient (Prov 10:19; 14:29; 16:32; 17:27; 19:11; Eccles. 5:1-2; 7:9; Gal 5:22-24; 1 Tim 3:2-3; 2 Tim 2:24-25; Titus 1:8; James 1:19).

I suspect that the final qualification, "he must manage his own household well" (1 Tim 3:4, ESV), is less about character than maturity expressed in action. All the relational attributes discussed in the first part of 1 Timothy 3 factor into an overseer's ability to manage his own household. "Manage" (προΐστημι, *proistemi*, 1 Tim 3:4) and "care" (ἐπιμελέομαι, *epimeleomai*, 1 Tim 3:5) both describe what the overseer does for the family and church, with care filling in what is perhaps ambiguous in "manage" (προΐστημι). "Manage" can refer to exercising leadership or rule, as it does in secular literature; this is supported by the primary identification of "managing" well in this context as having

[11] Tripp, *Dangerous Calling.*

children who submit (τέκνα ἔχοντα ἐν ὑποταγῇ, *tekna echonta en hupotage;* cf. "faithful," πιστός, *pistos*, in Titus 1:6). "Submission" (ὑποταγή, *hupotage*) is an authority word, used for those who are under someone's authority. We can perhaps fill out "see that his children obey him" with reference to Ephesians 6:1, where Paul commands children (τέκνα, *tekna*) to obey (ὑπακούω, *hupakouo*) their parents (cf. Col 3:20). Fathers are to treat their children gently, "not provoking them to anger" (παροργίζετε, *parorgizete*) but raising them up with care (ἐκτέφω, *ektepho*) "in the discipline and instruction of the Lord" (ἐν παιδείᾳ καὶ νουθεσίᾳ κυρίου, *en paideia kai nouthesia kuriou*) (Eph 6:4, cf. Col 3:21). As is evident from Ephesian 5:29, ἐκτέφω refers to a sort of "rearing" of children that is caring, that provides what they need to grow up. Fathers are to lead their kids, providing instruction and discipline in the ways of Christ, leading the kids in the right way to go, and they are to provide for their needs. This aspect of care is also present in 1 Timothy 3.

"Manage" (προΐστημι, *proistemi*), as it is used in the Bible, more often refers to the attention or sort of attention given to its object than "ruling" or "leading." It is doubtful that it ever means merely to lead without the connotations of care.[12] It is only used a handful of times, but elsewhere it appears to mean to care or show concern for something (Rom 12:8; 1 Thess 5:12; cf. 1 Tim 5:17). This is echoed in the final clause of 1 Timothy 3:4-5, "for if someone does not know how to manage his own household, how will he *care* for God's church" (ESV). Ἐπιμελέομαι (*epimeleomai*, "to care") only occurs elsewhere in the NT in Luke 10:34, where we are told the good Samaritan "took care" of the Jewish man he found on the side of the road. So, an overseer's management of their household is not leading alone but also

[12] See, for example, TDNT s.v. προΐστημι.

caring for their needs, as is their management of the church.

Paul appears to presume that if fathers manage their households well, their children will follow their lead: they will be "in submission" (ἐν ὑποταγῇ, *en upotage*; 1 Tim 3:4) and "faithful" (πιστός, *pistos*; 1 Titus 1:6). So, looking at a pastoral candidate's family reveals a lot about their character. At times, 1 Titus 1:6 is understood to mean "believers," but the parallel word in 1 Timothy 3:4 suggests that faithfulness is intended; a father cannot guarantee their children will believe in Jesus, but they must lead them and can expect them to obey. As in Proverbs 22:6, it is assumed that if the father leads well, the child will follow: "Train up a child in the way he should go, even when he is old, he will not depart from it" (ESV). 1 Timothy 3:4 and Titus 1:6 presuppose the sort of causal framework of the Proverbs (right inputs produce specific outputs), yet the Proverbs and the rest of Scripture affirm that one can train their child well and that child may still go their own way. As Bruce Waltke puts it,

> The proverb, however, must not be pushed to mean that the educator is ultimately responsible for the youth's entire moral orientation. "Rather, it gives a single component of truth that must be fit together with other elements of truth in order [to] approximate the more comprehensive, confused patterns of real life."[13]

Perhaps Cain is evidence of this (Gen 4:1-16); moreover, Josiah was a righteous king with faithless children (2 Kings 22:1-2; 23:31-32, 34-37; 24:18-20; cf. 2 Chron 34:1-2). We know little about Moses' children (Exod 2:22, 4:24-26, 18:2-4; 1 Chron 23:14-17), but they were not leaders of the people, and Gershom's descendants may have engaged

---

[13] Bruce K Waltke, *The Book of Proverbs: Chapters 15-31*, NICOT (Grand Rapids: Eerdmans, 2004). Quoting Ted Hildebrant, "Proverbs 22:6a: Train Up a Child?," in *Learning from the Sages: Selected Studies on the Book of Proverbs*, ed. Roy B. Zuck (Wipf and Stock, 2003), 290.

in idolatry (Judges 18:30). Samuel was a well-renowned man of God, yet his children were not like him (1 Sam 8:1-9). So, tentatively, I would suggest that children who are not submissive or "unfaithful" regularly reveal that a father is failing to lead his household, but, as is the case with Proverbs 22:6, closer scrutiny may reveal other factors involved, such as mental illness, trauma from a third party, or similar things. Nevertheless, a married overseer must manage his household well to qualify, and the state of their children often demonstrates the quality of their management.

It is evident why these qualities are important both for the spiritual health of the minister and the church. Strauch observes that

> The items focus on two areas: (1) personal self-discipline and maturity, and (2) ability to relate well to others and to teach and care for them. These two are intertwined, although there seems to be a tendency to move from the personal to the interpersonal.[14]

If we are going to *identify* godliness, it is apparent that we need to pay careful attention over some time and in various situations likely to test and reveal a person's character. The local church modelled in the NT epistles and interpreted by the historical tradition of pastoral care provides the ideal context for such observation: pastors who are intimately involved in the lives of their congregation, as Paul was with his, will have ample opportunity to discern the character of their congregation, perceive both where they are at and what they need to grow in. Identification is, therefore, only half the battle. The church's job is to grow together into maturity, so knowing where someone is at is not enough; we need to disciple our congregations so they grow in godliness—clergy and laity alike.

---

[14] Strauch, *Biblical Eldership*, 188.

C. Training in Godliness

I have argued that there is significant continuity between regular church discipleship and training pastors, though different issues will emerge in both cases. In regular discipleship, a pastor will often have to address sexual immorality and bad relationships, among many other problems; such disqualifying patterns of behaviour ought not to be present in the life of a pastor, so the issues that need growth will be different, perhaps the more subtle sins that we are easily blind to. In this section, we will sketch a broad framework for discipleship and then focus on the particular issues in the discipleship of pastors or pastoral candidates.

i. Discipleship in General

It should go without saying that discipleship is interpersonal: we are discipled by each other. Throughout the New Testament, training in godliness is *transitive*: God uses elders and fellow believers to disciple others. We see this in the apostle's letters as they teach, encourage, and rebuke those they care for and in Jesus's ministry towards the apostles and disciples. In Matthew 28, Jesus commissions his disciples to *make* disciples, *baptising* and *teaching* people to obey his commandments (19-20). In Ephesians 4, the leaders of local churches are charged with equipping the saints for the work of ministry, which is to build up the body of Christ (4:11-13). They are to speak the truth in love (4:15, 25), speak words that build up others (4:29), and be kind, forgiving and compassionate (4:32). These are things Christians do towards one another to see each other built up together into maturity. This is the goal of all the "one another" commands in the New Testament (Rom 12:10, 16; 14:13; 15:5, 7, 14; 1 Cor 12:21-26; 2 Cor 13:11-13; Gal 5:13-15; 16:2; Eph 4:2, 32; 5:19, 21; Col 3:13, 16; 1 Thess 3:12; 4:9, 18; 5:11, 15; 2 Thess 1:3; Heb 3:13-14; 10:24-25; James 4:11; 5:9, 16; 1 Pet 1:22; 4:8-11; 5:5; 1 John 3:11, 23; 4:7, 11-12; 2 John 5). God has given teachers so the body may be mature, enduring and accomplishing his purposes; leaders help the body of Christ mature by equipping all of

God's saints for the works of service towards one another. So, leaders with their various gifts disciple all of God's people so that they, in turn, disciple one another—so they challenge, encourage, help, and teach one another so they would all together persevere and grow in the faith.

Above, we identified the various characteristics that demonstrate someone to be Spirit-filled and to have a godly character. The goal in our relationships with other Christians is to grow together in godliness and preserve in faith through all the trials this life offers. To do this, we must move beyond merely commenting on and critiquing good or bad behaviour and understand a person's heart or character. In Luke 6:43-45, Jesus indicates that good or bad behaviour results from a good or evil heart, that there is a deeper cause to our actions than merely a choice we make; we are disposed to act this way by our heart. If we want to change what we do, we need to focus on why we do it. As Paul Tripp puts it,

> If my heart is the source of my sin problem, then lasting change must always travel through the pathway of my heart. It is not enough to alter my behavior or to change my circumstances. Christ transforms people by radically changing their hearts.[15]

The problem we face in discipleship is that "the heart can be veiled and difficult to know. We prefer to hide its less attractive thoughts and some of its hurts."[16] Discipleship happens when we get to the heart and can lovingly apply the truth of God's word. The commands Jesus through his apostles gives to his churches illustrate what Spirit-filled

---

[15] Paul David Tripp, *Instruments in the Redeemer's Hands: People in Need of Change Helping People in Need of Change*, Resources for Changing Lives (Phillipsburg, NJ: P&R Publishing, 2002), 62. Cf. Timothy S. Lane, *Unstuck* (Purcellville, VA: The Good Book Company, 2019), 83–93; Edward T. Welch, *Caring for One Another: 8 Ways to Cultivate Meaningful Relationships* (Wheaton: Crossway, 2018), 23–31.

[16] Welch, *Caring for One Another*, 24.

life looks like in the community of faith and show us how that life is to be nurtured and how we can understand who we truly are and spur one another on in faith, hope, and love.

Numerous aspects of the New Testament teaching focus on how we might grow together in Christ. To highlight some examples, God's people are to minister the word to one another, set an example for one another, listen to and instruct one another, and pray with one another. We do this when we gather together in worship and throughout the week, as we meet in each other's houses, enjoy fellowship, and read the word of God.[17]

a. Let the Word Dwell Richly Among You

In Colossians 3:16-17, Paul tells the Colossian believers,

> The word of Christ must dwell among you with abundance: with all wisdom, teach and admonish one another; sing psalms, hymns, and spiritual songs with thankfulness in your hearts towards God. [17]And whatever you do, in word or deed, do all things in the name of the Lord Jesus, giving thanks to God the Father through him. (My translation)

Verse 17 gives the framework within which the Colossians are to do everything, including having the word of Christ dwell abundantly among them. Among all the other ways they are to act towards one another as a united body (3:14-15), they are to foster an environment saturated in Christ's word (taking πλουσίως, *plousios*, quantitatively, i.e. abundance, rather than a rich quality). The NIV translates ὁ λόγος τοῦ Χριστοῦ (*ho logos tou Christou*, "the word of Christ") as "the message of Christ." However, as this is followed by a reference to "psalms" and "teaching," which are both closely linked to the Scriptures, I think it

---

[17] See Rutherford, *The Being of Churches*, sec. I.3-4, IV.D.1.

better to take this as Christ's word or the word that is about Christ, namely, the whole of Scripture interpreted in the New Covenant context. To do this, the Colossians must teach and admonish one another, presumably from the Scriptures. They are also to abound in rich, Scriptural songs towards one another. There may not be a firm distinction between the three words used for songs in verse 16; we get the idea of the abundance of Scriptural music addressed to one another (Eph 5:19).[18] The life of God's people together, which ought to be characterised by putting on the newness of life in Christ (Col 3:1-13), will be fostered and characterised by an overflow of the Scriptures addressed to one another in relationship.

This will undoubtedly happen when the church gathers, so we are encouraged to have gatherings saturated in the Scriptures read, taught, and sung. God permits various forms of songs, but the Psalms are explicitly indicated, and singing God's own songs is an obvious way to have the word of Christ dwell among us abundantly. However, the word of Christ does not "abundantly dwell among us" if we restrict the use of Scripture to our gatherings. The word of Christ should also abound in all our relationships, including with our families and friends. As our faith moves beyond the church gathered to all our relationships (Col 3:18-25), so we also ought to let Scripture abound in all our relationships with other believers. We are to address each other from the Scriptures with the goal of godliness. So, having the word dwell abundantly among us requires us to seriously engage with what God is saying in the text so that we would be transformed together. In ministering the word to one another, we aim at the sort of understanding that transforms: we want to properly understand God's word so that we will respond to it correctly. I suggest this is the proper object of the ministry of the word to one another, namely, the sort of understanding that produces transformation in terms of godliness.

---

[18] Douglas J. Moo, *The Letters to the Colossians and to Philemon*, The Pillar New Testament Commentary (Grand Rapids; Cambridge: Eerdmans, 2008).

In the contemporary Evangelical church, it is common for believers to gather in small groups to "study" the Bible, and it is also common to read the Bible one-on-one with other believers and unbelievers. This is consistent with Paul's exhortation in Colossians 3:16-17, but we perhaps need to think more clearly about this practice if we are to disciple well. In Chapters 5-9, I addressed various issues in contemporary and historic approaches to the Bible, yet these approaches have been highly influential on our approach to using the Bible in one-on-one and small group settings. The word "study" is revealing: the common inductive approach focuses on literacy and literate Bible reading skills, understanding words and phrases, answering comprehension questions, reflecting on the historical and literary background, and then moving to application. This is often adopted in deliberate contrast with an overly spiritualised or perhaps simplified approach that asks, "What does the text mean to me?" or "What is God saying to me in this text?" without a mechanism for critical feedback. In line with our conclusions in Chapters 5-9, I suggest we avoid treating the Bible as something to be studied *and* avoid oversimplifying the way God communicates to us in his word. I believe a similar approach could be used in both one-on-one and small-group settings. I propose that we 1) focus on an *oral* (as opposed to literate) approach to Scripture (we will discuss the role of literate study below, §12.C.iii), 2) choose a Bible translation and strategy conducive to oral learning, 3) establish expectations for feedback, 4) and use three basic sets of questions.

1) First, according to the nature of reading Scripture with others and the general demographics of our congregations, I propose we adopt an *oral* approach to reading the Scriptures. If we are reading Scripture one-on-one or in a small group, we are obviously communicating with one another. This moves us away from an introspective, internal (or silent) reading and reflection upon Scripture, which characterises the literate approach to reading and studying. The act of vocalising the text and reading it with others changes the way we interact with it. We will generally read it more slowly but will not stop

and re-read sections or pause and focus on individual words or phrases. In other words, reading out loud and in a communal setting moves us away from an analytic approach to the text (dissecting it and analysing its pieces) towards a synthetic approach (attempting to grasp and engage with the whole). Not only will our own engagement with the text be moved in an oral direction by the communal context, but our engagement with the text together will also be moved in this direction, evident in the use of questions and sharing reflections.

This may be intuitively unfamiliar and even uncomfortable for those of us who are used to literate forms of study, but this will be intuitive and comfortable—even ideal—for the majority of congregations across the world. It is suggested that 80% of the world's population are oral-preference learners; these are learners who struggle to or cannot learn through literate means.[19] Now, 'oral' versus 'literate' does not indicate 'learning styles,' a well-criticized concept, but rather competencies in learning based on the default approach to language across present and ancient societies, namely, orality, and the acquired skill of literacy.[20] The statistics for Australia indicate that only 15% of the population is highly literate (equivalent to a diploma or higher reading level), and the majority read at a level no higher than that

---

[19] "International Orality Network | Oral Learners: Who Are They?," accessed April 11, 2024, https://orality.net/about/oral-learners-who-are-they/.

[20] Walter J. Ong, *Orality and Literacy: The Technologizing of the Word* (New York: Routledge, 2002); Harold Pashler et al., "Learning Styles: Concepts and Evidence," *Psychological Science in the Public Interest* 9, no. 3 (December 2008): 105–19, https://doi.org/10.1111/j.1539-6053.2009.01038.x; Rick Sessoms, "Who Are Oral Learners?," *Freedom To Lead International*® (blog), April 12, 2012, https://freedomtolead.net/telling-story-great-commission-oral-learners/; Réka Vágvölgyi et al., "A Review about Functional Illiteracy: Definition, Cognitive, Linguistic, and Numerical Aspects," *Frontiers in Psychology* 7 (November 10, 2016): 1617, https://doi.org/10.3389/fpsyg.2016.01617.

expected of a Year 10 student.[21] We need to grapple with oral learning because this is the primary way our congregations learn, and this is not a bad thing. There is ample evidence from the Bible that it was intended to be read and engaged with in public, that is, orally (e.g. Deut 31:11; Neh 8:1-8; Luke 4:16-21; Col 4:16; 1 Thess 5:27; Rev 1:3).[22]

So, how do we do this? I propose that we focus on synthetic rather than analytic questions and reflection. Language processing occurs in chunks of text rather than in words, phrases, and even sentences (though a sentence is the most basic unit of comprehensible meaning): our minds do not hang on to, analyse, and then connect the individual pieces, but, like a ladder, they climb the individual pieces towards a synthesis—an understanding of what we read as a whole, not isolated parts.[23] In doing so, we are not purely objective observers but intuitively connect the text with our prior beliefs and experience, producing a range of syntheses or responses to the text, whether this is confusion (I do not understand), evaluation (this is good or bad), emotion (happiness, sadness, anger), comprehension (insight and understanding), the motivation to act (conviction, encouragement,

---

21 "Literary and Access," Government, *Australian Government Style Manual* (blog), February 27, 2024, https://www.stylemanual.gov.au/accessible-and-inclusive-content/literacy-and-access.

22 See Rutherford, "Church in an Oral World."

23 I draw this from years of reflection on numerous sources, but some places to start are, Catherine Walter, "Phonology in Second Language Reading: Not an Optional Extra," *TESOL Quarterly* 42, no. 3 (2008): 455–74, https://doi.org/10.2307/40264478; Stephen D. Krashen, *Principles and Practice in Second Language Acquisition*, 1st ed, Language Teaching Methodology Series (Oxford; New York: Pergamon Press, 1982); Stephen D. Krashen, *Second Language Acquisition and Second Language Learning*, Reprinted, Language Teaching Methodology Series (Oxford: Pergamon Press, 1985); Karen Lichtman, *Teaching Proficiency through Reading and Storytelling (TPRS): An Input-Based Approach to Second Language Instruction*, Routledge E-Modules on Contemporary Language Teaching (New York: Routledge, 2018); Ludwig Wittgenstein, *Philosophical Investigations*; Polanyi, *Personal Knowledge*; Polanyi, *The Tacit Dimension*; Frame, *The Doctrine of the Knowledge*.

realisation), action itself, etc. We will consider below the need for feedback because our intuitive responses to the text are not always correct, yet the fact that we respond to the text is not a bad thing: this means we have understood something (or in the case of confusion, realise we do not understand). Because this is how we naturally read and the only practical way to orally engage with a text (offering some advantages over a purely analytic reading, allowing us, for example, to understand the whole without understanding each part), we should focus our engagement on questions directed at this level, on drawing out, critiquing or analysing, and reflecting on our responses to the text. A leader's prior reflection on the text, whether this reflection is done through oral or literary means, prepares them to lead the group in critical reflection on their responses so that they are formed around the text.

2) Second, because we are adopting an oral approach to engaging with Scripture, I propose we adopt tools suitable for this approach. The first consideration is a Bible translation. God has gifted the English-speaking world with numerous Bible translations, and they have their merits and strengths; we often have our favourite translations, but (setting aside those that are methodologically flawed (e.g. the Passion translation and the Amplified Bible)) there is a place for all the principal Bible translations in local churches. In the context of oral engagement, we should choose a translation or translations (you do not have to always use the same one) that are suitable for reading out loud. Some biblical books are generally more challenging in this regard, but much of the Bible is written for an oral preferential world; some approaches to translation carry this forward into English, while others do not. The NIV is generally more readable than the ESV, though it is still translated for a highly literate audience. Though more readable (especially in the Old Testament), the NIV has the trade-off of being more interpretative relative to the ESV.[24] The more wooden

[24] All translation requires us to interpret the text, but different translations

NASB is sometimes difficult to understand in English, yet because it retains much of the repetition and coordinating syntax of the original texts, it can sometimes be friendly to oral reading. The KJV retains similar features, yet its dated language, syntax, and textual basis (the Greek and Hebrew texts used in translation) make it less useful than most modern translations. I am not familiar enough with the CSB to judge its merits for use in oral contexts, but the NLT is easier to read and understand than many of the previous translations. However, even more than the NIV, it forecloses ambiguities and makes more interpretative decisions than are strictly necessary for translation.

Each translation has its use, and the leader will need to weigh the strengths of each translation for the specific texts being read and for the audience that will listen. For pastors confident in their language skills, a specific translation (one oriented to a specific context rather than an entire language group) can be an excellent asset for oral study. Such translations should be produced in dialogue with the major translations.[25]

In addition to choosing a Bible translation that communicates orally, we must also consider how we will approach the Bible. In Part 2, I argued that Scripture communicates a portrait of God and communicates in various ways that cannot be reduced to the communication of propositions and theology (at least when theology is understood in the classical sense discussed above). If we accept that the Bible is literature (though not merely for the literate), then our reading must match the sort of literature it is. In practice, many of our

---

approach the ambiguities of the biblical text differently; the NIV tends to resolve ambiguities that the ESV maintains. I argue elsewhere that ambiguity in translation is not always a bad thing if it reflects genuine ambiguity in the text. Cf. Rutherford, *The Gift of Reading - Part 1*; Rutherford, *The Gift of Reading - Part 2*; Rutherford, *Habakkuk*.

[25] Cf. J. Alexander Rutherford, "A Defence of an Author's Translation - Part 1," Teleioteti, December 5, 2017, https://www.teleioteti.ca/2017/12/05/a-defence-of-an-authors-translation-part-1/; Rutherford, *Habakkuk*.

churches read the Bible as if it were a collection of statements about God or ethics (what we should do), reading and preaching passages or even verses isolated from their context. This is perhaps reinforced by the presence of chapter and verse notations, which may convey the idea that each verse is a self-contained thing, and similarly with chapters; however, verses and chapters were introduced much later (16th century AD).[26] It would be nearly impossible to reference specific verses in the early church without reference to the greater context, as we see in Jesus referring to the "account of the burning bush" to highlight a specific verse (Mark 12:26; cf. Mark 2:26). Moreover, for every text in the Bible, the context is significant. The epistles are written to specific churches and are woven through with themes (e.g. Ephesians uses the picture of the Church as Christ's body in every chapter. 1 Peter is framed by the designation of its audience as "sojourners" or "exiles"); the Psalms are complete songs, and the whole collection display deliberate organisation (as does the Proverbs). The narrative books tell a cohesive story with a purpose.[27]

This contrasts with a book like the Quran, which is a collection of often disconnected sayings and stories that lack cohesion and can be read without reference to the immediately surrounding material: selecting a random passage and reading it would make sense for a book

---

[26] Bart D. Ehrman, *The New Testament: A Historical Introduction to the Early Christian Writings* (Oxford University Press, 2000), 444.

[27] Long, *The Art of Biblical History*; Robert Alter, *The Art of Biblical Narrative* (London: Allen & Unwin, 1981); Sailhamer, *Pentateuch*; Thomas R. Schreiner, *Interpreting the Pauline Epistles*, 2nd ed (Grand Rapids: Baker Academic, 2011); C. Hassell Bullock, *Encountering the Book of Psalms: A Literary and Theological Introduction* (Grand Rapids: Baker Academic, 2004); Bruce K. Waltke, *The Book of Proverbs: Chapters 1-15*, NICOT (Grand Rapids: Eerdmans, 2004); Gerald Henry Wilson, *The Editing of the Hebrew Psalter* (Scholars Press, 1985); Jerome F. D. Creach, *Yahweh as Refuge and the Editing of the Hebrew Psalter* (A&C Black, 1996); Adam D. Hensley, *Covenant Relationships and the Editing of the Hebrew Psalter* (Bloomsbury Publishing, 2018).

like the Quran, but not a book like the Bible.[28] We would not read a sentence or two from a letter written by our spouse and ignore the rest, nor would we read the middle chapter of a novel and ignore the rest. We may read a textbook or reference resource this way, but not a letter, a song, or a story. As Dietrich Bonhoeffer reminds us in his reflections on Colossians 3, "Holy Scripture does not consist of individual passages; it is a unit and is intended to be used as such."[29] The idea of reading isolated sections of Scripture emerged in the Medieval church, following the liturgical calendar, and has featured in mainline Protestant, Catholic, and Orthodox traditions that employ lectionaries structured around this calendar. However, in the early church, *lectio continua* was practiced, namely, reading and preaching whole books of the Bible and the Bible itself in order. The Reformers retrieved this practice against the lectionary system and insisted on moving continuously through the Bible and the individual books. They saw this as essential to model the correct reading of Scripture and communicate its meaning. Reading across books and the whole Scripture is reading the Bible as it actually is. This practice is reflected within Scripture: Paul expected his letters to be read as wholes (Col 4:16; 1 Thess 5:27), and Ezra reads through the entire Law (Ezra 8:1-8).

We should, therefore, prioritise reading the Bible in its literary context, reading across the Bible (Genesis – Revelation) and, especially, reading across individual books.[30] There is a place for reading individual verses and chapters, yet if they are to be understood,

---

28 Cf. Rutherford, *The Gift of Revelation: A Biblical Perspective on the Bible.*

29 Dietrich Bonhoeffer, *Life Together* (New York: Harper & Row, 1954), 50–51, http://archive.org/details/lifetogether00diet.

30 I would suggest reading across the Bible using the Hebrew order of the Old Testament. In addition to the good argument that can be made for its originality, intentionality, and use in the New Testament, this order makes practical sense: you won't read 1 – 2 Chronicles right after 1 – 2 Kings, which bogs many readers down with the repetition. Cf. Rutherford, *The Gift of Revelation: A Biblical Perspective on the Bible.*

the big picture needs to be in place; perhaps counterintuitively, zooming in and studying individual parts of Scripture only makes sense if we have moved through and, consequently, understood the whole. One strategy that can be used for building a big picture framework alongside or as preparation for the lengthier and more difficult task of reading across Scripture is to read key moments in the Old and New Testament that reveal the critical themes, stories, and characters that make sense of the whole.[31] This is a valuable approach to small group study, whereas reading from Genesis to Revelation makes more sense in the context of the gathered church. Reading across individual books is also helpful in the context of small groups. Depending on the needs of a situation, it may be appropriate to read a particular part of a book to address specific issues. However, we should still model good interpretative practices by drawing attention to the context where that section is found. We should also, minimally, seek to read self-contained parts of Scripture; for example, the beatitudes are part of a larger sermon that gives them a particular meaning, and the differences between the beatitudes in Matthew and Luke are best explained by the different narrative strategies employed by each author. Therefore, a pattern I would suggest is making sure the main diet of a Christian is reading across Scripture; this will often be done in small groups and the church gathered.[32] However, within that regular diet, it can be useful to look at specific books or parts of books in various contexts. I would also suggest that we focus on *reading* across Scripture in these contexts, though we do not necessarily have to *preach* across Scripture.

---

[31] See my use of this approach to show who God is, J. Alexander Rutherford, *Portraits of the King: 20 Biblical Pictures of God* (Campbell River, BC: Teleioteti, 2024), https://www.teleioteti.ca/resources/books/portraits-of-the-king-20-biblical-pictures-of-god/.

[32] Tim Patrick and Andrew Reid, *The Whole Counsel of God: Why and How to Preach the Entire Bible* (Wheaton: Crossway, 2020); J. Alexander Rutherford, "Review of The Whole Counsel of God – Teleioteti Book Reviews," Teleioteti, May 18, 2020, https://www.teleioteti.ca/2020/05/18/review-of-the-whole-counsel-of-god/; Rutherford, "Church in an Oral World."

That is, if a church has New and Old Testament readings in the gathering and both are moving across the respective testaments, it may be helpful to preach on the NT passage one week and the OT passage another, or perhaps on a Psalm, if one passage is easily understood and as the minister perceives that God would speak to the congregation through the passages that week.

3) Third, I propose we establish expectations for feedback and implement them. It is a common experience in small groups for someone to share an opinion or belief about a passage that is entirely unrelated to that passage or false, yet a typical response is an awkward silence, not correction. None of us like to be told we are wrong in public, and we especially do not want to tell someone they are wrong. However, part of discipleship is developing humility, so being able to be corrected; developing gentleness, so being able to correct well; and growing in the knowledge of the truth, so pursuing a right understanding of God and his ways. Feedback is, therefore, essential to ministering the word to one another. When a person prophesies in the gathered church, when they apply the Scriptures to specific circumstances in a church's life, God expects us to judge that prophecy to be true or false (1 Cor 14:28-33); surely this applies to small group settings as well. Instead of reflexively and, perhaps, unexpectedly denouncing a perceived error, I propose we set clear expectations for giving and receiving feedback. We ought to make clear that feedback will be given but offer a considered way of doing so.

We should make clear *why* we give feedback and then model what giving good feedback looks like. It should go without question that we should give positive feedback and encourage people's engagement with God's Word and its meaning. However, there are times when we will need to give critical feedback, and this is hard. We should start by listening carefully and actively, asking clarifying questions and ensuring we understand what someone means before offering feedback. For example, someone may be angered by a passage like Romans 1:24-27; if this is the case, they have probably understood what Paul is saying, but the cause of their anger might not be so simple, and the implications of that anger are even more complex. Are they angry *that* God disproves of something, or are they perhaps angry about the implications that disproval has for their own life or someone they love? Maybe they are generally angry about passages like this because they perceive them to be barriers to communicating the Gospel. Anger, in this case, reveals something about the person, but it is not clear at first what that is.[33] Before we offer feedback, we need to know what we are offering feedback to. The Psalms demonstrate that we can be angry about God's decrees and wrestle with him from a place of genuine faith, but we also know that anger can produce or come from unbelief, so both cases need to be dealt with differently. Sometimes people will say something that sounds wrong, but it may turn out not to be wrong after we have understood them. So, good feedback starts with understanding what someone means by what they say and why they are saying it; we do not respond to words alone but to the people speaking them.

Next, we want to address what is wrong with what the person is saying. It is not wrong to be angry that God said something, but it is dangerous to be angry with God, and it is wrong to have a view of the world where you have the authority to judge God (Rom 9:14-24). God is the judge, and we are in no position to judge him; however, we often assume that we have an innate moral compass and that God must conform to that compass. It takes Christian maturity to humble ourselves and acknowledge that God is right and we are not; we need to help people get to the point, not shut them down because they are not there yet. This takes nuance and often many conversations over time.

Maybe someone responds to the passage about the rich young ruler and decides they must sell everything and pursue Jesus: are they wrong?

---

[33] See J. Alasdair Groves and Winston T. Smith, *Untangling Emotions* (Wheaton: Crossway, 2019).

This is a case that needs nuanced feedback. We must clarify what they intend to do and why. It would be good to ask if this was something they have thought about before (is the passage the source or just the trigger). Nevertheless, this response is not clearly wrong; we have ample evidence in the New Testament for people doing this very thing, but it is also not something someone should do spontaneously and without thought. In our feedback, we do not want to crush something that may genuinely come from God: God has called people throughout history to give up everything and follow him. However, we also would not want to hastily endorse what may turn out to be a foolish impulse. The expectation of receiving feedback gives us the opportunity to ask good questions, learn more about the response the person has given, and perhaps start a longer conversation in and beyond the group setting about what it looks like to follow Jesus and the cost that often comes with doing so. Again, is there anything wrong with this person's aspiration, and what exactly is it?

Finally, we want to offer feedback in a gentle and loving manner (Gal 6:1; 2 Tim 2:25). Having understood what someone has said and identified something that requires feedback, we seek to communicate in a way that will be heard. There is often something positive to say along with critical feedback; we can acknowledge that someone has engaged with God's word—which is a good thing—or maybe acknowledge that someone has rightly understood what God has said even though they have not identified a proper response. If we ask good questions and show that we have listened, we build trust to give feedback.[34] We must not refrain from giving feedback, but we should take care to do this well.

4) Fourth, I propose we analyse and develop our reflection on a text based on four responses and three types of questions used to promote synthetic understanding. We can model reflection through four basic

---

[34] For thinking through listening well, identifying issues, and responding, see Welch, *Caring for One Another.*

responses that may be given after a passage is read: someone may ask for the passage or part of it to be repeated, they may summarise or paraphrase what it said, they may share their response to the passage, or they may ask a question for clarification. If someone wants the passage to be re-read, this should be encouraged. If someone seeks clarification, they should be given space to ask (different groups will create that space differently). We may also invite someone to offer a summary or paraphrase of the passage or do so ourselves as leaders. However, the primary place for questions is in drawing forth and reflecting on our response to the passage, on the synthesis of understanding the passage and its relationship to our life. I suggest we use three basic types of questions to encourage this reflection. However, before considering these three types of questions, I want to discuss what these questions have in common.

Good questions are not too general, do not invite opinion or speculation, and do not foreclose on feedback; we should avoid questions that do so. A question like "What do you think?" is too general and is resistant to feedback. What we think differs from what God says to us and how we respond to that speech. We want to ask "open" questions, which prompt reflection and understanding, rather than "closed" questions:

> Open questions are those which open up discussion.... Closed questions are those which close down discussion. They have a single right answer (which is often embarrassingly obvious).[35]

Orlando Saer offers this example of a closed and open question: Mark 4:1-20, closed, "How many types of soil are there?" Mark 4:1-20; open, "How does Jesus describe the different types of soil?"[36] Also, asking

---

[35] Orlando Saer, *Iron Sharpens Iron: Leading Bible-Oriented Small Groups That Thrive* (Fearn, Ross-shire, Scotland: Christian Focus, 2010), 76.

[36] Saer, 76.

what the text says or means invites a paraphrase or summary of the text but does so in an ambiguous or general manner, so it would be better to ask specifically if someone would like to summarise the events in the narrative, the themes or progression of Psalm, or how an argument unfolds. We could also ask about a key phrase; Saer offers the example from Mark 8:29, "What is Peter really saying when he declares, 'You are the Christ'?"[37] Three specific types of questions that foster reflection on the text and our response to it, opening the door for good conversation, are questions that either 1) directly probe our response to the text, 2) zoom out to situate it in the biblical context, or 3) bring out an application.

First, we want to ask specific questions that address our response to the text. It is too general to ask, "How would you respond to God's word?" or "How should you respond to God's word"? However, more specific questions will foster transformative discussion that gets at our hearts, what we truly believe and love, and what God is saying. "How does this text make you feel?" is a genuine question, for many biblical texts will provoke an emotional response. We may get angry over something God does or what a character has done or feel sad over an event or a reflection on our condition before God. We may despair over the conviction of sin, we may feel frustrated that we still struggle with something the text discusses, we may be disgusted by behaviour described in the text, we may become uncomfortable with something, etc. These responses give us insight into our understanding of the text, which may be wrong or right, and our own beliefs or aspects of our character, which deserve consideration. We can ask questions about possible responses: e.g. should we sell everything we have? Why do we answer that in one way or another? When we ask questions about a reader's response, we are not asking what we *should* do (questions of application); rather, we are exploring how people intuitively synthesise the meaning of the text, that is, what our immediate perception of its

[37] Saer, 68.

implications for our lives is.

Second, we want to ask questions that seek a synthesis on a different level. We want to learn to understand specific passages within the context of the Bible, of God's covenant given to his New Testament People (see Chap. 8). We want to be specific about these questions. If we read an Old Testament passage, we can ask what that application would have looked like for Israel when they lived in the land or what it would have meant when they were in exile. We may then ask, "What has changed between these two situations?" For us today, if we isolate the features of having a land or home and an earthly king or kingdom, we can ask what changes for the New Testament people who are described as neither having a home nor an earthly kingdom. Another form of this type of question is to ask what problem or aspect of the broken world an Old Testament or New Testament passage reflects.[38] We may ask, "What do we have in common with those we read about in Scripture?" "What is our mutual condition?"[39] Jesus tells us we must take up our cross and follow him; we may ask, "What makes it difficult to do so?" "How does this command address something wrong in our patterns of thinking about the world and ourselves?" Asking how a passage points to Jesus is too general, but if we investigate a problem such as this, we can get to the problems that Jesus solves. Such questions are moving towards understanding, yet they attempt this at a whole-Bible level, seeking to integrate our responses and understanding of a passage read with our understanding of the whole Bible.[40]

Third, we want to ask questions that lead to reflection on how we

---

[38] Bryan Chapell, *Christ-Centered Preaching: Redeeming the Expository Sermon*, 2nd ed (Grand Rapids: Baker Academic, 2005), 48–57.

[39] Chapell, 52.

[40] See Gentry and Wellum, *God's Kingdom through God's Covenants*; Nick Roark and Robert Cline, *Biblical Theology: How the Church Faithfully Teaches the Gospel*, 9Marks: Building Healthy Churches (Wheaton: Crossway, 2018).

should respond to the text. We will get here often by reflecting on how we have responded, but sometimes, we need to ask questions that lead us to reflect specifically on how we should change in light of what we have read. Reading the passage on the rich young ruler, it is worth exploring the question, "Should we sell everything we have?" Similarly, reading the first four chapters of Acts, we may ask, "What would it look like if our churches had everything in common?" "How can we make concrete steps to ensure every need is met among our local church?" Reflecting on Matthew 6:33, it is worth asking, "What determines your choices?" "How do you decide what job you take, what house you rent or buy, where you live, whom you date or marry, what food you eat, or what you do with your time?" Reflecting on our responses to such questions, we may get an idea of our priorities, we can then ask, "What would it look like if we did not make providing for ourselves the first priority?" "Is this what Jesus is speaking about in these passages, worrying and, therefore, making decisions based on how bills will be paid rather than how we can best seek Christ's kingdom?" We may then ask, "What would it look like to choose where we live, whom we marry, how we live, what we do and where we do it, what we eat, and how we spend our free time in light of Jesus's challenge, 'seek first the kingdom of God and his righteousness'?"[41] We do not want to stay at the level of general or abstract applications but move towards responses we can and should make. It may be that our response should be a change in beliefs or thinking, so we might ask, "What does this passage say to somebody who thinks X [e.g. sex outside of marriage is okay, cohabitation is okay, we will get to heaven based on the amount of our good deeds]?" Saer gives a specific example for Romans 3:9-20, "What do these verses say to those of us who like to think of human beings as fundamentally good?"[42] If the

[41] Cf. J. Alexander Rutherford, *The Gift of Purpose: Orienting the Christian Life in Western Culture*, God's Gifts for the Christian Life - Part 3 1 (Ardrie, AB: Teleioteti, 2020); Rutherford, *The Being of Churches.*

[42] Saer, *Iron Sharpens Iron*, 86.

response is a change in action or habit, we can discuss steps to implement this change. We must not assume that change will be instantaneous. Just because someone feels conviction, their lives will not necessarily change from then on; we must be realistic that change takes time, but it is possible.

We are to have the word of Christ "dwell abundantly" among us; this happens as we sing, read, listen to, reflect on, and communicate God's word to one another. This happens in our gatherings and small groups, but the ministry of the Word is never alone. If we focus on merely reading and communicating the Bible, God may produce fruit as he wills, but we will rarely see growth. This is because change happens when we uncover and address the heart; God can address the heart through his Spirit (Heb 4:11-13), but he has instructed his people to do this work, to teach, encourage, rebuke, and instruct one another. To do this, we need to get at the heart, understand each other, and communicate God's word to people's hearts. In Scripture, this is often called prophecy, addressing people's circumstances, condition, or character from the Scriptures through the supernatural insight of God's Holy Spirit.[43] Today, we often call this discipleship or counselling.[44] God tells us to "speak the truth in love," seeking the growth of the whole body into maturity; we must speak the *truth*, so all discipleship is a ministry of the Word, but we are to do so with love (Eph 4:15). As we minister the word, in order that we would do so well and lovingly, we must set an example for, listen well to, encourage, and pray for one another.

---

[43] Rutherford, *The Gift of Revelation: A Biblical Perspective on the Bible*; Rutherford, *The Being of Churches*.

[44] Tripp, *Instruments in the Redeemer's Hands*; David Powlison, *Speaking Truth in Love: Counsel in Community* (Greensboro, NC: New Growth Press, 2005); Jeremy Pierre and Deepak Reju, *The Pastor and Counseling: The Basics of Shepherding Members in Need*, 2015; Welch, *Caring for One Another*; Powlison, *The Pastor as Counselor*.

b. Imitate Me as I Imitate Christ

> For though you have countless guides in Christ, you do not have many fathers. For I became your father in Christ Jesus through the gospel. I urge you, then, be imitators of me. That is why I sent you Timothy, my beloved and faithful child in the Lord, to remind you of my ways in Christ, as I teach them everywhere in every church. – 1 Corinthians 4:15-17 (ESV)

God's vision for the local church is a close community, like a body or a family. As we live in community, sharing our lives together during the regular gathering or throughout the week as we open our homes to one another, we will naturally see how others follow Christ. This stands to expose sin but to provide an opportunity to display godly behaviour to others. The value of a good example for discipleship is affirmed in numerous ways across Scripture. The biblical stories, Paul tells us, give examples of what to do and what not to do (1 Cor 10:6, 11). This is true of books like Genesis through Kings but even more so of Chronicles and Ezra-Nehemiah, which apply a so-called Deuteronomistic theology (i.e. righteousness brings blessing and unrighteousness curse) to the history of Israel, offering examples of righteousness to follow and unrighteousness as a warning. So, we can learn from the example of men and women who have followed God before us. So also in the New Testament, Jesus and the Apostles put themselves forward as examples for us to follow (John 13:12-20; 1 Cor 4:16; 11:1; Phil 3:17; 4:9; 2 Thess 3:7-9; 1 Tim 1:16; 2 Tim 3:10-11), and encourage church leaders to do likewise (1 Tim 4:12; Titus 2:7; 1 Pet 5:3). Paul also puts forth and speaks of different churches as examples (2 Cor 8:1-7; 1 Thess 1:6-7, 2:14). The example of others is presented as a significant aspect of discipleship, both positively and negatively. Church discipline provides a warning of the cost and ramifications of sin (1 Tim 5:20), and the life of a more mature Christian shows us both what a godly life looks like and the goodness of that life. Gregory the Great wrote in the 6th century, "The footprint of [the pastor's] good living should be that path that others follow rather than the sound of his voice showing them where to go."[45]

Setting an example of godliness also strengthens other aspects of our discipleship, opening the door for serious ministry, or it can shut down discipleship. Speaking to Pastors, David Powlison writes,

> Whether in casual interaction, a called meeting, or public worship, your attitudes, core values, and functional beliefs are continually on display. Other people listen, learn, watch, and decide whether to tune you in or tune you out. The fact that you are not hidden is a unique aspect of your pastoral calling [in contrast with professional counselors]. … [People] know (or have a pretty good idea) if you are a good counselor (or a busybody, a pontificator, a slacker, a pat-answer man). They know if you are the real deal (or a religious role player). … They know (or have an inkling) because you are not a "professional counselor" isolated in an office and self-protected by "clinical detachment." You live, move, and have your being in public space. If you fail the test, they won't seek you out, and they'll be guarded when you seek them out. If you pass, your counseling will gain a power for good that is unimaginable to other counselors.[46]

Our life, therefore, can further or hinder other aspects of discipleship and is itself a form of discipleship. We should, therefore, seek to both be an example to others and spend time with those who may be an example to us. Our lives should confirm the words we preach, giving an example of humility, repentance, faith, hope, and

---

[45] Gregory the Great, *The Book of Pastoral Rule*, 207.

[46] Powlison, *The Pastor as Counselor*, 38–39.

service towards others (among many other things).

c. Speak the Truth in Love

> Rather, speaking the truth in love, we are to grow up in every way into him who is the head, into Christ - Ephesians 4:15 (ESV)

> If you've arranged your pastoral ministry to avoid regular missions into the jagged and rocky places in people's lives, then you are not shepherding like Jesus. The grimy, sweat-streaked face of a pastor is but an image of that blood-streaked face we all love. – Jeremy Pierre and Deepak Reju[47]

Our actions can speak powerfully, but actions alone do not transform people: we are to *speak the truth* in love. Setting an example is powerful, but as we seek to see others transformed into the likeness of Jesus, we will need to listen carefully to understand them and communicate God's Gospel and words to them. In a previous section, we discussed having the Word of God dwell richly among us and some strategies to foster this ministry in small groups. In addition to mutually reflecting on and responding to Scripture, there are times when we will need to instruct, challenge, encourage, or rebuke others from Scripture (Col 3:16; 2 Tim 3:16-17; Titus 1:13; 1 Thess 4:18; Heb 3:13; 10:24-25). If we are to do so well, we must first listen and understand the person (2 Tim 2:24-25; James 1:19). Listen to Proverbs 20:5, "The purpose in a man's heart is like deep water, but a man of understanding will draw it out" (ESV). *Drawing out* what is in someone's heart takes time. Growing in Christ is difficult work, and it takes patience to listen and learn where people are struggling and where God is working in someone's life.

> Like any competent physician, the pastor doesn't know what interventions to provide for a distressed soul until

---

47 Pierre and Reju, *The Pastor and Counseling*, 34.

> he first listens to that soul. He needs an accurate diagnosis, so he begins with the symptoms. But like any good medical doctor, he doesn't treat the symptoms; he treats the illness.[48]

Learning to listen means learning who people are and not assuming we know,

> When you assume, you do not ask. If you do not ask, you open yourself up to a world of invalid conclusions and misunderstandings. You may try to be God's instrument but miss the mark because you are putting two and two together and getting five—and you don't even know it. Thanks to your assumptions, the person you *think* you are helping may exist only in your mind.[49]

Listening well deepens our understanding of someone and their needs and strengths and demonstrates that we love them and can be trusted to care for them. Once we have listened, we trust that God, through his Spirit, can and will lead us to respond wisely and lovingly. We do not listen so that we may speak. Sometimes, listening is all we need to do; other times, it is appropriate to offer biblical counsel to help someone grow in their faith and holiness.

Doing this, listening well and ministering the Gospel to a person is referred to in many ways in the Bible: we read of the sorts of things that are said, such as encouragement or rebuke, and the gift of the Spirit's insight into people's lives, prophecy (e.g. 1 Corinthians 12-14).[50] Throughout the history of the Church, this art of listening well and through the Spirit applying God's word to people was called "soul care." Gregory of Nazianzus (d. 390 AD) reminded his audience that

---

[48] Harold L. Senkbeil, *The Care of Souls: Cultivating a Pastor's Heart* (Bellingham, WA: Lexham Press, 2019), 67.

[49] Tripp, *Instruments in the Redeemer's Hands*, 168.

[50] On prophecy see, Rutherford, *The Gift of Revelation: A Biblical Perspective on the Bible*, 60–63; Rutherford, *The Being of Churches*, 153–72.

every exhortation is not suited for every audience, so Gregory the Great (d. 604 AD) writes that "the discourse of a teacher should be adapted to the character of his audience so that it can address the specific needs of each individual and yet never shrink from the art of communal edification."[51] To minister the Gospel, Gregory is saying, we need to know the person so that we can apply the Scriptures accurately. Martin Bucer describes soul care like this,

> This involves being concerned and through the word of God providing that Christ's lambs, who are still straying from his flock and sheep-pen, should be gathered in; seeing that those who have been brought in should remain with the flock and in the sheep pen, and when they do go astray again, leading them back again; and protecting those that stay with the flock against all temptations and afflictions, and helping them again if they fall prey to them; in other words, seeing that they are deprived of nothing which contributes to their continual growth and increase in godliness.[52]

Richard Baxter writes, again speaking to pastors,

> The object of pastoral care is all the flock, that is, the church and every member of it. We should know every person who belongs to our charge. For how can we take heed unto them if we do not know them? A careful shepherd looks after every individual sheep. A good schoolmaster looks to every individual student, both for instruction and correction. A good physician looks after every particular patient. And good commanders look after every individual soldier. Why, then, should the teachers, the pastors, the physicians, the guides of the churches of Christ not take heed unto

---

[51] Gregory of Nazianzus, *Apology for his Flight to Pontus* (*Or* 2.30); Gregory the Great, *The Book of Pastoral Rule*, 87.

[52] Bucer, *Concerning the True Care of Souls*, 69.

> every individual member of their charge?[53]

For each of these writers, across over a thousand years of the Church, pastoral care and discipleship involve getting to know God's sheep personally through listening, spending time with them, and ministering God's word individually and particularly to that person. Pastors must do this, yet pastors are instructed to equip all of God's saints for the work of ministry (Eph 4:11-12), so we also are to train God's people for the work of soul care, to minister God's word to one another as persons.

In contemporary literature, "soul care" or "pastoral care" is usually called "counselling." Essentially, the task before us is to actively listen to people in order to understand their struggles and circumstances and what is going on in their hearts amid these circumstances. It is important to listen and understand what someone is going through and how they are responding to it, but we know that circumstances do not determine our behaviour, for Christ calls us to endure suffering with joy and count it as a blessing when we are persecuted for his sake (Matt 5:1-12; Rom 5:1-11; 1 Pet 1:6-7; James 1:2-4). That is, we can have joy and be godly despite adverse circumstances; therefore, our sin problems are not problems with our circumstances, however much our circumstances are the occasions of our sins. As Paul tells the Philippians,

> Not that I am speaking of being in need, for I have learned in whatever situation I am to be content. I know how to be brought low, and I know how to abound. In any and every circumstance, I have learned the secret of facing plenty and hunger, abundance and need. I can do all things through him who strengthens me. (Phil 4:11-13, ESV)

A rebellious and disobedient child is not the cause of a father's anger.

---

[53] Baxter, *The Reformed Pastor*, 48.

No, the father's impatient, perhaps controlling, heart is the cause of his anger; the child's disobedience is the occasion for what has been there the whole time to emerge.[54] Jesus tells us that the source of our actions is our heart, our character (Matt 7:15-20), so if we want to change our behaviour, if we want to act differently and feel differently in response to the same circumstances, our hearts need to change. In other words, if we want to turn away from sin and begin to love God and our neighbour as ourselves, we need a deep change. It is not enough to merely change our beliefs, for we can believe anger is a sin and still get angry. We need to identify and address the sinful roots of our actions. James, for example, rebukes his audience for their divisiveness and identifies the heart of the problem:

> [1]What causes fights and quarrels among you? Don't
> they come from your desires that battle within you?
> [2]You desire but do not have, so you kill. You covet but
> you cannot get what you want, so you quarrel and fight.
> You do not have because you do not ask God. [3]When
> you ask, you do not receive, because you ask with
> wrong motives, that you may spend what you get on
> your pleasures. [4]You adulterous people, don't you
> know that friendship with the world means enmity
> against God? Therefore, anyone who chooses to be a
> friend of the world becomes an enemy of God. [5]Or do
> you think Scripture says without reason that he
> jealously longs for the spirit he has caused to dwell in
> us? [6]But he gives us more grace. That is why Scripture
> says: "God opposes the proud but shows favor to the
> humble." [7]Submit yourselves, then, to God. Resist the
> devil, and he will flee from you. [8]Come near to God
> and he will come near to you. Wash your hands, you
> sinners, and purify your hearts, you double-minded.
> [9]Grieve, mourn and wail. Change your laughter to
> mourning and your joy to gloom. [10]Humble yourselves

[54] Cf. Christopher Ash and Steve Midgley, *The Heart of Anger: How the Bible Transforms Anger in Our Understanding and Experience* (Wheaton: Crossway, 2021).

> before the Lord, and he will lift you up. (James 4:1-10, NIV)

The sins this church exhibits are fights and division. However, the real problem, the cause, is distorted desires. They have unmet desires, and their dissatisfaction with this state is expressed in envy and coveting what others have. These desires are not right, for they could ask God and receive what they needed if they desired rightly. No, they have replaced love and friendship with God with love for and friendship with the world. The answer to their divisions and fighting is not only to repent of their divisiveness and quarrelling, though they must do that, but also to repent and grieve their worldliness and devote themselves entirely to God. They must first humble themselves before God will restore them to the joy of his fellowship. In this case, the evident sin was a symptom of a deeper problem, a love of the world in the place of God; addressing the sin alone would not fix the real problem.

There are many ways of getting to the heart and seeing change. Right now, we are considering intentional, careful, interpersonal work of soul care, but this is not the only way we change. Seeing examples of godliness can not only model what to do but help us begin to do so: we may be encouraged to see someone who has successfully overcome sin or find greater success in walking with someone out of a pattern of sin rather than going at it alone. Growing in our knowledge of Jesus through his word and the fellowship of his people can also make this change. Jesus tells us that what we love shapes our actions; if we love comfort and material wealth—if this is what we truly want and if we are convinced this is what is truly good—we will act to increase our comfort and wealth or act out when our efforts are thwarted (Matt 6:19-24; Luke 12:34).[55]

---

[55] Cf. James K. A. Smith, *You Are What You Love: The Spiritual Power of Habit* (Brazos Press, 2016).

However, digging deep into our hearts to solve our disordered loves is not always helpful. If we were to feel that our love for a spouse had gone cold, or we were drawn away by the temptation to lust, we should not think more about the object of our lust or the things that distract us. No, we should engage in positive and appropriate relationships: we would arrange a date with our spouse and intentionally spend time with them. The answer to a disordered love is to do things that will help us love rightly—to love the one we should love more. If we find we love money more than God, we need to seek to strengthen our love for God (Matt 6:24). We can do this by spending time getting to know him through his word (see Chapter 6) or by spending more time with the people who reflect him, his church. Sometimes, we need to look away from ourselves and to God, but at other times, we need someone's help to uncover the roots of our sin and address these roots.

To listen and minister the word to others—to care for their soul—Paul Tripp uses a model of *love*, *know*, *speak*, and *do*. Care begins with loving the person before us: we spend time with them, listen to them, and share experiences with them. Tripp speaks of *entering the person's world, incarnating the love of Christ, identifying with their suffering*, and *accepting them to see them become like Christ.*[56] Love starts with hearing and understanding someone's state and being with them in their suffering. But if we stay there, we will not be able to offer counsel to see them change, for as we saw, the cause of sin is not our circumstance—important as they are (it was bad that the churches James addressed were fighting)! We need to get to know the person and understand their heart. Tripp speaks of the "redemptive importance of good questions." By listening to someone and asking good questions, we can discover the roots of sin or action; these roots are where change needs to happen.[57] We need to ask questions that clarify what someone is

[56] Tripp, *Instruments in the Redeemer's Hands*, 114–59.

[57] Tripp, 161–97; Powlison, *Speaking Truth in Love*, 55–60. Cf. Timothy S. Lane and Paul David Tripp, *How People Change*, 2nd ed (Greensboro, NC: New Growth Press, 2008); Lane, *Unstuck*.

saying and questions that help us develop insight into their experience and help them see their own experience in a new light. For clarification, we should get someone to define their terms; for example, if someone confesses to a "huge fight" in their marriage, get them to explain what a "huge fight" means.[58] Also, ask for concrete examples that explain terms they have used, such as "anger" or "frustration," and ask why they responded the way they did in these examples.[59] As with our ministry of the word, we want to ask *open* questions, questions that open the door to deeper relationships and better insight into a person's heart:

> Open questions require the other person to give a more detailed answer which requires thought and often story.... [Open questions are] questions designed to elicit a meaningful answer based on a person's feelings, thoughts and knowledge.[60]

Paul Tripp gives some examples of open-ended questions in the context of a marriage,

> What did you see in this person that made you want to marry him?
> What are your goals for your marriage when you were engaged?
> What things in your marriage make you sad?
> What things in your marriage make you happy?
> In what ways do you think God is honored by your marriage?[61]

He gives many more examples, but these show how questions can

---

[58] Tripp, *Instruments in the Redeemer's Hands*, 170–71.

[59] Tripp, 171.

[60] Anglicare Centre for Pastoral Development, "Introductory Pastoral Care Course Book" (Anglicare, n.d.), 10–11.

[61] Tripp, *Instruments in the Redeemer's Hands*, 175.

open discussion and lead to reflection on the circumstances someone faces and their heart amid those circumstances. Paul Tripp also helpfully describes five different classes of questions and the sorts of insights they reveal

> *What?* questions are the most basic, uncovering general information. ("What did you do?" "I talked to my wife.")
> *How?* questions reveal the way something was done. ("How did you talk to her?" "I yelled at her for fifteen minutes!") Notice how much more we know already, simply by asking a follow-up "how" questions.
> *Why?* questions uncover a person's purposes, desires, goals, or motivations. ("Why did you yell so long?" "I wanted her to know how angry I was at what she had done.") Here we have gone beyond the husband's behavior to examine the heart behind it.
> *How often?* and *Where?* questions reveal themes and patterns in a person's life. ("Where did this happen?" "At the supper table. Suppers are hard. We are both tired. We have young children. Meals are not relaxing at all! The evening meal always seems tense for us.")
> *When?* questions uncover the order of events. ("Tell me exactly when you began to yell during supper." "In the middle of the chaos my wife said, 'Well, how was *your* day?' She was obviously annoyed because I hadn't asked about hers. I said, 'Do you really care or are you just being nasty?' She said, 'Well, you're the only one here with an interesting and important life, right?' At that point I blew up.")[62]

We use good questions gently and patiently to get to know the heart.

If we know a person's heart in a specific situation, we can minister God's Word by his Spirit: we can speak the truth in love. Though all discipleship involves putting off sin and putting on righteousness, the

[62] Lane and Tripp, *How People Change*, 178–79.

causes of sin will not always themselves be sin; sometimes deep-seated beliefs lead us to act in sinful or unwise ways, so the *problem* behind sinful behaviour may not itself be clearly a sin. Perhaps it is a caricature, but contemporary models of pastoral soul care have been accused of reducing the myriad of issues that we may deal with in discipleship down to sin.[63] One pattern of doing this is to speak of the idols of the heart and false worship as the source of our problems.[64] Thinking through idols as false worship that distracts us from God and leads to sin can be helpful and reflects Paul's argument in Romans 1:18-32, yet it can be made too simplistic if an "idol" is the explanation of every issue in discipleship; this fails to understand the depth of human brokenness and complexities of restoration.

We need a thicker understanding of the roots of our sin, one that resists reducing the human condition to intellectual error (false beliefs), broken systems (as in Islamic and Marxist accounts of sin), or various unbiblical models of psychology, where human behaviour is reduced to a social-scientific model with some combination of environment and biology giving the entire account of the human condition, apart from spiritual and theological considerations.[65] Sin is not just what we

---

[63] This is frequent in discussions of Jay Adams and the origins of the biblical counselling movement and *nouthetic* counselling. See Heath Lambert, *A Theology of Biblical Counseling: The Doctrinal Foundations of Counseling Ministry* (Grand Rapids: Zondervan, 2016), 226–27; Heath Lambert, *The Biblical Counseling Movement after Adams* (Wheaton: Crossway, 2012), 49–80.

[64] Brad Bigney, *Gospel Treason: Betraying the Gospel with Hidden Idols* (Phillipsburg, NJ: P&R Publishing, 2012); Elyse Fitzpatrick, *Idols of the Heart: Learning to Long for God Alone*, Second edition (Phillipsburg, NJ: P&R Publishing, 2016). Cf. Johnson, *Foundations for Soul Care: A Christian Psychology Proposal*, 462–64.

[65] On the latter issue, see Edward T. Welch, *Blame It on the Brain? Distinguishing Chemical Imbalances, Brain Disorders, and Disobedience*, Resources for Changing Lives (Phillipsburg, NJ: P&R Publishing, 1998); Johnson, *Foundations for Soul Care: A Christian Psychology Proposal*; Powlison, *The Pastor as Counselor*.

do; it is a force at work in this world (see, for example, Romans 6:1-8:17). Sin describes our actions and failures to act but also the acts of others against us and the twistedness of created reality such that suffering is ever present, wickedness endures, sin comes naturally, and we are easily deceived into believing sin is good for us. If there were no Sin, there would be no sins, so Sin is our biggest problem, and sins are symptoms of that more significant issue. We not only have a twisted disposition, a proneness to sin (e.g. Ps 51; Jer 17:9; Rom 3:9-20), but we carry the effects of other's sins against us and face the assaults of an enemy who wants to drag us back into sin, including a world-system that fosters sin and discourages righteousness.[66] In discipleship, in caring for souls, we are addressing the whole range of Sin's effects in and on a person in order to walk with them into the freedom of Christ and growing obedience.

Because the causes of human thought and behaviour are complex, the way we approach discipleship must be nuanced. However, God has told us that he has in Scripture given us everything we need for life and godliness (2 Pet 1:3) so that we may be equipped for every good work (2 Tim 3:16-17). Therefore, the Bible is sufficient that we may live lives pleasing to God. Therefore, despite the complexities of the human soul, God has given his churches the tools they need to disciple each other in godliness. We will not be able to achieve every desirable end with the tools God has given us, especially with the broad understanding of soul care developed in the contemporary world; people in our churches will sometimes need help from the tools of psychology.[67] Medication alone, developing our resilience and

---

[66] On the first point, see Rutherford, *Prevenient Grace.* On the others, this is evident from the struggles of the Psalmists and Jeremiah in the face of sin, from the threat of the world-system to the believer in Revelation, from the nature of spiritual warfare in Ephesians 6, and elsewhere, e.g. 1 Peter 5:8-9.

[67] Powlison, *Speaking Truth in Love*, 141–52; Pierre and Reju, *The Pastor and Counseling*, 118–28. Cf. Powlison, *The Pastor as Counselor*; Johnson, *Foundations for Soul Care: A Christian Psychology Proposal.*

processing our experiences alone, changing our circumstances alone, or addressing our beliefs alone cannot fix the problems plaguing the human soul. However, each of these has its place. However, what we can do in the church is equip God's people to grow in godliness despite their struggles and circumstances.

In pastoral care, we address the problems of the heart from the word of God in the community of God's people. Deep-seated beliefs are hard to kill; if we identify the heart problem that leads to a discipleship issue, we need to identify it and offer a biblical perspective on it, but this is often not the end of the story.[68] Leading someone to confess a sinful disposition or problem, to acknowledge a wrong belief, or to label a concern or fear that leads to sinful behaviour does not produce change. Someone may struggle to trust God, and we may identify the problem as a terrible experience with a father being read onto God's claim to be our father (i.e. because my experience of fathers is that all fathers are **A** [e.g., jerks], so God as my father must be **A** [e.g. a jerk]). It is not so simple to tell them they are wrong and that God as a father is different from their experience of fathers. This must happen at some point, yet to change such a deep-seated belief (a concept of father), they must be exposed to an alternate vision of fatherhood consistent with the biblical picture. Perhaps this may come from the example of godly fathers in the church and from seeing how God acts as a father in the Scriptures. In discipleship, we help each other take concrete actions to change the roots of sin that dominate our lives. The tools we are given are the public gathering of God's people, the fellowship of the church, and the ministry of the word of God.

d. The Prayer of a Righteous Person Avails Much

> [13]Is anyone among you in trouble? Let them pray. Is

[68] Pierre and Reju, *The Pastor and Counseling*, 48–53; Tripp, *Instruments in the Redeemer's Hands*, 199–237.

> anyone happy? Let them sing songs of praise. [14]Is
> anyone among you sick? Let them call the elders of the
> church to pray over them and anoint them with oil in
> the name of the Lord. [15]And the prayer offered in faith
> will make the sick person well; the Lord will raise them
> up. If they have sinned, they will be forgiven.
> [16]Therefore confess your sins to each other and pray for
> each other so that you may be healed. The prayer of a
> righteous person is powerful and effective. – James
> 5:13-16 (NIV)

God is the one who achieves all change in us, so prayer is indispensable to our endeavours to care for one another and see each other grow in maturity. Prayer in Scripture does not consist of set words to be repeated (Matt 6:7) or a posture to be adopted. Instead, prayer is an offering of praise and thanksgiving, confession of sin and iniquity, a declaration of our state, and a request for God's intervention directly addressed to God himself. We are assured that through Jesus, our prayers are heard (Heb 5), and Jesus promises that through our prayers, God can achieve what appears impossible by human means (Matt 17:20; 21:20-22; Luke 17:5-6). Jesus assures us that God is a good Father who delights in giving good gifts to his children, so we do not need to worry that God will curse us when we ask him for a blessing (Luke 10:5-13). God hears our prayers and will answer the prayer of the righteous. James expects that elders will pray for the sick and that this will bring about healing (James 5:14). He also indicates that confession and prayer can play an important role in repentance and restoration (James 5:15). The role of prayer in discipleship is multifaceted.

We ought to pray that God would cleanse us, grant us repentance, and forgive us, as James indicates and we hear from David in Psalm 51. Not only do we pray for our sinful symptoms, but once we have identified that heart issues at work, we pray that God would renew our hearts and minds and transform our desires and dispositions in line with his word (Ps 51:10). God knows what we need before we ask (Matt 6:8), yet he nevertheless encourages us to make known our needs to him (e.g. James 1:5, 4:2); we ought to do so with specificity where known. The pattern of prayer Jesus gives us in Matthew differs from that in Luke, indicating that we are not being given a mantra or set prayer to repeat but a pattern of prayer (Matt 6:9-13; Luke 11:2-4). Jesus appears to make this point in Matthew 6:9 when he says "pray in this way [οὕτως, *houtos*]" rather than "pray this prayer." In Luke, the pattern of prayer is a prayer for the Lord's will, provision, forgiveness, and protection; the longer form of the prayer the Lord gives in Matthew has the same pattern. Given the emphasis of the Sermon on the Mount (Matthew) or Plain (Luke) on God's kingdom, the order is surely significant: we move from our desire for God's will to be done ("seek first the kingdom") to God's promises, which we are assured we will receive ("all these things will be added to you") (Matt 6:33). Therefore, the manner of prayer instructed by the Lord is itself a form of discipleship, teaching us to order our lives first around the kingdom of God and then around the reception of God's promises.

Jesus's promise that God will give good gifts to his children (Luke 11:5-13) makes sense in this pattern, for we are assured that as we seek God's kingdom, he will provide all of our needs (Matt 6:25-34; Luke 12:22-34). The teaching here also cautions our expectations: God has shown us that seeking earthly treasure and pleasure is not only incompatible with his kingdom but destructive for our souls (cf. Matt 16:24-28), so he will not grant a wish that is bent on self-destruction and opposed to his kingdom. Similarly, we are instructed to order our lives on the coming kingdom, so the prayer for healing from sickness may not always be answered with present healing, for the healing that comes through death and deliverance from the curse is, in the context of the Gospels, more significant than we could have asked for (cf. Phil 1:18-26). We are encouraged, nevertheless, to presume upon God's faithfulness to his promises so that when we ask, we have confidence that we will receive. In the case of discipleship, we ask in faith that God will not only forgive us our sins but also deliver us from the temptation to continue in sin and transform our lives in conformity with his will as we have asked him to transform the world (Matt 6:9-13). However, prayers of supplication, which ask God to realise his promises to us now, are not the only prayers useful for discipleship. We are also encouraged to pray prayers of thanks to God and to lament with one another, expressing our suffering to God and requesting his intervention.

Prayers can identify God's continued work in believer's lives and praise him for it. This is evident in Paul's pattern of thanksgiving prayers—which he prayed even for churches like the Corinthians with their serious issues (1 Cor 1:4-9). Thanksgiving is frequently conjoined with prayer in the New Testament epistles (e.g. Eph 1:16). This can be a source of encouragement for us and those for whom we give thanks: we draw attention to God's work and are reminded that he is indeed powerfully at work in the lives of his people, a fact that may be obscured by the trials and sins that emerge in the lives of God's people.

Prayers of lament are frequent across the Scriptures but are rarely prayed in our gatherings. However, they have an important purpose: corporately, prayers of lament acknowledge the reality of Sin and the brokenness of this world. They also demonstrate that Christians are emotionally moved by this world and that God does not expect or desire us to approach him after we have things together but wants to enter our mess to fix it. Mark Vroegop defines lament as "a prayer in pain that leads to trust."[69] He describes them as

> the historic biblical prayer language of Christians in pain. It's the voice of God's people while living in a broken world. Laments acknowledge the reality of pain

---

[69] Mark Vroegop, *Weep with Me: How Lament Opens a Door for Racial Reconciliation* (Wheaton: Crossway, 2020), 37. Cf. Vroegop, *Dark Clouds, Deep Mercy*; Vroegop, "Dare to Hope in God."

while trusting in God's promises.[70]

Prayers of lament also give us the opportunity to identify with the suffering of our fellow believers and, from that posture, approach God and request assistance. Though expressing anger and disappointment to God may appear, at first, to be a sign of unbelief, the logic of lament is that true faith is not blind to its own condition but is expressed in its constant orientation to God, even when it is beaten and bruised. The unbeliever refuses to even lament, for they either deny God's existence or refuse to believe he would listen. For the one who is in the midst of suffering or sin, the use of lament allows us to tear off the veil of self-righteousness and come to grips with the actual condition of our hearts, knowing that God is not deceived by our efforts to put forth a veneer of stoic faith. For those who would administer care, lament helps us show that someone can suffer greatly and struggle with God while still remaining faithful: the presence of frustration, anger, or doubt does not invalidate our faith. Consider Jeremiah's pray in the midst of persecution,

> [7] You deceived me, LORD, and I was deceived;
> you overpowered me and prevailed.
> I am ridiculed all day long;
> everyone mocks me.
> [8] Whenever I speak, I cry out
> proclaiming violence and destruction.
> So the word of the LORD has brought me
> insult and reproach all day long.
> [9] But if I say, "I will not mention his word
> or speak anymore in his name,"
> his word is in my heart like a fire,
> a fire shut up in my bones.
> I am weary of holding it in;
> indeed, I cannot.
> [10] I hear many whispering,
> "Terror on every side!

[70] Vroegop, *Weep with Me*, 37.

Denounce him! Let's denounce him!"
All my friends
are waiting for me to slip, saying,
"Perhaps he will be deceived;
then we will prevail over him
and take our revenge on him."

11 But the LORD is with me like a mighty warrior;
so my persecutors will stumble and not prevail.
They will fail and be thoroughly disgraced;
their dishonor will never be forgotten.
12 LORD Almighty, you who examine the righteous
and probe the heart and mind,
let me see your vengeance on them,
for to you I have committed my cause.

13 Sing to the LORD!
Give praise to the LORD!
He rescues the life of the needy
from the hands of the wicked.

14 Cursed be the day I was born!
May the day my mother bore me not be blessed!
15 Cursed be the man who brought my father the news,
who made him very glad, saying,
"A child is born to you—a son!"
16 May that man be like the towns
the LORD overthrew without pity.
May he hear wailing in the morning,
a battle cry at noon.
17 For he did not kill me in the womb,
with my mother as my grave,
her womb enlarged forever.
18 Why did I ever come out of the womb
to see trouble and sorrow
and to end my days in shame? (Jeremiah 20:7–18

NIV)[71]

Jeremiah, a man chosen by God before the foundations of the earth to minister his word to Judah, struggled with the calling God had given him (cf. Ezek 3:14-15). Throughout his ministry, Jeremiah expressed the struggles he experienced; in passages like this, he turns to God with frustration and even anger—"you deceived me!" is his claim. How was he deceived? From a young age, Jeremiah was commissioned to be God's prophet, yet little could he have understood the cost of his calling: he was God's chosen vessel, but earthly comfort did not accompany the favour God had shown him. Jeremiah expresses a sense of betrayal in the calling he received. Michael L. Brown describes it like this,

> "You drew me in and tricked me, Yahweh, and it worked. You overpowered me, took advantage of my youthful naivete. You were just too strong for me. You won!" And what a mismatch it was—almighty God enlisting an innocent young man (probably just a teenager!) in a lifelong, hapless task, not telling him up front that he would never be able to marry or have children, not telling him that he would, in fact, be beaten and imprisoned and publicly humiliated (didn't God promise that he would be rescued from his enemies?), not fully explaining to him the living hell he would experience, and not describing in detail the agonizing and personal nature of some of the oracles he would have to deliver.[72]

This passage is confronting, for we are forced to reckon with Jeremiah's perception of God as a foe who assails him and forces him to do something he no longer wishes to do. However, as we wrestle

---

[71] See also, Psalm 13, 77, 89; Job 3; Lamentations.

[72] Michael L. Brown, "Jeremiah," in *The Expositor's Bible Commentary Volume 7: Jeremiah-Ezekiel*, ed. Tremper Longman and David E. Garland, Revised Edition (Grand Rapids: Zondervan, 2010), 288.

with Jeremiah's words, we see that he is expressing his *perception*, not the reality. His words are those of one who suffers greatly and *feels* as though God is against him. In one sense, what he experiences is utterly real, but in another, it is not. What he feels is genuine, but it does not follow from what he feels that God is actually a manipulative and cruel God. Jeremiah himself knows this, so amid his angry and despairing prayer, he moves past the way he feels to the reality of God that is obscured by his tears: God is his protector. He calls on God's promises to avenge the wicked and protect his people (v. 12) and praises God, knowing that he will fulfil his promises (v. 13). Nevertheless, his present state is terrible, and he could even long that he was never born.

This is a prayer of faith, for Jeremiah has not abandoned God or transposed his feelings into convictions about God. Instead, he is brutally honest with how he feels; he has looked at his soul, and what he sees there is terrible. Nevertheless, he clings to the reality of God and his promises in his despair, simultaneously expressing what he feels and declaring the hope he has in the whirlwind that threatens to consume him. Many others in the Bible have felt like Jeremiah felt, so it should come as no surprise when Christians—even ministers—feel this way. Lament gives us the language to express the twin realities of how we feel and who God is simultaneously. Singing or praying such prayers in church normalises the reality of Christian suffering and the hope that we can cling to God in the midst of it.

Prayer is not only a tool in Christian discipleship as an instrument to access the riches of the spiritual blessings God has promised us in Christ (Eph 1:3) but also as a means to communicate the reality of the human condition and the Christian experience and to model genuine faith amid these realities.

ii. Discipling Pastors

In the previous sections of this chapter, we considered four significant aspects of discipleship discussed in Scripture. We approached them generally as a means for the entire Church to grow together into the fullness of maturity. The place of such a general discussion is justified in a volume devoted to the preparation of ministers because, as we have shown above, discipleship and ministry training are one and the same. These practices are equally applicable to pastors and are equally necessary for their spiritual development. However, we must consider the particularities of training pastors not because of any radical difference between their experience and the non-ordained Christian but because of the additional difficulties pastors face.

The continued discipleship of those in ministry or being prepared for ministry faces several challenges. Pastoral candidates may face fear about how they are perceived. Given the necessary qualifications for ministry, pastors may feel like imposters, as if they should never have qualified; in this case, they may fear that being truly vulnerable would end their ministry and damage the sheep in their care. Satan may use this as a tool to discourage genuine confession and repentance. As Senkbeil writes, "The threat of disciplinary consequence—whether imagined or real—is going to make a pastor somewhat hesitant to be transparent with his supervisor."[73] Pastors may fear that wolves could use their weakness in the church and outside of it to destroy their lives and ministry, as has happened to many pastors before them. Pastors may also face a situation where everyone in their church looks up to them: they may perceive a lack of peers or mentors to walk with them towards greater maturity. Discipleship for pastors continues in the same way as it does for all of us, but the specific burdens and challenges of pastoral ministry require extra attention.

Fear is a powerful tool in the hand of Satan, so discipling pastors requires creating contexts where they feel confident to confess their sins and submit themselves to the care of others. Part of this is developing a local church culture that recognises pastors are not perfect, is transparent about what is expected of a pastor, and upholds

---

[73] Senkbeil, *The Care of Souls: Cultivating a Pastor's Heart*, 239.

the biblical qualifications for a pastor. We have considered the qualifications above; what is called for is not perfection but a pattern of triumph over sin and genuine repentance. To be qualified for ministry, a pastor must be known to repent and confess their sins, not just in generalities but in specific confession to those they have hurt. To be above reproach is not to never sin but to ensure that no secret sin waits to be exploited by Satan to the detriment of God's people and the pastor himself. Pastoral transparency should be encouraged, so an atmosphere should be developed where pastors are given trust and encouraged to be open about their mistakes, not pressured with expectations only Jesus can meet.[74]

Pastors should also be expected to maintain pastoral relationships with other pastors, where they provide care for one another. The congregation will be able to minister the Gospel to their pastor, but it is also important that there are people empowered with Christ's authority as pastors to speak in their lives. In a multi-elder system, the elders ought to be expected to care for one another. In a system with a hierarchy of elders (with one leader) or a single minister per church, the pastor should be expected to develop these relationships with local pastors or others in their denomination who will spend time ministering the Gospel to them.

For pastoral candidates who are not yet qualified for ministry, it is essential to identify specific inadequacies and walk with them through these struggles, but this should be done within a broader pattern of discipleship, for a focus on one aspect may lead them to lapse in another or may promote false reporting (where they claim all is fine outside of the area of focus but let another aspect of their life slip).

D. Conclusion

Godliness is of essential importance to the health of a church and its

---

74 See further, Tripp, *Dangerous Calling.*

ministers, so we have dealt at length with this topic in this chapter. After identifying godliness as right character and showing how the local church is critical to correctly identifying the presence or absence of godliness, we then discussed at length several tools God has given us to disciple others. Throughout, we have seen that the godly character of a Christian, even a minister, is best discerned within a healthy local church. In this context, godly character may be developed among all of God's people, including its leaders. This chapter has provided a model for identifying and training ministers in the local church context; it begins by developing a robust and serious culture of discipleship within which character is identified and developed. We have accepted a qualified form of "inwardness" or self-knowledge (subjective) and knowledge of the self (objective) as an important component of discipleship.[75] Teaching others to obey Jesus's commands cannot be delivering a list of rules or telling them to stop what they are doing; no, since sinful actions proceed from a sinful heart (however much we must qualify this since we are new creations in Christ Jesus), true change requires addressing the cause of sin in the heart rather than the external behaviours. Therefore, to see genuine change our hearts—our inward self, our character—need to be assessed and our spiritual ailments diagnosed. The heart is not what we immediately perceive, our subjective sense of self and motivations, but something deeper. We rely on our perceived self to get at our heart, but these are related as an effect to its cause: when we *feel* angry, this reveals something about our heart, which is causing anger under the specific circumstances we face.[76] Because the heart is not equivalent to our immediate perception and feelings, we are not necessarily the best

---

[75] Johnson argues that inwardness is a Christian idea with a strong pedigree, and that it differs from corrupted forms of inwardness perpetuated through the 20th century until today. He appears to be broadly right and makes important observations on the implementation of inwardness in the context of soul care. Johnson, *Foundations for Soul Care: A Christian Psychology Proposal*, 415–538.

[76] Groves and Smith, *Untangling Emotions.*

judges of our own hearts, nor are we even the best equipped to understand the heart. Our heart is manifest not only in what we feel and perceive but also in what we say and do. Others are often more observant than we are about our actions and words, being able to identify things about ourselves that we miss entirely. For this reason, the inward element of discipleship is not introspective and individualistic but is "fundamentally social" and dialogical.[77] We need others to identify our true problems; so it is often in communion, as people see our reflexive words and actions and we share our observations, that we begin to truly understand our hearts. Thus, we have argued for a form of inwardness but have qualified this as an outward-looking, communal inwardness. Furthermore, though our problems are inside us, the tools to fix these problems are outside. In discipleship, we help others look inward to identify a problem and then lead them to God for the solution.

The Bible envisions pastoral candidates naturally arising within this context of serious discipleship. If we want to address the crisis the church is currently facing, we must start by seeking to lead our churches into the fullness of maturity. The first thing we must realise is that if discipleship and pastoral training are one and the same, the qualifications of a pastor are not extraordinary but are what Christ expects from every Christian in his church. Every Christian should be managing their household, living in a way that is above reproach, and actively growing in righteousness and helping others to do so. Every Christian must demonstrate genuine faith by taking up their cross and following Jesus (Matt 16:13-28; James 2:14-26).

We have not discussed the need for faith in this chapter, for godliness obviously presupposes genuine faith. So, demonstrated godliness is evidence of the genuineness and maturity of the pastoral candidate's profession of faith. Though faith is not directly addressed in the descriptions of pastoral competencies, it is clear that a pastor's

[77] Johnson, *Foundations for Soul Care: A Christian Psychology Proposal*, 433.

faith is not only to be expressed in godly character but also radical commitment to Christ. Faith manifests in following Christ, so a minister as a teacher and herald of genuine faith will set an example in following Jesus. As we know from the Gospels, following Jesus is a call to forsake worldly treasures and desires for the sake of the kingdom of God (Matt 6:24, 33). This sacrificial pursuit of Christ is implied in the qualifications to be free from the love of money and worldly vices, which we forsake in the pursuit of Christ. To pursue Christ is both rewarding and costly, for if Christ suffered how much more will those who follow him do so (Matt 10:24-25; John 15:20)?

For this reason (among others), Paul cautions against ordaining a "recent convert" to ministry, lest they fall into the sin of pride. Ordination can hinder a new convert's growth in godliness and Christian maturity. We must be cautious about putting new believers on a pedestal; embracing Christ late in life often comes at a great cost, so the devotion of those who make such a choice often puts those who have followed Christ for a long time to shame. However, qualification for ministry is not found in zeal alone but in demonstrated Christian character over time. Ministry is an endurance race, not a sprint. The temptation to give a platform and responsibility to new believers is seen when high-profile people come to Jesus, or in my own context, to Muslims who have become Christians (surely this happens with people coming from other religions or under-evangelised people groups). Doing this not only endangers the church, putting untested and ill-prepared people into a complex but vital role in the church, but it also—as is Paul's primary concern—puts them at risk from the Devil's schemes (1 Tim 3:6).

Further Reading

There are dozens of good books on Christian soul care and pastoral counselling and its use within the church. These are some examples of the overall discipline that I recommend. The first four books, from across Christian history, challenge us to take seriously the role of soul care in Christian ministry. See the bibliography for specific editions.

Gregory the Great, *The Book of Pastoral Rule*
This historical text provides an introduction to pastoral care and the pastor followed by instructions on the care to be administered to sets of opposing conditions (e.g. the sincere and the insincere, those who live in discord and those who live in peace). Gregory speaks of pulpit ministry, but his counsel extends to private care.

Martin Bucer, *Concerning the True Care of Souls*
This historical text addresses the lapse of pastoral care the Reformers identified in the medieval church. Using Ezekiel 34 as his base text, Bucer outlines pastoral ministry and then the care to be given to sheep in the different conditions described in Ezekiel 34.[78]

Richard Baxter, *The Reformed Pastor* (see the Crossway abridgement)
Richard Baxter pastored a large English church in the years following the Reformation; in this book, he argues that personal care is essential to the role of a pastor. He argues vigorously that pastors should visit each parishioner in their homes and addresses some of the practicalities of care. [79]

David Powlison, *Pastor as Counselor: The Call for Soul Care*
Powlison shows that pastors are counsellors, whether they like it or not; he argues that we must be intentional in this task and do it

---

[78] J. Alexander Rutherford, "Review of Concerning the True Care of Souls – Teleioteti Book Reviews," Teleioteti, November 3, 2021, https://www.teleioteti.ca/2021/11/03/review-of-concerning-the-true-care-of-souls/.

[79] J. Alexander Rutherford, "Review of the Reformed Pastor – Teleioteti Book Reviews," Teleioteti, November 10, 2021, https://www.teleioteti.ca/2021/11/10/review-of-the-reformed-pastor/.

well for the sake of God's sheep.[80]

Jeremy Pierre & Deepak Reju, *The Pastor and Counseling: The Basics of Shepherding Members in Need*

Pierre and Reju offer an outline of a formal counselling process in the context of the local church. They write primarily for pastors but have insights applicable to soul care in general. Like many books in the biblical counselling movement, they presume a high level of individuality and literacy, which will need to be critiqued in an oral and communal setting.[81]

Paul Tripp, *Instruments in the Redeemer's Hands: People in Need of Change Helping People in Need of Change*

This book is perhaps longer than it needs to be, but it is full of insights into how Christians can listen well to one another and care for each other by addressing the heart.

David Powlison, *Speaking Truth in Love: Counsel in Community*

Powlison provides an overview of soul care as a ministry of all Christians to one another.

Edward T. Welch, *Caring for One Another: 8 Ways to Cultivate Meaningful Relationships*

This short book gives an overview of mutual ministry among church members that gets to the heart of our problems. It is a helpful tool for equipping lay people for the work of soul care.

Harold L. Senkbeil, *The Care of Souls: Cultivating a Pastor's Heart*

This is a longer treatise addressing pastoral soul care specifically; it provides many insights into the pastor's role from a historical and theological perspective.

---

80 J. Alexander Rutherford, "Review of The Pastor as Counselor – Teleioteti Ecclesiology," Teleioteti, July 20, 2021, https://www.teleioteti.ca/2021/07/20/review-of-the-pastor-as-counselor/.

81 J. Alexander Rutherford, "Review of The Pastor and Counseling," Teleioteti, August 22, 2018, https://www.teleioteti.ca/2018/08/22/review-of-the-pastor-and-counseling/.

12

HOW DO WE IDENTIFY THE ABILITY TO TEACH AND TRAIN TO DO IT?

> And the Lord's servant must not be quarrelsome but must be kind to everyone, able to teach, not resentful. Opponents must be gently instructed, in the hope that God will grant them repentance leading them to a knowledge of the truth, and that they will come to their senses and escape from the trap of the devil, who has taken them captive to do his will. – 2 Timothy 2:24-26 (NIV)

A. What is Teaching?

The primary qualifications for a pastor pertain to godliness, but they are also required to teach. Teaching is undeniably an important aspect of pastoral work, yet our current pathways to ministry spend inordinate amounts of time and effort on this single qualification. We have argued that the amount of time spent on training pastors to teach is not justified by Scripture, for our current approach rests on an understanding of teaching that is different from the teaching in the biblical context. In this chapter, we will unpack our claims about teaching made above (e.g. §7.B.c) and consider how we can equip people in our churches to do this. This first section will be primarily synthetic, drawing together our argument in Parts 1 and 2. The following sections will attempt to take this view of teaching on a walk in the life of a church, looking at how we can identify and develop the ability to teach. We have already looked closely at the presuppositions of contemporary institutions, so I do not intend to revisit them here. Instead, I want to consider what goes into "teaching," which we identified in Chapter 7 as the public ministry of the word and, by extension, the private ministry. That is, though "teaching" is primarily a public act in the New Testament, the content of teaching, namely, the application of the Word of God to people in specific circumstances, is the same as an elder-overseer's private ministry.

Above, I argued that "able to teach" means to have demonstrated the ability to do so, which raises questions about the characteristics of teaching and how an ability to teach can be demonstrated. I will argue that *skill* is not intended by this phrase: Paul does not require demonstrated rhetorical abilities or charismatic and persuasive public presence (see §ii below). If it is presumed that communicative ability is not a prerequisite for ministry and the Spirit can fill in what is lacking in someone's speaking proficiency, then we must investigate what is necessary for someone to be *able to teach*. I will argue that teaching requires wisdom and discernment (knowing how and what to communicate), godly character (living a life consistent with one's message and being able to exercise wisdom in communication), and knowledge. I will then argue that skill in speaking and communicating is not required.

i. Teaching Requires Wisdom

> Him we proclaim, warning everyone and teaching everyone with all wisdom, that we may present everyone mature in Christ. For this I toil, struggling with all his energy that he powerfully works within me.
> – Colossians 1:28-29 (ESV)

Wisdom, in the Bible, often refers to the skill of living in the world as

God has created it. In other words, it is knowing how to go with the grain of the created order instead of against it. Wisdom is the skill of living well. Wisdom in Paul's writings is often a form of knowledge or a way of thinking; God's wisdom is demonstrated in his administration of the created order and is utterly foreign to this world's wisdom yet is intrinsically best. Like godliness, wisdom presupposes a proper posture towards God—the "fear of the Lord"—but it is not only knowing how to do what is right in the eyes of God but also how to live rightly in God's world, to live in the world in a way corresponding to God's governance and administration of creation. In the case of teaching, wisdom is knowing *how* to administer God's saving word. There is a way of speaking the truth that is wise and, therefore, loving; there is another way that is cumbersome and clumsy, often wreaking more damage than it does good. In 2 Peter 3:16, we are told of those who twist Paul's words and the rest of Scripture to their own destruction; Paul speaks wisdom, but these men are characterised by lawlessness, by a refusal to submit to God's instructions, and are therefore unstable (v. 17). There is much in the Scriptures about *speaking* wisely; there is a way of speaking which conforms to the way God has ordered the world.

James instructs us to be "quick to hear, slow to speak, slow to anger" (James 1:19); teaching requires the wisdom to listen first and then speak, to understand before acting. The servant of God is to be gentle in his instruction so that the sinner might turn from their ways (2 Tim 2:24-26; Gal 6:1): a harsh word will not bring such a response. It takes wisdom to know how to be gentle in specific circumstances and to avoid being drawn into arguments (Titus 3:2). "A gentle answer turns away wrath, but a harsh word stirs up anger," and "The soothing tongue is a tree of life, but a perverse tongue crushes the spirit" (Prov 15:1, 4 NIV). There is a way of speaking that commends the truth: "The tongue of the wise adorns knowledge, but the mouth of the fool gushes folly" (Prov 15:2, NIV). Not only does wisdom identify how a word is spoken, but it also leads us to speak the right words at the right time, "A person finds joy in giving an apt reply—and how good is a timely word!" (Prov 15:23, NIV). A teacher is not to be swayed by the mood of the age; they are to communicate God's truth at all times (2 Tim 4:1-2), but wisdom is knowing the right time to speak a specific word. A wedding can be an amazing opportunity to communicate the truth of God's Gospel, but a message on the coming judgment and the need for repentance before that day would be ill-timed. Similarly, there are many reasons to rejoice in the death of a believer. However, there is great grief over the loss of life, and death confronts us with the evilness of death, so trite words that fail to reckon with the reality of death's evil most often cause more damage than good.

Wisdom helps us interpret our audience and know what to say to them. The Proverbs highlight the difficulty of responding to someone foolish—who walks contrary to God's way—like this,

> Do not answer a fool according to his folly,
>   or you yourself will be just like him.
> Answer a fool according to his folly,
>   or he will be wise in his own eyes. (Prov 26:4-5)

How do you speak the truth of God to someone who will feel justified by your silence but lives in an utterly incoherent manner that resists the truth? As one commentator explains, "These two verses are put together to show that human problems are often complicated and cannot always be solved by appealing to a single rule."[1] Bruce Waltke speaks of the wisdom needed in these circumstances,

> It is unfitting to meet the fool's insult with insult (2 Pet. 3:9). Should the disciple reply vindictively, harshly, and/or with lies—the way fools talk—he too—"yes, even you"—would come under the fool's condemnation. Rather, without lowering himself to the

[1] Allen P. Ross, "Proverbs," in *The Expositor's Bible Commentary, Volume 6: Proverbs-Isaiah*, ed. Tremper Longman and Garland David E, vol. 6 (Grand Rapids: Zondervan, 2008). Summarising R. N. Whybray, *The Book of Proverbs* (Cambridge: Cambridge University Press, 1972), 152.

> fool's level in a debate, but by overcoming evil with good (25:21f), the wise must show the fool's folly for what it is. The wise do not silently accept and tolerate the folly and thereby confirm fools in it.[2]

Wisdom also guides us as we seek to present a rebuke to or instruct a person, as Jesus shows his disciples, "Do not give dogs what is sacred; do not throw your pearls to pigs. If you do, they may trample them under their feet, and turn and tear you to pieces" (Matt 7:6 NIV). There are times when presenting the precious truths of the Kingdom will incite anger and a bad response; we are not to seek such confrontations but take care in how we speak and to whom we speak that we might commend the Gospel and not lose the opportunities God grants us to speak a word to a brother or sister (cf. Matt 7:3-5).

Relationships take wisdom; communication takes wisdom. Teaching as relational communication requires us to use "all wisdom" so that, by God's grace, "we might present everyone mature in Christ" (Col 1:28-29 ESV). As demonstrated by Solomon, wisdom alone is not sufficient to be able to teach, for it is possible to know the way one should go and fail to do so. Thus, besides wisdom, a teacher needs to be godly to teach well.

ii. Teaching Requires Godliness

> And the Lord's servant must not be quarrelsome but must be kind to everyone, able to teach, not resentful. Opponents must be gently instructed, in the hope that God will grant them repentance leading them to a knowledge of the truth, and that they will come to their senses and escape from the trap of the devil, who has taken them captive to do his will. – 2 Timothy 2:24-26

---

[2] Waltke, *NICOT: Proverbs 15:31*, 136.

(NIV)

We have already considered the importance of godliness for ministry at length, but consider with me the specific application of godliness to the act of teaching. It is possible to know the wise path but have insufficient character to take it: we can know a harsh word stirs up anger but still use harsh language out of impatience and a lack of self-control. We can know how to interpret God's Scriptures and apply them to our lives but fail to do so because we do not desire or have the discipline to actually change. At each step of communicating the Bible to ourselves and to others, we take steps that are themselves moral: we make choices to do what is right and wrong as we seek to act with wisdom and not foolishness. In 2 Timothy 2:24-26, Paul shows Timothy that a teacher must be kind and free from resentment; he shows that gentle instruction will see genuine change and repentance. The implication is that a lack of gentleness, kindness, and forgiveness—a lack of developed Christian character—will affect the outcome of one's teaching. Because Christian teaching is teleological, not just focused on what is said but the end for which we say it (i.e. to see people built up in Christ and enduring to the final day), godly character is essential to the task. Furthermore, if teaching expresses the elder-overseer's authority, then he must have the godly character to wield that authority. A Christian teacher must, thus, have wisdom and godliness, but teaching will also require that they teach *something*; they need knowledge to communicate.

iii. Teaching Requires Knowledge

> I charge you in the presence of God and of Christ Jesus, who is to judge the living and the dead, and by his appearing and his kingdom: preach the word; be ready in season and out of season; reprove, rebuke, and exhort, with complete patience and teaching. – 2 Tim 4:1-2 (ESV)

In Matthew 28:18-20, Jesus commissions his apostles to make disciples; one thing they are to do is "[teach] them to observe all that I have commanded you" (v. 20). The content of teaching in this verse is Jesus's commandments, and it is oriented to obedience. So, teaching involves ethical instruction and is, therefore, *concrete*, relating to specific people in specific circumstances (see the application of this command in the NT Epistles). Similarly, in Colossians, Paul speaks of the church's proclamation of Christ consisting of both warnings and 'teaching'; this teaching concerns "all wisdom" with the intended result of maturity (Col 1:28-29). In 2 Timothy 4, teaching is a manner by which Timothy ought to "preach the word… reprove, rebuke, and exhort" (4:2). Teaching here pertains to the public ministry of the word and relates to the concrete instructions to people. In each case, 'teaching' involves knowledge of God and his word and the knowledge of the people who will be taught.

In the previous chapter, we considered the relationship between ministering God's word and knowing the people we minister to. In summary, teaching people to obey Christ is not only telling them what to do but also helping them to do it. Doing this requires diagnosing the heart and addressing the roots of sin with God's word. Therefore, the ability to teach requires personal involvement in people's lives; teaching cannot be easily separated from pastoring, as Paul speaks elsewhere of those who pastor and teach (Eph 4:11). In previous chapters, we already addressed discipling people and the qualifications of godliness (i.e. being able to set a good example and lead people in it), which are critical components of being able to teach (cf. Eph 4:12). In the rest of this chapter, we will address the components of teaching that we have not talked about already, namely, the knowledge requirements and skill requirements. The latter is rarely a concern in Scripture, but 1 Corinthians does speak about it negatively (as in, lacking skill). In line with what we have argued above, I want to indicate that teaching requires the teacher to know God and his Word and live out obedience to God so that they might instruct others to do the same. We have already discussed knowing God and his word above, so in this section, we will briefly apply that discussion to the pastor's qualifications to teach. We will then discuss the potential skill component of being able to teach.

Because God has made himself known primarily in his word (and the knowledge of God with which we are born is distorted by sin), knowing God and his word are intimately connected. We know God by listening to what he says in his word, and we can only rightly understand God's word when we know him.[3] Growing in our knowledge of God and his word is, thus, a circle (or a spiral): as we read the Scriptures, we grow in our knowledge of God. This knowledge deepens and corrects our reading of Scripture. To enter this circle, we need to know something about the word and something about God. Though God occasionally enables people to grow in special and irregular ways, the regular means he has chosen to help us grow are local churches.[4] More mature believers are not only able to answer questions we may have but also give us a framework to understand Scripture, namely, an overview of God and his Bible, enabling us to understand and grow through reading it. They do this as Philip was able to help the Ethiopian man understand the Scriptures by showing him Jesus the Messiah (Acts 8:26-40). To be able to teach, a minister will need to know God and his word such that he can equip others with a framework to begin to read God's word with understanding.

This knowledge of Scripture is not mere facts—knowing verses,

---

[3] On this latter point, see Rutherford, *The Trinity and the Bible: How All Scripture Testifies to One God in Three Persons*; Rutherford, *The Gift of Knowledge.*

[4] This is harder to see in Western culture where, for many years, nonbelievers shared a conceptual framework with the Scriptures, so their cultural upbringing gave them certain presuppositions about God and his word that enable them to understand it when they read it. However, people from other cultures who have a different view of God, of God's communication, or written texts struggle to understand God's word without the help of God's people.

dates, and significant events. No, we need to understand the *meaning* of events. It is a fact that the Israelites practised sacrifices; it is a critical theme in Scripture that the sacrifices illustrate the severity of sin and point forward to the need for a substitute to cover human sin and reconcile humans to God. It is a fact that God made a covenant with Abraham; it is a critical theme in Scripture that covenants are mutual relationships between two parties that lay forth the expectations of behaviour and promise reward or blessing for those who uphold the relationship and curses for those who break it (Genesis 15, cf. Jeremiah 34; Deuteronomy 27-29). The sort of knowledge here is the ability of a minister to connect a passage in Scripture with the rest of Scripture, to understand its purpose and place and then connect it with the hearts of those to whom they minister. It is hard to quantify this knowledge, but we have seen that the fundamental role of a pastor is to apply the word of God to the hearts of God's people and equip them to do so as well and to live for God in the world. A pastor needs to know the Bible well enough to apply it to their own hearts and the hearts of others. To do this, they will need to know the storyline of Scripture (creation through restoration), the differences between the Old and New Testaments, how Christians relate to each testament, and how Christ is the subject of the whole of Scripture. One can know these things to varying depths. So, a pastor will grow in his knowledge throughout his life, but he must begin with sufficient knowledge to apply God's word to his people. We will give more concrete details about the content taught in the following two sections (§§B-C). As discussed in the previous chapter, to apply God's word to God's people we need to know people well.

This is the essential body of knowledge required for Christian ministry: knowledge of God and his word paired with the knowledge of persons in and outside the church who are the subject of the Bible's commands. There is room here for additional knowledge that is not necessary but may be helpful in some contexts: the knowledge found in cultural analyses that can move beyond personal issues and problems to shared trends and patterns in culture. Having this type of insight is not indispensable but can greatly help the ministry. Similarly, knowledge from various disciplines is valuable as we engage with those disciplines theologically, that is, as we seek to communicate God's word to all life. However, helpful as the knowledge of culture and various disciplines is, we must not presume God can only work where such knowledge is present. A difficulty that emerges at this point is quantifying the knowledge requirement for teaching: a pastor needs to know God, the Bible, and specific people, but it is challenging to identify how much of or how well a pastor needs to know these. This is best addressed, I believe, in the context of identifying the ability to teach and adopting strategies for training teachers (see §§B-C below). However, before we do so, we must consider the role of skill in teaching.

iv. Teaching Does not Require Communication Skills

> For they say, "His letters are weighty and strong, but his bodily presence is weak, and his speech of no account." Let such a person understand that what we say by letter when absent, we do when present. Not that we dare to classify or compare ourselves with some of those who are commending themselves. But when they measure themselves by one another and compare themselves with one another, they are without understanding. – 2 Cor 10:10-12 (ESV)

The phrase "the ability to teach" appears to speak of a skill, namely, the skill of teaching. "I am able to bike," for example, appears to presuppose a measure of skill, though not extraordinary skill; this is the case with many instances where we speak of an 'ability.' It seems counter-intuitive to suggest that someone may be able to teach without being skilled at teaching: as many of us have experienced, someone can be very knowledgeable but a lousy teacher! When I say that teaching does not require communication skills, I have something particular in mind. I do not mean skill in the sense that "I am able to bike" implies a measure of skill but in the sense of excellence, as in "he is a skilled hockey player." So, I argue that pastors do not need to be *excellent* teachers. Even here, there is ambiguity, for if someone is extraordinarily godly, loves people, and has the knowledge to teach, they would seem to be excellent teachers already—at least from the Bible's perspective. Peter was an excellent teacher because he effectively communicated God's word to God's people, as were Paul and the other apostles. So, when we say that the ability to teach does not mean that one is skilled at teaching, we mean that people do not have to be skilled in the world's understanding of 'skilled' and possess worldly excellence to be a teacher. Teaching is a demonstration of spiritual power, not worldly power, and spiritual power is manifest in worldly *weakness*. Therefore, worldly power may actually be a hindrance to good teaching.

What is worldly power? It is teaching skill or excellence that fits the world's tastes. To be an excellent teacher according to the Bible, I contest, is to be demonstrably filled with the Spirit's power. This is visible in genuine love and care for God's people and in the ministry of God's word. This contrasts with worldly excellence that prizes depth and ingenuity of thought—unique ideas and penetrating insight—eloquent and captivating speech, ambition and achievement, capacity and vision, and boldness with power. The person of worldly excellence is listened to because of their novelty: they are outside the box and willing to confront the stagnant patterns of life; they have something new to say. They are listened to because of their charisma: how they speak captures their audience. They are listened to because of their ambition and achievement: they cast a vision that people want, and they demonstrate by their accomplishments that they have made it, that they have already arrived at the place they are leading people to. Finally, the worldly teacher is listened to because they are bold, willing to say what others will not, and they exude strength, not weakness—they do not show cracks and are quick to put others in their place. Surely dozens of bad teachers come to mind when we begin to think in these terms; these are men or women who have caused terrible harm not because they were humble and meek but because they were powerful and charismatic, building a following and leading them to destruction. Yet, someone may object, "Some of our heroes sound a bit like this!" Indeed, I contend that many 'heroes' in church history are celebrated as heroes because of their boldness, charisma, ambition, novelty, achievement, vision, captivating (though perhaps not eloquent) speech, and depth of insight.[5] Men like this are put forth as examples to follow for up-and-coming Gospel ministers and theologians, men like Athanasius, Basil, Cyril, Augustine, Maximus the Confessor, Martin Luther, etc.

However, whatever idols we present for the adoration of the young and zealous, the Bible is clear that this is not the model of excellence Christ gave us.[6] When God took up flesh to dwell among us, he did not become excellent. No, he shone as the light, but the dark world neither recognised nor embraced him; he was not the sort they liked (John 1:1-14). Jesus was neither attractive nor bombastic. He was not physically desirable (Isaiah 53:2-3), and he was meek: he was gentle with a humble heart (Matt 11:29; 2 Cor 10:1). We have no indication he spoke with eloquence and charisma (unless we first assume that only someone who spoke in such a way could draw a crowd), and he certainly did not attract the sort of crowd that would be drawn to such a spectacle. Though heir of unspeakable treasure, Jesus did not demonstrate reckless ambition to achieve greatness but the firm commitment to accomplish the task set before him and reap the rewards for doing so (Luke 9:51; Heb 12:2). During his earthly life, he

---

[5] E.g. Judith Smart, "The Evangelist as Star: The Billy Graham Crusade in Australia, 1959," *The Journal of Popular Culture*, January 1, 1999, https://www.academia.edu/45510173/The_Evangelist_as_Star_The_Billy_Graham_Crusade_in_Australia_1959; Piggin and Linder, *Attending to the National Soul*, 278–89.

[6] For an alternate picture of ministry, consider D. A. Carson's account of his father, a faithful minister who did not receive great fame. D. A. Carson, *Memoirs of an Ordinary Pastor: The Life and Reflections of Tom Carson* (Wheaton: Crossway, 2008).

did not achieve much: for 30 or so years, he was known as a carpenter—not the greatest local carpenter, let alone a world-renowned carpenter. His ministry lasted about three years, and the most significant moments were in the final week before his crucifixion. Jesus did not model radical ambition and achievement but humble godliness and tenacity in the face of opposition. He endured 30 years of lowliness (the model for us to imitate) before being exalted to his throne. The response of those among whom he lived for those first 30 years suggests that he lived a normally un-extraordinary life: "Is this not the carpenter's son?" and, We know his family, don't we? were their surprised response to his miracles and claims (Matt 13:53-58).

Lest we think it is his heavenly glory that we ought to imitate, Jesus made crystal clear the model he was setting for us. After stooping down to wash the dirty, stinking feet of his disciples, Jesus confronts them, "Do you understand what I have done for you?" (John 13:12, ESV) The rest of the Gospels suggest that they did not, at least not yet. If Jesus, their Lord, would do the work of a servant, they ought to do likewise, "For I have given you an example, that you also should do just as I have done to you" (John 13:15). When certain disciples seek glory and power over the others, Jesus rebukes them. In contrast with worldly leaders, Jesus tells the disciples,

> whoever wants to become great among you must be your servant, and whoever wants to be first must be your slave—just as the Son of Man did not come to be served, but to serve, and to give his life as a ransom for many. (Matt 20:26-28, NIV)

Jesus, who suffered on the Cross for those he loved, demonstrated decisively that biblical leadership is antithetical to the world's pattern of authority and power, of teaching. If the world hated Jesus, it would undoubtedly hate those who imitate him (John 15:20). Far from commending itself to an eager audience, the Gospel would be repugnant to their sensibilities and tastes.

This is what Paul tells us in 2 Corinthians 2: the Gospel we preach does not tickle ears and draw the masses. No, it offends them. It is a great insult and carries a putrid stench, odious to the world's sensibilities (vv. 14-17; cf. 1 Cor 1:18). Skill is unnecessary and is, indeed, destructive, for the skilled medium would undermine the message.[7] The world has a standard of wisdom (in fact, different standards, one for the Jews and numerous for the nations) radically different from the wisdom of God in Christ Jesus our Lord, so when we preach the Gospel, we are called fools (1 Cor 1:14-31). The right messengers for a message that abases human pride and exalts God are messengers with nothing to offer but God, who are nothing without God. Moses complained of his lack of eloquence, but he would not be first (Exod 4:10; cf. Jer 1:6). To speak with eloquence and worldly wisdom, Paul writes, risks emptying the cross of its power (1 Cor 1:17)! Whom does God use to achieve his purposes?

> Brothers and sisters, think of what you were when you were called. Not many of you were wise by human standards; not many were influential; not many were of noble birth. But God chose the foolish things of the world to shame the wise; God chose the weak things of the world to shame the strong. God chose the lowly things of this world and the despised things—and the things that are not—to nullify the things that are, so that no one may boast before him. It is because of him that you are in Christ Jesus, who has become for us wisdom from God—that is, our righteousness, holiness and redemption. Therefore, as it is written: "Let the one who boasts boast in the Lord." (1 Cor 1:26-31, NIV)

God, it appears, delights to use weak tools.

In 2 Corinthians, Paul confronts a group of false teachers that he

---

[7] Cf. Marshall McLuhan, *Understanding Media: The Extensions of Man* (McGraw-Hill, 1964).

calls "super-apostles" (2 Cor 11:5, 12:11). They were skilled in speaking—unlike Paul (11:6)—and were bold and powerful in person, exploiting the Corinthians (2 Cor 11:20). They boast in their spiritual credentials as Jews (2 Cor 11:21-23). False teachers elsewhere in Scripture are described by their novelty, charisma, and worldly "power." They dare to speak about what they are ignorant about—and do so with boldness (2 Pet 2:10-11, 18). They speak the world's wisdom, so they are listened to (1 John 4:5). They invent novelties about the Gospel and Jesus Christ (Gal 1:8; 2 Cor 11:1-6; 1 John 2:18-25; 4:3). They engage in speculation and impose a worldly spirituality (1 Tim 1:3-4; 4:7; 2 Tim 4:4; 6:4; Titus 1:14; 2 Pet 1:16; Col 2:20-23).

God's apostles were not like this; no, they were like Jesus. Paul was weak and unaccomplished in his speaking (2 Cor 10:10; 11:6). Not only did he lack the polish of the false teachers, but he was also beset with affliction (2 Cor 11:16-33; 12:1-10). What demonstrated Paul's apostleship was not the eloquence of his speech or profundity of his speculation but his love for God and the saints shown in the depths of his suffering and perseverance (2 Cor 11:16-30, 12:1-10, 12:12).

God delights to use weak tools, and as his Spirit is sufficient to turn fishermen like Peter into mighty evangelists, so through the Spirit of God a godly man who knows God and his Scriptures is competent to minister the saving Gospel of Christ. If this is what teaching is and what it requires, how do we identify the ability to teach?

B. Identifying the Ability to Teach

Because being able to teach is not showy and visible as charisma, power, and rhetorical eloquence are, it is not immediately evident how we may identify those who can teach. Indeed, it would seem like it would be easier to be taken in by unqualified people than to recognise those God is raising up. Worldly excellence is much more evident than Spiritual excellence. The former stands out in the crowd and draws attention to itself; the latter is quiet and humble, active, yes, but invisible. Spiritual excellence does not offer public displays of devotion, eloquent prayers, and public demonstrations of godliness, for Jesus forbids such displays (Matt 6:1-7). Spiritual excellence prays in the background constantly and actively delights in God's word, especially when others cannot see it. What we seek cannot be found by identifying who can preach the best or who is most eager to take up the opportunity to serve; it cannot be found by quizzing Bible knowledge or demanding a university degree. When we think carefully about what the ability to teach consists of and what it is not, we are led back to godliness as the fundamental evidence of this ability.

There is a sort of Bible knowledge that yields no growth in holiness; this knowledge is inadequate for ministry. However, a genuine connection exists between godliness and the growth in the knowledge of God's word fostered in an authentic relationship with him. Where godliness is present, knowledge is necessarily present as well. We have here inverted the conventional practice. The traditional approach to ministry emphasises tests of knowledge to verify one's qualifications, with some measure of character testing. However, put in this order, there is no definite connection between knowledge and character. The presence of knowledge does not guarantee the presence of character, but the logic does not cut the other way. Biblically speaking, we know God through his Word, and we grow in godliness as we behold the face of God reflected in the face of Jesus Christ (2 Cor 3:12-4:6). So, knowledge does not reveal character, but character reveals knowledge.

So, the first thing we are looking for is godliness; in the previous chapter, we discussed how godliness is identified. To summarise the argument, godliness is best identified in long-term relationships within the local church. For this reason, the current education system undercuts the best evidence for identifying the ability to teach by undercutting the primary context for demonstrating godliness. However, we can add to our discussion in the previous chapter. The ability to teach involves not only knowledge of God and his word but also of people and the wisdom to navigate relationships and communicate God's word to others. So, we are looking for a particular demonstration of godliness, namely, the evident love for others.

An elder-overseer is entrusted with God's authority to pastor the flock, to care for their souls and lead them. This authority is accompanied by responsibility. However, elder-overseers are to train others for the work of ministry, so it is expected that mature Christians will pastor each other. We should expect mature Christians to care for one another's souls. Mature Christians will minister the Gospel to one another in word and deed; they will communicate the good news and offer rebuke and encouragement as is appropriate. The elder-overseer has a particular role in the economy of the church, to lead and ensure that the whole church is growing together into maturity, but the nitty gritty work of actually loving one another is shared with the whole church (Eph 4:1-16). For this reason, we should expect that genuine godliness and maturity—not only the desire to love others but the wisdom and insight to actually do so—will result in mature Christians caring for others. They will demonstrate hospitality, listen well, care for others, be eager to evangelise, and seek opportunities to disciple others. We will certainly need to encourage and train them to do so, but as we do this for the whole congregation (which is our job, Eph 4:12), we should notice those who are able to do so. In this way, a church that actively seeks to develop its members in the love of God and their neighbour demonstrated in care and service simultaneously institutes a robust system for identifying those who are mature in their faith.

I am suggesting (supported by our argument so far) that we do not develop diagnostic tests to measure the breadth of someone's knowledge, their godliness, their wisdom, or the knowledge of and insight into other people, but instead devote our time to encouraging and enabling the congregation to do the things that require all these features. In other words, if we give people opportunities to care for one another and come alongside them so that they are enabled to do so, we will identify those who already possess the knowledge, wisdom, and character to teach and will have an accurate assessment of those areas that people need to grow in. If we give people opportunities and training so they can apply the Word of God to each other's lives one-on-one or in small groups, if we give them opportunities to prophecy (in the sense we have discussed above, to apply the Word of God to individuals under the direction and illumination of the Holy Spirit), we will not only discover who can teach but also equip more people to do so. We can then run courses or meet one-on-one to develop a deeper knowledge of the Bible, grow in the ability to understand and relate to others, and develop wisdom to communicate in a godly manner. Thus, identifying who can teach and training people to teach are intimately connected with the act of teaching itself.

Teaching as the activity of an elder is intrinsically tied to their position, so teaching in the sense of the elder's teaching ministry cannot be performed by those who are not themselves elders. However, as I argued in *The Being of Churches*, teaching and prophecy are two ways of looking at the same act, one rooted in the authority Christ has given an elder through ordination and the other in the immediate authority of the Holy Spirit's work. If we view teaching as the pulpit ministry alone, we radically undercut the connection between the teaching ministry of ordained ministers and the prophetic ministry of the whole body of Christ. As public teaching is closely related to pastoral care given in private, so prophecy may happen in public or private. Teaching and prophecy differ in the act's authority, not the act itself. By identifying the connection between the public act of teaching and the private ministry of the elder, the public act of prophecy, and the private act of prophecy, we identify numerous practical routes to determine if someone is able to teach. To conclude this chapter, we will consider some ways to help our congregation develop the ability to teach.

C. Training for Teaching

Because of the close relationship between teaching and godliness, many of the approaches to discipleship we discussed in Chapter 11 are applicable here. As Christians minister the word to one another amid life, they will grow in their knowledge of one another, of God, and of his word, as well as the wisdom to communicate well. The ministry of the gathered church can also develop a deep and broad Bible knowledge base throughout someone's life. If a church is dedicated to reading and singing the whole word of God regularly, accompanies this with good teaching, and uses prayer and liturgical elements to communicate the Bible and its application, the congregation will benefit from the regular diet of Scripture and its themes and application. A church could realistically read the entire Bible every five years in the gathered church (though it would require developing a culture of longer Bible readings than the average Western church today) and accompany this with Bible-based preaching, singing, and liturgy, providing broad exposure to the whole Bible in regular cycles. Preaching that is soul-care and focused on the heart and good mutual ministry in small groups and one-on-one will foster a depth of applied biblical knowledge. However, in addition to the approaches to growing in godliness we have already discussed, which employ the Scriptures and lead to growth in understanding, we can also introduce methods targeted directly at increasing the knowledge of God and his word. I want to suggest that we use the categories of systematic, biblical, and exegetical theology to think about these targeted strategies and then look at the use of adult Sunday school programs and literate study to grow in depth. In conclusion, I will also propose that we should encourage and provide opportunities for people in our congregations, especially those who desire to enter ministry, to learn the biblical languages.

i. Systematic, Biblical, and Exegetical Theologies

A helpful way to think through the structured presentation of biblical knowledge, or ways to help someone grasp the Christian faith as presented in the Bible, is to think about three uses we make of the Bible and how they can facilitate a deeper understanding of the word of God.[8] Focusing, with John Frame and D.A. Carson, on theology as "the application of Scripture" or the "study of what Scripture says" (rather than the broader field of Christian intellectual endeavours), these three "theologies" are three ways of engaging with Scripture to better understand it and to move from Scripture to our lives.[9] In each sense of theology, I want to maintain that we are not attempting to get beyond Scripture or attain something behind it (which we critiqued above) but instead are developing tools to better understand the Bible and its interactions with all of life. Systematic and biblical theology provide shortcuts (though not in a negative sense) for good exegetical theology; they facilitate our understanding of a specific passage's application. Biblical theology provides the proper context for sound exegesis on which systematic theology is built, so these three senses of theology are not independent but necessary to one another.[10] On this understanding, systematic and biblical theology are both disciplines directed at the Bible itself, while exegetical theology is a movement away from the Bible and towards the issues we face in everyday life: it draws *out* the meaning of Scripture. I understand that these are not necessarily the standard uses of these terms. Still, I maintain that understanding theology this way is similar to the more conventional use of these terms but developed within the criticism of theology developed in this book.

a. Systematic Theology

Systematic theology, as I am using the term here, means synthesising or articulating the whole Bible's contribution to a question emerging from the Bible. "Systematic theology seeks to bring all the aspects of

[8] Frame, *The Doctrine of the Knowledge*, 206–14.

[9] D. A. Carson, "Unity and Diversity in the New Testament: The Possibility of Systematic Theology," in *Scripture and Truth*, ed. John D. Woodbridge and D. A. Carson (Grand Rapids: Baker Book House, 1992), 69; Frame, *The Doctrine of the Knowledge*, 81–85.

[10] Frame, *The Doctrine of the Knowledge*, 213.

Scripture together, to synthesize them."[11] That is, if a passage speaks of the "spirit" of a man, systematic theology is the attempt to draw the passage into a discussion with the rest of Scripture over the concept of a "spirit" and the constitution of humanity. We might seek to synthesise a theology of the seventh day of rest from all relevant passages of Scripture. This assumes the Bible has coherence and relies on concepts and themes expressed in multiple passages. The basis of this coherence is the Christian confession that God is the author of Scripture through his Spirit moving the human authors (2 Pet 1:19-21): all Scripture is God's words (2 Tim 3:16-17). When we talk about concepts and themes expressed through the synthesis of biblical passages, we are not talking about word studies (which overestimate the role of words in conveying meaning and assume too rigid a connection between words and concepts) but wrestling with the implications of specific teachings for questions raised by the Bible.[12] An example of a question from outside the Bible is, "Are humans trichotomous (i.e. body, soul, and spirit), or is there another account of their constitution (e.g. dichotomous, body and soul)?" A similar question raised within the Bible is, "How do spirit and soul in a person relate to one another and other constitution terms used in the Bible, such as mind and flesh?" We can ask what it means for God to be unchanging or that God foreordained the world from before the foundations of the world. Unlike in exegetical theology, we are not asking what a specific passage has to say but what picture emerges from drawing together all the threads of Scripture. To do this well, we need to understand each passage drawn together, for which we need biblical and exegetical theology.

---

[11] Frame, *The Doctrine of the Knowledge*, 212.

[12] On the problems of careless word studies, Moisés Silva, *Biblical Words and Their Meaning: An Introduction to Lexical Semantics*, rev. and expanded ed. (Grand Rapids: Zondervan, 1994); Carson, *Exegetical Fallacies*.

b. Biblical Theology

If systematic theology has to do with unity, biblical theology has to do with order and development. Biblical theology attempts to track themes across the Scripture and detect development and narrative. We presuppose that themes are developed across the Scriptures, so the meaning of one passage might not be what the whole Scripture has to say on a subject; we want to recognise and respect the meaning of a particular passage rather than making it an opportunity for systematic theology. Biblical theology recognises that the order of passages matters—that there is an unfolding story across the Bible. It matters that the Tabernacle came after the Garden, for the Tabernacle (and Temple) is an attempt to regain the Garden. It matters that the Prophets come after Deuteronomy, for the Prophets convict Israel of their failure to uphold the laws and declare the curses given there. In these cases, order matters. Biblical theology helps us recognise this. Biblical theology also pays attention to the relation that specific passages have to one another, such as the prophetic tradition and the book of Revelation. Among other things, biblical theology concerns the overarching narrative of Scripture and traces themes as they unfold across the narrative of Scripture. As a result of this effort, biblical theology identifies key structural elements of the Bible as a book and offers overarching interpretive categories for doing exegetical and systematic theology; the debate between Covenant Theology and Dispensationalism happens on this level.[13]

c. Exegetical Theology

Whereas systematic theology seeks to synthesise the teaching of many texts, and biblical theology seeks to understand the narrative threads that run through them, exegetical theology seeks to understand the

---

[13] See Gentry and Wellum, *Kingdom through Covenant (2nd Ed)*; Craig A. Blaising and Darrell L. Bock, *Progressive Dispensationalism* (Grand Rapids: Bridgepoint Books, 2000).

texts themselves. Exegetical theology situates the text in its biblical and systematic theological contexts and asks what that text is saying, that is, how and what it communicates. In this way, exegetical theology turns from the Bible to everything outside of the Bible, for the meaning of a text is its implications and applications to the life and thought of God's people. Exegetical theology is not only involved in systematic and biblical theology (we understand texts to understand their contribution to these theologies) but is the primary form of theology found in local church ministry, as we preach and teach from the pulpit or apply Scripture in the context of discipleship and counselling. Systematic and biblical theology are also features of preaching as we seek to help people understand their lives and the Scriptures. However, the primary diet of a Christian is exegetical theology.

For local church ministry, we can view exegetical theology (i.e. the understanding and application of Scripture to all life) as the primary endeavour a pastor will engage in; our goal is to equip pastors to do exegetical theology. Systematic and biblical theology are tools to equip the pastor to understand individual texts. When we think about targeted strategies to develop a pastor's understanding of the Bible, we want them to develop the skills needed for good exegetical theology and give them the background knowledge of Scripture through systematic and biblical theology. Practice in reading and applying the word is essential for developing the skills of good exegetical theology, yet classroom-style learning and reading books can be used to develop a systematic and biblical-theological knowledge base.[14]

---

[14] My yet unfinished series "God's Gifts for the Christian Life" is intended to equip people for exegetical, systematic, and biblical theology. Using all three approaches, I attempt give an overview of how to do exegesis, the biblical framework for Christian intellectual engagement, which is one aspect of the "outward" movement of exegetical theology, and the basis for doing good systematic theology. The series is contextualised to the condition of the church in the Western World, so it is intended to address the barriers raised by conventional approaches to theology as discussed in the book. For

ii. Sunday School

To the list of tools we identified in the last chapter for discipleship, we can add the more information-oriented approach of Sunday school. Sunday school is only secondarily concerned with godliness, which will result from growing in the knowledge of God, the primary purpose of Sunday school. In many Western churches, "Sunday school" refers to something offered to children. However, for many in the Reformed tradition, Sunday school is not only for children but also includes classes run for members of the congregation to deepen their understanding of God and his word. Sunday school for children and adults has similar goals: to equip people to live for God by helping them understand the Gospel and God's word. Adult Sunday school often focuses on equipping men and women with exegesis skills, systematic theology, and biblical theology. Sunday school classes are often conceived similarly to seminary classes, with lecturers and activities accompanied by set readings. However, unlike seminary classes, Sunday school is offered locally, for free, and can be pitched appropriately for the audience (accreditation not being an issue).

The concept of Sunday school is well known, and the tools for executing a Sunday school program are abundant. In the model we have identified, the primary use of Sunday school models is to develop the knowledge of Scripture through the study of biblical and systematic theology and to develop exegetical skills through hands-on practice. Studying history can also contribute to these skills by understanding how Christians from across the ages have understood and exercised these theological disciplines, addressing the chronological arrogance and blindness we often have.

Many ministers object to Sunday school programs because of the

---

exegetical skills and biblical theology, see *Part 1 – The Gift of Knowledge* (complete) and *Part 2 – The Gift of Truth* (incomplete). Systematic theology is woven throughout, but especially in *Part 3 – the Gift of Wisdom* (incomplete).

work they require and the lack of expertise available in their churches. Both objections result from confusion over what we mean by theology. As discussed throughout this book, this theology is not the abstract, academic theology taught in many seminaries (the sort of theology that requires a PhD). We have argued that the Bible is written to be understood by men and women from all walks of life; if theology is a reflection on the Bible, then it should likewise be doable and communicable by many. Sunday school does not have to look like a formal, academic lecture but can simply be an opportunity for a pastor to apprentice his congregation in the practices of biblical interpretation he uses every Sunday. There are also many resources online from bible colleges, seminaries, and para-church groups that could be adapted for use in the church under a flipped classroom or hybrid learning approach.[15] In the flipped classroom model, a digital lecture can be viewed when the members have time during the week, and then in-class exercises in application and problem-solving can help solidify and employ what was learned. In the hybrid learning model, a lecture could be watched as a group with an opportunity for question and interaction accompanied by exercises to engage with the content. Caution should be used in adopting content designed for a seminary or college setting, for this content often presupposes the approaches to theology and ministry we have critiqued throughout this book. However, with some effort to curate and contextualise them, the resources available digitally are invaluable.

Digital resources will be particularly helpful for churches located in remote locations. For churches located in cities, a simple solution may be present for a pastor who does not feel up to teaching a Sunday school class. Someone in another local church would likely have the skills or knowledge to teach the desired subject. Because of the ample resources God has given us in fellow churches, coordinating adult Sunday school classes with other churches can be an effective way to

---

[15] Some resources are, https://biblicaltraining.org, https://thirdmill.org, and the Reformed Theological Seminary app (by Subsplash Inc).

split the workload and collaborate to fulfil God's mission.

Whatever approach is taken to Sunday school, learning goals are better achieved if there are opportunities for participants to exercise what they have learned and receive feedback. Opportunities to preach for the group and essay or blog writing projects can provide opportunities for students to put what they have learned to use and for the leader to determine the effectiveness of the class. Several considerations will come into play for planning a Sunday school class:

What is the goal? For each class, we want to start with the goal we are aiming for. In all things, we want to see God glorified through growth in the lives of our church members. We want to see them grow in their knowledge of God and in godliness. However, we want a specific goal that explains why we are hosting *this* class. A grasp of what we are trying to achieve will help us identify the tools and resources to use to achieve that goal and how we can measure if we have accomplished the goal.

Who are the learners? The local church setting allows us to focus on the areas where particular students need to grow and develop a strategy that matches their competencies and schedules. A Sunday school class for a primarily illiterate church should look different from one in a literate context.

What is the context? A church's physical and cultural context will also impact how a Sunday school class is organised. If a church only has access to their building for a handful of hours on a Sunday, they may need to run the class in a house. Doing so will suit different styles of classroom learning, particularly informal approaches, over a larger classroom setting. Though group learning is valuable in all contexts, in a cultural context that is communal rather than individualistic, group learning (such as collaborating on verbal projects) will be more effective than individualistic approaches (such as writing an essay). If a particular culture views Sundays as a day for family and fellowship, a Sunday school class run immediately after church may not find many participants. However, a class run before or after work during the week may be more successful. Knowing your context will be critical to getting people on board with a Sunday school class and ensuring it will be effective.

Who are the teachers? Knowing the teachers and their skills, knowledge, and availability will determine the teaching methods used. For example, online resources will be necessary if no teachers are available with the knowledge needed to achieve the goal.

What content will be taught? In light of the expressed goal, the learners, and the teachers (as well as cultural considerations), you will need to determine what content will be used in teaching. At this point, with content, you must also ask what methods will be used (a lecture is only one of many possible approaches).

How will you evaluate the success of the class? After a class is run, it is crucial to implement assessment procedures to determine the effectiveness of the class in achieving its goals. A good assessment process will allow for the fine-tuning of future classes and identify the growth of particular students and their areas of weakness.

iii. Good Books and Essays

Recommending good books or essays can also be an effective way to help someone grow in their knowledge of the Scriptures. Numerous good books are available and options for people with various degrees of reading skill and time. Audiobooks can be good for someone who is not great at reading or does not have the time, though the effectiveness of audiobooks often depends on whether the book was written in an oral-friendly way. For the outcomes we seek, recommending a book is not enough; we are not merely looking for someone to finish a task but to learn and grow. Various approaches can be taken to help someone engage with a book. We want to encourage readers to evaluate their reading and synthesise their learning.

a. Evaluating Books

We evaluate books when we step back to determine if the argument has persuaded us and (whether we have been persuaded or not) if it makes a cogent argument. Sometimes, we are persuaded by books with a persuasive style but lacking in substance: we want to teach readers to evaluate why they find a book persuasive. For Christians, the fundamental basis of persuasion is the exegetical basis of an argument: we should be persuaded by arguments that are rightful applications of the Scriptural teaching. Even books written by non-believers still need to be evaluated by the biblical teaching in its broad and specific contours, so we bring Scripture to bear in our evaluation of all things. We will bring our skills and knowledge of systematic, biblical, and exegetical theology to bear on each book we read. For this reason, reading the same book at different seasons in our learning may lead us to evaluate it differently. From a learning perspective, this is why evaluation is subjective, pertaining to *persuasion,* rather than objective, pertaining to the overall correctness of the book. We will not often be in a position to judge the correctness of a book, but all of us can evaluate the persuasiveness of a book. Analysing a book's persuasiveness is an exercise in understanding the book and ourselves.

There are many dimensions to persuasion from a biblical foundation. We evaluate the coherence of the book's claims with the Scriptures as a whole and in their parts. We want to identify the accuracy of the author's treatment of individual passages but also how they integrate them into a picture of the whole, so we attend to the exegetical, systematic, and biblical theological dimensions of the argument.

We evaluate its tone and attitude for coherence with the biblical teaching. The Bible instructs us to be kind, gentle, wise, patient, fair, free from gossip and slander, not argumentative, and generous, so Christian writing should express these virtues. This does not mean writers cannot be *passionate* in their writing (see the Psalms, Romans 9, and Galatians 5:7-15), but passion must be married with Christian virtue. Christian books should be edifying, not mean, slanderous, or bitter. Martin Luther is notorious for the abuse in his works; we want to contextualise this in his time and understand that there were different standards of discourse (and different stakes), yet his writing is nevertheless not a model to follow. It is not appropriate in Christian discourse to say of one's opponents, "You sophistic worms, grasshoppers, locusts, frogs and lice!"[16]

We evaluate the reasonableness of its application of Scriptural teaching to the claims it makes. A book may make a persuasive exegetical point but fail in the connection it makes between that point and the broader argument. In his book *Through New Eyes,* James B. Jordan introduces Hebrews 1:7, "And of the angels He says, 'Who makes His angels winds, and his ministers a flame of fire.'" He then concludes that "at least sometimes angels are involved in running the weather." He has rightly identified the connection between angels and heavenly phenomena, which we associate with the weather, yet he draws a more substantial point from this than the text asserts: that angels are related to heavenly phenomena does not make them the cause of heavenly phenomena. From the general point that this text is saying that angels appear as or are associated with heavenly phenomena (which is debatable), he concludes that they are at least sometimes *the causes* of the regular patterns of weather we encounter

---

[16] Martin Luther, "Against Latomus," in *Luther's Works: Career of the Reformer II*, ed. Helmut T. Lehmann, vol. 32 (Philadelphia: Muhlenberg Press, 1955), 150.

and then universalises this to conclude, "It is likely that gravity-angels either pulled or pushed [a falling watch] down at that rate."[17] Some scholars have made a lengthy argument along these lines.[18] However, Jordan here pins a weighty conclusion on far too weak exegetical evidence, evidence that could more conservatively uphold the claim that angels can, at times, appear as wind or fire.

We evaluate its use of supporting evidence: does it quote any supporting evidence? Is the evidence from a trustworthy source? Is the source used well? It is not usual to find someone using a source only to discover on closer reading that the source does not support the argument. At other times, an untrustworthy source may be used, perhaps poorly researched or written with an agenda in mind. For example, you will find many sources online claiming that the Quran contains advanced scientific insight, yet further investigation reveals that these so-called "scientific" insights are forced upon the text, and what is there reflects the state of knowledge in the 6th Century.[19] Finally, we evaluate its treatment of alternate positions (does it present "straw men," caricatures of an opposing position, or the strongest objections possible?).[20]

---

17 James B. Jordan, *Through New Eyes: Developing a Biblical View of the World - Theopolis Institute* (Eugene, OR: Wipf & Stock, 1999), 110–11, https://theopolisinstitute.com/books/through-new-eyes-developing-a-biblical-view-of-the-world/.

18 E.g. Edward Epsen, *From Laws to Liturgy: An Idealist Theology of Creation* (Brill, 2020).

19 E.g. Dr. Zakir Naik, *The Quran And Modern Science* (Islamic Research Foundation, 2000), http://archive.org/details/thequranandmodernscience_201910; James Wilberding, "Embryology," in *A Companion to Science, Technology, and Medicine in Ancient Greece and Rome*, ed. Georgia L. Irby, 2 vols., Black Companions to the Ancient World (Chichester, West Sussex: Wiley Blackwell, 2019), 329–42, https://www.academia.edu/10295752/Embryology_Wiley_Blackwell_.

20 For resources on evaluating and reading well, see Frame, *The Doctrine of*

John Frame provides this list of nine areas by which to judge *theological* writings,

1. *Scripturality*. Are the ideas teachings of Scripture? Are they at least consistent with Scripture? This is, of course, the chief criterion.
2. *Truth*. Even if an idea is not found in Scripture, it may be true—for example, a theory about the influence of Bultmann on Pannenberg.
3. *Cogency*. Is the author's case adequately argued? Are his premises true, his arguments valid?
4. *Edification* (Eph. 4:29). Is it spiritually helpful? Harmful? Hard to say?
5. *Godliness*. Does the text exhibit the fruit of the Spirit, or is it blasphemous, gossipy, slanderous, unkind, and so forth?
6. *Importance*. Is the idea important? Trivial? Somewhere in between? Important for some but not for others?
7. *Clarity*. Are the key terms well defined, at least implicitly? Is the formal structure intelligible, well thought out? Are the author's positions clear? Does he formulate well the issues to be addressed and distinguish them from one another?
8. *Profundity*. Does the text wrestle with difficult, or only with easy, questions? (Robert Dick Wilson, the great Old Testament scholar, used as his motto, 'I have not shirked the difficult questions'—a good motto for all theologians to remember.) Does it get to the heart of the matter? Does it note subtle distinctions and nuances that other writers miss? Does it show extraordinary insight of some kind?

---

the Knowledge, 369–70; Carson, *Exegetical Fallacies*; John Piper, *Think: The Life of the Mind and the Love of God* (Wheaton: Crossway, 2010); Poythress, *Logic*, 125–32. This article has some good points, C. Michael Patton, "Seven Common Fallacies of Biblical Interpretation," *Credo House Ministries* (blog), July 1, 2024, https://credohouse.org/blog/seven-common-fallacies-of-biblical-interpretation.

9. *Form and Style.* Is it appropriate to the subject matter? Does it show creativity?[21]

Frame is writing for a somewhat academic context, so his points are not wholly transferable to the context we are discussing. Many books we will read do not make a profound point; sometimes, we will recommend simple but relevant books. Form and style help evaluate the quality of a book but not necessarily its usefulness, for a profound and clearly biblical book may suffer from stylistic liabilities.[22] Our goal in evaluating a book is to ensure we are being persuaded by what is true, not what sounds good or desirable. Evaluating a book asks whether we should learn from it, and the evaluation process brings forth what the book has to say, but learning from it happens when we synthesise the book with our current beliefs and actions.

b. Synthesising learning

I use the term "synthesis" for the act of integrating what we are reading with our greater body of beliefs and actions. Some of us do this intuitively, but there are things we can do to facilitate this integration. The point of synthesis is that we are not reading merely to understand what someone is saying (though we certainly want to do that) but to understand the effect their words should have on our lives (and the lives of those we minister to). We can know what they are saying and even if it is true or not without acting on this knowledge.

Sometimes synthesis happens as we read; maybe we highlight interesting points or jot down notes engaging with the author's claims. Some people journal about the effects that their reading has on their beliefs or what they feel. At other times, learning from a book or article

---

21 Frame, *The Doctrine of the Knowledge*, 369–70.

22 The style of John Owen, Meredith Kline, and Cornelius Van Til is often lamented, but the works of these authors contain profound insights into God's word and his world. In these cases, there are sometimes edited versions of these books

involves engaging with it more formally. I engage best with the Bible when I write sermons or books, thinking about how the Bible interacts with my beliefs and actions or those of people in my church. Writing a critical book review that moves from evaluation to application can achieve something similar, or engaging with a book as part of a research essay or blog post can force us to slow down and bring a book into engagement with our prior knowledge. Many people benefit from discussing the themes and argument of a book.

c. Helping Readers Engage with Books

There are many strategies we could use to encourage engagement with books. Someone comfortable with reading and writing could be asked to write a book review or use it with other books to prepare an essay (with various formats and styles possible here, from a blog post to an academic article). A group could read the book together and discuss its themes, or a pastor could regularly meet with the person reading the book to talk it through. The person reading could be asked to give a presentation on the book for a small group of people reading the same book or working through similar issues. Reading a book could also be paired with related exegetical exercises, giving the opportunity to use the knowledge from the book in engagement with Scripture. We do not want to merely test someone to determine if they have accomplished the task or grasped what the book says, but we want to move towards evaluation and synthesis. We want to encourage the reader to understand the text on its own terms and then wrestle with its implications and apply it to their life and thought.

d. Choosing Good Books

At least in the English-speaking world, it is not hard to find a book that would help someone engage with the Bible and their faith; indeed, the problem is often choosing the right books. There are thousands of good books—too many for anyone to read—and they often overlap in their themes and content. We are often not choosing between a good or bad book but between dozens of good choices. So, our choice of books to give someone will depend on what books we know of. It is essential to know what books are available if we are to use them for training. Part of this can be achieved by reading broadly, but also by following book reviews and paying attention to what is being put out by good publishers. Many books are written for very immediate issues and are soon dated; it is good to pay attention to the books that last, which were worth reading 10 years ago and are still worth reading today. Many authors recommend alternating between ancient and modern Christian books; there is some wisdom in this.

We want our assumptions confronted and to be forced to consider alternatives we would not otherwise consider. Reading old books chastens our chronological arrogance, our belief that newer is inherently superior.[23] Yet, in favour of reading contemporary books is their relevance to our concerns and the fact that contemporary books often build upon the heritage received from older generations. Older books can often be dense and challenging to read; however, labouring through difficult, old books may be valuable at times. We are reminded that God has been faithful throughout the ages, and we are not the first generation to read and apply God's word. Each generation of Christians has faced its own issues and addressed them from the Scriptures with the same mixed success as our generation. We will read old books and find problems contemporary authors have shed light upon, but we will also find solutions to contemporary issues that we would not have considered.

iv. Training in the Biblical Languages

The original Scriptures well deserve your pains, and

[23] C. S. Lewis, "God in the Dock," in *The Collected Works of C.S. Lewis: The Pilgrim's Regress, Christian Reflections, God in the Dock* (New York: Inspirational Press, 1970), 434–38, http://archive.org/details/collectedworksof00csle.

will richly repay them. – John Newton[24]

There was a time when ministers of the Gospel were required to study Hebrew and Greek, but this is no longer the case in many institutions. Many colleges require students to Study New Testament Greek but make Hebrew optional. This book has critiqued many tendencies in contemporary pastoral education for demanding too much, but here, I want to sound the alarm in the opposite direction. Our churches are disadvantaged when at least one of their ministers cannot access the original Scriptures. However, in line with what we have argued throughout this book, the alternative to our present situation is not to demand Bible College and Seminary students take classes in Koine Greek and Classical Hebrew. This is bound to fail, for students already face extensive study burdens, and learning both languages in this setting is too difficult for many students. Furthermore, there is a way of teaching Greek and Hebrew in academic institutions that contributes to the issues we have been addressing in this book. This way treats the original Scriptures as texts to be analysed and decoded rather than read.[25]

Instead, I want to suggest that prospective ministers should be trained in the biblical languages. While we are doing this, anyone in our congregations who is interested should be given the opportunity to learn the languages. I do not think we should train in the biblical languages because translations are biased and twist the original Scriptures or hide something we should know, as some might claim. No, I think we should train in the biblical languages because God's work is deep and rich; by its very nature, translation requires limiting the scope of God's words to a specific dialect and situation so that it is understandable to the native speaker. This is right and good, but it

[24] John Newton, "Letter 2: To Student in Divinity," in *The Works of John Newton. Vols 1-6*, ed. Richard Cecil, 3rd Ed, vol. 1 (Edinburgh: Banner of Truth, 1985), 143, http://archive.org/details/worksofjohnnewto0001newt.

[25] See the appendices.

means that a pastor relying on translations alone is reading something that has already been interpreted and applied. Possible applications of the text and possible interpretative ambiguities are dismissed because a translation's goal is, rightly, to communicate to English speakers. Our contemporary translations are a gift from God, yet Martin Luther reminds us of the danger of neglecting the original languages,

> And let us be sure of this: we shall not long preserve the Gospel without languages. Languages are the sheath in which this sword of the Spirit is contained. They are the case in which we carry this jewel. They are the vessel in which we hold this wine. They are the larder in which this food is stored. And, as the Gospel itself says, they are the baskets in which we bear these loaves and fishes and fragments.[26]

God's Word is powerful and necessary for the success of the Church's mission and, therefore, for the sake of the world. The neglect of God's word through the neglect of the languages in which it was written should concern us. The connection between knowledge of the languages and revival in the Church has often been made; the Reformation occurred in the context of the Renaissance and its commitment to *ad fontes*, returning to the sources. The resurgence of Christian engagement with Greek and Hebrew led to new Bible translations, particularly in the common languages, and theological renewal. After hundreds of years, God's people heard the Word as it was written and not as it was interpreted. Heinrich Bitzer, a layman who learned the original languages and edited a popular original-language devotional resource, reflected on this reality and wrote,

---

[26] Martin Luther, "To the Councilmen of All Cities in Germany That They Establish and Maintain Christian Schools," in *The Christian in Society II*, ed. Walther I Brandt, trans. Albert T. W. Steinhaeuser and Walther I Brandt, Luther's Works 45 (Philadelphia: Muhlenbeg, 1962), 360. Cf. Jason S. DeRouchie, "The Profit of Employing the Biblical Languages: Scriptural and Historical Reflections," *Themelios* 37, no. 1 (2012): 32–50.

> The more a theologian detaches himself from the basic Hebrew and Greek text of Holy Scripture, the more he detaches himself from the source of real theology! And real theology is the foundation of a fruitful and blessed ministry.[27]

A good translation is of great value, and the ability for the Scriptures to speak clearly in translation is essential for the Evangelical claim that Scripture is clear and sufficient for the entire Christian life, not just the lives of the intelligentsia. However, no translation is perfect, and new translations are continually required as language evolves. We need translators with a strong competency in these languages if we want good translations. As I have argued elsewhere, translations are good but not ideal; translations always involve a restriction of the text's meaning—i.e. interpretation and application—and so, by their very nature, eclipse potential ways that the text could speak to the lives of a specific congregation or minister.[28] For this reason, biblical languages are essential for excellent pastoral ministry, for only through acquaintance with the original languages will the *whole* counsel of God be available to the pastor.

In the case of the Old Testament, each of these issues is magnified. The inadequacies of our best English translations of the Old Testament saddens me. For one reason or another (often a clearly identifiable one) our translations leave things wanting. For example, my wife, Nicole, recently drew my attention to what she perceived to be a significant difference between the ESV and NIV's translation of Hosea 3. In the ESV, Hosea is instructed to go and marry "a woman," in the NIV, "his wife." Neither is wrong, but the problem is exemplified. The ESV is attempting to be faithful to the Hebrew text,

---

27 Heinrich Bitzer, ed., *Light on the Path: Daily Scripture Readings in Hebrew and Greek* (Grand Rapids: Baker Book House, 1982), 10. See Piper, *Brothers We Are Not Professionals A Plea to Pastors for Radical Ministry.*, 81–88.

28 J. Alexander Rutherford, *The Gift of Reading – Part 1 & Part 2* (Vancouver, Teleioteti 2019).

which is ambiguous at this point. In doing so, the ESV is doing what it says it would do. The NIV has followed the dominant interpretation of Hosea and translated the ambiguous Hebrew in a way that excludes other interpretations. Reading the ESV, my wife did not make the connection that "a woman" could very well be Hosea's wife; reading the NIV, one would easily be led to believe that the Hebrew is decisive on this matter. The ambiguity is true to the Hebrew text, and a pastor needs to wrestle through such questions in his preaching.

In other instances, the major translations have followed commentaries or lexicons that often come from questionable methodological and theological biases. In Habakkuk 3:13, for example, nearly every modern English translation has "to save your anointed" where the syntax clearly favours "to save with your anointed" (cf. KJV).[29] Furthermore, the resources that pastors and students, even scholars, rely upon to interact with the Hebrew text of the Old Testament (primarily commentaries but also the BHS and BHQ, handbooks, grammars, and lexicons) are dominated by methodologies and theological assumptions that are arguably incompatible with or, at least, objectionable to Evangelicalism. If we are going to wrestle through these texts without the guiding hand of higher criticism and Modern or Postmodern philosophies, we need sufficient knowledge of the languages (and, I pray, better tools) to interact critically with these resources. Similar problems emerge in the study of the New Testament, yet they are most pronounced in the study of the Hebrew Bible. We need better commentaries and translations; if this is to happen, we who have a high view of Scripture need a better understanding of the languages. Most pastors may not be writing commentaries or Bible translations (this is perhaps a place where the academic study of the Bible has an important place), but knowing the languages will allow them to engage critically with secular and non-Christian resources.

[29] For a defence of this claim, see Rutherford, *Habakkuk*.

Pastors should learn Greek and Hebrew, but doing so is not as difficult as it is sometimes made out to be. Those of us who aspire to train pastors will first need to learn the languages ourselves, and the most expedient way to do so may be through classes in a local seminary or Bible College or online through programs like Bible Mesh (https://biblemesh.com), https://greekforall.com, or https://freehebrew.online (as of November 2024). However, once we have learned the languages, I would advocate adopting a different approach than is usually used in seminaries and Bible colleges.

We should aim for literary fluency rather than the ability to use Bible software to translate biblical texts. "Literary fluency" is not nearly as scary as it sounds and offers several advantages over the traditional model. Merriam-Webster defines fluency along the lines of "being capable of using a language easily and accurately."[30] In the realm of a living, spoken language, "use" means being able to recognise and act in response to what is being said and to be able to respond verbally or initiate and maintain conversation. In its application to a language that will not often be spoken, like Biblical Hebrew, or where fluent speech seems unattainable, like Koine Greek, "use" will have a somewhat restricted sense. It means being able to recognise and respond to written communication. Being able to respond in writing is another level of skill and yet intimately connected with the ability to read well. We can define the skill level we seek, fluency in Koine Greek and Biblical Hebrew, as *the ability to recognise and respond to written communication with ease and accuracy.*[31]

In this book, we have stressed that Christian ministry is not reliant on literacy, though it is helped by it. On the current state of things,

---

[30] This combines the definitions of "fluent" and "fluency." Inc Merriam-Webster, *Merriam-Webster's Collegiate Dictionary.*, Eleventh ed. (Springfield, MA: Merriam-Webster, Inc., 2003).

[31] See Appendix 1 for my attempt to unpack this. Cf. Appendix 2 for some context to this claim.

learning the biblical languages requires literacy. However, as living language approaches grow more popular, it may be possible to teach Greek and Hebrew as oral rather than literary languages (allowing an illiterate pastor to study the Greek and Hebrew Testaments in audio format). However, I am not aware of resources that exist to do this.[32] This is also an area where the individual gifts of pastors in a team of co-elders may factor in: the biblical languages are invaluable to the ministry of the local church, but it may be the case that one pastor on a team is proficient in Greek, Hebrew, and Aramaic and will be able to help the other pastors who are not so adept.

D. Conclusion

In Chapter 7, we argued that teaching refers primarily to the public ministry of the word and is closely related to the private ministry of the word and prophecy. In this chapter, we argued that this sort of teaching does not require excellence in public speaking but wisdom, godliness, and knowledge. Teaching requires knowing how and when to communicate, not just what to communicate; teaching needs to be reinforced by a life that lives out what is taught; and teaching requires knowledge of God, his word, and the people being taught. The categories of systematic, biblical, and exegetical theology help us to understand the knowledge required for teaching and to consider ways to communicate that knowledge to others. In addition to one-on-one discipleship, regular church teaching, and small groups, we considered Sunday school, written study resources, and the importance of learning the biblical languages for an effective local church teaching ministry.

---

[32] As of November 2024, there is a recording of the New Testament read in Modern Greek according to the Orthodox Ecumenical Patriarchate text (1904), https://live.bible.is/bible/ellape/mat/1?audio_type=audio (also available in the Bible app), and in reconstructed Koine pronunciation, https://www.koinegreek.com/audio. For Hebrew, a recording of the Hebrew Bible can be found at https://mechon-mamre.org/p/pt/ptmp3prq.htm.

CONCLUSION

> Then he said to his disciples, "the harvest is plentiful, but the workers are few; therefore, intently ask the Lord of the harvest to send workers into his harvest." (Matt 9:37-38)[1]

Looking out at the cities of his time, Jesus identified a great harvest, many people ready to receive God's word and enter his Church. Pray—ask God eagerly—that he would raise up the workers necessary to reap that harvest, Jesus told his followers. All Christians are called to be part of the great harvest God is reaping, yet Christian ministers have a unique and essential role in the mission Jesus is completing. Pastors are a gift from God to equip all of God's people to do the work of ministry, to help them grow in godliness and knowledge, and to protect them from the schemes of the evil one. Therefore, Gospel ministers are essential for completing Jesus's mission and reaping the great harvest the Spirit has prepared. However, it is here that our Western churches are terribly weak.

There is a problem in our Western churches. We lack Gospel ministers in our churches, let alone for the vast communities around us that need to receive God's Gospel. The initial problem we identified

[1] My translation

is that pastors have been equated with scholars and theologians, and 'theology' has been carefully defined so that only scholars qualify for Christian ministry. By redefining the core task of pastors as 'teachers' (where 'teaching' involves communicating an academic theology) and redefining the competencies of pastoral ministry in line with this definition, the Western church has succeeded in producing generations of pastors ill-equipped for the reality of pastoral ministry and ill-equipped for the realities of the Christian life in a culture that is growing more and more hostile to the central tenets of the Christian faith. We have also excluded from ministry the vast number of Christians who would fail in the academic environment of our seminaries and Bible colleges.

In Part 1 of this book, we traced our contemporary problems across the history of the Church. In Chapter 1, we argued that early church theologians (for lack of a better word) in the time between Nicaea and Chalcedon identified orthodoxy with a philosophical formulation of the Bible's teaching. In Chapter 2, we argued that the Reformation continued this trend and identified the pastoral task with a highly intellectual form of theology. We saw that these trends continued into contemporary Evangelicalism in Chapter 3. Evangelicalism continues to identify pastoral ministry with an intellectual approach to the Bible and theology, and it treats ministry as a profession like other white-collar professions rooted in higher education. We summarised in Chapter 4 the trends we saw across Christian history: we argued that 1) orthodoxy was defined by adherence to philosophically thick doctrinal formulations as found in the Creeds; 2) the highest form of the knowledge of God was an abstract, intellectual knowledge; 3) pastors were identified as teachers; 4) the Bible was seen as the source or principle for doing theology rather than a work of theology itself; 5) and that the academy has been given a central place in the life of the church and training its ministers.

Having identified these presuppositions in contemporary Evangelicalism—assumptions developed across the history of the

Church—we set out in Part 2 to offer alternate accounts of each of these presuppositions. First, in chapter 5, we defined 'orthodoxy' as the question of who is in and out of God's people and argued that orthodoxy involves both right beliefs and right character. Character is the primary criterion God has given us for judging orthodoxy. We did not deny that there is such a thing as right beliefs. However, we challenged the assumption that it was possible to produce a list of right beliefs that qualify someone for the kingdom of God. Therefore, relying on the affirmation of belief to verify someone's orthodoxy does not work. Instead, character is a much more reliable judge of a person's standing before God. We saw from the Bible that Christian community and context were essential for properly evaluating someone's orthodoxy.

In Chapter 6, we argued that the knowledge of God in Scripture is person-knowledge, like the knowledge we possess of a friend or spouse. This is not proposition-less knowledge but knowledge that cannot be resolved into a list of propositions. Because knowledge of God is personal, it resists intellectualism and is accessible to all who meet God in his churches and Scriptures. In Chapter 7, we observed that the primary qualifications for a pastor pertained to character and that pastoral care was essential to the pastor's task. We identified teaching as communicating the word of God to people, primarily in public but, by extension, also in private. In this way, we saw that teaching did not neatly align with academic theology or intellectual activity. 'Teaching' is not the sort of thing that requires academic expertise. In Chapter 8, we argued that the Bible presents itself as the document of God's New Covenant and that it is both essential and sufficient for a Christian to live a life pleasing to God. We concluded Part 2 by arguing that serious intellectual engagement with the world, including academics, has a role in the kingdom of God; we argued that secular universities, liberal arts colleges, and research centres based in local churches were appropriate places for this engagement.

Building upon the foundation established in Part 2, Part 3

considered recognising, ordaining, and training leaders. In Chapter 10, we argued that leaders are best trained by pastors in the context of the local church; against the dominant trends in Western churches, we argued that training may follow ordination. We argued that there is continuity between regular Christian discipleship and the training of pastors, so the same tools for discipleship in the local church apply to training pastors. In Chapter 11, we considered the nature of godliness and how we could identify and develop godly character in our congregations and potential ministers. In Chapter 12, we analysed the components of being able to teach and considered how to identify and develop this ability.

The conclusion we have reached should be shocking: we already have the tools for training pastors in our congregations, but the lack of competent ministers in the Western Church reveals a deeper problem, namely, the lack of discipleship in our churches. We observed that the New Testament epistles expect us to find godly men and women in our churches ready for ministry: it does not take extraordinary means to identify and develop competencies for ordained ministry. No, if a Christian grows consistently in godliness and knowledge, it is expected that they would be competent for ministry. Not everyone who qualifies will pursue ministry, yet if we were discipling our congregations well, we would expect to find men and women qualified for Christian ministry. The New Testament teaches us to recognise those who are ready and to ordain them; after this, we are expected to train them further, as Paul trained Timothy and Titus while they were on the job. Therefore, *the most fundamental cause of our crisis in pastoral ministry is the failure of serious discipleship in our local churches.* This problem is exacerbated by an academic and intellectual approach to pastoral ministry, which communicates that higher education is necessary not only to be qualified as a minister of God but to know God and be godly.

If we are to repair pastoral training, we need to start by investing in serious discipleship in our local churches, with the expectation that every Christian could become qualified for ministry. Again, that does not mean everyone should enter ordained ministry. It does mean that the standard God sets for ministers is not extraordinary but a picture of the mature Christian life. Men and women filled with God's spirit can develop godly character and the wisdom and knowledge to prophesy and offer pastoral care to one another. When they do so, we should not send them to seminary but encourage them and, eventually, ordain them for service in local churches. At this point, they can continue to grow in godliness and their ability to communicate God's word in public and private.

APPENDIX 1 – TOWARDS FLUENCY WITH THE BIBLICAL LANGUAGES

Merriam-Webster defines fluency along the lines of "being capable of using a language easily and accurately."[1] In the realm of a living, spoken language, "use" means being able to recognise and act in response to what is being said and to be able to respond verbally or initiate and maintain conversation. In its application to a language that will not often be spoken, like Biblical Hebrew, or where fluent speech seems unattainable, like Koine Greek, "use" will have a somewhat restricted sense. It means being able to recognise and respond to written communication. Being able to respond in writing is another level of skill and yet intimately connected with the ability to read well. We can define the skill level we seek, fluency in Koine Greek and Biblical Hebrew, as *the ability to recognise and respond to written communication with ease and accuracy*. This appendix briefly breaks down this definition and elucidates some of its ambiguities and components.

---

[1] This combines the definitions of "fluent" and "fluency." Inc Merriam-Webster, *Merriam-Webster's Collegiate Dictionary.*, Eleventh ed. (Springfield, MA: Merriam-Webster, Inc., 2003).

A. Ability

Though this should not be controversial, we should observe that fluency is an attribute of skill or ability, not knowledge. By aiming at *fluency*, we are not aiming at any set of knowledge. Knowledge is implied in fluency, but our goal is not imparting this or that piece of knowledge but such knowledge as is requisite for recognition and response with ease and accuracy. Recognising this fact ought to shape our pedagogy regarding content and evaluation. In terms of content, content is defined not by the total body of what could be known (vocabulary, morphology, grammar, or syntax) but by what is necessary for fluency. These may not be equivalent. As concerns evaluation, since content is subordinate to the goal of an ability, evaluation should concern the achievement of that goal and not necessarily the learning of content. If our goal is fluency, then evaluation should be oriented to testing whether or to what degree that goal has been attained. This may involve some measure of content, yet the goal of assessment should be skill-based.

B. Recognition and Response

In our definition, fluency as an ability is defined by "recognition" and "response." Recognition and response are not distinct acts but, rather, two sides of the same coin: recognition requires response and response recognition. That is, the sort of recognition implied by fluency is recognition that leads to proper interpretation; if our goal is fluency, recognising the language, symbols, pronunciation, or even morphological features of the text is not sufficient. The recognition required for fluency is the sort that recognises the meaning of a text as a whole and the relations each part has to one another to ascertain the force of the whole. Recognition occurs at the level of the clause, the minimal unit of meaning.[2] Recognition is the perception of what the

---

[2] Every unit of a clause has meaning only in a context; the clause is the

text could mean; response is reacting to what the text should mean within the context of the reader's interaction with the text. Response is the connection of the text's meaning potential with a pre-existing set of beliefs and circumstances resulting in action. This action may occur intuitively or intentionally, depending on the nature of the response required.[3] A response may involve the confirmation of a belief, the adoption of a new belief, the revision of a belief, an emotional response, refraining from a course of action, or adopting a new course of action. Meaning, the realisation of the potential of a text, involves both aspects, recognition of what the text may say and actualising an element of this meaning potential. Without recognition, a response will inevitably be false; without a response, recognition is inevitably superficial.[4] Our goal must be both.[5]

---

minimal context sufficient for meaning. That is, a clause, whether a single word (Tom!; go!) or multiple words (he went), is necessary for meaning to be present, for this is the minimal requirement for the use of language in communication. However, a clause is not *sufficient* for meaning. A clause independent of a system of symbols and grammar for intelligible combination has infinite meaning: it could mean anything. There must also be a referential context to specifying what is meant. "Tom!" printed on a rock in the woods is practically meaningless; "Tom!" uttered in the context of a wife greeting her husband returning from war is highly meaningful. Vern Poythress identifies these as three subsystems involved in communication, reference, phonology (or graphology), and grammar. For 'meaning' in this context, see my book *The Gift of Reading – Part 2*. Vern S. Poythress, *In the Beginning Was the Word: Language: A God-Centered Approach* (Wheaton: Crossway Books, 2009), 259–69; Rutherford, *The Gift of Reading - Part 2*.

[3] Drawing on Polanyi's account of knowing, meaning is found in the focal-subsidiary integration. Polanyi, *Personal Knowledge*.

[4] Cf. Frame, *The Doctrine of the Knowledge*, 93–98.

[5] In *The Gift of Reading – Part 1 & 2*, I outline meaning as defined in this sense and identify the criteria for a justified use or meaning of a text in terms of its reference, grammar, and contextual force.

C. With Ease

Given enough time, many of us who have received a seminary education can recognise and respond to a Hebrew, Aramaic, or Greek text. However, fluency is marked by the ability to recognise and respond to the text with ease, intuitively, without moving the pieces into the centre of our focus and analysing them. The skills of analysing a clause, performing a word study, or analysing the syntax of a passage can be of great help in exegesis, but they are not characteristic of good reading. These skills find their place in dealing with difficulties in the text, not in reading the text for edification, catching a narrative, or interpreting the symbolic rhythm of poetry. Ease is, of course, a subjective value, so there may be varying degrees of fluency. However, ease can be defined as proficiency in interpreting significant textual units—such as pericopes, paragraphs, and poetic strophes or verses—in the original language (that is, without having to first translate the text and work with this translation). A beginning reader of Hebrew may be able to do so with the books of Samuel and not with Chronicles or Isaiah, so there may be fluency concerning parts of Scripture without fluency concerning the whole. Our ultimate goal must be whole-Bible fluency, though fluency in more manageable sections may be the best stepping stone to get there.

Drawing on psycholinguist research, Randall Buth argues that

> The biggest and most compelling issue for Christian scholarship is to have the fluency in speech that enhances high-level textual processing and macro-comprehension in reading.[6]

Research suggests that our cognitive faculties for language involve a

---

[6] Randall Buth, "The Role of Pronunciation in New Testament Greek Studies," in *Linguistics and New Testament Greek: Key Issues in the Current Debate*, ed. David Alan Black and Benjamin L Merkle (Grand Rapids: Baker Publishing Group, 2020).

component of the working memory that retains phonological data and repeats it, enabling us to comprehend texts as they are read; this is called the "phonological loop."[7] This loop is integral to our ability to grasp a text. Because it works in short intervals, reading that produces comprehension must be relatively rapid, comparable to speech.[8] The research suggests that reading is closely integrated with hearing (hence "phonological" loop), so language pedagogy that aims at fluency must regard pronunciation and verbal expression.[9]

D. And Accuracy

The final element of fluency is recognising and responding to the text with accuracy. Accuracy encompasses all levels of the text, accurately identifying morphology (correctly identifying the subject or object of a verb, the mood or tense of the clause), the syntax of clauses, the function of the clause, sentence or paragraph in the greater text and so the appropriate response to it. In *The Gift of Reading – Part 1* and *Part 2*, I identified three criteria for identifying a justified use, or true meaning, of a text, *validity, appropriateness,* and *fittingness*:

> We could say that an application [broadly defined to include any use of a text] is justified when it is a *valid* use of the text that is *appropriate* for the function of the text and *fits* its field of reference. An application is valid when it is consistent with the text interpreted in its context. An application is *appropriate* when it is consistent with the force or intent of the text. An application is fitting when it is consistent with the referents of a text.[10]

---

[7] Walter, "Phonology in Second Language Reading," 456–58.

[8] Cf. Walter, "Phonology in Second Language Reading."

[9] Buth, "The Role of Pronunciation in New Testament Greek Studies."

[10] Rutherford, *The Gift of Reading - Part 1*, 93–94. Cf. Ibid. 77-95, 203-208 and Rutherford, *The Gift of Reading - Part 2*, 69–80.

If our aim is fluency, part of our task will be to equip our students with the appropriate tools not only to recognise and respond to the text but also to evaluate their responses and to sustain them with argument. Part of the constructive task of Greek and Hebrew grammar may just be to outline the parameters and criteria for justifying a particular reading of morphology, grammar, and syntax, given the lack of ontological reality for language beyond the texts that compose the context of its discourse (see Appendix 2).

APPENDIX 2 – AGAINST THE NORMATIVE MODEL OF BIBLICAL LANGUAGES[11]

The 20th and 21st centuries have seen a boom in language studies; linguistics has been particularly fruitful for the study of the biblical languages. Whatever biases may affect their decision-making, the primary Hebrew and Greek lexicons published in these centuries are testimonies to the advances in the discipline of lexical semantics and the ways computers can aid in language analysis. Lexical semantics is one area that has yielded unambiguous fruit. Another area that has received great attention is the Greek and Hebrew verbal systems. Studies on these systems did not begin in these centuries, but the 20th and 21st centuries have witnessed a growing consensus concerning these languages. Today's primary model for verbal systems is TAM, the coordinating values of Tense, Aspect, and Mood. *Tense* describes the time value of a verb (though it should be observed that this value relates to presentation, not reality). *Aspect* can be described as the

[11] I intend this appendix to contribute to the previous appendix and, with that appendix, to Ch.12.C.iv.

perspective given on an action, often either as perfective, viewed as a whole, or imperfective, considering the action closely, according to its internal structure. *Mode* could be summarised as the presentation of a verbal event's relation to actuality, whether indicative (presented as actual) or modal (subjunctive indicating potentiality, etc.). Sometimes, especially in the discussion of the Greek verbal system, spatiality is added: a verb can be remote or proximate. The TAM(S) values of a specific verb in a context manifest *aktionsart*, the type of action presented (continuous, iterative, etc.). It is thought that verbal forms or conjugations and verbal systems manifest these values in different ways. It is thought that they *encode* these abstract values, and these values manifest in concrete ways when used. Some consider Hebrew to have a perfective and non-perfective aspectual system;[12] the Greek "tenses" are often thought to encode aspect and maybe spatiality, not tense.[13] Newer Greek grammars present the conjugations within this

---

[12] Waltke and O'Conner provide a helpful overview of the discussion until the late 20th century. Bruce K. Waltke and Michael Patrick O'Connor, *An Introduction to Biblical Hebrew Syntax* (Winona Lake: Eisenbrauns, 1990). For the developments since then, see John A. Cook, *Time and the Biblical Hebrew Verb: The Expression of Tense, Aspect, and Modality in Biblical Hebrew*, Linguistic Studies in Ancient West Semitic 7 (Winona Lake: Eisenbrauns, 2012); Aaron D. Hornkohl, "Biblical Hebrew Tense–Aspect–Mood, Word Order and Pragmatics: Some Observations on Recent Approaches," in *Studies in Semitic Linguistics and Manuscripts: A Liber Discipulorum in Honour of Professor Geoffrey Khan*, ed. Nadia Vidro et al., Studia Semitica Upsaliensia 30 (Uppsala Universitet, 2018), 27–56; John A. Cook, *The Biblical Hebrew Verb: A Linguistic Introduction* (Grand Rapids: Baker Academic, 2024).

[13] Fanning and Porter provide the seminal analysis of the issues surrounding the Greek verbal system, with the former favouring including tense within the system and the latter arguing that aspect is primary and tense is not a factor. More recently, Campbell has modified Porter's proposal and offered an extended argument for aspect and spatiality (which Porter also ascribes to the Greek tenses) in the Greek tenses. His short book on aspect provides an entry-level discussion of these issues and a model for identifying the *aktionsart* of a verb. Buist M. Fanning, *Verbal Aspect in New Testament Greek*, Oxford Theological Monographs (Oxford: New York: Clarendon; Oxford University Press, 1990); Stanley E. Porter, *Verbal Aspect in the Greek of the New*

framework.[14] This is where I want to address a theoretical issue. I believe the TAM system gives us an insight into an underlying theoretical issue with linguistics (at least as applied to our pedagogy of biblical languages) and the way we approach the phenomenon of language in Biblical Studies (and, perhaps, beyond).

My journey started in the 3rd year of my MA in Theological Studies at Regent College, for which I specialised in biblical languages. I majored in Hebrew but wanted to round out my skill set by doing an extracurricular research project in Greek. My object of study was the Greek Perfect conjugation. I spent nearly two years, alongside my requisite Hebrew studies and ThM thesis, reading the primary literature on the issue and thinking through the problems. Essentially, the conventional understanding of the Perfect as resultative did not quite

Testament, with Reference to Tense and Mood, Studies in Biblical Greek 1 (New York: Peter Lang, 2003); Constantine R. Campbell, *Verbal Aspect, the Indicative Mood, and Narrative: Soundings in the Greek of the New Testament*, Studies in Biblical Greek, v. 13 (New York: Peter Lang, 2007); Constantine R. Campbell, *Verbal Aspect and Non-Indicative Verbs: Further Soundings in the Greek of the New Testament*, Studies in Biblical Greek, v. 15 (New York: Peter Lang, 2008); Constantine R. Campbell, *Basics of Verbal Aspect in Biblical Greek* (Grand Rapids: Zondervan, 2008). See the response to Porter's approach in Steven E. Runge, "Contrastive Substitution and the Greek Verb," *Novum Testamentum* 56, no. 2 (March 18, 2014): 154–73, https://doi.org/10.1163/15685365-12341446; Steven E Runge, "Markedness: Contrasting Porter's Model with the Linguists Cited as Support," *Bulletin for Biblical Research* 26, no. 1 (December 31, 2016): 43–56; Stanley E Porter, "What More Shall I Say?: A Response to Steve Runge and Benjamin Merkle," *Bulletin for Biblical Research* 26, no. 1 (December 31, 2016): 75–79; Benjamin Merkle, "Response to Porter," *Bulletin for Biblical Research* 26, no. 1 (2016): 83; Steven E Runge, "Response to Porter," *Bulletin for Biblical Research* 26, no. 1 (December 31, 2016): 81–82.

[14] E.g. Andreas J. Köstenberger, Benjamin L. Merkle, and Robert L. Plummer, *Going Deeper with New Testament Greek: An Intermediate Study of the Grammar and Syntax of the New Testament* (Nashville: B&H Academic, 2016).

work within an aspectual oriented, TAM system.[15] Nor did the categories of perfective and imperfective necessarily lend themselves to the way the Perfect seems to work—though Campbell has offered a valiant attempt to interpret the Perfect as imperfective.[16] Some, like McKay, have suggested that the Perfect manifests a third aspect, "perfect" or "stative"—to which others respond that stativity is an *aktionsart* not an aspectual value.[17] Which is it?

I isolated the indicative Perfect and worked through every instance in the New Testament, interpreting it in its context. While working one night at the John Allison Library, a potential solution to the problem of the Perfect (what it meant and what encoded value explained its peculiar *aktionsart* values) offered itself to me. I had observed that in the most peculiar instances of the Perfect indicative (those where it did not resemble the Present or Aorist in its function), it seemed to have stative *aktionsart* with a transitive or intransitive verb. None of the TAM values seemed to explain this difference between Present and Aorist (and Imperfect). This seemed to favour MacKay's analysis—that it is a distinct aspect—yet MacKay's "perfect" aspect could not easily explain all the times the Perfect resembled an Aorist verb. If aspect is the perspective on an event, then the Perfect must have a rather strange aspect, for it focuses not on the happening of the event but the mere fact that it happened with reference to the subject. It even did this with actions that continued into the time of writing or speaking; it presented them in terms of their result concerning the

15 Fanning and Köstenberger, et al. both present something like the traditional understanding within the framework of modern verbal linguistics. Köstenberger, Merkle, and Plummer; Fanning, *Verbal Aspect in New Testament Greek*.

16 Campbell, *Verbal Aspect*; Constantine R. Campbell, *Advances in the Study of Greek*, New Insights for Reading the New Testament (Grand Rapids: Zondervan, 2015).

17 Kenneth L McKay, "On the Perfect and Other Aspects in New Testament Greek," *Novum Testamentum* 23, no. 4 (October 1981): 289–329.

subject. I concluded that this third aspect was *telic* or "closed," focusing not on the action as a whole but on its completion, whether that "completion" was actual (a past event) or theoretical (for a continuing event). In this way, it could present a past action just like the Aorist or create a stative *aktionsart* out of a transitive verb, with a focus on either the object (scarce, e.g. "Someone has shot Tom, so he is in the hospital") or subject ("Tom has been shot, so he is in the hospital"). I attempted to get the resulting paper published but received the feedback I expected: I needed to present a clear and distinct methodology. Without a background in linguistics, I had adopted a general abductive or scientific method for my study, presenting a hypothesis and testing it through an extensive examination of the evidence.[18] It was only when I re-examined the matter in search of an adequate method that I discovered a serious flaw not only in my argument but, I contend, the whole TAM(S) theory.

Method ought to be shaped by the available data and the desired goal, shaped to reach a goal in a manner that is consistent with the relevant data. In many disciplines, that goal will be something that is true. In the search for an explanation for the Perfect, I and others were searching for the actual or true description of the cause for the varied phenomena we encountered. So, if I was to prove that my theory was better than the others, I needed to show that it was true over against the others. The problem I encountered was that there is no ground for the truth of any TAM(S) claim. This has been recognised within linguistics, especially among proponents of cognitive and functional linguistic schools. It is recognised that the goal of finding an abstract cause or meaning for any morphological form or lexeme, its

---

[18] I have been pleased to see that some of what I observed intuitively and by analysing the data from the Greek New Testament has been echoed in recent and more methodologically refined works. See David Alan Black and Benjamin L Merkle, eds., *Linguistics and New Testament Greek: Key Issues in the Current Debate* (Grand Rapids: Baker Publishing Group, 2020).

"semantic" core, is misguided.[19] However, this issue is worth probing beyond the disagreements among schools of linguistics.

To be overly simplistic, we can identify three broad theories of truth in the history of philosophy, three claims of what it means for any claim to be true. In reverse order, some have claimed that something is true if it *works*. However, this definition is seriously problematic. Though many truths will "work," such as scientific theories, this pragmatic approach is insufficient; a true analysis of art does not "work" or have pragmatic value, yet we would not deny that someone could correctly or falsely interpret a work of art. Furthermore, though many (or if we stretch the definition enough, all) truth "works," this does not mean that everything that works is true. Believing in Atheism may lead to a productive and joyful life, but that result by no means justifies the belief; believing in Christ may do the same, yet these beliefs are contradictory. So, a pragmatic theory of truth does not work with how we usually think of "truth" and cannot uphold exclusive claims to truth. The next theory, coherence, has similar issues. According to coherentists, something is true if it is completely consistent with all known data—or, better, a worldview. However, there could be many contradictory beliefs that cohere with the same worldview; are they all true? Also, if another worldview is adopted, truth changes. So, though all truth will cohere with a correct worldview or all the data, not everything that coheres with a correct worldview or all the data is true. The last theory, and the most important from a Christian perspective, is the correspondence theory of truth. The correspondence theory of truth claims that something is true if it corresponds in some sense with

---

19 See, for example, Silva, *Biblical Words and Their Meaning: An Introduction to Lexical Semantics*; Poythress, *In the Beginning Was the Word*; Alexander Andrason and Christian Locatell, "The Perfect Wave: A Cognitive Approach to the Greek Verbal System," *Biblical and Ancient Greek Linguistics* 5 (2016): 7–121; Nicholas J. Ellis, "Biblical Exegesis and Linguistics: A Prodigal History," in *Linguistics and New Testament Greek: Key Issues in the Current Debate*, ed. David Alan Black and Benjamin L Merkle (Grand Rapids: Baker Publishing Group, 2020).

reality. Correspondence theory has been dominant in the history of philosophy and Christian thought, yet it has come into serious problems as of late. It is not clear to what a true statement corresponds. The most defensible theory, with a strong biblical basis, is the view that something is true if it coheres with God's interpretation of reality. On this theory, any truth is an interpretation of reality, a description of it, and to be true it must agree without error with God's interpretation of that reality.[20] As John Frame argues, we should not choose between these three theories but see them as different ways of viewing the same reality, truth.[21]

Returning to the topic at hand, one thing should be immediately apparent: that truth is more complicated than it seems. Most arguments for TAM(S) claims are *coherentist* arguments; such an argument seeks to demonstrate that the claim is consistent with all the available evidence. However, as we saw briefly, such a claim does not make the claim "true" in any conventional sense. If a TAM(S) claim is to be true, it must correspond to some reality, yet to what reality does it correspond? If we suggest it is the author's intention, we encounter an immediate problem: I know of no person (this is certainly true of me) who thinks about what they read and write in terms of TAM(S). You are not reading this book and thinking about the verbs used in terms of tense, aspect, mode, (and spatiality), or even *aktionsart.* There is no reason to believe that the author of a text had these things in mind and a great reason to be suspect of such a claim. So, the correspondence is not with an author's intention. Nor is it clear that there is a subliminal intention (whatever that might mean). TAM(S) claims do not correspond to the text for they are looking beyond the text to a hypothesised cause for it. If we have no reason to think people interpret and create texts in terms of TAM(S), we have less reason to

---

20 See J. Alexander Rutherford, *The Gift of Knowledge* (Airdrie, AB: Teleioteti, 2021).

21 Frame, *The Doctrine of the Knowledge.*

believe that God would interpret texts in these categories. So, TAM(S) claims have no correspondence value. Simply put, a claim about TAM(S) cannot be true in any conventional sense of the word. A claim may or may not work better or cohere better with the data, but this is a claim about pedagogy or heuristic value, not truth.

What I saw as I considered method was exactly what I encountered in my philosophical work. TAM(S), and verbal linguistics in general, assumes that its claims have truth value; the only possible correspondence is an abstract essence, a unifying core that causes all the various functions a verbal form takes. However, like the Platonic Universals or the Aristotelian formal cause, we have no reason to believe this abstract essence exists. At this point, I identified another correlation: this is exactly the conclusion that was reached in the 20th-century discussion of lexical semantics, and it is similar to various theories within cognitive linguistics. It was long thought that every word had a core meaning that could explain all its uses; however, 20th and 21st-century studies on how words work put this claim to death. Instead of a single meaning, words have a semantic range, a range of ways they *have been* used. The different points in this range may be explained by the evolution of a word over time or by analogy with other uses; sometimes, we have no explanation for why a word is used in a particular way. The point is that a single word can have many meanings that may be loosely related or not at all related; a word has no abstract essence that causes all its uses.[22] In cognitive linguistics, ontology has been treated as a mental habit by which we group particulars, perhaps with one particular exemplar, such as in prototype theory.[23] In the same way, a verbal form has no abstract essence that

22 Cf. Silva, *Biblical Words and Their Meaning: An Introduction to Lexical Semantics*; Poythress, *In the Beginning Was the Word.*

23 Kathleen Callow, *Man and Message: A Guide to Meaning-Based Text Analysis* (Lanham, MD: Summer Institute of Linguistics, University Press of America, 1998); Ellis, "Biblical Exegesis and Linguistics: A Prodigal History"; Andrason and Locatell, "The Perfect Wave: A Cognitive Approach to the

causes all its uses. Therefore, our analysis of a verbal form cannot describe its essential meaning—for it has none. Instead, a verbal analysis considers the phenomena of the verb and describes them, creating a semantic range. Part of this descriptive task will be identifying points of relation on this range, how different uses are related, and whether they evolved through time (diachronically) or are naturally related to the other uses. This points to another goal, namely, pedagogy; as pedagogy, the task is drawing connections within this semantic range so that we need not memorise every use of a word—or verb, or clause—to recognise its uses.

If this is true—that TAM(S) claims have no truth value—then we cannot evaluate them as true or false, only as useful or not. If TAM(S) claims fail in the realm of correspondence, they may have heuristic or explanatory value as they cohere with our worldview and the relevant data or as they are found useful. Unfortunately, it is in these various areas that these theories are weakest.

Greek Verbal System."

SELECT BIBLIOGRAPHY

Adams, Liam. "Christian Colleges Are Changing to Survive. Is It Working?" News & Reporting. Christianity Today, September 9, 2020. https://www.christianitytoday.com/news/2020/september/enrollment-crisis-christian-college-cccu-evangelical-humani.html.

Alter, Robert. *The Art of Biblical Narrative*. London: Allen & Unwin, 1981.

Anderson, Terry. "The Hidden Curriculum in Distance Education: An Updated View." *Change: The Magazine of Higher Learning* 33, no. 6 (November 1, 2001): 28–35. https://doi.org/10.1080/00091380109601824.

Andrason, Alexander, and Christian Locatell. "The Perfect Wave: A Cognitive Approach to the Greek Verbal System." *Biblical and Ancient Greek Linguistics* 5 (2016): 7–121.

Anglicare Centre for Pastoral Development. "Introductory Pastoral Care Course Book." Anglicare, n.d.

Aristotle. "Metaphysics." In *The Works of Aristotle*, edited by W. D. Rose and J. A. Smith, Logos Edition. Vol. 8. Oxford: The Clarendon Press, 1908.

Armstrong, Brian G. *Calvinism and the Amyraut Heresy: Protestant Scholasticism and Humanism in Seventeenth-Century France*. University of Wisconsin Press, 1969.

Ash, Christopher, and Steve Midgley. *The Heart of Anger: How the Bible Transforms Anger in Our Understanding and Experience*. Wheaton: Crossway, 2021.

Athas, George. *Bridging the Testaments: The History and Theology of God's People in the Second Temple Period.* Grand Rapids: Zondervan Academic, 2023.

Australian Government Style Manual. "Literary and Access." Government, February 27, 2024. https://www.stylemanual.gov.au/accessible-and-inclusive-content/literacy-and-access.

Ayres, Lewis. "Athanasius' Initial Defense of the Term Homoousios: Rereading the De Decretis." *Journal of Early Christian Studies* 12, no. 3 (2004): 337–59. https://doi.org/10.1353/earl.2004.0035.

———. *Nicaea and Its Legacy: An Approach to Fourth-Century Trinitarian Theology.* 1st ed. Oxford: Oxford University Press, 2004. https://doi.org/10.1093/0198755066.001.0001.

B. B. Warfield. "The Religious Life of Theological Students," February 25, 2011. https://bbwarfield.com/works/sermons-and-addresses/the-religious-life-of-theological-students/.

Baptist Churches Western Australia. "Accreditation - BCWA," October 31, 2021. https://www.baptistwa.asn.au/accreditation/.

Barna Group. "Pastors Share Top Reasons They've Considered Quitting Ministry in the Past Year," April 27, 2022. https://www.barna.com/research/pastors-quitting-ministry/.

Barrett, Matthew. *None Greater: The Undomesticated Attributes of God.* Grand Rapids: Baker Books, 2019.

Basil of Caesarea. *Against Eunomius.* Translated by Mark DelCogliano and Andrew Radde-Gallwitz. The Fathers of the Church, v. 122. Washington, DC: Catholic University of America Press, 2011.

Baxter, Richard. *The Reformed Pastor: Updated and Abridged.* Edited by Tim Cooper. Wheaton: Crossway, 2021.

Bebbington, David W. *Evangelicalism in Modern Britain: A History from the 1730s to the 1980s.* London: Routledge, 2003.

Beckwith, Roger T. *The Old Testament Canon of the New Testament Church and Its Background in Early Judaism.* Grand Rapids: Eerdmans, 1986.

Behr, John. *The Nicene Faith: Vol 2 of Formation of Christian Theology.* Crestwood, NY: St Vladimir's Seminary Press, 2004.

———. *The Way to Nicaea.* The Formation of Christian Theology, v. 1. Crestwood, NY: St. Vladimir's Seminary Press, 2001.

Benevich, Grigory. "God's Logoi and Human Personhood in St Maximus the Confessor." *Studi Sull'Oriente Cristiano* 13, no. 1 (2009): 137–52.

Berger, Peter L. *The Sacred Canopy: Elements of a Sociological Theory of Religion.* New York: Doubleday, 1967.

Bethune-Baker, J. F. *Nestorius and His Teaching: A Fresh Examination of the Evidence.* Cambridge: Cambridge University Press, 1908.

Bigney, Brad. *Gospel Treason: Betraying the Gospel with Hidden Idols.* Phillipsburg, NJ: P&R Publishing, 2012.

Bilezikian, Gilbert. "Hermeneutical Bungee-Jumping: Subordination in the Godhead." *Journal of the Evangelical Theological Society* 40, no. 1 (March 1997): 57–68.

Bird, M. F., and R. Shillaker. "Subordination in the Trinity and Gender Roles: A Response to Recent Discussion." *Trinity Journal* 29, no. 2 (2008): 267–83.

Bird, Michael F., and Robert Shillaker. "The Son Really, Really Is the Son: A Response to Kevin Giles." *Trinity Journal* 30, no. 2 (Fall 2009): 257–68.

Bitzer, Heinrich, ed. *Light on the Path: Daily Scripture Readings in Hebrew and Greek.* Grand Rapids: Baker Book House, 1982.

Black, David Alan, and Benjamin L Merkle, eds. *Linguistics and New Testament Greek: Key Issues in the Current Debate.* Grand Rapids: Baker Publishing Group, 2020.

Blaising, Craig A., and Darrell L. Bock. *Progressive Dispensationalism.* Grand Rapids: Bridgepoint Books, 2000.

Boersma, Hans. *Heavenly Participation: The Weaving of a Sacramental Tapestry.* Grand Rapids: Eerdmans, 2011.

———. *Nouvelle Théologie and Sacramental Ontology: A Return to Mystery.* Oxford; New York: Oxford University Press, 2009. https://doi.org/10.1093/acprof:oso/9780199229642.001.0001.

———. "Up the Mountain with the Fathers: Evangelical Ressourcement of Early Christian Doctrine." *Canadian Theological Review* 1, no. 1 (2012): 3–22.

Bonhoeffer, Dietrich. *Life Together.* New York: Harper & Row, 1954. http://archive.org/details/lifetogether00diet.

Brown, Michael L. "Jeremiah." In *The Expositor's Bible Commentary Volume 7: Jeremiah-Ezekiel*, edited by Tremper Longman and David E. Garland, Revised Edition. Grand Rapids: Zondervan, 2010.

Bucer, Martin. *Concerning the True Care of Souls*. Translated by Peter Beale. Edinburgh: Banner of Truth Trust, 2009.

Bullinger, Heinrich. *The Decades of Henry Bullinger*. Cambridge: Cambridge University Press, 1849. http://archive.org/details/decadesofhenrybu0000bull_n6r5.

Bullock, C. Hassell. *Encountering the Book of Psalms: A Literary and Theological Introduction*. Grand Rapids: Baker Academic, 2004.

Bultmann, Rudolf. *New Testament and Mythology and Other Basic Writings*. Translated by Schubert Miles Ogden. Philadelphia: Fortress Press, 1989.

Burton, Simon J. G. *Ramism and the Reformation of Method: The Franciscan Legacy in Early Modernity*. Oxford Studies in Historical Theology. New York: Oxford University Press, 2024.

Buth, Randall. "The Role of Pronunciation in New Testament Greek Studies." In *Linguistics and New Testament Greek: Key Issues in the Current Debate*, edited by David Alan Black and Benjamin L Merkle. Grand Rapids: Baker Publishing Group, 2020.

Butner, D. Glenn. "Eternal Functional Subordination and the Problem of the Divine Will." *Journal of the Evangelical Theological Society* 58, no. 1 (March 2015): 131–49.

Callow, Kathleen. *Man and Message: A Guide to Meaning-Based Text Analysis*. Lanham, Md: Summer Institute of Linguistics, University Press of America, 1998.

Calvin, John. *Commentary upon the Acts of the Apostles*. Translated by Henry Beveridge. Bellingham: Logos Bible Software, 2010.

———. *Institutes of the Christian Religion*. Translated by Henry Beveridge. Logos Digital Edition. Edinburgh: The Calvin Translation Society, 1845.

Campbell, Constantine R. *Advances in the Study of Greek*. New Insights for Reading the New Testament. Grand Rapids: Zondervan, 2015.

———. *Basics of Verbal Aspect in Biblical Greek*. Grand Rapids: Zondervan, 2008.

———. *Verbal Aspect and Non-Indicative Verbs: Further Soundings in the Greek of the New Testament*. Studies in Biblical Greek, v. 15. New York: Peter Lang, 2008.

———. *Verbal Aspect, the Indicative Mood, and Narrative: Soundings in the Greek of the New Testament*. Studies in Biblical Greek, v. 13. New York:

Peter Lang, 2007.

Carson, D. A. *Exegetical Fallacies*. Grand Rapids: Baker Books, 1996.

———. "Matthew." In *The Expositor's Bible Commentary: Matthew–Mark (Revised Edition)*, edited by Tremper Longman III and David E. Garland, Vol. 9. Grand Rapids: Zondervan, 2010.

———. *Memoirs of an Ordinary Pastor: The Life and Reflections of Tom Carson*. Wheaton: Crossway, 2008.

———. "Unity and Diversity in the New Testament: The Possibility of Systematic Theology." In *Scripture and Truth*, edited by John D. Woodbridge and D. A. Carson, 61–94. Grand Rapids: Baker Book House, 1992.

Carter, Craig A. *Contemplating God with the Great Tradition: Recovering Trinitarian Classical Theism*. Grand Rapids: Baker Academic, 2021.

———. *Interpreting Scripture with the Great Tradition: Recovering the Genius of Premodern Exegesis*. Grand Rapids: Baker Academic, 2018.

Chapell, Bryan. *Christ-Centered Preaching: Redeeming the Expository Sermon*. 2nd ed. Grand Rapids: Baker Academic, 2005.

Cheung, Vivian W. "Called 'My People' by God's Sovereign Grace: A Study of the Calling Motif in Romans." PhD Thesis, Moore Theological College, 2023.

Christian Reformed Church. "Paths to Ordination | Candidacy in the Christian Reformed Church." Accessed February 23, 2024. https://www.crcna.org/candidacy/paths-ordination.

Collett, Don C. *Figural Reading and the Old Testament: Theology and Practice*. Grand Rapids: Baker Academic, 2020.

Constas, Maximos. "Maximus the Confessor, Dionysius the Areopagite, and the Transformation of Christian Neoplatonism." *Analogia* 2, no. 1 (2017): 1–12.

Cook, John A. *The Biblical Hebrew Verb: A Linguistic Introduction*. Grand Rapids: Baker Academic, 2024.

———. *Time and the Biblical Hebrew Verb: The Expression of Tense, Aspect, and Modality in Biblical Hebrew*. Linguistic Studies in Ancient West Semitic 7. Winona Lake: Eisenbrauns, 2012.

Cowan, Christopher. "The Father and Son in the Fourth Gospel: Johannine Subordination Revisited." *Journal of the Evangelical Theological Society* 49, no. 1 (March 2006): 115–35.

Creach, Jerome F. D. *Yahweh as Refuge and the Editing of the Hebrew Psalter.* A&C Black, 1996.

Cvetković, Vladimir. "'All in All' (1 Cor 15:28): Aspects of the Unity Between God and Creation According to St Maximus the Confessor." *Analogia* 2, no. 1 (2017): 13–28.

Cvetkovic, Vladimir. "Re-Interpreting Tradition: Maximus the Confessor on Creation in Ambigua Ad Ioannem." In *Questioning the World. Greek Patristic and Byzantine Question and Answer Literature*, edited by Bram Bemulder and Peter Van Deun, 147–80. Lectio 11. Turnhout, Belgium: Brepols, 2021.

Dahms, John V. "The Subordination of the Son." *Journal of the Evangelical Theological Society* 37, no. 3 (September 1994): 351–64.

Daley, Brian E. "Divine Transcendence and Human Transformation: Gregory of Nyssa's Anti-Apollinarian Christology." In *Rethinking Gregory of Nyssa*, edited by Sarah Coakley, 67–76. Malden, MA: Blackwell, 2003.

Danker, Frederick W. *A Greek-English Lexicon of the New Testament and Other Early Christian Literature.* 3rd ed. Chicago: University of Chicago Press, 2000.

De Ste. Croix, G. E. M. "The Council of Chalcedon with Additions by Michael Whitby." In *Christian Persecution, Martyrdom, and Orthodoxy*, edited by Michael Whitby and Joseph Streeter. Oxford ; New York: Oxford University Press, 2006.

Dekker, Willem-Maarten. "John Webster's Retrieval of Classical Theology." *Journal of Reformed Theology* 12, no. 1 (2018): 59–63. https://doi.org/10.1163/15697312-01201004.

Dempster, Stephen G. "Canons on the Right and Canons on the Left: Finding a Resolution in the Canon Debate." *Journal of the Evangelical Theological Society* 52, no. 1 (March 2009): 47–77.

DeRouchie, Jason S. "The Profit of Employing the Biblical Languages: Scriptural and Historical Reflections." *Themelios* 37, no. 1 (2012): 32–50.

Dewhurst, Emma Brown. "How Can We Be Nothing?: The Concept of Non-Being in Athanasius and Maximus the Confessor." *Analogia* 2, no. 1 (2017): 29–34.

Dockery, David S., and Christopher W. Morgan, eds. *Christian Higher Education: Faith, Teaching, and Learning in the Evangelical Tradition.* Wheaton: Crossway, 2018.

Dolezal, James E. *All That Is in God: Evangelical Theology and the Challenge of Classical Christian Theism*. Grand Rapids: Reformation Heritage Books, 2017.

———. *God without Parts: Divine Simplicity and the Metaphysics of God's Absoluteness*. Eugene, OR: Pickwick Publications, 2011.

Dr. Zakir Naik. *The Quran And Modern Science*. Islamic Research Foundation, 2000. http://archive.org/details/thequranandmodernscience_201910.

Dragas, George D. "The Anti-Apollinarist Christology of St Gregory of Nyssa: A First Analysis." *The Greek Orthodox Theological Review* 42, no. 3–4 (1997): 299–314.

Draguet, René. "La Christologie D'Eutychès D'après Les Actes Du Synode de Flavien (448)." *Byzantion* 6, no. 1 (1931): 441–57.

Duby, Steven J. *Divine Simplicity: A Dogmatic Account*. T&T Clark Studies in Systematic Theology, volume 30. London ; New York: Bloomsbury, 2016.

———. *Jesus and the God of Classical Theism: Biblical Christology in Light of the Doctrine of God*. Grand Rapids: Baker, 2022.

Dunbar, David G. "The Biblical Canon." In *Hermeneutics, Authority, and Canon*, edited by D. A. Carson and John D. Woodbridge. Grand Rapids: Academie Books, 1986.

Duncan III, Ligon J. "The Covenant Idea in Ante-Nicene Theology." Ph.D. Thesis, University of Edinburgh, 1995.

Duvall, J. Scott, and J. Daniel Hays. *Grasping God's Word: A Hands-on Approach to Reading, Interpreting, and Applying the Bible*. 3rd ed. Grand Rapids: Zondervan, 2012.

Earls, Aaron. "22 Vital Stats for Ministry in 2022 - Lifeway Research." Lifeway Research, January 5, 2022. https://lifewayresearch.com/2022/01/05/22-vital-stats-for-ministry-in-2022/.

Ehrman, Bart D. *The New Testament: A Historical Introduction to the Early Christian Writings*. Oxford University Press, 2000.

Ellis, Nicholas J. "Biblical Exegesis and Linguistics: A Prodigal History." In *Linguistics and New Testament Greek: Key Issues in the Current Debate*, edited by David Alan Black and Benjamin L Merkle. Grand Rapids: Baker Publishing Group, 2020.

Epsen, Edward. *From Laws to Liturgy: An Idealist Theology of Creation*. Brill,

2020.

Erickson, Millard J. *Who's Tampering with the Trinity? An Assessment of the Subordination Debate*. Grand Rapids: Kregel Academic & Professional, 2009.

Eunomius. *The Extant Works*. Translated by Richard Paul Vaggione. Oxford Early Christian Texts. Oxford; New York: Clarendon Press; Oxford University Press, 1987.

Evans, William B. "Whither the Seminary Model?" Reformation21, April 29, 2012. https://www.reformation21.org/blogs/whither-the-seminary-model.php.

Fanning, Buist M. *Verbal Aspect in New Testament Greek*. Oxford Theological Monographs. Oxford: New York: Clarendon; Oxford University Press, 1990.

Ferguson, Hazel. "Regional and Remote Higher Education: A Quick Guide." Government. Parliament of Australia, April 27, 2022. Australia. https://www.aph.gov.au/About_Parliament/Parliamentary_Departments/Parliamentary_Library/pubs/rp/rp2122/Quick_Guides/RegionalRemoteHigherEducation.

Feuerbach, Ludwig. *The Essence of Christianity*. Translated by George Eliot. Amherst, New York: Prometheus Books, 2010. https://doi.org/10.1017/CBO9781139136563.

Fitzpatrick, Elyse. *Idols of the Heart: Learning to Long for God Alone*. Second edition. Phillipsburg, NJ: P&R Publishing, 2016.

Forsyth, Alasdair, and Andy Furlong. "Socio-Economic Disadvantage and Experience in Higher Education | Joseph Rowntree Foundation." Joseph Rowntree Foundation, May 16, 2003. https://www.jrf.org.uk/socio-economic-disadvantage-and-experience-in-higher-education.

Foster, M. B. "The Christian Doctrine of Creation and the Rise of Modern Natural Science." *Mind* 43, no. 172 (1934): 446–68.

Fowler, Megan. "Fuller Seminary Won't Leave Pasadena After All." News & Reporting. Christianity Today, October 31, 2019. https://www.christianitytoday.com/news/2019/october/fuller-seminary-pasadena-campus-cancel-move-pomona.html.

Frame, John M. *Apologetics: A Justification of Christian Belief*. Edited by Joseph E. Torres. Second edition. Phillipsburg, NJ: P&R Publishing, 2015.

———. *Cornelius Van Til: An Analysis of His Thought*. Phillipsburg, NJ: P&R Publishing, 1995.

———. "Proposal for a New Seminary." *Journal of Pastoral Practice Winter 1978*, January 1, 1978. https://frame-poythress.org/proposal-for-a-new-seminary/.

———. "Seminaries and Academic Accreditation." In *John Frame's Selected Shorter Writings*, Vol. 2. Phillipsburg, NJ: P&R Publishing, 2014.

———. "The Academic Captivity of Theology." In *John Frame's Selected Shorter Writings*, Vol. 2. Phillipsburg, NJ: P&R Publishing, 2014.

———. *The Doctrine of God*. A Theology of Lordship. Phillipsburg, NJ: P&R Publishing, 2002.

———. *The Doctrine of the Christian Life*. A Theology of Lordship 4. Phillipsburg, NJ: P&R Publishing, 2008.

———. *The Doctrine of the Knowledge of God*. A Theology of Lordship. Phillipsburg, NJ: P&R Publishing, 1987.

———. *The Doctrine of the Word of God*. A Theology of Lordship. Phillipsburg, NJ: P&R Publishing, 2010.

Gaddis, Michael. *There Is No Crime for Those Who Have Christ: Religious Violence in the Christian Roman Empire*. The Transformation of the Classical Heritage 39. Berkeley: University of California Press, 2005.

Gaddis, Michael, and Richard Price. *The Acts of the Council of Chalcedon*. 3 vols. Translated Texts for Historians 45. Liverpool: Liverpool University Press, 2005.

Gaebelein, Frank E. *The Pattern of God's Truth: The Integration of Faith and Learning*. New York: BMH Books, 1985.

Gavrilyuk, Paul L. *The Suffering of the Impassible God: The Dialectics of Patristic Thought*. Oxford University Press, 2004.

Geehan, E. R., ed. *Jerusalem and Athens: Critical Discussions on the Theology and Apologetics of Cornelius Van Til*. Presbyterian and Reformed, 1971.

Gentry, Peter J., and Stephen J. Wellum. *God's Kingdom through God's Covenants: A Concise Biblical Theology*, 2015.

———. *Kingdom through Covenant: A Biblical-Theological Understanding of the Covenants*. 2nd Ed. Wheaton: Crossway, 2018.

Giles, Kevin. "Response to Michael Bird and Robert Shillaker: The Son Is Not Eternally Subordinated in Authority to the Father." *Trinity Journal* 30, no. 2 (Fall 2009): 237–56.

———. *The Trinity & Subordinationism: The Doctrine of God and the Contemporary Gender Debate*. Downers Grove: InterVarsity Press, 2002.

Graumann, Thomas. "Orthodoxy, Authority and the (Re-) Construction of the Past in Church Councils." In *Invention, Rewriting, Usurpation: Discursive Fights over Religious Traditions in Antiquity*, edited by Jörg Ulrich, Anders-Christian Jacobsen, and David Brakke. Early Christianity in the Context of Antiquity, v. 11. Frankfurt am Main: Lang, 2012.

———. *The Acts of the Early Church Councils: Production and Character*. Oxford University Press, 2021.

Gray, Patrick T. R. "Covering the Nakedness of Noah: Reconstruction and Denial in the Age of Justinian." *Byzantinische Forschungen* 24 (1997): 193–205.

———. "'The Select Fathers': Canonizing the Patristic Past." In *Studia Patristica*, 21–36. Louvain: Peeters, 1989.

Gregory of Nyssa. *Anti-Apollinarian Writings*. Translated by Robin Orton. The Fathers of the Church, a New Translation, volume 131. Washington, DC: The Catholic University of America Press, 2015.

Gregory the Great. *The Book of Pastoral Rule*. St. Vladimir's Seminary Press "Popular Patristics" Series, no. 34. Crestwood, NY: St. Vladimir's Seminary Press, 2007.

Groves, J. Alasdair, and Winston T. Smith. *Untangling Emotions*. Wheaton: Crossway, 2019.

Grudem, Wayne A. *Systematic Theology: An Introduction to Biblical Doctrine*. 2nd Ed. Grand Rapids: Zondervan Academic, 2020.

Guthrie, George H. "George H Guthrie: Helping You Read the Bible Better." George H Guthrie, July 29, 2023. https://georgehguthrie.com.

———. "The Study of Holy Scripture and the Work of Christian Higher Education." In *Christian Higher Education: Faith, Teaching, and Learning in the Evangelical Tradition*, edited by David S. Dockery and Christopher W. Morgan, 81–100. Wheaton: Crossway, 2018.

Hanson, R. P. C. *The Search for the Christian Doctrine of God: The Arian Controversy 318-381*. Edinburgh: T. & T. Clark, 1988.

Harvey, David T. *The Plurality Principle: How to Build and Maintain a Thriving Church Leadership Team*. Wheaton: Crossway, 2021.

Henry, Carl F. H. *The Uneasy Conscience of Modern Fundamentalism*. Grand Rapids: Eerdmans, 2003.

Hensley, Adam D. *Covenant Relationships and the Editing of the Hebrew Psalter*. Bloomsbury Publishing, 2018.

Hildebrant, Ted. "Proverbs 22:6a: Train Up a Child?" In *Learning from the Sages: Selected Studies on the Book of Proverbs*, edited by Roy B. Zuck, 277–92. Wipf and Stock Publishers, 2003.

Himes, Paul A. "Rethinking the Translation of Διδακτικός in 1 Timothy 3.2 and 2 Timothy 2.24." *The Bible Translator* 68, no. 2 (August 2017): 189–208. https://doi.org/10.1177/2051677017715676.

Hopfensperger, Jean. "Fewer People Are Entering the Seminary as Need Declines, Church Budgets Shrink." News & Reporting. Star Tribune, August 19, 2018. https://www.startribune.com/fewer-people-are-entering-the-seminary-as-need-declines-church-budgets-shrink/490381681/.

Hornkohl, Aaron D. "Biblical Hebrew Tense–Aspect–Mood, Word Order and Pragmatics: Some Observations on Recent Approaches." In *Studies in Semitic Linguistics and Manuscripts: A Liber Discipulorum in Honour of Professor Geoffrey Khan*, edited by Nadia Vidro, Rony Vallandt, Esther-Miriam Wagner, and Judith Olszowy-Schlanger, 27–56. Studia Semitica Upsaliensia 30. Uppsala Universitet, 2018.

https://www.sbc.net/. "Colleges and Universities - SBC.Net." Accessed February 23, 2024. https://www.sbc.net/resources/directories/colleges-and-universities/.

https://www.sbc.net/. "Theological Seminaries - SBC.Net." Accessed February 23, 2024. https://www.sbc.net/resources/directories/theological-seminaries/.

"International Orality Network | Oral Learners: Who Are They?" Accessed April 11, 2024. https://orality.net/about/oral-learners-who-are-they/.

Jakimow, Liz. "Is Australia Losing Religion: The State of the Church." Education. Australian Centre for Christianity and Culture. Accessed February 2, 2024. https://about.csu.edu.au/community/accc/about/latest-news-assets/2023/is-australia-losing-religion-the-state-of-the-church.

Jamieson, Bobby. *The Path to Being a Pastor*. Wheaton: Crossway, 2021.

Johnson, Eric L. *Foundations for Soul Care: A Christian Psychology Proposal.* Downers Grove: IVP Academic, 2007.

Johnson, Jeffery D. *The Failure of Natural Theology: A Critical Appraisal of the Philosophical Theology of Thomas Aquinas.* New Studies in Theology. Free Grace Press, 2021.

Johnson, Keith E. "Trinitarian Agency and the Eternal Subordination of the Son: An Augustinian Perspective." *Themelios* 36, no. 1 (May 2011): 7–25.

Jordan, James B. *Through New Eyes: Developing a Biblical View of the World - Theopolis Institute.* Eugene, OR: Wipf & Stock, 1999. https://theopolisinstitute.com/books/through-new-eyes-developing-a-biblical-view-of-the-world/.

Kähler, Martin. *The So-Called Historical Jesus and the Historic, Biblical Christ.* Vancouver: Regent College Pub., 1998.

Keener, Craig S. "Is Subordination within the Trinity Really Heresy? A Study of John 5:18 in Context." *Trinity Journal* 20, no. 1 (Spring 1999): 39.

Kelly, Charles J. "Classical Theism and the Doctrine of the Trinity." *Religious Studies* 30, no. 1 (March 1994): 67–88.

Kelly, J. N. D. *Early Christian Creeds.* New York: Bloomsbury Academic, 2006.

Kelsey, David H. *Between Athens and Berlin: The Theological Education Debate.* Grand Rapids: Eerdmans, 1993.

Kierkegaard, Søren. *Provocations: Spiritual Writings of Kierkegaard.* Edited by Charles E. Moore. Maryknoll, NY: Orbis, 2002. http://archive.org/details/provocationsspir0000kier.

Kilby, Karen. "Perichoresis and Projection: Problems with Social Doctrines of the Trinity." *New Blackfriars*, October 2000. http://theologyphilosophycentre.co.uk/papers/Kilby_TrinNBnew.pdf.

Kinzig, Wolfram, and Markus Vinzent. "Recent Research on the Origin of the Creed." *The Journal of Theological Studies* 50, no. 2 (October 1999): 534–59.

Kline, Meredith G. *The Structure of Biblical Authority.* Rev. ed. Grand Rapids: Eerdmans, 1975.

———. *Treaty of the Great King: The Covenant Structure of Deuteronomy; Studies and Commentary.* Grand Rapids: Eerdmans, 1963.

Köstenberger, Andreas J., Benjamin L. Merkle, and Robert L. Plummer. *Going Deeper with New Testament Greek: An Intermediate Study of the Grammar and Syntax of the New Testament.* Nashville: B&H Academic, 2016.

Kovach, Stephen D., and Peter R. Schemm. "A Defense of the Doctrine of the Eternal Subordination of the Son." *Journal of the Evangelical Theological Society* 42, no. 3 (September 1999): 461.

Krashen, Stephen D. *Principles and Practice in Second Language Acquisition.* 1st ed. Language Teaching Methodology Series. Oxford; New York: Pergamon Press, 1982.

———. *Second Language Acquisition and Second Language Learning.* Reprinted. Language Teaching Methodology Series. Oxford: Pergamon Press, 1985.

Kuhn, Thomas S. *The Structure of Scientific Revolutions.* Fourth edition. Chicago; London: The University of Chicago Press, 2012.

Kurz, Jess. "When the Pastor Baptizes His Wife." The Gospel Coalition, February 17, 2021. https://www.thegospelcoalition.org/article/when-the-pastor-baptizes-his-wife/.

Lacoste, Jean-Yves. "Homoousios et Homoousios: La Substance Entre Théologie et Philosophie." *Recherches de Science Religieuse* 98, no. 1 (January 2010): 85–100. https://doi.org/10.3917/rsr.101.0085.

Lambert, Heath. *A Theology of Biblical Counseling: The Doctrinal Foundations of Counseling Ministry.* Grand Rapids: Zondervan, 2016.

———. *The Biblical Counseling Movement after Adams.* Wheaton: Crossway, 2012.

Lane, Timothy S. *Unstuck.* Purcellville, VA: The Good Book Company, 2019.

Lane, Timothy S., and Paul David Tripp. *How People Change.* 2nd ed. Greensboro, N.C: New Growth Press, 2008.

Lewis, C. S. "God in the Dock." In *The Collected Works of C.S. Lewis: The Pilgrim's Regress, Christian Reflections, God in the Dock.* New York: Inspirational Press, 1970. http://archive.org/details/collectedworksof00csle.

Lewis, C. S. *The Complete C.S. Lewis Signature Classics.* New York: HarperOne, 2007.

Liberia Editrice Vaticana. "Catechism of the Catholic Church." Vatican.

Accessed March 8, 2024. https://www.vatican.va/archive/ENG0015/__P17.HTM.

Lichtman, Karen. *Teaching Proficiency through Reading and Storytelling (TPRS): An Input-Based Approach to Second Language Instruction*. Routledge E-Modules on Contemporary Language Teaching. New York: Routledge, 2018.

Long, Bridget Terry. "Addressing the Academic Barriers to Higher Education." Brookings. Accessed February 7, 2024. https://www.brookings.edu/articles/addressing-the-academic-barriers-to-higher-education/.

Long, V. Philips. *The Art of Biblical History*. Foundations of Contemporary Interpretation, v. 5. Grand Rapids: Zondervan, 1994.

Lossky, Vladimir. *In the Image and Likeness of God.* Crestwood, NY: St. Vladimir's Seminary Press, 1974. http://archive.org/details/inimagelikenesso0000loss.

Ludwig Wittgenstein. *Philosophical Investigations*. Translated by G. E. M. Anscombe. New York: Macmillan, 1958.

Luther, Martin. "Against Latomus." In *Luther's Works: Career of the Reformer II*, edited by Helmut T. Lehmann, 32:48–128. Philadelphia: Muhlenberg Press, 1955.

———. *The Bondage of the Will.* Edited by J. I Packer and O. R Johnston. Grand Rapids: Fleming H. Revell, 2003.

———. "To the Councilmen of All Cities in Germany That They Establish and Maintain Christian Schools." In *The Christian in Society II*, edited by Walther I Brandt, translated by Albert T. W. Steinhaeuser and Walther I Brandt. Luther's Works 45. Philadelphia: Muhlenberg, 1962.

MacIntyre, Alasdair C. *After Virtue: A Study in Moral Theory*. 2nd ed. Notre Dame, Ind: University of Notre Dame Press, 1984.

Mari, Tommaso. "Greek, Latin, and More: Multilingualism at the Ecumenical Council of Chalcedon." *Journal of Latin Linguistics* 19, no. 1 (July 2020): 59–87. https://doi.org/10.1515/joll-2020-2003.

———. "The Latin Translations of the Acts of the Council of Chalcedon." *Greek, Roman & Byzantine Studies* 58, no. 1 (March 2018): 126–55.

Marshall, Colin, and Tony Payne. *The Trellis and the Vine: The Ministry Mind-Shift That Changes Everything*. Sydney, NSW: Matthias Media, 2021.

Maspero, Giulio. "Isoangelia in Gregory of Nyssa and Origen on the

Background of Plotinus." In *Papers Presented at the Seventeenth International Conference on Patristic Studies Held in Oxford 2015 Volume 10 Evagrius between Origen, the Cappadocians, and Neoplatonism*, 77–100. Studia Patristica 84. Leuven: Peeters, 2017.

Mbewe, Conrad. *God's Design for the Church: A Guide for African Pastors and Ministry Leaders*. Wheaton: Crossway, 2020.

McCarthy, Dennis J. *Treaty and Covenant: A Study in Form in the Ancient Oriental Documents and in the Old Testament*. Pontifical Biblical Institute, 1963.

McCormack, Bruce Lindley. *The Humility of the Eternal Son: Reformed Kenoticism and the Repair of Chalcedon*. Cambridge University Press, 2021. https://doi.org/10.1017/9781009000123.

McGilchrist, Iain. *The Master and His Emissary: The Divided Brain and the Making of the Western World*. New expanded edition. New Haven: Yale University Press, 2019. https://doi.org/10.12987/9780300247459.

McGuckin, John A. "'Perceiving Light from Light in Light' (Oration 31.2): The Trinitarian Theology of St. Gregory the Theologian." *Greek Orthdox Theological Review* 39, no. 1 (1994): 7–32. https://doi.org/10.7916/D8GF144P.

———. *St. Cyril of Alexandria, The Christological Controversy: Its History, Theology, and Texts*. Supplements to Vigiliae Christianae 23. Leiden: Brill, 1994.

McKay, Kenneth L. "On the Perfect and Other Aspects in New Testament Greek." *Novum Testamentum* 23, no. 4 (October 1981): 289–329.

McLuhan, Marshall. *Understanding Media: The Extensions of Man*. McGraw-Hill, 1964.

Meek, Esther L. *Loving to Know: Introducing Covenant Epistemology*. Eugene, OR: Cascade Books, 2011.

Merkle, Benjamin. "Response to Porter." *Bulletin for Biblical Research* 26, no. 1 (2016): 83.

Merkle, Benjamin L. "Are the Qualifications for Elders or Overseers Negotiable?" *Bibliotheca Sacra* 171, no. 682 (April 2014): 172–88.

Merleau Ponty. *Merleau Ponty Phenomenology Of Perception*. Translated by Colin Smith. London: Routledge & Kegan Paul, 1962. http://archive.org/details/merleaupontyphenomenologyofperception.

Merleau-Ponty, Maurice. *Consciousness and the Acquisition of Language.* Translated by Hugh J. Silverman. Evanston, IL: Northwestern University Press, 1973.

———. "The Primacy of Perception and Its Philosophical Consequences." In *The Primacy of Perception: And Other Essays on Phenomenological Psychology, the Philosophy of Art, History, and Politics*, translated by James M. Edie, 3–11. Evanston, IL: Northwestern University Press, 1964.

Merriam-Webster, Inc. *Merriam-Webster's Collegiate Dictionary.* Eleventh ed. Springfield, MA: Merriam-Webster, Inc., 2003.

———. *Merriam-Webster's Collegiate Dictionary.* Eleventh ed. Springfield, MA: Merriam-Webster, Inc., 2003.

Moleski, Martin X. "Polanyi vs. Kuhn: Worldviews Apart." *Tradition and Discovery: The Polanyi Society Periodical* 33, no. 2 (2006): 8–24. https://doi.org/10.5840/traddisc2006/200733219.

Moo, Douglas J. *Galatians.* Baker Exegetical Commentary on the New Testament. Grand Rapids: Baker Academic, 2013.

———. *The Epistle to the Romans.* NICNT. Grand Rapids: Eerdmans, 1996.

———. *The Letters to the Colossians and to Philemon.* The Pillar New Testament Commentary. Grand Rapids; Cambridge: Eerdmans, 2008.

Moore Theological College. "Bachelor of Divinity (BD) – In Teach-Out." Accessed February 23, 2024. https://moore.edu.au/courses/bachelor-of-divinity-bd/.

Morris, Leon. *The First and Second Epistles to the Thessalonians.* Grand Rapids: Eerdmans, 1991.

Muehlenberg, Bill. "Evangelical Seminaries in Decline." Blog. Culture Watch. Accessed February 2, 2024. https://billmuehlenberg.com/2022/05/18/evangelical-seminaries-in-decline/.

Mühling, Markus. "Immanent/Economic Trinity." In *Religion Past and Present.* Brill, April 1, 2011. https://referenceworks.brillonline.com/entries/religion-past-and-present/immanenteconomic-trinity-SIM_10307.

Muller, Richard A. *After Calvin: Studies in the Development of a Theological Tradition.* Oxford: Oxford University Press, 2003.

———. *Prolegomena to Theology.* 2. ed. Post-Reformation Reformed

Dogmatics: The Rise and Development of Reformed Orthodoxy, ca. 1520 to ca. 1725, Vol. 1. Grand Rapids: Baker Academic, 2003.

———. *The Divine Essence and Attributes*. Post-Reformation Reformed Dogmatics: The Rise and Development of Reformed Orthodoxy, ca. 1520 to ca. 1725, Vol. 3. Grand Rapids: Baker, 2003.

———. *The Unaccommodated Calvin: Studies in the Foundation of a Theological Tradition*. Oxford: Oxford University Press, 2001.

Nash, Ronald H. *The Word of God and the Mind of Man*. Grand Rapids: Zondervan, 1982.

Nestorius. *Nestoriana: Die Fragmente Des Nestorius*. Edited by Friedrich Loofs. Halle: Max Niemeyer, 1905.

———. *The Bazaar of Heracleides: Newly Translated from the Syriac and Edited with an Introduction, Notes & Appendices*. Translated by G. R. Driver and L. Hodgson. Oxford: Clarendon, 1925.

Newton, John. "Letter 2: To Student in Divinity." In *The Works of John Newton. Vols 1-6*, edited by Richard Cecil, 3rd Ed. Vol. 1. Edinburgh: Banner of Truth, 1985. http://archive.org/details/worksofjohnnewto0001newt.

Noll, Mark A. *The Scandal of the Evangelical Mind*. With New Preface and Afterword. Grand Rapids: Eerdmans, 2022.

Ong, Walter J. *Orality and Literacy: The Technologizing of the Word*. New York: Routledge, 2002.

Palmer, Parker J. *To Know as We Are Known: Education as a Spiritual Journey*. New York: Harper Collins, 1993.

Parker, Garrett. "Why You Should Never Stay at a Job For Too Long." Money Inc, September 1, 2016. https://moneyinc.com/why-you-should-never-stay-at-a-job-for-too-long/.

Parsons, Mikeal C. *Acts*. Paideia Commentaries on The New Testament. Grand Rapids: Baker Academic, 2008.

Pashler, Harold, Mark McDaniel, Doug Rohrer, and Robert Bjork. "Learning Styles: Concepts and Evidence." *Psychological Science in the Public Interest* 9, no. 3 (December 2008): 105–19. https://doi.org/10.1111/j.1539-6053.2009.01038.x.

Patrick, Tim, and Andrew Reid. *The Whole Counsel of God: Why and How to Preach the Entire Bible*. Wheaton: Crossway, 2020.

Patton, C. Michael. "Seven Common Fallacies of Biblical Interpretation."

Credo House Ministries (blog), July 1, 2024. https://credohouse.org/blog/seven-common-fallacies-of-biblical-interpretation.

Payne, J.D. "An Overlooked Reason for Decline in Seminary Enrollment." *ChurchLeaders* (blog), July 21, 2023. https://churchleaders.com/outreach-missions/455242-an-overlooked-reason-for-decline-in-seminary-enrollment.html.

Peckham, John. *Divine Attributes: Knowing the Covenantal God of Scripture*, 2021.

Pierre, Jeremy, and Deepak Reju. *The Pastor and Counseling: The Basics of Shepherding Members in Need*, 2015.

Piggin, Stuart, and Robert Dean Linder. *Attending to the National Soul: Evangelical Christians in Australian History 1914-2014*. The Fountain of Public Prosperity, Vol. II. Clayton, Victoria: Monash University Publishing, 2020.

Piper, John. *Brothers We Are Not Professionals A Plea to Pastors for Radical Ministry*. Updated&Expanded. Nashville: B&H, 2013.

———. *Think: The Life of the Mind and the Love of God*. Wheaton: Crossway, 2010.

Polanyi, Michael. *Personal Knowledge: Towards a Post-Critical Philosophy*. First Harper Torchbook Edition. New York: Harper Torchbook, 1964.

———. *The Tacit Dimension*. Chicago; London: University of Chicago Press, 2009.

Porter, Stanley E. *Verbal Aspect in the Greek of the New Testament, with Reference to Tense and Mood*. Studies in Biblical Greek 1. New York: Peter Lang, 2003.

Porter, Stanley E. "What More Shall I Say?: A Response to Steve Runge and Benjamin Merkle." *Bulletin for Biblical Research* 26, no. 1 (December 31, 2016): 75–79.

Powlison, David. *Speaking Truth in Love: Counsel in Community*. Greensboro, NC: New Growth Press, 2005.

———. *The Pastor as Counselor: The Call for Soul Care*. Wheaton: Crossway, 2021.

Poythress, Vern S. *In the Beginning Was the Word: Language: A God-Centered Approach*. Wheaton: Crossway Books, 2009.

———. *Logic: A God-Centered Approach to the Foundation of Western Thought*. Electronic. Wheaton: Crossway, 2013.

———. *Redeeming Science: A God-Centered Approach.* Wheaton: Crossway Books, 2006.

———. *Symphonic Theology: The Validity of Multiple Perspectives in Theology.* Grand Rapids: Academie Books, 1987.

Prestige, G. L. *St Basil the Great and Apollinaris of Laodicea.* London: SPCK, 1956.

Price, Richard. "The Council of Chalcedon (451): A Narrative." In *Chalcedon in Context: Church Councils 400-700*, edited by Richard Price and Mary Whitby, 70–91. Liverpool: Liverpool University Press, 2011.

Price, Richard, and Michael Gaddis, trans. *The Acts of the Council of Chalcedon.* Vol. 2. 3 vols. Translated Texts for Historians. Liverpool: Liverpool University Press, 2005.

Radde-Gallwitz, Andrew. *Basil of Caesarea, Gregory of Nyssa, and the Transformation of Divine Simplicity.* Oxford Early Christian Studies. Oxford; New York: Oxford University Press, 2009. https://doi.org/10.1093/acprof:oso/9780199574117.001.0001.

Radner, Ephraim. *Time and the Word: Figural Reading of the Christian Scriptures.* Grand Rapids: Eerdmans, 2016.

Ramelli, Ilaria. "Gregory Nyssen's and Evagrius' Biographical and Theological Relations: Origen's Heritage and Neoplatonism." In *Papers Presented at the Seventeenth International Conference on Patristic Studies Held in Oxford 2015 Volume 10 Evagrius between Origen, the Cappadocians, and Neoplatonism*, 165–231. Studia Patristica 84. Leuven: Peeters, 2017.

Religion News Service. "Theological Schools Report Continued Drop in Master of Divinity Degrees." The Presbyterian Outlook, December 5, 2022. https://pres-outlook.org/2022/12/theological-schools-report-continued-drop-in-master-of-divinity-degrees/.

Rinquest, Linzay. "Caught and Not Taught: A Journey in Integrating the Hidden Curriculum in a South African Seminary." In *Making Connections: Integrative Education in Africa*, edited by Marilyn Naidoo. African Sun Media, 2021. https://www.academia.edu/111133180/Caught_and_not_taught_A_journey_in_integrating_the_hidden_curriculum_in_a_South_African_seminary.

Roark, Nick, and Robert Cline. *Biblical Theology: How the Church Faithfully Teaches the Gospel.* 9Marks: Building Healthy Churches. Wheaton: Crossway, 2018.

Robinson, Haddon W. *Biblical Preaching.* 2nd ed. Grand Rapids: Baker Academic, 2001.

Rodrigues, Adriani Milli. "The Rule of Faith and Biblical Interpretation in Evangelical Theological Interpretation of Scripture." *Themelios* 43, no. 2 (August 2018): 257–70.

Rogers, Jack B, and Donald K McKim. *The Authority and Interpretation of the Bible: An Historical Approach.* Eugene, OR: Wipf and Stock Publishers, 1999.

Ross, Allen P. "Proverbs." In *The Expositor's Bible Commentary, Volume 6: Proverbs-Isaiah*, edited by Tremper Longman and Garland David E, Vol. 6. Grand Rapids: Zondervan, 2008.

Runge, Steven E. "Contrastive Substitution and the Greek Verb." *Novum Testamentum* 56, no. 2 (March 18, 2014): 154–73. https://doi.org/10.1163/15685365-12341446.

Runge, Steven E. "Markedness: Contrasting Porter's Model with the Linguists Cited as Support." *Bulletin for Biblical Research* 26, no. 1 (December 31, 2016): 43–56.

———. "Response to Porter." *Bulletin for Biblical Research* 26, no. 1 (December 31, 2016): 81–82.

Rutherford, J. Alexander. "A Defence of an Author's Translation - Part 1." Teleioteti, December 5, 2017. https://www.teleioteti.ca/2017/12/05/a-defence-of-an-authors-translation-part-1/.

———. "Authority Structures and Biblical Education – Teleioteti Articles." Teleioteti, April 14, 2021. https://www.teleioteti.ca/2021/04/14/authority-structures-and-biblical-education/.

———. "Church in an Oral World – Teleioteti Articles." Teleioteti, April 30, 2024. https://www.teleioteti.ca/2024/04/30/church-in-an-oral-world/.

———. *God's Gifts for the Christian Life — Part 1: The Gift of Knowledge.* Airdrie, AB: Teleioteti, 2021.

———. *God's Kingdom through His Priest-King: An Analysis of the Book of Samuel in Light of the Davidic Covenant.* Teleioteti Technical Studies 1. Vancouver: Teleioteti, 2019.

———. "Of Metaphysics and Theology." *Journal of The Evangelical Theological Society* 66, no. 4 (2023): 727–49.

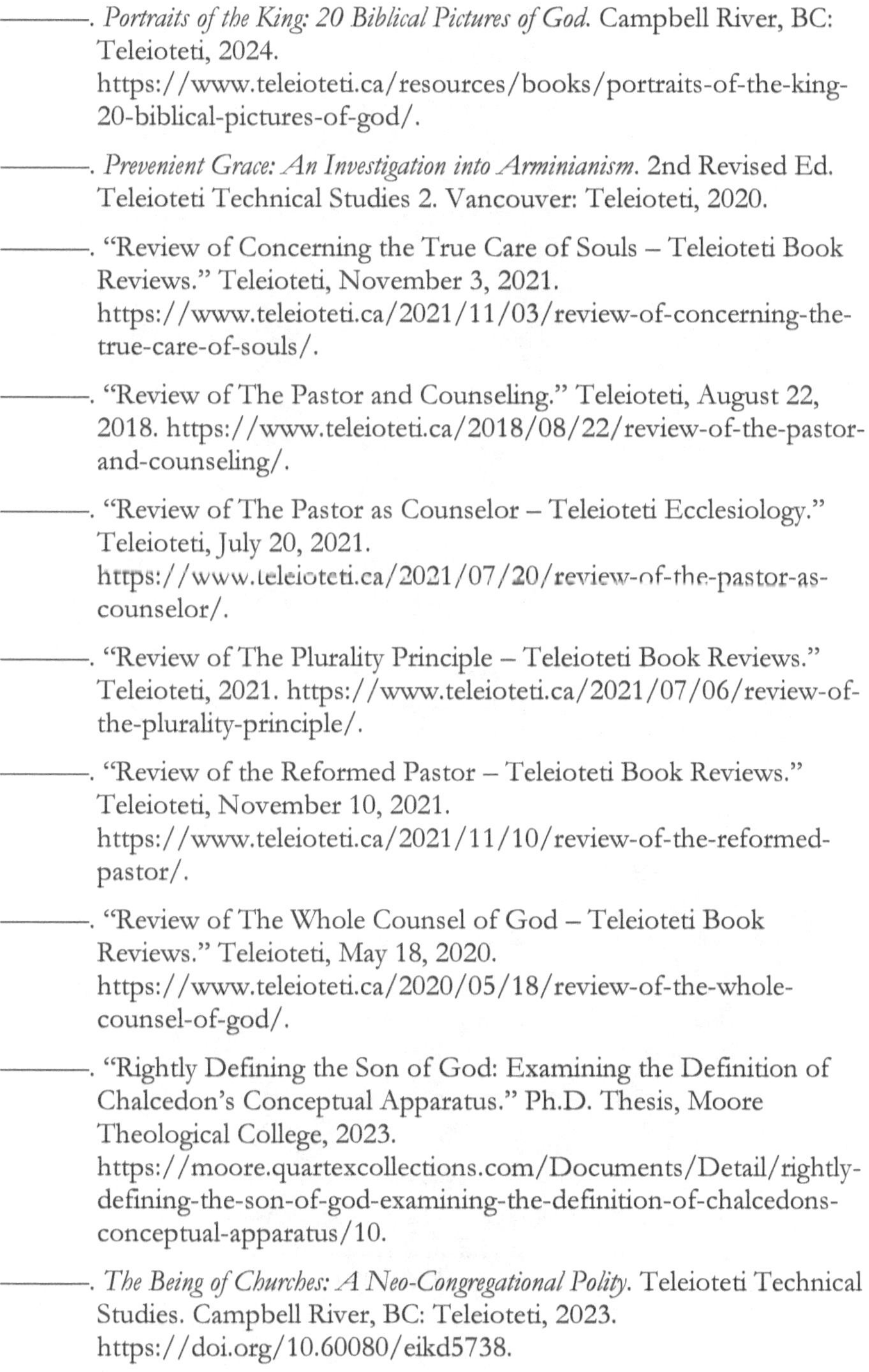

———. *Portraits of the King: 20 Biblical Pictures of God.* Campbell River, BC: Teleioteti, 2024. https://www.teleioteti.ca/resources/books/portraits-of-the-king-20-biblical-pictures-of-god/.

———. *Prevenient Grace: An Investigation into Arminianism.* 2nd Revised Ed. Teleioteti Technical Studies 2. Vancouver: Teleioteti, 2020.

———. "Review of Concerning the True Care of Souls – Teleioteti Book Reviews." Teleioteti, November 3, 2021. https://www.teleioteti.ca/2021/11/03/review-of-concerning-the-true-care-of-souls/.

———. "Review of The Pastor and Counseling." Teleioteti, August 22, 2018. https://www.teleioteti.ca/2018/08/22/review-of-the-pastor-and-counseling/.

———. "Review of The Pastor as Counselor – Teleioteti Ecclesiology." Teleioteti, July 20, 2021. https://www.teleioteti.ca/2021/07/20/review-of-the-pastor-as-counselor/.

———. "Review of The Plurality Principle – Teleioteti Book Reviews." Teleioteti, 2021. https://www.teleioteti.ca/2021/07/06/review-of-the-plurality-principle/.

———. "Review of the Reformed Pastor – Teleioteti Book Reviews." Teleioteti, November 10, 2021. https://www.teleioteti.ca/2021/11/10/review-of-the-reformed-pastor/.

———. "Review of The Whole Counsel of God – Teleioteti Book Reviews." Teleioteti, May 18, 2020. https://www.teleioteti.ca/2020/05/18/review-of-the-whole-counsel-of-god/.

———. "Rightly Defining the Son of God: Examining the Definition of Chalcedon's Conceptual Apparatus." Ph.D. Thesis, Moore Theological College, 2023. https://moore.quartexcollections.com/Documents/Detail/rightly-defining-the-son-of-god-examining-the-definition-of-chalcedons-conceptual-apparatus/10.

———. *The Being of Churches: A Neo-Congregational Polity.* Teleioteti Technical Studies. Campbell River, BC: Teleioteti, 2023. https://doi.org/10.60080/eikd5738.

———. *The Book of Habakkuk: An Exegetical-Theological Commentary on the*

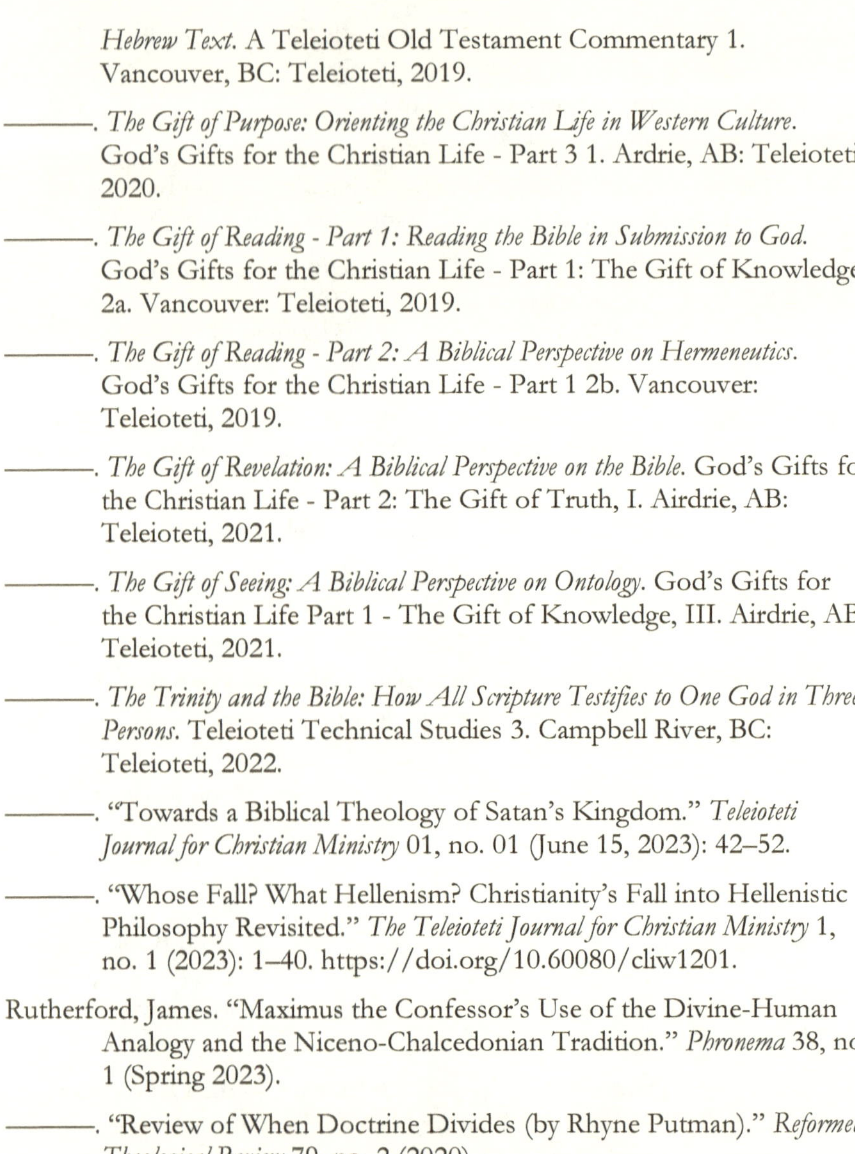

Hebrew Text. A Teleioteti Old Testament Commentary 1. Vancouver, BC: Teleioteti, 2019.

———. *The Gift of Purpose: Orienting the Christian Life in Western Culture.* God's Gifts for the Christian Life - Part 3 1. Ardrie, AB: Teleioteti, 2020.

———. *The Gift of Reading - Part 1: Reading the Bible in Submission to God.* God's Gifts for the Christian Life - Part 1: The Gift of Knowledge 2a. Vancouver: Teleioteti, 2019.

———. *The Gift of Reading - Part 2: A Biblical Perspective on Hermeneutics.* God's Gifts for the Christian Life - Part 1 2b. Vancouver: Teleioteti, 2019.

———. *The Gift of Revelation: A Biblical Perspective on the Bible.* God's Gifts for the Christian Life - Part 2: The Gift of Truth, I. Airdrie, AB: Teleioteti, 2021.

———. *The Gift of Seeing: A Biblical Perspective on Ontology.* God's Gifts for the Christian Life Part 1 - The Gift of Knowledge, III. Airdrie, AB: Teleioteti, 2021.

———. *The Trinity and the Bible: How All Scripture Testifies to One God in Three Persons.* Teleioteti Technical Studies 3. Campbell River, BC: Teleioteti, 2022.

———. "Towards a Biblical Theology of Satan's Kingdom." *Teleioteti Journal for Christian Ministry* 01, no. 01 (June 15, 2023): 42–52.

———. "Whose Fall? What Hellenism? Christianity's Fall into Hellenistic Philosophy Revisited." *The Teleioteti Journal for Christian Ministry* 1, no. 1 (2023): 1–40. https://doi.org/10.60080/cliw1201.

Rutherford, James. "Maximus the Confessor's Use of the Divine-Human Analogy and the Niceno-Chalcedonian Tradition." *Phronema* 38, no. 1 (Spring 2023).

———. "Review of When Doctrine Divides (by Rhyne Putman)." *Reformed Theological Review* 79, no. 2 (2020).

Rutherford, James Alexander. "Interpreting the Definition of Chalcedon." Presented at the Australia & New Zealand Association of Theological Studies Annual Conference, 2022, Sydney, June 2022. https://www.academia.edu/82687829/Interpreting_the_Definition_of_Chalcedon.

Ryan, Liz. "Ten Reasons Successful People Change Jobs More Often." Forbes, 2016.

https://www.forbes.com/sites/lizryan/2016/10/28/ten-reasons-successful-people-change-jobs-more-often/.

Saer, Orlando. *Iron Sharpens Iron: Leading Bible-Oriented Small Groups That Thrive*. Fearn, Ross-shire, Scotland: Christian Focus, 2010.

Sagan, Carl. *The Demon-Haunted World: Science as a Candle in the Dark*. 1st Ed. New York: Ballantine Books, 1997.

Sailhamer, John H. *The Pentateuch as Narrative*. Grand Rapids: Zondervan, 1992.

Schreiner, Thomas R. *Interpreting the Pauline Epistles*. 2nd ed. Grand Rapids: Baker Academic, 2011.

Schwartz, Eduard, ed. *Acta Conciliorum Oecumenicorum II: Concilium Universale Chalcedonense*. 6 vols. Berlin: Walter de Gruyter, 1914.

Senkbeil, Harold L. *The Care of Souls: Cultivating a Pastor's Heart*. Bellingham, WA: Lexham Press, 2019.

Sessoms, Rick. "Who Are Oral Learners?" *Freedom To Lead International®* (blog), April 12, 2012. https://freedomtolead.net/telling-story-great-commission-oral-learners/.

Shaw, Perry W. H. "The Hidden Curriculum of Seminary Education." *Journal of Asian Mission* 8, no. 1–2 (2006): 23–51.

Shchukin, Timur. "Matter as a Universal: John Philoponus and Maximus the Confessor on the Eternity of the World." *Scrinium* 13, no. 1 (2017): 361–82. https://doi.org/10.1163/18177565-00131p23.

Shellnutt, Kate. "The Pastors Aren't All Right: 38% Consider Leaving Ministry." News & Reporting. Christianity Today, November 16, 2021. https://www.christianitytoday.com/news/2021/november/pastor-burnout-pandemic-barna-consider-leaving-ministry.html.

Sheridan, Alison, Andrew Harvey, Buly Cardak, and Matt Brett. "Four Barriers to Higher Education Regional Students Face – and How to Overcome Them." The Conversation, October 27, 2015. http://theconversation.com/four-barriers-to-higher-education-regional-students-face-and-how-to-overcome-them-49138.

Silliman, Daniel. "Facing Financial Challenges, TEDS Cuts Faculty Positions." News & Reporting. Christianity Today, April 12, 2022. https://www.christianitytoday.com/news/2022/april/teds-financial-trouble-crisis-perrin-faculty-cuts.html.

———. "Gordon-Conwell to Sell Main Campus, Move to Boston." News

& Reporting. Christianity Today, May 17, 2022. https://www.christianitytoday.com/news/2022/may/gordon-conwell-sell-campus-financial-enrollment-struggle.html.

Silva, Moisés. *Biblical Words and Their Meaning: An Introduction to Lexical Semantics*. Rev. and Expanded ed. Grand Rapids: Zondervan, 1994.

Smart, Judith. "The Evangelist as Star: The Billy Graham Crusade in Australia, 1959." *The Journal of Popular Culture*, January 1, 1999. https://www.academia.edu/45510173/The_Evangelist_as_Star_The_Billy_Graham_Crusade_in_Australia_1959.

Smith, James K. A. *You Are What You Love: The Spiritual Power of Habit*. Brazos Press, 2016.

Smith, Mark S. *The Idea of Nicaea in the Early Church Councils, AD 431-451*. Oxford: Oxford University Press, 2018. https://doi.org/10.1093/oso/9780198835271.001.0001.

Southern Cross. "Vacant Parish List." March 2024. https://issuu.com/sydneyanglicans/docs/sc24_02-03.

Stamps, Luke. "The New Evangelical Subordinationism? Perspectives on the Equality of God the Father and God the Son/The Eternal Generation of the Son: Maintaining Orthodoxy in Trinitarian Theology." *Journal of the Evangelical Theological Society* 59, no. 4 (December 2016): 874–81.

Stang, Charles M. "The Two 'I's of Christ: Revisiting the Christological Controversy." *Anglican Theological Review* 94, no. 3 (2012): 529–47.

Stark, Rodney. *The Rise of Christianity: A Sociologist Reconsiders History*. Princeton University Press, 1996.

Stead, George Christopher. *Divine Substance*. Oxford: Clarendon Press, 1977. https://doi.org/10.1093/acprof:oso/9780198266303.001.0001.

Stott, John. *Between Two Worlds*. Grand Rapids: Eerdmans, 2017.

Strauch, Alexander. *Biblical Eldership: An Urgent Call to Restore Biblical Church Leadership*. Rev. and Expanded. Littleton, CO: Lewis and Roth Publishers, 1995.

Sullivan, Robert David. "Parishes without Pastors Decline, but Only Because More Churches Have Closed." America Magazine, June 14, 2019. https://www.americamagazine.org/faith/2019/06/14/parishes-without-pastors-decline-only-because-more-churches-have-closed.

Sweeney, Douglas A. "A Call and Agenda for Pastor-Theologians." Blog.

The Gospel Coalition, June 16, 2017. https://www.thegospelcoalition.org/article/a-call-and-agenda-for-pastor-theologians/.

Sydney Anglicans Ministry and Development. "Considering Ordination - Policy." Accessed February 23, 2024. https://www.mtd.org.au/considering-ordination/policy/.

Taylor, Charles. *Modern Social Imaginaries*. Public Planet Books. Durham: Duke University Press, 2004. https://doi.org/10.1215/9780822385806.

"The Chicago Statement on Biblical Inerrancy." ICBI. Accessed April 16, 2014. http://library.dts.edu/Pages/TL/Special/ICBI_1.pdf.

"The Well Training." Accessed October 31, 2024. https://thewelltraining.org.au/.

Thompson, Mark D. *A Clear and Present Word: The Clarity of Scripture*. New Studies in Biblical Theology 21. Downers Grove: IVP Academic, 2006.

———. "The Clarity of Scripture." The Gospel Coalition. Accessed August 18, 2020. https://www.thegospelcoalition.org/essay/the-clarity-of-scripture/.

Treier, Daniel J. *Introducing Theological Interpretation of Scripture: Recovering a Christian Practice*. Grand Rapids: Baker Academic, 2008.

Tripp, Paul David. *Dangerous Calling: Confronting the Unique Challenges of Pastoral Ministry*. 1st edition. Wheaton: Crossway, 2012.

———. *Instruments in the Redeemer's Hands: People in Need of Change Helping People in Need of Change*. Resources for Changing Lives. Phillipsburg, NJ: P&R Publishing, 2002.

Trueman, Carl R. *The Rise and Triumph of the Modern Self: Cultural Amnesia, Expressive Individualism, and the Road to Sexual Revolution*. Wheaton: Crossway, 2020.

Turretin, Francis. *Institutes of Elenctic Theology*. Edited by James T. Dennison, Jr. Translated by George Musgrave Giger. Vol. 1. 3 vols. Phillipsburg, NJ: P&R Publishing, 1992. http://archive.org/details/institutesofelen0001turr.

Union Theological Seminary. "Ordination Process by Denomination." Accessed February 23, 2024. https://utsnyc.edu/academics/career-paths/ordination-process/.

Vágvölgyi, Réka, Andra Coldea, Thomas Dresler, Josef Schrader, and Hans-

Christoph Nuerk. "A Review about Functional Illiteracy: Definition, Cognitive, Linguistic, and Numerical Aspects." *Frontiers in Psychology* 7 (November 10, 2016): 1617. https://doi.org/10.3389/fpsyg.2016.01617.

Van Pelt, Miles. *A Biblical-Theological Introduction to the Old Testament: The Gospel Promised.* Edited by Miles Van Pelt. Wheaton: Crossway, 2016.

———. "Structure of the Christian Bible." Education. Biblical Training. Accessed August 29, 2017. https://www.biblicaltraining.org/library/structure-christian-bible/biblical-theology/van-pelt-blomberg-schreiner.

Van Ruler, Han. *The Crisis of Causality: Voetius and Descartes on God, Nature and Change.* Leiden: Brill, 1995.

Van Til, Cornelius. *A Christian Theory of Knowledge.* Phillipsburg: Presbyterian and Reformed, 1969.

———. *Essays on Christian Education.* Phillipsburg: Presbyterian and Reformed, 1979.

———. *The Defense of the Faith.* Edited by K. Scott Oliphint. 4th ed. Phillipsburg, NJ: P&R Publishing, 2008.

Vanhoozer, Kevin J. *Biblical Authority after Babel: Retrieving the Solas in the Spirit of Mere Protestant Christianity.* Grand Rapids: Brazos, 2016.

———. *Remythologizing Theology: Divine Action, Passion, and Authorship.* Cambridge Studies in Christian Doctrine 18. Cambridge, UK ; New York: Cambridge University Press, 2010.

"Vocational Bible College." Accessed October 31, 2024. https://www.vbc.edu.au.

Vroegop, Mark. "Dare to Hope in God: How to Lament Well." Desiring God, April 6, 2019. https://www.desiringgod.org/articles/dare-to-hope-in-god.

———. *Dark Clouds, Deep Mercy*, 2019.

———. *Weep with Me: How Lament Opens a Door for Racial Reconciliation.* Wheaton: Crossway, 2020.

Wagschal, David. *Law and Legality in the Greek East: The Byzantine Canonical Tradition, 381-883.* Oxford University Press, 2015.

Walter, Catherine. "Phonology in Second Language Reading: Not an Optional Extra." *TESOL Quarterly* 42, no. 3 (2008): 455–74.

https://doi.org/10.2307/40264478.

Waltke, Bruce K. *The Book of Proverbs: Chapters 1-15*. NICOT. Grand Rapids: Eerdmans, 2004.

Waltke, Bruce K. *The Book of Proverbs: Chapters 15-31*. NICOT. Grand Rapids: Eerdmans, 2004.

Waltke, Bruce K., and Michael Patrick O'Connor. *An Introduction to Biblical Hebrew Syntax*. Winona Lake: Eisenbrauns, 1990.

Watkin, Christopher. *Biblical Critical Theory: How the Bible's Unfolding Story Makes Sense of Modern Life and Culture*. Grand Rapids: Zondervan Academic, 2022.

———. *Thinking through Creation: Genesis 1 and 2 as Tools of Cultural Critique*. Phillipsburg, NJ: P&R Publishing, 2017.

Watts, Rikk E. *Isaiah's New Exodus in Mark*. Biblical Studies Library. Grand Rapids: Baker Books, 2000.

Webster, John. "On the Theology of the Intellectual Life." In *God Without Measure: Working Papers in Christian Theology*, II:141–56. T&T Clark Theology. London; New York: Bloomsbury T&T Clark, 2016.

———. "Principles of Systematic Theology." In *The Domain of the Word: Scripture and Theological Reason*, 133–49, 2013.

———. "What Makes Theology Theological?" In *God Without Measure: Working Papers in Christian Theology*, Vol. I. T&T Clark Theology. London ; New York: Bloomsbury T&T Clark, 2016.

Welch, Edward T. *Blame It on the Brain? Distinguishing Chemical Imbalances, Brain Disorders, and Disobedience*. Resources for Changing Lives. Phillipsburg, NJ: P&R Publishing, 1998.

———. *Caring for One Another: 8 Ways to Cultivate Meaningful Relationships*. Wheaton: Crossway, 2018.

West, M. L. "The Metre of Arius' 'Thalia.'" *The Journal of Theological Studies* 33, no. 1 (1982): 98–105. https://doi.org/10.1093/jts/XXXIII.1.98.

Westerholm, Stephen. *Perspectives Old and New on Paul: The "Lutheran" Paul and His Critics*. Grand Rapids: Eerdmans, 2004.

Westminster Assembly (1643-1652). *A Directory for the Publique Worship of God throughout the Three Kingdoms of England, Scotland, and Ireland: Together with an Ordinance of Parliament for the Taking Away of the Book of Common-Prayer and for Establishing and Observing of This Present*

Directory throughout the Kingdom of England and Dominion of Wales: With Propositions Concerning Church-Government and Ordination of Ministers. London: Printed by T.R. and E.M. for the Company of Stationers, 1651. http://archive.org/details/directoryfo00west.

Westra, Liuwe H. *The Apostles' Creed: Origin, History, and Some Early Commentaries.* Instrumenta Patristica et Mediaevalia 43. Turnhout, Belgium: Brepols, 2002.

Whybray, R. N. *The Book of Proverbs.* Cambridge: Cambridge University Press, 1972.

Wilberding, James. "Embryology." In *A Companion to Science, Technology, and Medicine in Ancient Greece and Rome*, edited by Georgia L. Irby, 329–42. Black Companions to the Ancient World. Chichester, West Sussex: Wiley Blackwell, 2019. https://www.academia.edu/10295752/Embryology_Wiley_Blackwell_.

Williams, D. H. *Evangelicals and Tradition (Evangelical Ressourcement): The Formative Influence of the Early Church.* Grand Rapids: Baker, 2005.

Williams, Rowan. *Arius: Heresy and Tradition.* 2. ed. London: SCM, 2001.

Williams, Rowan D. "The Quest of the Historical Thalia." In *Arianism: Historical and Theological Reassessments: Papers from The Ninth International Conference on Patristic Studies*, edited by Robert C. Gregg, Reprint., 1–35. Patristic Monograph Series, V. 11. 2006: Wipf and Stock Publishers, 2006.

Wilson, Gerald Henry. *The Editing of the Hebrew Psalter.* Scholars Press, 1985.

Wittgenstein, Ludwig. *Preliminary Studies for the "Philosophical Investigations," Generally Known as the Blue and Brown Books.* Oxford: Blackwell, 1958.

Wright, N.T. *Justification: God's Plan & Paul's Vision.* Downers Grove: IVP Academic, 2009.

———. *The New Testament and the People of God.* Christian Origins and the Question of God 1. Minneapolis: Fortress, 1992.

———. *What Saint Paul Really Raid: Was Paul of Tarsus the Real Founder of Christianity?* Grand Rapids; Cincinnati: Eerdmans; Forward Movement Publications, 1997.

Young, Frances M. *From Nicaea to Chalcedon: A Guide to the Literature and Its Background.* 2nd ed. London: SCM Press, 2010.

Zachhuber, Johannes. "Derivative Genera in Apollinarius of Laodicea." In *Apollinaris Und Die Folgen*, 93–114. Studien Und Texte Zu Antike

Und Christentum 93. Tübingen: Mohr Siebeck, 2015.

———. *The Rise of Christian Theology and the End of Ancient Metaphysics: Patristic Philosophy from the Cappadocian Fathers to John of Damascus.* Oxford University Press, 2020.

ABOUT TELEIOTETI

Teleioteti (Τελειοτητι, te-ley-o-tey-tee)—meaning "unto maturity"—is dedicated to faithful, thoughtful ministry. We create resources for Christian discipleship, resources that address theological and pastoral concerns from a Biblical worldview. Our purpose is to see Christ's Church mature in its understanding of God and His Word. We do this through the production of Gospel-centred materials that connect the Bible with the heads, hearts, and minds of Christians. We hope to enable Christians from all walks of life to better understand and glorify God through service in His Church.

To achieve this purpose, Teleioteti publishes online materials and books researched with academic rigour yet based upon Biblical presuppositions. That is, we are neither academic nor lazy. We use methods, or epistemology, informed by the Bible along with the hard work usually associated with professional research and study. We produce resources directed towards all Christians, but most of our resources are directed towards students, pastors, and theologically inclined lay Christians.

To learn more about us and what we are doing, please visit us at https://teleioteti.ca or contact us at info@teleioteti.ca. If you have found this resource helpful, prayerfully consider supporting us by giving a review on the web (e.g. Amazon, Goodreads, etc.), praying with and for us, or giving financially so that we can produce more resources like this one. For more information on how you can support us, visit us at https://teleioteti.ca/ about/partner/ or at our page on Patreon, https://www.patreon.com/teleioteti.

Other Books by J. Alexander Rutherford

The Being of Churches: Neo-Congregational Polity (Teleioteti, 2023)

What is a church? Are denominations churches? Who has the authority to ordain ministers of the Gospel? How do we determine what a church gathering should look like? These are the questions of "polity," or the principles and foundations for the organisation and conduct of a church. Nearly 400 years ago, Christians in New England produced a clear articulation of polity based on the Bible, called The Cambridge Platform of Discipline. This document offers much insight into the way God would have churches act. In this book, the author engages with the Bible in the tradition of the Cambridge Platform to offer a new congregational polity, an account of the being and conduct of churches that retrieves the best insights of the Cambridge Platform while attempting to improve upon it in light of the later failings of American congregationalism and the 400 years of Christian reflection on the church that has followed that document.

It is the author's prayer that this book would help churches engage with the Bible as they think about what it means to be a church and would give them the tools to do so with faithfulness and clarity.

The Trinity and the Bible: How All Scripture Testifies to One God in Three Persons (Teleioteti, 2022)

To write on the Trinity is to enter a minefield of presuppositions-presuppositions of theology, exegesis, grammar, logic, philosophy, etc. However, at the heart of God's self-revelation in the Bible is God's tri-unity, that God is three, Father, Son, and Holy Spirit. Confessional Christians would identify this claim, that God is Triune, as a necessary condition of true Christian faith. To be Christian is to follow Christ who is the 2nd person of the Trinity. Yet, does following this Christ mean following the 2nd hypostasis who is eternally begotten of the Father, sharing with him his ousia? That is a more difficult question, isn't it? Indeed, many faithful men and women in my life could not make heads or tails of the latter claim while worshipping and following the Christ of the former. So, what does it mean to be Trinitarian? This book is about that question, what does it mean to be a Christian who worships a triune God, to be "Trinitarian"? Is the Trinity a doctrine, arrived at through second-order reflection on the biblical data several hundred years after the canon closed, or is it something else? Is it, perhaps, a presupposition about the reality of God that has shaped the Christian imagination, that has shaped the framework Christians bring to the world, throughout created history?

Prevenient Grace: An Investigation into Arminianism, 2nd Revised Edition (Teleioteti, 2020)

When a building is built on a poor foundation, the inevitable result is its collapse. But this isn't a book on architecture; foundations are found in thought structures as well as in material structures. In theology, a bad foundation will produce results as catastrophic as a bad foundation in architecture. How we think about God and His work in the world will profoundly affect how we live and work out our Christian faith; is your foundation strong? This book evolved from the conviction that a prominent theological system rests on a fragile foundation.

Endorsements:

> This book is a fine piece of scholarship. Rutherford presents his arguments with admirable clarity. His intention is to offer guidance for pastors and teachers who may be faced with questions about whether human beings have the freedom to accept or reject God. The great strength of Rutherford's book is his knowledge of biblical texts and an appropriate interpretation of them. He successfully shows that the claims of Arminianism with its view that prevenient grace allows an acceptance or rejection of God are not supported by biblical texts. Nor are they justified by philosophical arguments. They layout of the book and its careful treatment of arguments both for and against prevenient grace is a model of excellent writing. His chapters are supplemented by a Glossary that explains all specific terms and Appendices where detailed theological discussions are given. Most helpful is his Index of Scripture passages discussed.
>
> - Dr. Shirley Sullivan, FRSC (elected), Professor Emeritus of Classics, University of British Columbia

Habakkuk: An Exegetical-Theological Commentary (Teleioteti, 2019)

It is all too common to find commentaries that miss the forest for the trees, commentaries that get so caught up in the minutiae of scholarly controversies that they miss what God is saying for His church today. This is especially evident when it comes to the book of Habakkuk.

The Teleioteti Old Testament Commentaries series is an attempt to attain theological depth, to pay attention to the forest, without neglecting the details of the text, without missing the trees. To do this, a Teleioteti Old Testament Commentary seeks to bring scholarly rigour and thoughtfulness together with faithful attention to the purpose and significance of each book for God's people today. It strikes a balance between technicality, working through the Hebrew text and its difficulties, and practicality, applying each major section of the text to contemporary needs.

Reviews:

Habakkuk is a solid commentary. The emphasis upon the text of Habakkuk and its address of key theological issues presented in the text make it a worthy addition to the collection of commentaries on Habakkuk already in print. Habakkuk will fit nicely on the bookshelf in the pastor's library.

- Daniel Wiley, Adjunct Professor Clarks Summit University in Journal of Ministry and Theology, Spring 2020, Vol. 24, No. 1.

www.ingramcontent.com/pod-product-compliance
Lightning Source LLC
Chambersburg PA
CBHW030351130626
46549CB00004B/1446

9781989560792